# Gull Island

=== AND OTHER STORIES ===

# Gull Island

### AND OTHER STORIES

Elvin Hooper

*Elvin Hooper*

*tight lines*            *fresh bait*

CHAPEL HILL

FULL-SERVICE · BOOK-MAKERS
ESTD · 1995

PRESS

PUBLISHED BY
The Chapel Hill Press, Inc.

————

ISBN 978-1-59715-123-8
Library of Congress Catalog Number 2015911926

First Printing
Printed in the United States of America

*To my only brother,*
*Burtis Hooper,*
*who has been like a father to me.*

# CONTENTS

Acknowledgments . . . . . . . . . . . . . . . . . . . . . . . . . . ix
Prologue . . . . . . . . . . . . . . . . . . . . . . . . . . . . . . . xi

Chapter 1    Summer Vacation . . . . . . . . . . . . . . . . . . .1
Chapter 2    The Dirt Clod War . . . . . . . . . . . . . . . . . 9
Chapter 3    Shack on the Island . . . . . . . . . . . . . . . .17
Chapter 4    The Curtain Boxes . . . . . . . . . . . . . . . .23
Chapter 5    The Finishing Touches . . . . . . . . . . . . . .29
Chapter 6    Decoy Monday . . . . . . . . . . . . . . . . . .37
Chapter 7    The Feeding Geese Decoys . . . . . . . . . . . 45
Chapter 8    The Grain Truck . . . . . . . . . . . . . . . . .53
Chapter 9    The First Hunt . . . . . . . . . . . . . . . . . .61
Chapter 10   The Bluebird Hunt . . . . . . . . . . . . . . . .71
Chapter 11   The Deepwater Blind . . . . . . . . . . . . . . .79
Chapter 12   A Gull Island Christmas . . . . . . . . . . . . .87
Chapter 13   Torpedoes in the Channel . . . . . . . . . . . .95
Chapter 14   Island Changes . . . . . . . . . . . . . . . . . 103
Chapter 15   The Tow . . . . . . . . . . . . . . . . . . . . .111
Chapter 16   Painting the Boats . . . . . . . . . . . . . . . 119
Chapter 17   Bulkhead and Docks . . . . . . . . . . . . . . 127
Chapter 18   The Diving Duck Hunt . . . . . . . . . . . . . 135
Chapter 19   The Lost Crank . . . . . . . . . . . . . . . . . 143
Chapter 20   Holiday Pranks . . . . . . . . . . . . . . . . . 151
Chapter 21   The Big Freeze . . . . . . . . . . . . . . . . . 159
Chapter 22   Stranded Game Warden . . . . . . . . . . . . 167
Chapter 23   Box of Ducks . . . . . . . . . . . . . . . . . . 175

Chapter 24  New Boats . . . . . . . . . . . . . . . . . . . . . . . . . . 183
Chapter 25  The Lost Navy Pilot . . . . . . . . . . . . . . . . . . . 191
Chapter 26  Market Gunning . . . . . . . . . . . . . . . . . . . . . . 199
Chapter 27  The Lacey Act . . . . . . . . . . . . . . . . . . . . . . . .209
Chapter 28  Live Decoys . . . . . . . . . . . . . . . . . . . . . . . . . 217
Chapter 29  The New Clubhouse . . . . . . . . . . . . . . . . . . . 225
Chapter 30  November Trout . . . . . . . . . . . . . . . . . . . . . . 233
Chapter 31  Black Duck Moon . . . . . . . . . . . . . . . . . . . . . 241
Chapter 32  The *Contraption* . . . . . . . . . . . . . . . . . . . . . .249
Chapter 33  Campground Girls . . . . . . . . . . . . . . . . . . . . 257
Chapter 34  Gas Episode . . . . . . . . . . . . . . . . . . . . . . . . .265
Chapter 35  The *Ramadancer* . . . . . . . . . . . . . . . . . . . . . 273
Chapter 36  Chowder . . . . . . . . . . . . . . . . . . . . . . . . . . . 281
Chapter 37  Lost Hunters . . . . . . . . . . . . . . . . . . . . . . . . 289
Chapter 38  Bottlenose Dolphins . . . . . . . . . . . . . . . . . . .297
Chapter 39  Coffin Boxes . . . . . . . . . . . . . . . . . . . . . . . . .305
Chapter 40  Warmer Winters . . . . . . . . . . . . . . . . . . . . . . 313
Chapter 41  Record Catch . . . . . . . . . . . . . . . . . . . . . . . . 321
Chapter 42  Outdated Scales . . . . . . . . . . . . . . . . . . . . . . 329
Chapter 43  Blues Blitz . . . . . . . . . . . . . . . . . . . . . . . . . . 337
Chapter 44  Rockfish . . . . . . . . . . . . . . . . . . . . . . . . . . . .345
Chapter 45  Ash Wednesday . . . . . . . . . . . . . . . . . . . . . . 353
Chapter 46  Breeches Buoy Drill . . . . . . . . . . . . . . . . . . . 361
Chapter 47  Too Much Powder . . . . . . . . . . . . . . . . . . . .369
Chapter 48  Island Band . . . . . . . . . . . . . . . . . . . . . . . . . 377
Chapter 49  Shenanigans . . . . . . . . . . . . . . . . . . . . . . . . . 385
Chapter 50  Jersey Connection . . . . . . . . . . . . . . . . . . . . 393
Chapter 51  New Regulations . . . . . . . . . . . . . . . . . . . . . .401
Chapter 52  Drifting Along . . . . . . . . . . . . . . . . . . . . . . . 409

Epilogue . . . . . . . . . . . . . . . . . . . . . . . . . . . . . . . . . . . . .417
About the Author . . . . . . . . . . . . . . . . . . . . . . . . . . . . . .419

## ACKNOWLEDGMENTS

I have incorporated many of my childhood friends as characters in these stories. Some of these tales are true and some not so true. I hope they approve of how I used them to bring these fictional episodes to life. First, I would like to thank my wife, Debra, for putting up with me for the past forty-two years. The countless hours she spent researching the proper spelling and meaning of words helped to make this work possible, and a thanks for just being there whenever I needed her over the years. I would like to recognize several other folks who helped make this possible as well. Hugs, kisses, and a great big thank-you go out to Lovie Heilig, Suzanne Jennette, and Randy Ratliff. Their endless hours of editing, rewriting, and formatting brought this work together. Thank you, Gee Gee Rosell, of Buxton Village Books, for her continuing support and encouragement. Thanks to Michael Halminski for his research and photography on the cover and inside the book. Also, many thanks to Edwina Woodbury and the folks of Chapel Hill Press for their assistance in making this book a reality. The encouragement and willingness of all these folks to share their experience and knowledge helped make this work possible. I would like to thank each and every one of them from the bottom of my heart.

## PROLOGUE

From an early age, no matter where I went on the island or anywhere in the county, I was referred to as a Rodanther. It was to no avail to protest and tell folks that I grew up in Salvo and was extremely proud of that fact. Whenever folks saw me coming toward them they would say, "Here comes that Rodanther." As I grew older I realized that everyone who lived in the villages of Rodanthe, Waves, or Salvo would be referred to as Rodanthers. I have lived in the village of Buxton for twelve years. To the rest of the island folk, I am still a Rodanther. I gave up the lengthy explanation of where I was from and let it go.

I grew up in a much simpler era. I hunted, fished, and gathered shellfish with my father, brother, cousins, and friends. It was pounded into our gray matter that if you took the life of an animal, it was your responsibility to dress and eat it. It was okay to share your bounty with your relatives, friends, and neighbors. If you offered it to older folk, it was your responsibility to clean or dress the fish, game, or shellfish. Over the years we all shared waterfowl during good hunting winters. If there was a run of speckled trout, drum, or spots, they were caught and shared. I remember drum fishing with my friends and catching dozens of big drum during an angling session. We took them to the villages and gave them away. If a few of us had drum, almost everyone got at least a large enough piece to make a meal for their family. Boiled drum, potatoes, meat cracklings, cornbread, coleslaw, cucumbers, and iced tea. This combination of food is nectar for the gods. Once you take on a load of this, it's time to rub your stomach and tell everyone within earshot that it's good to be full. The next step is to find a place to take a nap.

We always used everything we harvested. Nothing was ever thrown away or went to waste. The entire island was wide open, and fun was encouraged.

The church that I attended sponsored several summertime beach parties. The kids were allowed to roast hotdogs and marshmallows over fires on the beach. That is an experience that I will never forget. The kids growing up here now will never have the opportunity to experience things of that nature. There are so many new rules and regulations, it's hard to keep them all straight, much less obey them. I have often thought it would be proper to erect a sign on the south end of the bridge crossing Oregon Inlet. The sign should read, "Welcome to Hatteras Island, where no fun is allowed."

Now let me transport you back in time to 1957. An eight-year-old boy was riding a school bus home from school. It was the last day of school before the beginning of summer vacation. Welcome to the fantastic lifestyle I enjoyed growing up on Hatteras Island, in the village of Salvo, truly the land of paradise.

# CHAPTER ONE

# Summer Vacation

Finally it was here. After spending nine months confined in a classroom I was finally liberated for at least the summer season of 1957. The school bus came to a halt adjacent to the sandy one-lane road that led to my house and continued on to the sound. I ran all the way up the lane and entered the front porch area that enveloped the inner portion of the house. "Elvin Hooper, don't slam that screen door," Mother hollered too late; the door followed me with a bang. Whenever she addressed me by my full name I knew she meant business. My mother was a beautiful woman although along in years. She was raised on Island Beach in coastal New Jersey. She was of German-Irish descent. Her name was Eleanora Worth before she became Eleanora Hooper after she married my father. My father had met her when he was in the Coast Guard stationed at Island Beach Station. She always told me I was God's little unexpected gift; my brother was sixteen years old when I was born.

Off came the school clothes and shoes; a pair of cutoff dungarees and a straw hat were all I needed. I was out the front door with another bang, and she yelled, "Be careful and make sure you don't get in the way of the work men. Let your father know you have come to the landing. You make sure you go straight to him; if I find out different you are in for it." I ran straight up to my father and let him know I was home.

My father was a short, powerful-looking man in his late fifties, aged from the sun and many hours of making a living on the water. His name was

Edward Hooper, born and raised in Salvo, a small village on Hatteras Island in coastal North Carolina. He was an ordained Holy Roller preacher with the International Assembly of God Conference of Ministers. Also he was a hunting guide and a commercial fisherman. He told me to be careful and stay out of the way. He wanted me to remain close to him if I wanted to watch the work that was in progress. The work consisted of a large drag line, or a harbor digger outer as an eight-year-old boy such as I saw it. This big, powerful machine was digging out our harbor, making it much larger and deeper. It piled the mud and sand on the side of the creek as it crawled along on large wooden mats. Boy, was this exciting. Black smoke bellowed from the stack as another few yards of dirt crashed on the marsh with a soft plop. Large mounds of fill began to mount up in a straight line along the ditch bank like oversized anthills. Both of us watched without speaking until the drag line crawled from the marsh onto high ground and the bucket was placed on the ground with a thud. The engine was shut off and all was silent. Out of the cabin door came a big, redheaded, rugged-looking man. He walked up to us and told my father that he would return the next day to continue working.

As my father and I walked to the house for supper, I asked him what was up with all the digging and making the harbor larger. He told me that a sportsman named Alexander Kotarides from Norfolk, Virginia, had leased our harbor and we were going to work for him. Mr. Kotarides was the owner and operator of the Mary Jane Bakery in Norfolk and was an avid hunter. His company was paying for all the improvements to our harbor, and my father was going to become the hunting guide for Gull Island Gunning Club. I knew where Gull Island was from the many fishing trips we had taken together. I also knew that there was only a small, run-down shack located there.

My father came from a long line of commercial hunters. As a boy he and his father, Aaron Hooper, harvested waterfowl and shipped them to the northern markets. They had ten- and eight-gauge punt guns mounted on the bows of my grandfather's hunting skiffs. They would go fire lighting ducks, geese, brant, and swan at night. In those days this method was a customary way of making a living for waterfowlers. When my father was a boy this area had an abundant supply of fish and fowl. He told me that his hunting work was about to change. During the season this year he would be working for Mr. Kotarides and the newly formed Gull Island Gunning Club. He would be turning his two curtain boxes over to Fair Payne and Perry Farrow, the one on Opening Shoals and the one on Sheep's Head Shoals; they would manage these for us. "Come on, Son. Need to hustle. Your mother is cooking stewed crabs and pie bread for supper. We need to go in and get washed up, and I will answer all your questions and fill you in after supper," he told me.

That night after evening prayers and a Bible story, my father told me all the exciting things that were going to take place during my summer vacation from school. I could not believe my ears; it was going to be an exciting time indeed. I was busting at the seams. I could hardly wait until the next day to tell my friends what was going on at our harbor. In my childhood imagination, I knew with all that sand and mud piled up, we would be able to choose sides and have long and enjoyable dirt clod wars.

The next morning dawned as a hot, muggy day in the early part of June. I was up early and out of the house even before breakfast. This morning I was off to tell all of my friends about the big goings-on at the harbor. I ran over to my grandpop's house to tell my cousin Elwood all about it. He and his family lived with my grandparents. We had a family conference, and I filled him in on what was going on. We agreed that I would go down the road to my friend Larry Midgett's house to share the news. He would go up the road to Richard Austin's house, one of our cousins, to tell him of what we had planned. Soon we had a group of six young boys running down the lane, headed for the harbor and the digging machine. We were laughing, pushing, and tripping each other as kids do. We could hear the noise and see the smoke from the monster that was digging out our creek. Just before we rounded the bend that separated our house from the harbor, there stood my mother in the center of the road, hands on her hips and a frown on her face, blocking all access to the water. "Elvin Hooper, where do you and your partners in crime think you are going?" she asked.

"Off to the harbor to check out the digging machine," I replied.

"Not before you all come in and wash up and have breakfast." We all moaned and complained, said we were not hungry, but to no avail. "Now move," she said. "Each and every one of you go on the front porch after you wash your hands, and you can eat at the picnic table." My father had built a picnic table and placed it on the front porch so that we could have the evening meals in the cool air away from the heat in the kitchen. We gulped down the servings of ham, scrambled eggs, toast, and milk. We then tore out the door and headed to the harbor, slamming the screen door behind us. "What have I told you boys about slamming that screen door?" my mom yelled after us. "One of these days it is going to come off the hinges if you don't watch out. Then you will be in for it."

We ran the rest of the way to the harbor. When we came to the end of the road there was the drag line, dipping the large bucket in the water, then swinging around and dumping the load of sand on a growing pile. "Man, would you look at that thing," was one comment.

"Look at the wheels it rides on," was another. None of us had ever seen a digger this size in the Salvo area; we had only seen things such as this on television. All of the ditches we were used to were dug by hand, straight from the sound up a few yards toward the houses. These were a result of trying to drain the surrounding marshes to control the mosquito population. The ditches were dug by the Works Progress Administration or the Civilian Conservation Corps encampments by the Roosevelt administration. "Man, look at your harbor," one of my friends said. "You could probably put a hundred boats in there." It did look massive compared to what it used to look like. Before this transformation it was just a straight narrow ditch. My father could only get his boats up the creek when the wind was from the southwest and the water was up. On a nor'easter you could not get a boat in there; the creek would be nearly dry. "Boy, look at that thing go," said someone; it had dug a huge basin to the north and south about fifty to sixty feet wide and was now widening the access toward the sound. "Look how it moves those big pieces of wood to make its own road," was a comment as we watched the monster grab a large flat of wood by a hook attached to the large boom and drag it in front of itself, and then move onto it to make forward progress. We all agreed that this ditch digger was something to behold.

We could see my father and another man walking in our direction from the drag line. He walked up to us. His nephew Floyd was with him. Floyd was a rather friendly sort, and for some reason his nickname was Pudding Head. My father said someone named him that when he was young and the name stayed with him. "The harbor will probably be finished in a couple of days; then you boys can have some fun," said my father. "It will be about two weeks before Ray and Dick begin the bulkhead work. Once they begin pumping those creosote pilings, I want you boys to stay out of the harbor. Those chemicals in that wood will burn you up and blister your skin," my father informed us. "The pilings will not be delivered until the end of next week, but the men will be bringing their pumps and barge as soon as the harbor is completed to the shore side," he told us.

This was all we needed to know. This would give us ample time to complete our planning and notify our friends in other villages about the upcoming fun. We watched the digging for a while but soon became bored. After watching it swing and dump many times, cousin Elwood said, "Man, I'm over this. We have seen all there is to see here, and the day is still young." He was a little older and was the ringleader of our small group.

"What do you suggest, Woody?" asked Richie, as we called him. He was the next in line of age and command. "Man, let me see, do you boys remember where we hid the corncob pipes we made last week?" he asked. "If I remember right they are in a plastic bag about halfway back up the landing road," he said. It was decided that we would go get them, walk up and down the road and pick up cigarette butts and smoke the tobacco in our pipes.

"If we can't find any butts we can always fall back on rabbit tobacco," Woody said. We could search the trash piles for liquor bottles, and if we could find about a dozen or so we could pour all them into one and have ourselves a little drink. No matter how you try, when you finish a bottle there is always a little still left in the bottom. Elwood had taught us this in an earlier get together.

"What do you think, men?" he asked. A little smoke, a little drink could polish the morning off. We all agreed but decided to be extremely cautious. The last thing we wanted was to get caught by some grownup.

We located the pipes and soon had enough tobacco to pack them. The whiskey in a Holy Roller community was another thing entirely. We searched several trash piles and only found three bottles containing a small amount of liquid. Elwood poured all the liquid in one bottle. "I will have a little drink and tell you boys how good it was," he said with a laugh. Before we could say anything he drained the bottle and flung it back in the trash pile. He started laughing and staggering around as if he were drunk. We all laughed because we knew he was acting up. "Might not have on," he said, "but I have the smell of one on my breath, next best thing, now let's go and have that little smoke." We went back to the landing road and settled in a small clearing, all lit up our pipes and were having us a time. All of a sudden, I looked up and in the entrance of the clearing there stood my father. I had a lung full of smoke, when he said, "Hello, Son. What are you boys up to?" I had the pipe in my hand, my lungs full of smoke, and all I could do was hold my breath and nod. "You have to breathe sometime I suspect," he said to me. "This time I won't tell your mother or the rest of you boys' parents. Just put that mess out and be careful with those matches. I don't want to fight a marsh fire today. Boy, your mother would peel the skin off your back and probably try to whip the lot if she had caught you."

At this point I let out the smoke in a choking breath. "Thanks, Pop," I said.

As he turned to leave us he reminded us, "Remember what I said." It had been a very dry spring and the weeds would easily burn.

"Man, Uncle Ed is alright," Elwood said.

"Yes, but he said, 'This time,'" I reminded the group. "I think we need to choose a better location, maybe the beach next time we smoke," I said.

"Okay, cats, a near miss is as good as a mile," began Elwood. "Now we need to get down to business. We will meet right here tomorrow and check on the progress of the ditch digger," he said. "That will give us an idea when the digging will be completed," he added.

"We will need more people in order to have a decent dirt-flinging war," Woody said.

Richie added, "I think we should come up with a plan to send word to our buds in Waves and Rodanthe of the upcoming war of the dirt clod."

"That is a great idea, Rich," Woody responded.

"How are we going to get word to them?" someone in the group asked. A voice from the back of the group responded, "We could walk up there and tell them."

"Man, you must be out of your mind," Woody said. The village of Waves is only about two miles away, but Rodanthe is another two.

"Yes," Richie added, "that would be a total of eight miles there and back. That would take us hours probably all day just walking.

"In order to make such a walk we would have to pack a lunch to take along," Rich said. We were in a quandary, almost to the point of despair. "Just relax a few minutes, cats," Woody said. "Let's give this thing a little more thought. If we put our heads together I am sure we can come up with an idea to spread the word. Let's sleep on it tonight and see what we can come up with tomorrow."

"Let's walk back to the creek for a last look at the ditch digger," someone said. So back to the creek we went. When we got there the dragline operator was in the process of quitting for the day. He had shut down the machine and was walking toward us. "You boys need to stay off those sandpiles until all the water runs out of them," he told us. "If you walk on them this afternoon, you are liable to sink to your waist in mud," he added. "They need at least a whole day of sunshine to dry them out and firm them up," he said as he walked toward the truck.

# CHAPTER TWO

# The Dirt Clod War

The next morning we met at the harbor. The digger was almost at the end of the marsh with large amounts of sand and mud piled up in high mounds on both ditch banks. "Boy, look at all those nice dirt clods," said Woody. "Do any of you birds know if your folks are headed up to the other villages today?" he asked.

"Not today," came a response from someone in our group. "It's Saturday."

"So, it's Saturday. What does that have to do with anything?" asked Woody.

"Because tomorrow is Sunday, and Fair Haven Methodist Church has its homecoming the second Sunday of June each summer," was the answer he got.

"Boy," said Richie, "all those fine eats, cakes, pies, and any dessert you can imagine," he added.

"Yeah, but we will have to put long pants on and wear shoes and sit through a whole church service. All you cats know how long-winded that fat preacher up there is," Woody said.

"A small price to pay to get one of the best meals of the summer, and we will have time before the meeting to spread the word about the dirt clod war," I said.

All of a sudden, a gleam came in Woody's eyes. "Perhaps we could slip out and polish off a bunch of those Pepsi-Colas they ice down in that large skiff each year," he exclaimed. "All right, that is the plan. All you birds make sure your folks are planning to go to homecoming at Fair Haven Methodist Church tomorrow. We will feast on pies and cakes and have our fill of Pepsi-Cola. Then we can spread the word about our upcoming fun."

"Now what are we going to do for the rest of the day? Man, it's still early yet," Woody said. A few of our group said they had to return home to help their parents with Saturday chores around their homes. All who were left standing at the edge of the newly dug out basin were myself, Elwood, and Richie.

"Well, I guess it is just the three of us with absolutely nothing to do," I said as I slid off the bank and sank up to my knees in water. We heard someone holler, and all of us turned to see who was coming toward us. It was my father and Mr. Perry Farrow.

"Stay out of the creek today," my father said to us. "It is still not settled out yet. The water is thick with silt and not fit for swimming yet. It needs another day to clear. Why are you three standing here looking like you lost your last friend?" he asked.

"We don't have anything to do today," I responded.

"Well, do I have news for you all," he said. "Perry and I have just finished a terrapin pound back of the house. We will pay you boys a quarter for each cow terrapin you catch that is at least six inches long and put in the pound."

"Boy, let's go cats," Elwood said. "We are employed."

"I am not finished yet," said my father. "We will pay you fifty cents for each stingray you can catch to be used for crab pot bait. Perry and I set fifty pots a few days ago, but the tide has been too low to fish and rebait them. You boys go over to Pop's ditch and you will find my shove skiff there. The stingray gigs are in the skiff, also a shove paddle. Catch us some terrapins and stingrays for bait, and we will pay you. Before you put any stingrays in the skiff, make sure you cut off their tails and get rid of the stinging barbs. I don't want to have to cut barbs from your feet," he said. "Perry and I have work to do on a few more pots we plan to set, so we need fresh bait. We will collect the terrapins all summer and ship them to the northern markets in the fall. I suggest you all go home and tell your folks what you are up to. Make sure you pack a lunch because you will be gone most of the day," he added.

We were off in a flash and soon met at Grandpop's ditch with our lunches in hand. Sure enough, there was my dad's shove skiff tied to the dock. My grandfather was mending net close to the ditch bank. "Where are you boys off to in such a hurry?" he asked. We told him of our plans. "You boys mind them barbs," he warned. "You know what will happen if you get one in your foot." We promised to be careful and piled into the skiff.

Elwood was the best paddler of all three of us, and we began sliding smoothly toward the mouth of the creek. Soon we were out of the creek, and Elwood turned the skiff to the north. He shoved it along the marsh close to the shore. He said, "If you see a terrapin, dive on it and grab it by the end of the shell near the tail." All of a sudden, he was over the side of the skiff with a splash. He surfaced with a large grin on his face and a terrapin that was at least ten inches long. "That is how you do it, boys," he said. Then it was Richie's turn. Over he went and returned with a terrapin large enough to keep. Then I saw one swim under the boat, and I dove on it, returning to the skiff with it. "Man, we have hit the honey hole," Woody said. "There are terrapins everywhere." Soon we had about thirty of them in the back of the boat. A couple of them tried to climb over the stern. They have long claws good for climbing on a slanted wood surface. "Let's gather some wet seaweed to keep them cool and shade them from the sun. This should calm them down and stop their climbing," said Woody. As usual, he was right. As soon as we placed the wet seaweed on them, they stopped moving around so much.

"Now let's stop and have lunch," said Richie. "Man, I am hungry after catching all those terrapins." So we pulled up to the shore and ate.

After we finished, Woody said, "All right, cats. It's on to the gigging." He headed the skiff offshore to the grassy beds where the stingrays forage for small crabs, fish, shrimp, and anything they can catch for food. As a rule, they are bottom feeders. It was decided that I would remain in the stern of the skiff and keep an eye on the terrapins, keeping them wet and cool as well as stop any attempt to escape. Elwood moved to the center of the skiff. Richie was on the bow, and the hunt was on.

"Okay, Rich, when you see one, point the way to it, and I will head the boat in that direction. When you are stingray gigging, an element of surprise is necessary. If you bang the side of the skiff with the paddle, your quarry is off in an instant; however, if you remain quiet they can be approached if you use extreme caution."

"Man, here comes a barn door," shouted Richie, a name for a very large stingray, comparing it to the size of a barn door. "He is headed right for us. Just to the left a little, Woody," said Rich, then he flung the gig. "Hit," yelled Richie as the handle of the gig sped off ahead of the skiff. Then Woody gave chase. Soon we had our first big stingray in the front of the boat. Elwood placed the end of the paddle on its tail and pinned it to the bottom of the skiff, and Rich hacked it off with a hatchet and threw it over the side. This process was repeated several times with each of us taking turns and trading jobs until we were completely worn out. We had caught about twenty large stingrays; this would provide plenty of bait for the pots. Dusk was coming, so we headed back. Mr. Perry was waiting for us at Grandpop's ditch.

"You boys did really well today," he said. "Give me the hatchet and help me off-load the stingrays. I need to cut them to bait pocket size and salt them down in this vat. Then we can put the terrapins in the pound. I will pay you for a job well done," he said.

"Where is my dad?" I asked Mr. Perry.

"He has gone up to Asa Gray's store to buy gas for us on Monday. Elwood and Richie can help me with the stingrays, and you can take the terrapins to the pound," he said to me. I dropped the terrapins off and came back just as they were removing the last ray from the boat. Grandpop helped me wash out my dad's skiff and store the gear in the fish house. Just then my father drove up in Uncle Dick's truck, Richie's father, and rolled a barrel of gas out on the ground. "Son," he said to me, "you can help me gas up the crab boat, then we need to get home. We are all going to the Methodist homecoming tomorrow. Elwood, you and your sisters, Rachael and Alpean, will be staying at our house tonight and going with us up to the homecoming. Your folks are catching the ten o'clock ferry and going to Wanchese to spend a few days with your mother's folks. As soon as you finish helping Perry, you, Rich, and Elvin climb in the back of the truck."

"Okay, Uncle Ed," Woody said. My dad and I gassed up the boat, just about the same time Elwood, Rich, and Mr. Perry finished packing the stingrays. All three of us climbed in the back of the truck tired but happy. We were headed to one of the biggest and best feeds of the summer, and we would see all our buds before church started.

The next day my house was a ball of energy. My mom was busy helping the girls put their hair up and fixing us a light breakfast of toast and cream of wheat. "Don't you kids eat too much now and spoil your dinner later," my father warned. "There will be everything you could possibly imagine there to eat," he said.

"Elvin, I better not see you and Elwood set up camp at that boat full of drinks," warned my mother. Woody and I just looked at each other. "Did you hear me?" she asked.

"Yes, Mom," I responded.

"Okay, Aunt Nudge," Elwood said. To this day Elwood and my father are the only two people who called my mother by that nickname. My father, mother, and Rachael sat in the front seat of the 1953 Henry-J my father owned. Alpean, Elwood, and I sat in the back seat and we were off. Lying on the floor by my feet was a small electric fan my father had been repairing. There was a large nail near the fan blade. I slipped the nail through the hole in the blade and held it up to the window to spin in the breeze. Everything was fine until the spinning blade began to build up friction and burn my fingers. It got so hot I had to drop the blade. It landed on the back of the seat and popped my father in the back of his head. He yelled in surprise, "For God's sake, Son, what are you trying to do? Kill me?" My mother turned and swung at me. I dove for the cover of the floor. She landed a few blows to my back, partially blocked by the high seats.

"You could have seriously cut your father's head open," she screamed at me.

"Calm down, Nudge," my dad said. "He did not mean to hit me with that fan blade. He was only playing with it."

"All the same he needs to think before he does things like that." Saved by my father again, I rubbed his head where the blade had hit him. There was a knot already. He looked at me in the mirror and softly smiled.

As we pulled in the Fair Haven Church yard, my mother said to Elwood and me, "You boys be careful and don't get dirty before services. You have a few minutes to spend with your friends before we have to go inside." Elwood and I were out of the car as soon as it stopped. We searched the church yard for our friends. We found them on the north side of the church away from the grown folks. There was a group of about a dozen kids sitting on the church yard fence. Soon Woody had everyone's attention. He told them about the planned dirt clod war. Everyone said they would be there after lunch the next day. The plans were finalized, and we began fooling around. Of course we got a little dirt on us. As we entered the church, my mother was waiting for us. She grabbed Woody first and said to me, "Don't you dare move, young man." She began to give him a spit bath. I was next in line for the same treatment. A spit bath is when an adult wets a handkerchief. If there is an absence of water it is permissible to wet it with your tongue.

When she finished scrubbing on us she directed us up to where my father and the girls were seated. She placed us on the inside of the pew so we had to pass by her to get out. Woody groaned, "She has got us, bud," he said to me. Rachael snickered at us; she knew what we had on our minds. Alpean was seated next to my father. When her boyfriend, Leland Midgett, came in, she was allowed to leave us and sit with him during the service. We sat there while that long-winded preacher went on and on. Finally, he invited my father up to the podium for a few words and to bless food. Then we were dismissed to the church yard for the feed.

We made straight for the boat of drinks. They had a skiff in the yard filled with soft drinks and shaved ice. They were so cold it was all you could do to hold one in your hands. Man, did we have a feast. There was everything there you could think of to eat. All of it was all very good. The ladies of the villages were excellent cooks. All types of cooked meats, vegetables, salads, and dessert were there for the taking. The older folks always said, "Take all you want, but be sure you eat all you take." Man, my friends and I ate until we could not eat anymore. We said our good-byes and piled into the car. Alpean was the last to get in as Leland stood by the car near my father's open window. He asked my father if she could ride home with him. "It will be okay by me, son," my father told him, but he looked over at my mother.

"Straight to our house," was my mother's reply. "You two can visit there for the rest of the afternoon."

All the digging had been finished by the end of Saturday afternoon. When Woody and I walked to the harbor early Monday morning, the drag line was being loaded on a large flatbed trailer to be taken to its next scheduled job. The harbor digging was finished, the water was clear, and the dirt was piled high and waiting for us. Just after lunch, our buds began to arrive. We divided and chose sides for the battle. We set up positions across the ditch banks on the portion that heads out to the sound. The basin was so wide that not one of us could throw across it. Then the battle began; a steady barrage of mud and dirt was thrown with many successful targets.

The dirt was a little dry from the sun and hard to pack; water was needed to form the desired clod for good throwing. A trip down to the water's edge was required. It was during these trips that the opposing team plastered you. When you ran out of ammo and needed water, you made them suffer. Half of the fun was forming wet slides down the mounds of dirt and mud for easy access to the water. You could slide head first into the creek, grasp some wet mud, and come up firing. We dodged behind mounds of dirt, ran to the top, and pummeled the opposition. Sometimes you would take a sound hit and roll all the way down to the water. This was a paradise for kids our age.

"Hold your fire, men," was a call we all heard. We looked toward the mouth of the harbor, and there was my father and Mr. Perry coming in the crab skiff powered by an air-cooled motor. We all stopped to watch them. Just as they got to us they reached in the bottom of the skiff and came up with dirt clods and pummeled us on both sides. We were caught without any ammo and they got us good. My father throttled up the boat, and they cruised up into the basin laughing.

"Come on boys," Woody said. "They have to come out by us; let's be ready for them. We will gang up on them when they come back by," he said. We gathered up plenty of ammo and waited to ambush them. Soon we heard them coming. "Get ready, men," was the battle cry. They came at an idle up toward us. "Let them have it," Woody cried. Just as we began to give it to them, both men ducked below the gunnels of the skiff. When we had exhausted ourselves and used all of our ammo, they reappeared and caught us wide open at the edges of both sides of the creek. They peppered us again. We were hit in the back, legs, neck, all over. Before we could recover and get more ammo, they were out the creek laughing at us again. We all gathered dirt and ran down the bank after them. It is really hard to run in mounds of soft sand with dirt clods in both hands. Some of us fell down, dropping our ammo. A few of us were able to launch, but our barrage fell short of the skiff near the stern. That made them laugh harder. After they were out of range we continued maneuvers until dark was approaching. That day I discovered that dirt clod fun was not just reserved for the young.

We all washed in the harbor and walked up to my house. My mother was waiting with the water hose, towels, and a change of dry clothes for all. We had a satisfying afternoon of fun. The boys' parents began to arrive to pick them up. "We are going to roast hot dogs tonight and eat on the porch," my mother announced. As we were eating, my mother asked my father, "What in the world were you and Perry laughing about when you came from the creek?" He just winked at Woody and me.

"Oh, nothing," he said.

# CHAPTER THREE

# Shack on the Island

My father got Woody and me up early the next morning. "Come on, boys," he said. "We are going to the island today to check out that shack to see what condition it is in."

I had seen the shack many times from a distance. We had crab pots set in the Gull Island channel. We also had nets there, and we had navigated the channel many times during long net fishing sets. The plan was to take carpentry tools with us to see if we would be able to repair the shack and begin work on the blinds for the upcoming hunting season.

We had to take a small skiff from Grandpop's ditch and paddle out to the *Gray Dolphin*; she was tied at one of the boat stakes offshore. The *Gray Dolphin* was my father's run boat from his long net rig. She was painted battleship gray and was twenty-six feet long and about six feet wide. A grown man could stretch out at her mid-ship area. She was decked over inside above the bottom so she could hold a complete load of fish from a long net catch. She had a 327-cubic-inch short block Chevrolet motor, tunnel stern, and a wet exhaust. Under her bottom was a screened intake port that allowed salt water to be pumped through her jacket for cooling purposes, and then pumped overboard. She had a clutch with reverse and forward and a throttle control. The steering consisted of a large homemade tiller and rubber. She got her name because my father had put flair in her bow when he built her. Her bow was capped about four feet back; she could glide through large waves on rough days. Even if she went down by the bow, she would come up without taking on any water.

We climbed aboard the *Dolphin*, tied the skiff to the boat stake, and soon we were skimming along the waves, headed southward toward the island. Soon we had passed No-Ache Marsh, Cedar Hammock Marsh, and the outer point of Cedar Hammock Island. Then we began to cross over Bay Shoals and head out to Cedar Hammock Channel, then Gull Shoal Channel, and soon we were approaching the island itself.

Gull Island is located six miles south of the village of Salvo and about a mile and one half offshore. It rises out of the sound at the end of the reef. The reef extends all along the Outer Banks a mile or two offshore. This barrier separates the deeper waters of the sound from the shallow in-shore water. The island itself is about a mile wide by a mile and a half long. It is separated from all activity the shore of Hatteras Island provides. It is a perfect habitat for wildlife to seek seclusion and provides natural food for all species of fish and fowl. The island is an ideal location for a gunning club.

As we approached the island, thousands of birds took flight; all types of gulls were screeching at us, announcing our approach. The *Dolphin* began to bump bottom about fifty yards from the island. We had to go cut the motor, go over the side and pull the boat up to the bank abreast the shack.

The shack was about twelve feet wide and sixteen feet long. It had one door and two windows, and a porch surrounded all sides. It was located in a small cove on the northwest point of the island. Inside the shack were four built-in bunk beds and a gas stove, and in one corner there was a crude table and benches on both sides. My father decided with a little work it would do for the first season. He made a list of the materials he would need to fix up the shack.

We pulled the *Dolphin* back into deep water and went off to mark the locations of shore blinds. My father wanted to start working on the shack and the shore blinds right away. He picked the locations for four shore blinds. He wanted to situate two of the blinds to be hunted on north winds and two for south wind hunts. We marked the locations by driving four stakes in the marsh, one for each corner. The first location was on the northwest point of the island. He named this the northwest point box. The second location was at the mouth of a small creek that ran back for a short distance in the island itself. He said this was the Thara-Fair Creek box. The third location was at a natural cane field; he named it the cane field box. The fourth location was located out on the back of the island on a white sand beach. He named this spot the sandbox. My father had a name for everything. I have often heard him say it was bad luck for a boat of any size not to be named, and never change the name of any boat.

"This is where we will dig to bury the boxes for the blinds."

"What boxes?" was my question.

"The boxes we are going to build and bring here," was my father's response. Then we went to the north reef near the island, and he marked a location for a curtain box with four weighted floats made from glass bleach bottles. He marked the position of a stilt blind in the same manner. At this point we went to the south reef. The wind was from the southwest and the south reef was covered. All three of us got out of the boat and walked to the middle of the reef. It was covered with water about knee deep. "We will place a curtain box here," he told us. "This will be the south reef high-water box," he said. "We will only hunt it when the south reef is completely covered with water." The third curtain box location we marked on the edge of Bay Shoals.

"Remember, boys," he told us, "all fowl must have a source of fresh water and gravel for their gizzards to survive. They can drink water off their backs when it rains, but they must find gravel for their gizzards to help digest their food."

When he was satisfied with his marked blind locations, we dropped off in the channel for a little fishing. We had angle poles along with peeler crab for bait. This time of year the channel was full of types of edible fish. An angle pole is a homemade fishing pole usually made from bamboo found washed up on the beach. It consists of a nine- to ten-foot pole with fishing line attached, with a bobber or cork, light lead weight, and a fish hook. The line is tied off at the small end and extends the length of the pole. The bobber or cork is allowed to slide up and down on the line and has a small wooden peg in the center of the cork to lock it into position, adjusting the bait just off the bottom. The peeler crab bait is a stage in the shedding process of all crabs as they grow too large for their exterior shells. They are excellent bait for all species of fish. The hook is baited and tossed over the side. When the cork goes under, usually a fish is on the line. Soon we had a nice catch of panfish, and satisfied, we headed for home. It was almost dark when we arrived back to the boat stake. We had just enough time to clean the fish, then it was time to wash up for supper.

Woody's parents arrived home from visiting relatives off the island. His father was my father's younger brother. His name was Luther, and he worked on the Oregon Inlet ferry. Woody and the girls returned to Grandpop's with their parents. The next day my father woke me up early to help him fish the crab pots. He had about seventy-five pots set from the beginning of Scotts Reef to the northwest edge of Gull Shoal Channel. We were back to the creek before lunchtime. The framing he had ordered arrived late that afternoon. We covered it with several canvas tarps to protect it from the rain and sun.

The creosote lumber for the curtain boxes and plywood for the stilt blinds and shore boxes arrived early the next morning. For the next two weeks every afternoon after we crabbed the pots, my father and I built the boxes for the hunting blinds. We built four shore blind boxes, three stilt blind boxes, and three curtain boxes from the creosote lumber. When all the boxes were finished, he told me he had to hire three me to help us install them. He decided that his nephew, Pudding Head, would become a full-time employee, and the two other men would work only until the blinds were ready and the shack was complete for the first season's hunt. He used Mr. Perry Farrow, his crabbing partner, and Uncle Bill, one of his sister's husbands who was retired from the Norfolk Navy Yard. He fashioned a platform on the *Dolphin*, also on his net skiff from the long net rig.

The first morning before crabbing we loaded one of the shore boxes on the *Dolphin* and two on the net skiff, and tied them down with ropes. Mr. Perry and Uncle Bill were off crabbing. Pudding Head, my father, and I headed out with the three shore boxes. When all the pots were fished Uncle Bill joined us on the island to help with the work, and Mr. Perry took the crabs to market. We took the first box to the cane field and rolled it off on the marsh near its location. Then it was on to Thara-Fair Creek, and we rolled the second one off. On we went to the northwest point of marsh and rolled the third one off. But at this location we pumped four creosote pilings down in the marsh with an air-cooled water pump and bolted the box to them about three feet above the marsh. There was a natural growth of reed grass on this point; the box was almost concealed. With little effort, we tied up branches of reed grass and covered the box, blending it in with the natural surroundings.

"Alright, men," my father said. "I am satisfied with these doings. Let's go." He told me to make sure the bottom was clear and able to float up if we had a storm tide. All the boxes he placed as shore blinds had the bottom just lying in place inside them and could be lifted out with very little effort. When a storm came with extremely high tides, the bottoms would float up and out of the box. The boxes or the pilings were not subjected to the water pressure trying to lift them off location. His boxes always stayed in place; he drilled a small hole in one corner of the bottom and tied it to the back of the box. If it floated out of the box, it would be just outside, tied by a nylon decoy cord. I checked the bottom to make sure it was free and easily removable. Satisfied, I got in the net skiff, and we paddled out to the *Dolphin* and returned to Salvo. When we arrived at the harbor, my father told us, "Okay, men, same thing tomorrow." We repeated this process until all four shore boxes were installed.

Then we began work on the stilt blinds. A stilt blind is a solid plywood box about eight feet above the water equipped with peep holes supported on four creosote pilings. We had to pump the pilings down in the bottom, then bolt the boxes to them. They were not grassed or brushed, just painted with nonreflective green-gray paint. Normally placed on a reef so that the hunters can walk and collect their downed fowl, they have a vertical ladder attached to the underside for access. In the stilt blinds we installed, my father had removable bottoms in them. At the end of the season you could remove a few screws and the bottoms would lift out. During the off-season, gulls, cormorants, and all type of fish-eating birds would land on the stilt blinds. If they dropped their food inside the box they would go in after it. The creatures would be trapped inside and die if the box had a bottom in it. All of these large fish-eating birds have to take flight, much like airplanes. They have to take off into the wind to become airborne. They are unable to achieve flight with a vertical takeoff. When you returned to the blinds at the beginning of a new hunting season, there would be a mess inside the boxes. Dead birds, fish scraps, and rainwater resulted in a putrid soup that would have to be cleaned out before the hunters could occupy the blinds again. In the stilt boxes my father built with the bottoms removed during the off-season, the food dropped by the birds would simply drop to the water below, passing through the box. All that was needed at season's beginning was to scrub the inside walls, check the hinges on the peep hole flaps, and install the bottom containing the trapdoor. We placed a stilt blind on the northwest edge of Gull Shoal Channel, one directly behind the island on the west point of the south reef, and one on Bay Shoals.

At this point my father decided to work on the shack to make it livable for the first season's hunt. We added a small twelve-by-twelve-foot kitchen and built in four more bunk beds. This made it possible to sleep five hunters and three workers. The addition of the kitchen made it possible to install a small gas cookstove and wash sink. The table was moved from the main portion of the building into the kitchen area. Rainwater was collected from the roof runoff, stored in a tank, and gravity fed into the kitchen.

# CHAPTER FOUR

# The Curtain Boxes

The curtain boxes had three main components: a buried box that was installed below the bottom into the sand, a curtain that was smaller and was adjustable by raising and lowering it inside the buried box, and a wing or sea breaker to keep the wind-driven waves from washing over inside the box. My dad built the submersible boxes on the shore at Salvo. A man by the name of Sam Boomer from Norfolk, Virginia, came to Salvo and made the adjustable curtains. He used white cedar or juniper, as it was locally called, and waterproof canvas to make the curtains. These curtains were made to fit the boxes my dad built. These curtains were constructed with a wooden flange on the bottom to match up with the flange on the top of the box to be buried. The curtain was covered on the outside by waterproof canvas. The top was wooden, about two and one half feet deep with a vertical four-foot leg attached one to each corner. Each one of these legs had a round hole drilled in the bottom with a piece of rope passing through the holes that were attached to the underside of the buried box. A cleat was attached to the top of each leg, allowing a pull upward on the rope to raise the top of the curtain above the water and be tied off to the cleat. A sea breaker, or wing as it was called, made from one-by-four slats of wood with an open section that was fashioned to fit around the box was the third component of the setup. When it was set up properly the hunters were actually below the surface of the water, and from a short distance it resembled a raft of fowl sitting on the water. When the curtains were finished they were fitted to the creosote boxes on the shore at Salvo. If the flanges lined up properly, holes were drilled through both surfaces and bolts were installed in the holes, bolting both flanges together.

When Mr. Boomer and my father were satisfied with the results, they marked the flanges so that they could be aligned properly when they were installed at their location. We took them apart and loaded the creosote boxes on the boats, one on the *Dolphin* and the other two on the net skiff. We took them to their locations that we had marked earlier. The first one was the Bay Shoal location. We anchored one box there to allow the water to swell up the wood and make it waterproof. We dropped the next one off near the center of the north reef at its marked location. The last one we took as close to the center of the south reef as we could get. The water was much too shallow to get to its marked location.

"We will have to come back on a southwest wind to work on this one," my dad told us. "It will only be hunted in stormy conditions when everything else is covered over from strong south winds and the water is too deep to wade and hunt the other locations."

We anchored the box at the edge of the reef and went back to the Bay Shoals to begin installing the creosote box. Pudding Head and I went over the side and began filling the box with water by bailing it in with a five-gallon bucket. We bailed until the box settled on the bottom in knee-deep water. My dad and Uncle Bill took the *Dolphin* over to the desired box location and anchored her off with two anchors over the stern. Then the boat was put in forward gear and they began to blow a hole out with the prop, large enough to sink the box in. Pudding Head and I bailed on the box until it would float and moved it over the hole that was kicked out by the boat. Then we bailed it full of water again until it sank and rested on the bottom of the hole in its location. My father got into the water and checked the box. When he was satisfied that it was deep enough in the sand and level, he had us fill burlap bags with sand and place them on a platform that was fastened to the bottom on all sides of the box. When we had sand bags halfway up the sides of the box, he repositioned the boat and washed sand back around the box until it was completely covered. He moved the boat and marked all four corners of the box with floats. Then he told us that we would come back and put the curtain on when the tide was lower. Darkness was coming, and we headed back to the ranch, as my father called it. We were going home for the day.

The next day when Dad woke me, the wind was blowing ten to fifteen miles per hour from the southwest. It was a perfect day to place the curtain box in the center of the south reef at Gull Island. By the time I got dressed and washed up, my mom had breakfast on the table and a lunch packed for us. As we were walking to the harbor, Uncle Bill and Pudding Head joined us. We exchanged greetings and boarded the *Dolphin*. We arrived at the anchored box to the north edge of the reef just after daybreak. The water was not deep enough for us to tow the creosote box to the center of the reef where my dad had marked the location. The *Dolphin* had a tunnel stern in her and could operate in the shallow water with no problem. But the creosote box with the platforms attached to the bottom soon began to drag and bottomed out, quickly becoming stuck on the reef. We were about one hundred yards from its desired location. My dad studied the situation for a few minutes. He told Pudding Head and me to go to the island and bring back four of the empty barrels we had taken there to collect rainwater for outside use around the club. As we were leaving, he yelled to us, "Make sure you bring four that we haven't cut the tops out of yet." Pudding Head and I left to fetch the barrels.

By the time we returned with the barrels Uncle Bill and my father had worked the box out to about knee-deep water again. We rolled the barrels over the side, and the three of us climbed on the platform opposite my dad. He positioned one of the barrels under the platform opposite us. We repeated this procedure, placed all four barrels, tied them in place, and now the creosote box was riding high in the water with about one quarter of the barrels above the surface. We towed the box to its location with ease. We removed the barrels, dug the hole with the boat, placed the sand bags, used the boat on all sides, and the prop blew the sand around the bags and covered the box and settled it into position. We marked the corners of the box with floats, and Dad said we would come back and install the curtain when the sand settled around the box. Then it was off to the north reef. We completed the same process, and the last creosote box was buried. We would have to wait a few days for the reef to settle, and then we could install the curtains on all the buried boxes.

"Boy, your pop knows his stuff," Pudding Head said to me as we walked back to the *Dolphin* to leave.

The next day we were involved in the long process of towing the sea breakers or wings to the curtain box locations. They were slid along the bank until we could push then into the harbor. We tied all three together and headed out into the harbor with them. The wind was still from the southwest at about twenty miles per hour. My dad turned the *Dolphin* southward as we rounded the outside boat stake marking deep water. Our speed had to be extremely slow as the waves from a southwester such as this could easily separate the one-by-four pieces of wood from the two-by-fours and trash the wings. It took us about two hours to reach the first buried box at the Bay Shoal location; the Bay Shoal wing was anchored, and we headed for the edge of the northwest reef to the second location. We anchored this wing, then dropped the last one off at the center of the south reef. Pudding Head and I got overboard and had to walk this last wing position and anchored it near the box. By this time it was about lunchtime.

"Boy," my father said, "what do you think about some steamed crabs to add to our midday meal? Let's fish a couple of the crab pots and try out that new gas stove at the camp. We will be able to get out of the sun for a while and eat on the screened porch and enjoy the breeze," he added. We all agreed, and we spread out our lunches and the crabs on the picnic table and everyone helped themselves.

When we had eaten our fill and relaxed for a few minutes, my father said, "Boys, we have the wings in place, finished the shore blinds, and the stilt blinds are ready. All we have left to do is to install the curtains on the sink boxes. We will go home and load the curtains, all the iron ducks and the window weights, and all the materials needed to set the curtains." When we got back to the harbor we loaded one curtain on the *Dolphin* and the other two on one of the net skiffs. We were ready for the next day's work.

"All right, boys, we will take the rest of the day off with pay. Get a good night's sleep. Tomorrow will be a busy day," said my father.

The next day the wind had pulled around to the west and diminished somewhat. The water levels were high, and we headed for the box near the center of the south reef. With the wind falling out, my dad warned, "We will leave the net skiff at the edge of the channel with the two curtains in it just in case the water runs off." We loaded all the materials to set the curtain on the *Dolphin* and rode right alongside the buried box. The conditions were ideal for setting this curtain. The water level was about six inches above the top of the buried box. I positioned the bolts through the holes in the flange of the buried box while Pudding Head and Uncle Bill spread the roofing tar on the flange of the curtain. Uncle Bill and I held the bolts in place while my dad and Pudding Head lifted and lowered the curtain, lining up the aligning marks, and set the curtain in place. Uncle Bill and I tightened up the bolts until the roofing tar was visible on both sides of the flanges, and we knew we had a watertight seal. At this point the curtain was in its highest upward position. I got inside the box and began to bail the water out with a five-gallon bucket. As I bailed, the curtain could be lowered. The box was about half full of sand, which also had to come out. We had a reliable seal with no apparent leaks.

My father told me to off-load the iron ducks with the floats attached to them, along with the canvas-covered window weights, and move the *Dolphin* to deeper water. The water was running off fast, and he did not want her to be stuck on the reef. As I moved the *Dolphin* to the edge of the reef, the three of them completed setting the curtain. They let the curtain down, allowing it to fill with water, and placed an iron duck on each corner cleat, holding the curtain below the surface of the water. Then a window weight covered in canvas was placed in the folds of the curtain to prevent chafing and wearing a hole in the folded canvas. The wing was moved about one hundred yards away to a safe distance so that there was no way it could make contact with the box, even if the wind shifted as it drifted on its anchor line.

When they were convinced the jobs were completed, they walked toward me as I held the *Dolphin* at the edge of deep water. We took the net skiff in tow and went to Bay Shoals and installed that curtain in the same manner. My father decided the water was too high to install the curtain on the north reef box. "We will have to come back another day. That is a low-water box, and the wind has to be from the northeast in order to put this curtain on," he said to us. "We will take the net skiff into the creek at the clubhouse and leave her here with the curtain and the materials to set it, and come back on a northeaster," he told us. "Let's drop off in Cedar Hammock Channel and see if we can catch some of them big hog fish for our supper on the way home," he said.

# CHAPTER FIVE

# The Finishing Touches

Almost all the work had been completed on the hunting blinds, except for a few finishing touches. We returned to all the stilt blinds and checked them. We checked the shore blinds and the curtain boxes; all was ready for hunters. There were no built-in seats in any of the boxes. My father always used adjustable stools as seats. They adjusted in the vertical direction; you could pull a pin and raise or lower them to the desired height. Also, each blind was equipped with a signal flag attached to a long sticklike handle. If any hunter wanted to come to the camp for any reason during the hunt, all he had to do was wave the flag. The hunting guides kept a watchful eye with field glasses on any blinds that were occupied during all hunts. These stools and flags remained in the decoy skiffs until they were needed. We checked all aspects of the camp and pumped down three boat stakes outside the entrance of the clubhouse creek. These stakes would be used to tie up larger boats when the water was low. Smaller skiffs would be used to enter the creek, ferrying passengers and supplies to the camp. The first one we installed about one hundred feet from the entrance of the creek. The others were also spaced about one hundred feet apart to reach the edge of deeper water. As we finished the most off-island stake, my dad looked at me and said, "Son, this is the most worrisome aspect about this whole operation. We will miss many good hunting days because of this low water. Somehow the creek here at the club needs to be dug out and a bulkhead put in, and docks be built for the decoy skiffs as well as the powerboats." When he was satisfied that everything was ready, we headed back to the ranch for the day.

It had taken us most of the summer to finish up the task of making the island ready for the hunters. I was crushed when the end of August was near and I would have to start school the day after Labor Day in September. My adventures at Gull Island, with the exception of weekend excursions and Christmas vacation, were rapidly coming to an end. I positioned myself on the large bow cap of the *Dolphin* as we were steaming home. She was skipping along; my dad had her at about half throttle. I was lying on my stomach looking down as she was splitting the water in fine fashion. It was a beautiful afternoon in the latter part of August; the water was crystal clear. Every now and then you could catch sight of a flash of white on the bottom from a clam shell. As we came out of Cedar Hammock Channel, on the edge of Scotts Reef, the *Dolphin* leaped ahead. She was feeling the effects of entering much shallower water. My dad laughed and gave her a little more throttle. The wind was almost calm. With all the tools, three men, and a eight-year-old boy, she came up, and now we were "balling the jack," as my dad called it. Lying there on the bow as we were skimming along made you feel like you were on top of the world: no worries, no cares, just you, the boat, the sky, and water. Life was good. This was the end of a perfect workday on a Friday afternoon in late August. The *Dolphin* was a workboat, but she cut a swath through water. At that time she was one of the fastest sound-class vessels in the Chicamacomico area, to my recollection.

The next day was Saturday; my dad woke me up at seven in the morning. "I have a surprise for you today," he said. "You and I are taking the *Dolphin* to Avon to see Mr. Willie Austin. He has been building two decoy skiffs, numerous paddles, and scoops for Mr. Kotarides and the club." The skiffs were built from juniper or white cedar lumber. The paddles or push sticks were made from oak. The scoops were made from juniper also. They were used for bailing water out of boats or the curtain boxes when the water level was bailed to a point that a bucket was no longer effective. Scoops had a round handle centered in the back of them. They had two angled sides that intersect at the front on a thin bottom. The front of the bottom was beveled to a thin slope that made it an effective low-water bailing tool.

These scoops have been replaced by plastic bleach one-gallon jugs, with the handle and caps left in place and cut with a sharp knife to the shape of a scoop. Everyone who owns a small boat or skiff these days has a five-gallon plastic bucket and several scoops made from plastic gallon jugs on board as standard equipment.

After breakfast my dad and I boarded the *Dolphin* and headed out of the harbor. When we reached the entrance of the harbor we encountered a stiff southwest wind. "The water is high enough this morning we can go down the inside close to the marsh, cross Bay Shoals, and duck behind the southward reef and be in the calm," he said to me. As we rounded the boat stake, he turned her south and gave her about half throttle. She jumped above the three-foot chop and leveled slick as a whistle. Soon the mouth of the harbor was fading fast over our port stern. We shot past No-Ache Marsh, then Cedar Hammock Marsh. We entered the edge of Bay Shoals; the water was so shallow, she really took off. We were moving so fast, she began to lope from sea to sea. When the stern came out of the water, the engine would race. Dad had to back off the throttle until she settled into a nice plane. Before long, we scooted past Bay Landing, nearing the Little Hills Marsh. Then we passed Little Kinnakeet Coast Guard Station about one hundred yards offshore. Now we could see the houses of Avon plainly. It seemed like no time at all; we were entering Avon Harbor. We tied up near the two decoy boats; Mr. Austin had painted them a drab gray color, copper painted the bottoms, and pushed them in to swell up. They were bailed out, and the paddles and scoops were inside the boats.

We walked a short distance to Mr. Austin's boat shop. We found him in his shop working on a boat. The floor was covered with juniper shavings, and the smell of cedar was in the air. Anyone who works with wood could relate and enjoy this environment. He had a sign up in his shop that read, "Boats built, one hundred dollars per foot. If you stay and watch, five hundred dollars per foot." My dad and Mr. Austin exchanged greetings. He knew why we were there. Mr. Austin and Dad went into his small office off to the side to conduct the settlement for the skiffs and the accessories. They decided to walk back to the harbor; there were a few things Mr. Austin wanted to show my father about the boats. As we walked out of the boat shop, I saw Miss Rachael, as we all call her. She was Mr. Austin's wife. Also, she was the head cook in our cafeteria at school. She had feed buckets in her hands and was headed to feed their things. I ran over to her. "Elvin, for land's sakes, son, what are you doing here today?" she asked.

"I came down here with Dad to get decoy boats from Mr. Willie for the club," I answered.

"Yes," she said, "I heard something about that."

"Can I help you feed your things?" I asked.

"If it is okay with your father, I would welcome the help," she said.

I asked my dad. He said, "Okay, but stay with Rachael and don't wander off." Her things consisted of chickens, ducks, turkeys, even a couple of peacocks.

"Ed," she said to my father, "when you and Will get finished at the harbor, I'll expect you and Elvin to take dinner with us before you leave."

"I don't know, Rachael," he began.

She cut him off, "Fried bluefish, boiled potatoes, coleslaw, fresh-baked cornbread, and poor man's pudding for dessert," she said.

"I am kind of hungry, Pop," I said.

"Don't want you to go to no trouble," he answered her.

"No trouble," she said. "Just don't get involved in a heavy conversation at the harbor and let my food get cold. It's not going to take Elvin and me long to feed and water the things." As we walked toward the small feed shed, she said, "I have a surprise for you." The other day a man was leaving the island and he gave Willis a baby goat. The goat's mother for some reason refused to feed him; he was in pretty bad shape when he brought him here. Willis has been feeding him warm milk from a baby bottle, and he is beginning to come around. After we feed and water the fowl, you can give him a bottle."

Feeding that little goat was really fun. As I finished, Dad and Mr. Willie were returning from the harbor. "I see you have made friends with Little Billy," he said to me.

"Yes, sir," I responded. "Miss Rachel let me feed him."

"Let me show you something about Little Billy," he said to me. "Place your hands on his head and see if you can push him backward." I put my hands on the goat's head and applied pressure in a backward motion. He stiffened his legs and I could not budge him. The harder I pushed, the more he resisted. "Now get down on your hands and knees and push him," Mr. Willie told me. As soon as I got down on all fours, he began to butt me anywhere he could make contact. I stood up, and he continued to butt me to the point of chasing me around the yard. My father and Mr. Willie just rolled in laughter.

Miss Rachael appeared at the screen door and said, "All right, you three come on in and get washed up for dinner. Elvin, take the goat back to his pen," she said.

"How?" I asked.

"Just run toward the pen and he will follow you," she said. So I ran toward the pen with Billy at my heels; my dad, still laughing, came behind us as we entered the pen and closed the gate for me. I climbed over the fence and started toward the house. Billy started crying. "He is calling you," Mr. Willie said. "Son, Little Billy wants you to come back and play some more." So I walked back to the fence. Billy came over, and I scratched his head. "Scratch him under the chin. He likes that," Mr. Willie told me.

"Come on in and eat before it gets cold," Miss Rachael called to us. "Elvin, make sure you wash your hands good where you have been playing with that goat," she said to me.

"Yes, ma'am," I responded. I left Little Billy, washed up, and enjoyed a delicious midday meal with Mr. Willie, Miss Rachael, and my dad.

"We have to be shoving off," Dad said. "The wind is supposed to switch to the north late this afternoon. I want to be home before the shift. Thank you for the fine meal," he said to Miss Rachael.

"You are certainly welcome," she responded. "Elvin, come here, son. I have something for your boat ride home," she said to me. I walked over to her, and she handed me two large pieces of poor man's pudding. "See you in school in a

few days," she called to me as we left the yard for the harbor. Mr. Willie walked
to the harbor with us. He helped us with the tow ropes, and soon we were
out of Avon harbor and headed northward toward Salvo. The wind was off
our port stern quarter; we had an easy ride all the way home. We entered the
harbor in the early part of the afternoon. We secured the boats to the docks.

My dad said, "Son, we are finished for today. Check with your mother
to see if she has anything for you to do. If not, you are free as far as I am
concerned." I checked with my mother. I had to take out the garbage, which
consisted of separating all the paper for a burn barrel, placing all the food
scraps on a compost heap, and digging a hole for all the cans and glass. I
placed all the cans and all the glass in the bottom of the hole and covered
them up. Then I was free to go and find my friends before the evening meal.

I took off, headed for my grandfather's house. His house was located
on the highest hill in Salvo, near the center of the village. There must have
been a dozen kids there playing tag hide and seek. This is a game where one
person who is called counts to fifty near a place called the base. During the
count you could remain on base if you were tired, or you could go hide in
the surrounding bushes, porch roof—anywhere you might think you would
be hard to find. If you were spotted by the person searching for those who
were hid, they called out your name and location. They would have to tag
you before you beat them in a foot race back to the base. If you could avoid
the tag and outrun the person back to the base, you were safe. If not, you
were it, and you became the counter and the searcher. We played until we
were called in for the night. Whenever my mother called, I took off for
home right away because I knew she meant business. The next day was
Sunday, and we always ate at my grandfather's house. My mom always
talked to Grandmother, and they coordinated the Sunday dinner. Mom
always cooked on Saturday night and took the food over there. No one did
any type of work on Sunday. We all went to church and then gathered for
dinner and attended church on Sunday night.

Labor Day came on Monday, September 2, my last day of freedom for
that summer. After church on Sunday night, my father told me that he had

a surprise for me. He told me that I could hire one of my friends if any wanted to work all day long the next day. He said he was willing to pay three dollars per hour for a ten-hour day. Each kid would make thirty dollars. "What will we be doing?" I asked.

"Mr. Kotarides will be sending a tractor trailer truck full of decoys here tomorrow. First, all the decoys have to be unloaded and stacked. Then we will have to attach the decoy spans, leathers, and weights to them and stack them in the decoy skiffs." The spans are the name of the cord that attached the weights to the decoys. My dad always used short pieces of leather that passed through the holes in the bottom of the decoys. The leathers had a hole in their ends to attach the cord. He used this method to prevent the cords from being chafed off as the decoy drifts, controlled by the wind. I ran over to Grandfather's and told Woody.

"Man, thirty bucks," he said. "I am in." So three men and two boys would be the decoy crew for my father the next day.

# CHAPTER SIX

# Decoy Monday

We heard a noise and all three of us looked up. Coming across the road, we saw Richie and his father in an old Chevrolet. The car had the back and the fenders cut off it. Richie's father had cut the car off just behind the front seat and built a wooden trucklike bed on it. He had equipped it with split rims and oversized tires where the fenders used to be. This creation is exactly what most Islanders did to their old cars when they purchased a new vehicle. On the island in those days there were hardly any four-wheel-drive vehicles. Everyone modified their older vehicles into beach buggies. With this type of modification there wasn't any problem driving on the beach. These buggies floated across the surface of the sand on oversize tires with reduced air pressure. This gave the islanders the ability to drive to the beach instead of walking the long distance to get there. This opened up the possibilities of beach parties, fishing trips, sand hauling, and limited beachcombing adventures. Richie and his dad had the wooden bed piled high with sand. Richie was driving. He stopped the buggy next to the growing sandpile. Woody and I were off the porch in a flash. "Hey, man," Woody shouted. "Your dad lets you drive that thing?

Richie smiled and said, "He lets me drive on the beach, but not the road." Woody and I helped Richie unload the sand. Richie's father gave us two rakes, and we leveled the sandpile out for him. He looked at the low spot, rubbed his chin, and said, "I think we need one more load. Son, can I trust you and your friends to get another load for us?"

"You mean just the three of us?" Richie asked his father.

"As long as you drive carefully," came his dad's reply. "Just stay in first gear, keep on the sand road past Burgess's house, then very slowly on to the beach and back." The three of us piled into that buggy before you could slap a tick. Richie started her up and drove out to the road very slowly. We then proceeded past Burgess Hooper's house and on to the sand road that led to the beach. Just as soon as we were out of sight of the houses, Woody began to beg Richie to let him have a go at driving. He just wouldn't let up, "Oh, come on, man," he said. "Just for a short distance." Richie finally gave in to him. "Remember what my dad said: first gear only and very slow," Richie told him.

"I got this," replied Woody. "Now, come on, man; let me have this thing," he said, almost pushing Richie from the driver's seat. Richie got out and walked around the back and I slid over, trapping me in the middle. "Hold on, cats," Woody shouted and floored it. All three of us were thrown violently backward, almost to the point of ripping the seat out. The buggy went flying across the sand as Woody shifted the buggy into second gear. He down-wheeled the buggy to the left. Sand flew clean over the top of our heads. Then he made a hard turn to the right, throwing sand all over the buggy and us. In the next instant he slammed on the brakes. All three of us lurched forward, and then we were slammed backward in the seat. We came to a sliding stop right next to a large sand dune. All three of us were hollering and laughing uncontrollably. "Man, where did you learn to drive like that?" Richie asked Woody.

"Just watching my dad drive his buggy after a few drinks," replied Woody. We leveled the bed off with sand, and Richie drove back to his house. While we were off-loading the sand, Richie's father came over to where we were shoveling.

"Well, I declare, how in the world did you boys and the buggy get completely covered in sand?" he asked, smiling. After we finished leveling out the sand, I asked Richie if he wanted in on the decoy work. "We will each get paid thirty bucks," he said.

"Yes," I said. "But that is for ten hours work. We will all have to get up early," I added. "The workday will begin at seven in the morning with an hour off for lunch; my mom will feed us. Back to work from one until five in the afternoon."

"Count me in," he replied. Three boys and three men were involved in the decoy work.

The next day came early. My dad woke me at six o'clock. I could smell ham cooking as I came downstairs. As I washed up I could hear strange voices coming from the dining room. I took a shower and dressed. Then I went to the dining room. As I entered, my dad introduced me as his son to two strangers sitting at the dining room table, drinking coffee. The first one was named James Johnson; he was the truck driver. The other man was much older, probably in his middle seventies; his name was Harry Bowman.

James Johnson was a regular truck driver for Mr. Kotarides and the Mary Jane Baking Company. James was a big man: six feet tall and 250 pounds. He was good natured and jolly. His job was to haul flour from Richmond to Norfolk. The flour he hauled was used in Mr. Kotarides's bakery. He told us he made the trip three days per week.

Mr. Bowman was a retired lieutenant commander from the navy; he was much more serious than James. He had a stern face and everything he said was precise and to the point. He told us that since his retirement, he had hunted the Back Bay area as a waterfowl hunter, and during the off-season he had worked on and painted decoys. For years he had worked for three of the best decoy makers in the states of Virginia, Delaware, and Maryland. It seemed he was a lifelong friend of Mr. Kotarides.

At that time my mother brought in a platter of scrambled eggs, bacon, ham, and grits. She instructed everyone to help themselves. She told me to mind my manners, then she added some fruit, fresh-baked biscuits. and a variety of jellies and butter. My father blessed the food, then the platters were passed, conversation resumed, questions about truck driving were answered by James, and decoy making and painting by Mr. Bowman. The conversation drifted to the school here on the island. I answered their questions the best I could.

After a hearty breakfast we left the harbor. We walked down the small path from the back door of the kitchen; the path opened up into the single-lane dirt road that ended at the harbor. The path access was just large enough to walk down, and the road was just large enough to drive along. My dad let all the crape myrtle bushes, scrubby oaks, water bushes, and larger shrubs become entwined with briars and grow very thick; he only trimmed enough to keep the access open. His theory was that during hurricanes, as the wind shifted from the west, the thickly grown marsh provided a buffer during times of sound-side flooding, protecting the dwellings. All the villagers practiced this same type of protection, and many times it proved itself. The sound flooding in the tri-village has become much more severe since so many off-island people have moved in, purchased property, built multistory homes and clear-cut all the way to the sound. It seems they have to be high enough to see the sun rise in the morning, and cut enough to see it set in the afternoon. The view seems to have become more important than the protection of their property.

As we came out of the path, we were joined by Uncle Bill, Pudding Head, Woody, and Richie. We all continued along to the harbor. When we reached the harbor, we saw a large silver tractor trailer with a white cab. On the doors of each side was a picture of a young girl's face in the center of a loaf of bread painted in red, with the words "Mary Jane Bread" beneath it. James opened the large back door, and all you could see was decoys. They were a sight to see. There were stacks of them; this large truck was completely filled to the brim with them.

"Man," Woody said. "There must be a million of them in there."

"No, son," said Mr. Bowman, "a few hundred maybe." Compared to the decoys we were used to, they looked really good. "Floyd, I have a question for you, but I really don't want to upset you or make you uncomfortable," said Mr. Bowman.

"Ask away," was Pudding Head's response.

"How in the world did you get a nickname like Pudding Head?" asked Mr. Bowman.

"Well, it seems Pudding Head began when I was a small child. My family was attending a homecoming, which is a large church feed. I ate five helpings of poor man's pudding. One of the older ladies commented that my head was going to turn into pudding. Some of my friends took it from there and started calling me Pudding Head, and the name stuck." Our cousin Floyd has been gone for many years now, but when the family conversation drifts back to him, he is still Pudding Head.

"That is an interesting story, and you are okay with me calling you 'Pudding Head'?" Mr. Bowman asked.

"Absolutely," answered Pudding Head. "I'm used to it. That's what everyone calls me."

Then he turned to Woody. "How about you, Woody?" he asked. "Where does the nickname Woody come from? Does calling you that give you problems?" he asked.

"Heck no!" Woody answered. "It is short for Elwood. I have my cousin's middle name, and Elvin has his first name. We had a cousin; his name was Elvin Elwood Hooper. He was killed on a PT boat in the Second World War. His name appears on a World War II monument located at the county seat in Manteo. There is a list of names of all the Dare County military folks who gave their lives in that war."

"So, Elvin, what would you like me to call you?" Mr. Bowman asked me.

"Just Elvin," was my response.

"We call him Nate. That's his nickname," Woody chimed in. "Richie—that is the other kid standing over there— and Uncle Edward, his father, we call Uncle Ed; all the grownups call him Ed."

"Okay," said Mr. Bowman. "You can call me Harry."

"That is fine for the grown-ups, but E and I will have to call you Mr. Harry, or Uncle Ed will box our ears," replied Woody.

"And what is your name, young man?" he asked Richie.

"My name is Richard Austin, but everyone calls me Richie," he told Mr. Bowman.

"Alright," Mr. Harry said. "This is James; he is a truck driver for Mr. Kotarides's bread company. Okay, boys, today is decoy day." Then he turned to my father and said, "Ed, you can take over and organize this operation."

My father placed Woody and myself up in the truck. We began to hand the first row of decoys down to the waiting men. There were rows of canvas geese decoys. They were all handmade; the bottoms were flat with a weighted keel on each one to make them self-right if they became overturned. These flat bottoms had a series of copper wire ribs attached to each side. Each piece of wire fit in a groove along a wooden back support that began at the base of their necks and ended near their tails. They were covered with light canvas called ticking. This ticking was attached all along the rim of the bottoms with small hand-driven copper tacks. It was folded around their necks and ended in a precise fold at their tails and was tacked in place. There was a small hole near the front of the keel for cord attachment. Each one was a thing of beauty, a creation of art. They were painted with a drab, nonreflective paint. They would be valuable in today's market; each one would bring several hundred dollars.

"Boys," Mr. Harry said to us, "please don't pick those up by their necks. That's the most fragile part of them. Place your hands under the front and the tails as you lift them. We will take them in the same manner and stack them where Ed wants them," Harry instructed us.

Woody and I handled them carefully. When we had all the geese decoys off-loaded, my father told us there were 75 of them. Then we began to off-load the duck decoys. These decoys were a mixture of redheads, blackheads, and canvasbacks. Unlike the geese decoys, all the duck decoys were factory made. They were made from balsa wood and came from the Herter's Manufacturing Company in Minnesota. They had wide backs, a curve that matched folded wings, and perfectly carved heads and tails. They had weighted keels with a hole for cord attachment. They were top-of-the-line diving duck decoys. Woody and I meticulously loaded all of the diving duck decoys. My dad had a count of 250 of them. The term "diving ducks" refers to those ducks that dive all the way under the water to feed. They can feed in knee-deep water or in great depth. They feed on eel grass, which is a natural food, or on any type of grain that may be provided for them. These decoys are used on the offshore blind locations such as stilt blinds, curtain boxes, and float blinds.

Next came the paddle duck decoys. These include ducks such as sprig-tails, black ducks, widgeons, blue and green wing teal—any type of marsh or pond ducks. These ducks feed by dipping their bodies halfway under the water and stretching their necks. Most species of these ducks have long necks and feed in shallow water. They will eat small insects, worms, frogs, tadpoles, and anything shallow ponds and shallow shoreside waters provide for them. They will feed on all types of grains they find. These decoys are used in the blinds that are located on the shoreside areas. My father had a count of 50 of these decoys. That was the last of the decoys that were in the truck.

James said his good-bye to us and started out the harbor road toward the highway. At that moment I could hear my mother calling me from the house.

"Boy," my father said, "you better see what your mother wants if you know what's good for you."

I ran toward the house. She met me at the path that opens up into the harbor road and handed me a paper sack. "Catch that truck," she said to me, "before he reaches the road and give the driver his lunch."

"But, Mom," I said, "it's ten-thirty."

"Don't 'but' me," she said. "He is in a hurry to catch that eleven o'clock ferry at Oregon Inlet and won't have time to stop for food. Now get a move on, boy." I was lucky there was a car coming up the road from the south and James had to wait for it. I ran up to the driver's side of the truck and banged on the door, and he rolled down the window.

"My mom sent you a lunch," I told him.

"Thank your mother for me, son. I got to roll trying to catch the next ferry," he replied. He turned onto the road and was gone.

"Okay, boys," my dad said, "we need to get started spanning these decoys." He bought out a five-gallon bucket full of four-inch-long pieces of leather that he had been soaking in oil with holes in each end. "Son, you and Woody begin running a piece of leather through each hole in the keels at the end of the geese decoys. Take them over to your Uncle Bill and Pudding Head; they will tie a bowline knot after passing the cord through the hole in the leathers. Then Mr. Bowman and I will attach the weights and restack them near the decoy skiffs," my dad said to us. We repeated this process until my mom called us all to the midday meal. We had spans on all the geese decoys, and about half of the diving ducks when we broke to eat.

After we returned from eating we soon worked our way to the end of the diving duck stack and began on the puddle ducks. By three o'clock we had spanned all the decoys and were ready to load the decoy skiffs. My father wanted to load the new decoy skiffs that we picked up from Mr. Willie's boat shop in Avon. He instructed us to load twenty geese decoys near the bow seat on each skiff. Then he wanted to load about seventy-five diving duck decoys and five puddle duck decoys near the stern seats on each skiff. After that he directed us to load two adjustable stools and one signal flag in each skiff. "These rigs will be for the offshore hunts in the stilt blinds and curtain boxes," he told us. The rest of the decoys he wanted us to load in his net skiff from his long net rig. He had us load eight stools and eight flags in the net skiff. "We will divide up the remaining geese and puddle duck decoys among the shore blinds," he said to us. They would be left behind the shore blinds at their locations. The stools and flags would be left inside the blinds until they are ready to be set out, he informed us. All the decoys were spanned, weighted, and loaded on the skiffs by six-thirty. My father was very pleased; he gave us all ten hours of work time. I was tired but happy. Woody, Richie, and I were discussing what to purchase with the money we earned.

# CHAPTER SEVEN

# The Feeding Geese Decoys

When I got off the school bus the next afternoon, I ran all the way to the house. As I entered the front door, my mom called, "Elvin, is that you?"

"Yes, Mom," I responded.

"Take off those clothes, make sure they hit the hamper and not the floor," she said.

"Yes-um," I answered her.

"Your father and Pudding Head will be returning from the island soon, but he left instructions for you. He wants you to get the hand pump from the crib and pump the rainwater out of the decoy skiffs. They pumped them this morning before they left, but it has rained mostly all day. If the water is deep enough inside them to float the decoys off their stacks, he wants you to clear the cords and restack them."

"What are we having for supper?" I asked.

"Fried pork chops," was her response. "If you are hungry, I made some molasses cookies today. Take a couple with you. Look in the icebox on the back porch. There are small cartons of milk in there to go with the cookies," she said.

"Thanks, Mom," I said, and was out the kitchen door. She heard me walking across the kitchen roof where I kept an angle pole and a dip net.

"I hear you up there," she said. "Absolutely no fishing until you have pumped out those skiffs and straightened up those decoys."

"Yes-um," I said. I walked to the crib, opened the door, and found the pump leaning against the wall. The pump is a long, thin, round, cylinder-shaped piece of pipe with its top spread out like a large funnel. About twelve inches down from the top it has a fitting that allows the water to be pumped overboard. It had a long, round-shaped piece of wood with a T-shape attached at the top completing the handle. This handle travels vertically all the way to the bottom of the cylinder, where a small, funnel-shaped piece of leather is attached. The bottom of the cylinder has a one-way flapper that lets the water in. After the pump is primed, the handle is drawn up, which opens the valve and pulls the water up into the cylinder and then overboard. When the handle is pushed toward the bottom, the valve closes, trapping the water in the cylinder until the handle is pulled up, expelling the water over the side. On the way to the harbor I noticed stacks of about twenty-five wooden triangle-shaped objects located on a large worktable. The table was located under a large oak tree to provide shade from the heat of the sun. When I got to the harbor, the decoy boats were about half full of water. They had floated from their stacks, and the cords were in a tangled-up mess. The first thing I had to do was pump the water out of the boats. This proved to be quite a task; the decoy cords kept fouling the flapper valve at the bottom of the pump. I would have to stop pumping and clear the cord, then continue removing the water from the boat. This proved to be a time-consuming process. I finished pumping both boats, and I had to untangle all the cords and restack the decoys. I finished this process just as my dad and Pudding Head came into the harbor from their day's work. As they pulled up to the dock, I met them and helped them tie up the boat. My father asked me if I had finished bailing out the decoy boards. I told him I had, and he asked how bad the decoy spans were tangled. "They were in a mess," I told him.

"I was afraid of that," he said.

"Didn't get much fishing in this afternoon, did you?" asked Pudding Head.

"No," I responded. "I have been bailing and untangling all afternoon, but now I am finally finished."

"Well," my father said, "you have helped us considerably, Son, and I appreciate that. Now Pudding Head and I can rest and enjoy the rest of the evening without worrying with those boats. It is getting late, and we should go on to the house and see what your mother has for supper," he said.

"I know it's fried pork chops with all the trimmings. She told me when I came home this afternoon," I responded.

"Let's go on up to the house and get washed up before the food gets cold," said my dad. When we reached the path, Pudding Head went on down the landing road; his house was directly across Highway 12 from ours. "Oh, by the way, Pop, what are the wooden triangles on the worktable at the oak tree for?" I asked.

He said with a twinkle in his eye, "I will explain their function to you after supper. Bet I can beat you to the house," he said, and placed his arm in front of me and pushed me backward to gain a head start and took off running. I was right on his heels. I caught him and tried to pass; he grabbed and held me back. We reached the porch about the same time, both of us laughing.

"What in the world are you two doing?" my mother asked.

"Just having some fun," my dad answered.

"Fun you call it. You two sound like a herd of elephants just landed on the back porch. I thought the whole house was coming down. Come on in now and wash up; the food is ready," she said. We partook of the chops, baked sweet potatoes, pickled beets, and cornbread. Supper was accompanied with a tall glass of tea made from rainwater, caught in a cistern or rain tank with a gutter system from the roof and gravity fed into the kitchen. "Dinner" to us was the midday meal. (As I have grown up and been corrected properly now, I know that the midday meal is called "lunch," and the evening meal is called "dinner.") My father always broke out the Bible and read a few verses from a chosen chapter to my mother and me, and he always explained the passages to us with a story I could understand. I loved my father's Bible stories. When he was telling them, you could visualize the particular situation he was talking about. That night it was about Noah and the ark. In my mind I could see the animals boarding this large ark. After he finished we always had an evening prayer. We joined hands, and he prayed for our continuing health and the problem we faced daily at that time. When he was finished, my mother said, "Alright, boy, it's time for homework. When you are finished I will check it for you."

"But Pop said he was going to explain the wooden triangles on the work-table to me."

"Alright, but as soon as he is finished, it's homework time at the Hoopers," she said. "Do I make myself clear?"

"Yes, ma'am," I said.

"Alright, Son," he began, "those triangles you saw at the harbor are a part of a brainstorm I had about making geese decoys appear to be feeding. On the northwest part of Gull Island Reef during a winter northeast blow, the water is low enough to allow the geese to dip their bodies halfway under the water and feed on the eel grass. They have long enough necks to reach the grass and feed." He asked Mom for a pencil and paper. He drew the tri-angles with measurements and continued his explanation. "These triangles are four feet from tip to tip," he said. "I had your Uncle Bill and Perry make them from juniper one-by-six I got from Willie Austin when you and I were at his house in Kinnakeet. There are twenty-five of them. Your grandfather and I have roughly chopped seventy-five tail sections of geese decoys from juniper blocks. If you go over to Pop's tomorrow you can see them. He has them bolted to a large workbench, and he is finishing shaping them with a drawing knife and wood rasp." A drawing knife is a hand tool with a sharp blade made of steel with ninety-degree corners turned back in the same direction. The corners have wooden handles attached; the user does all the cutting by drawing the blade back toward their body. This is why it is called a drawing knife. "When they are finished they will resemble the lower half of a goose decoy, from the mid body section to the tail. We will attach these tail sections to the triangles, one on each point. A weight and span will be attached; they will resemble geese dipping and feeding from a distance," he said. "As the geese fly from the south and round the back side of the island, they will see the North Reef low-water curtain box set up with a few of these triangles in place with their white tails in the air, resembling feeding geese," he told me.

"Where did you get that idea from?" I asked.

"It came to me the other day when Pudding Head rounded the back side of the island on a nor'easter. I had field glasses in my hand, and all I could see were white tails in the air from geese feeding on the eel grass there. We stopped the boat and let it drift into that small cove below the northwest point of the island. We watched flock after flock of geese land next to the ones already there. I thought, *If I see those white tails in the air, so do the geese.*" I have never seen any of these triangles used anywhere except by my father, and he was very successful while using them.

"You better get to work on your lessons," he told me. "Your last report card left a lot to be desired," he said with a chuckle. "Your mother will be in here soon as she finishes in the kitchen, and she has high hopes for you. She wants something better for you than beating out a living in the sound."

"But that is what I want to do. I love the sound," I responded.

"I know, Son," he said, "but your mother has a mindset of you becoming an educator like her side of the family." My mom's family was all about education; one of her aunts was a principal of an elementary school in New Jersey and actually had the school named after her. Several of her cousins were classroom teachers. At the table our place mats were in the shape of the United States, with each state's name and the capital city printed on it. As we ate she would ask me the capital city of various states; I did not have to know them by heart. I was allowed to use the mats to answer.

The next afternoon when I got home I asked Mom if Dad had left any jobs for me.

"Not today," she answered. "As far as I know you are free until supper." I changed and ran over to my grandfather's house. He was in the side yard shaping juniper blocks that were going to be the feeding geese decoys. He had just over half of them shaped except for final hand-sanding smooth. We exchanged greetings, and he asked me to take a wheelbarrow and take the finished blocks to the harbor where they could be sanded, attached to the triangles, and then painted. I loaded fifteen of them in the wheelbarrow and struck out for the harbor. He told me to stack them under the table where the triangles were stacked. When I returned he had finished up five more of them. He showed me how to smooth the sharp edges off the blocks using a wood rasp. These edges were left by the rough shaping using the drawing knife. A wood rasp is a large filelike hand tool. The grooves are much deeper in the metal and located farther apart than in a metal file. It is an excellent tool for smoothing wood just before the sanding phase begins. As my grandfather finished shaping, he gave me the block for continued smoothing with a wood rasp. We soon finished, loaded the last ten in the wheelbarrow, and both of us went to the harbor.

We hand-sanded the rough spots from the blocks, and soon we had all twenty-five tail sections of the feeding geese decoys finished. They were shaped with a wing groove in the middle of their backs, and their bellies were rounded plump and smooth. At a glance it was easy to distinguish the front from the back and which way they would be arranged on the triangles, so they would resemble dipping geese in the act of feeding. "That is just what Bud Ed wanted," my grandfather said to me. Bud Ed was the nickname my grandfather always called his son, Edward, my father. "Okay, bud," he said to me, "when we have the last of the blocks stacked under the table, we are finished for the evening. Your father is going to mix up some paint for me when he gets home tonight, and you can help me again tomorrow."

"Okay, Grandpop," I said, and we began to walk back toward the house. Just as I was about to enter the back door of the kitchen to my house, my cousin Richard Austin came running down the path toward me.

"Hey, Nate," he yelled. "Let's go over to cousin Les's house. He has brought his kids a big chestnut mare. I just saw her, and I'll bet she is eighteen to twenty hands high. She is much taller than the little scrubby ponies we are used to riding bareback. He has a saddle for her; all the kids are over there, and he is letting everyone ride her." Nate was the nickname cousin Richie always called me by, and still does to this day. My mom heard his conversation, and before I could ask permission, she said, "Go on, but be back before it gets dark. I'll put your supper in the oven and keep it warm for you." We ran through the path toward Grandpop's house, overtook and passed him. Cousin Les's house was directly across the road from my grandfather's.

"Where are you pair going in such a hurry?" my grandfather asked. We told him, and he called after us, "You boys be careful around such a large animal. If she accidentally steps on your bare feet, she could cause some damage." When we reached the road we could see her. She was the biggest horse I had ever seen. I asked cousin Les where she came from and what her name was. He told me she came from a farm in Edenton, and her name was Champ.

"She is very gentle and easy to ride. You boys can have a turn," he told us. When it was my turn, he told me she was neck trained. You didn't have to pull on the reins to turn her head. Just touch the reins to the opposite side of her neck in the direction you wanted to go. After we all rode this big mare, Richie and I volunteered to cool her down by walking her and giving her a rubdown. While we were rubbing her down, cousin Les cleaned the inside of her hooves. I learned that day that horses have an area inside their hooves that is called a frog. He smoothed around the edges of her hooves with a course rasp.

"It's important to take care of her legs and hooves," he told us. "If you tend to her properly, she is much more comfortable and will be in a good mood. That makes her easy to get along with and manage. I am going to try to break her to a cart," he said. "There is a man in Manteo who has a small horse cart for sale. I believe it will fit in the back of my truck. I have talked to him on the phone, and I plan to go up there tomorrow and purchase it. You boys might want to come over this weekend. That is when I plan to introduce her to the cart. Everything might go smoothly and be just fine. With these things you never know. I plan to ask Grandpa to come over," he said.

Grandpa had broken many a horse to a cart. He had that big stallion he named Barnacle trained so well that he never used a bit in the horse's mouth. There weren't any reigns to guide the horse. When Grandpa wanted to go to the beach and get a cart load of firewood, he simply hitched him up and said, "Come on, Barnacle." The horse followed, pulling the cart along behind him. When they came to a piece of wood to be loaded, Grandpa said, "Stop, Barnacle," and the horse stopped.

"It beats anything I have ever seen," cousin Les told us. "If anyone can help introduce Champ to the cart, it will be Grandpa." We thanked him for letting us ride, and he invited us again to return on the upcoming weekend. Richie and I made plans on the school bus ride home on Friday afternoon to meet at cousin Les's house early the next morning.

We arrived around eight o'clock on Saturday morning at cousin Les's house. My grandfather and Les were already at the carrel with the big mare. My grandfather put a lead rope bridle over her head. He attached the cart carrier strap over her head and adjusted it to her chest. Then he snapped buckles to a wide back band that held the cart poles. He talked to her in a gentle, soothing voice and stroked her head during the entire process. The big horse looked at him and shook her entire body. "She is just getting a first time feel for her new lash up," my grandfather told us. He took the lead rope that was fastened to the bridle and led her off a few yards and brought her back. She never flinched. "You won't have any trouble with her as long as you talk to her and reassure her each time you hitch her to the cart," he told Les. After that, all the kids flocked to cousin Les's house for cart rides. This went on all day long on Saturday and after church on Sunday. Champ responded like a true lady; I think she truly liked kids. Sunday afternoon Rich and I left for home. Rich turned and said, "See you on the bus in the morning."

"Nate, see you," I answered.

# CHAPTER EIGHT

# The Grain Truck

The remaining afternoons of September were spent with my grandfather finishing up the geese feeding triangles. We attached one of the feeding blocks to each point on the triangles. The backs of the blocks with the wing groove were placed forward, with the smooth bellies and tails positioned toward the rear. We painted them, balanced them, and placed the cords and weights on them. We tried them out in the harbor; they floated perfectly. We turned them bottom up, and they righted themselves. When they were viewed from a distance, they looked like three geese with their heads and half of their body under water, with their tails in the air feeding. They were ready to be set out in a stand of decoys on a hunt. On the very afternoon when we finished testing the last triangle in the harbor, my cousin Richie showed up and said, "Hey, Nate, let's go over to Les's again and get another look at that large mare he has."

"Boys," my grandfather began, "I think they went to Manteo today and won't be back until late this afternoon."

"If they are not home, we'll come back to the harbor and mess around until Uncle Ed and Pudding Head return," Rich said. As we approached the back porch to my house, I called for my mother; she came out and greeted us. I asked permission to go, and she said, "Okay, but I heard they are off island today. If they are, you boys come straight back here." As we approached cousin Les's house it appeared that no one was home. We walked up on the front porch and called out; no answer came in return. "We had better go, Rich," I said.

"Not so fast, Nate," he replied. "Let's go around back to the stable and take a look at the horse."

"I don't think we should," I added.

"Ah, come on, don't be so afraid. Nothing is going to happen," he said. So around back we went. The stable door was open, and it was empty.

The horse pen was large and extended all the way to the back of cousin Les's property. There were small bushed and tall grasses inside the fence. The horse was nowhere to be seen. "This is boring," Rich said. "Let's go back to the harbor.

"Hey, Nate, check this out," he said. He had a large yellow balloon in his hand. He blew it up and pinched the mouth of the balloon together. The escaping air made a high-pitched screeching sound. From under the shed, cousin Les's large Chesapeake Bay retriever came bounding out between us: all one hundred pounds of his growling, snarling teeth showing. He grabbed Rich by the seat of his pants as he tried to run. I leaped forward and grabbed the dog by the tail. Rich was spinning his wheels and yelling, "Hold him, Nate, hold him." His teeth ripped the entire seat of his pants out, allowing Rich to escape. Then the dog turned to me. I immediately yelled, "Fondy," as loud as I could. That was the dog's name. He recognized me from the many sticks I had thrown in the harbor for him to retrieve. He came over and allowed me to pet him. "I think he bit a chunk of my butt off," Rich said.

"He was asleep under the shed and that screeching from the balloon startled him," I said, as we ran all the way to my house. My mother heard us coming, and she said, "I know you pair have been up to something. Now what have you done?" We told her the whole story. She examined Rich and told him he was bruised a bit, but the skin was not broken. She gave him a pair of my father's pants to wear home.

"See you tomorrow," he said, and left for home. I told my father that night, and he laughed and laughed. My mother scolded me and said we should have left as soon as we determined that no one was home. "We have a truck load of grain coming from Mr. Kotarides's bakery. It is Saturday. Do you think you could get three of your friends to help unload the grain truck tomorrow? Same deal as the decoys: three dollars per hour, a ten-hour day, thirty bucks for each of you," he said.

"I am sure I can," I responded. "But I will have to go and ask them tonight before bedtime."

"I will drive you," he said. "Your mother needs a few things from the store in Waves." We stopped at my friend Larry Midgett's house, then at my grandfather's house to see Woody, and then to Richie's house. Larry, Woody, and Rich indicated they were interested in the grain truck unload. We continued on up to Mr. Asa Gray's store for my mother's shopping.

The next morning one of the tractor trailers from the Mary Jane Bakery showed up at the harbor loaded with grain. James was the driver of the grain truck. My dad wanted to off-load the grain bags as soon as we could so that James could catch the earliest possible ferry back across Oregon Inlet. We off-loaded whole-grain corn, wheat, and milo in ninety-pound burlap sacks. All four of us boys got up in the truck and rolled the sacks toward the tailgate and off onto the yard. The truck was completely empty in about three hours' time. James was headed back up the road by ten o'clock, and we still had to move the grain. We carried it to my father's fish house, converted into a grain storage area. My dad and Pudding Head used wheelbarrows to bring the bags to us. We all four grabbed a corner of each bag; it was all we could do to lift and stack the bags. Soon the fish house was filled near to the ceiling with bags of grain. There was just enough room left to store a dozen pair of waders and matching slickers hung up on nails by the door. There were about fifty bags left in the yard. My father had us load ten bags on the *Dolphin*, and we covered the rest with a tarp. My mom made lunch for us. We ate under the shade of a big oak tree near the water's edge. While we were eating, Woody asked my father what he was going to do with all the feed.

"We are going to feed the fowl at the island heavily during the month of October, not only to draw them in, but to hold them in the area. Anyone is allowed to feed or bait wildlife as much as they choose, and as often as they wish. However, it is against the law to shoot over a baited area. Any blind must be located at least five hundred yards away from the grain or baited area. It is perfectly fine to hunt an area after all the bait has been eaten," he told us.

As we finished storing the grain, he paid us all for our work. "I also have some tricks up my sleeve that your grandfather taught me," he said. He got some of his ideas from a good friend of his who lived over in Fairfield on the mainland. This old fellow was not only a waterfowl hunter, he was also a bear hunter. He guaranteed all his hunters a bear, or they didn't have to pay for the hunt. One of his methods was to use honey poured into small wooden containers that he had made and painted red. He did this three days before each hunt. On the day of the hunt, he retrieved his containers, washed them out, and returned them to the field. The bears came the next day to the containers, looking for the honey, and they were empty. There were no regulations about bear hunting with empty red containers. My grandfather's friend had some successful methods of attracting waterfowl and keeping them in the area where he wanted them to stay. My dad told us that animals are creatures of habit. If you can get them in the habit of using the areas where your hunters are, it is much easier to harvest them. He promised to share some of his methods with us in the future. The next afternoon after the church service, my father and I took the ten bags of the grain and emptied them near the stilt blinds, the curtain boxes, and the shore blinds.

"We need to get them in the habit of feeding near these blinds," he told me. The whole month of October he fed the fowl heavily. Near the end of the month he would begin to alter his methods of feeding and begin to manipulate the fowl and prepare for hunting. Our hunting season began November 1 and lasted until the last of January. He had to be extremely careful around the shore blinds. He used a ten-foot-long stake with a small cedar tree wired to it. He baited around the cedar tree five hundred yards away from the shore blinds. On the day of the hunt he pulled up the stake, marked the bait location with a buoy, and moved the stake next to the blind. The fowl were used to feeding near the stake with the cedar tree attached, so they came to the tree to feed, and the bait was still a legal distance away from the blinds.

When he baited the offshore blinds, he had several different methods. He used a small wooden float painted white with an open compartment that he used in the off-season as a clam storage box while clamming. He anchored one of these floats a legal distance away from the offshore blinds and placed the bait around them. On the day of the hunt, he buoyed their location and anchored the clam float at the head of his decoy layout. He also made large, round balsa wood floats, painted them red, and used them the same way he used the white clam floats. The methods he used were successful for him. All the hunters were happy, and he never violated any gunning laws or regulations.

All the experts share a common belief that animals are colorblind. It is believed that their eyes are absent of rods and cones, the parts of the eye that distinguish color. If so, why does a bull attack a red cape and ignore a white cape? On some fishing trips, speckled trout only hit certain color jigs at certain times. I know that the grain was the draw for the fowl to the structures, but I still believe, as did my ancestors and their friends, that color had something to do with it.

My father had many successful seasons on Gull Island using these techniques. He used them from my earlier childhood years up to my college days, when he finally had to retire from commercial gunning because of his age and health. The game wardens had numerous pictures taken from the air of him and his crew spreading feed for waterfowl, but not one hunter was ticketed while hunting over baited gunning areas.

On this particular Sunday afternoon, Dad and I were spreading wheat for the rafts of diving ducks that been feeding on the northwest reef of Gull Island Channel. He had a stilt blind there on the outer edge of the reef, and a curtain box in the middle of the reef. He was using the balsa wood round buoys there, and we spread the wheat heavily around them. I helped him place a grain bag halfway over the stern of the boat, and he cut a hole in the bag with his pocket knife. The grain began to spill over the stern into the water. I went back up front to steer the boat until the bag was empty, and we replaced it with another one. The wheat was dumped into the prop wash of the boat, which helped spread it out before it settled to the bottom. We went around and around in a circle, close to the balsa wood float, widening the circle as we went until we had dumped fifteen bags of wheat at that location. The other locations were baited in the same manner. It was nearing the end of October, and my father had diving ducks, swan, geese, and puddle ducks working the Gull Island reefs in abundance.

The next weekend I helped my father and Pudding Head all day on Saturday take the final materials over to the island to make ready for the hunters. We took all the bedding, towels, and toiletries, made the beds, and cleaned the shack up well. We unloaded cases of gun shells, stored the gun cleaning supplies, and stocked the small pantry with canned goods. The perishable food would be brought over when the party arrived. We placed sand into some of the empty grain bags and placed them on the bottom near the entrances to the blinds. My father worried about the hunters walking through the soft mud. If they became stuck, it was possible they might fall face first in the cold water. This could be a disaster on the first day of a hunt. He wanted to make it as easy as possible for the hunters to access the blinds. He wanted to get off to a good start on his first hunt. When he was satisfied that all was well with the island, we headed back home to clean and prepare the boats to be ready to transport the hunters when they arrived late Sunday afternoon for the hunt. Pudding Head and I worked the rest of the afternoon gassing up the two powerboats. The houseboat, *Vivian Marie*, from my father's long-haul rig, would be the crew boat down to the island. My father would take her so that he could meet the hunters and answer any questions they might have. The *Dolphin* would be taken by Pudding Head. She would be the supply boat, transporting all the perishable food, hunting gear, and any other supplies needed for the hunt. When all was ready at the harbor, the three of us walked toward our houses. My father and I parted company with Pudding Head where our path branched off toward our house. "See you tomorrow, Pudding," my father said to him as we entered the path.

"What time will we be going over for the hunt?" he asked my dad.

"We will have plenty of time to attend church and have Sunday dinner with our families before we leave," my dad responded. I watched him walk until he was out of sight toward his house, before I mumbled in a low tone, "Wish I could go."

"You will have plenty of hunts with me in the future, Son," my dad said. "You know you have school."

"I know," I responded, "but that doesn't make me feel any better about this first hunt. Besides we learned in school that farmers' sons are allowed to miss school during harvest times as long as they make up their school-work—if it is a benefit to their family or their fathers need help to complete the harvest."

"And it's not counted against them as far as attendance is concerned?" Dad asked me.

"No, sir," I said. "They are considered excused absences."

"Well, which one of us is going to run this by your mother for her approval?" asked my dad.

"I was hoping for a little help from you in that department," I responded.

"You plant the seed, and I will do what I can," he said. We were about fifty feet from the back door to the kitchen. I had to come up with something fast to persuade my mother to let me go on the hunt. As I walked in the door she said, "Elvin, is that you?"

"Yes, Mom," I replied.

"Did you, Floyd, and your father finish up everything to make ready for the first hunt?"

"Yes, Mom," I answered. She had provided me with just exactly what I needed; she had brought up the hunt. "Oh, by the way," I began, "Dad said he might need my help on the first hunt of the season."

"Excuse me," she said. "Just what are you talking about? The first hunt is tomorrow, on a Monday, and where do you go on Mondays from September to June each year?" she asked.

"To school," was my response.

"To school, exactly right," she said. "What in the world makes you think you can go hunting instead of going to school?"

"It's like we learned in school: with the farmers, if your parents need you to help work for short periods of time, you can be excused from school and allowed to make up your work."

"I believe that has to do with a very short time to gather the harvest of a year's work before the crop is spoiled. That is the case, right?" she asked.

"Yes, ma'am," I replied.

"What makes you think that applies to hunting with your father?" she asked. "Where is he anyway?"

"He is feeding the things," I replied. Feeding the things refers to feeding the chickens, ducks, pigeons, and any other livestock one might have.

"Well, we will see what he has to say about this when he comes in. You wash up for supper, then I have some problems I selected from your math book for you to complete. Your last grade left a lot to be desired. But I can tell you this: No matter what you or your father come up with, you are not missing school to go to Gull Island hunting. So you can put that in your pipe and smoke it," she said. No matter what plea I used, including begging, she would not budge. "I know you helped unload the grain truck, helped make ready for the first hunt, but Monday morning you will board the school bus as usual. Sorry," she said to me.

Man, I felt terrible. The very first hunt to my beloved island, and I would not be included. I felt as if my whole world was about to come crashing down on me. I mulled it over and over in my mind. Finally, I just gave up and sulked.

# CHAPTER NINE

# The First Hunt

Normally on Sunday morning I pop out of bed and beat everyone to the breakfast table. This particular Sunday I moped around and was slow to the table. "What is ailing you this morning?" my mother asked.

"It's about the hunt," I began.

"Don't even go there," she said to me. "You are not missing that much school to go hunting with your father. What makes you think he needs your help? He would need to look after you as well as the hunters. You are only eight years old."

"I turn nine this summer in July," I said. "Besides, I am a lot of help to him. He takes me everywhere he goes."

"He takes you because you are his son. I don't want to hear any more about this. Finish your breakfast and get ready for Sunday school; you are late already."

Sunday school began a quarter to ten with the ringing of the church bell by Edward, a cousin named after my father. He rang a late bell five minutes after the hour. The *bong, bong, bong* of that old church bell could be heard all over the Salvo neighborhood on Sunday mornings. I squirmed all through church this particular morning; it was the day the hunters were coming. I knew they would be leaving for the island without me. I suffered through Sunday dinner and asked to be excused early. I went to the harbor and made a last check of the boats. Everything looked prepared and ready. Then around three o'clock the hunters arrived. In the first party was

Mr. Alexander Kotarides, my father's new boss; Mr. Harry Bowman, the decoy guardian; and two of Mr. Kotarides's very close friends, Mr. Thomas Hodges and Mr. Roy Brown. My father introduced me to all the hunters, and I helped them load the boats with the gear. Mr. Bowman asked my father if I was going on the hunt. *Ah*, I thought, *a ray of hope*. All my father said was "school."

"Education is a very important aspect of a young child's life," replied Mr. Bowman.

As I pushed the houseboat away from the dock, my dad looked at me and said, "I will tell you everything on Friday when I pick you up at Bay Landing." My mother had agreed that I could obtain permission from school and be let off the school bus at Bay Landing about five miles south of Salvo. My dad would be waiting there with a pair of waders for me, and we would walk out to the anchored *Dolphin* just off the marsh. I would be able to join in a half-day hunt on Saturday.

"Don't forget me," I yelled, as my father headed the house out of the harbor. The wind was blowing fifteen to twenty from the northwest, and all the hunters scampered for the cover of the cabin. I helped Pudding Head load the remaining supplies on the *Dolphin*, then I pushed him off the dock and he headed out behind my father and the houseboat. I watched them until they faded from site behind No-Ache Point; the water was high because of the wind direction. They were taking the inside route near the shore, following the marsh line until they reached the end of Cedar Hammock Island, then out across Cedar Hammock Channel, and across Gull Shoal Channel. Then they would approach the island. The water levels were high enough that they would have no trouble getting the larger boats in the small island creek next to the dock.

As I started walking back toward the house I could see flock after flock of diving ducks on the horizon out back of the reef headed south. I knew if they tied out on the north reef they would have a successful hunt. I sat on a bench that was fastened to the dock and watched the horizon for a while. Then my mind drifted to the hunters. I wondered how far Mr. Hodges and

Mr. Brown had to travel to come to the hunt. I thought I heard them say Mr. Hodges was from Pennsylvania, and Mr. Brown from Tennessee.

All the hunters had to cross the Oregon Inlet ferry to get to Hatteras Island. This was about a forty-minute crossing over the inlet on a state-maintained ferry system. Before the state took over the ferry, it was privately owned by a man named Toby Tillett from Wanchese. He had a flat-bottomed bargelike craft that could hold three vehicles. It stayed more on the north side of the inlet. He had a tall flagpole equipped with a large red flag on the south side of the inlet that he watched with field glasses. If anyone wanted to cross, they raised the flag. Mr. Tillett would come over and transport them across for a fee. His ferry was named the *Barosolona*. I have no earthly idea where he got the name from. When the state took over they established scheduled crossings until the inlet was bridged in 1963.

Dusk was coming on, and I had to get to the house. I still had to get the things, and bring in two buckets of coal from the coal bin to last my mother and me through the night. In those days it got cold in November and stayed cold until April. As I entered the kitchen door, my mother asked if I had fed the things and got the coal in; I told her I had finished both tasks. She told me to wash up for supper. That night I tossed and turned in bed thinking about the hunt. The morning finally arrived. At the table eating breakfast, my mother commented, "You look as if you haven't slept a wink all night."

"I was thinking about the hunt."

"Well, Friday will be here soon enough, and you will be with your father back on that island. Both of you act as if that place is paradise itself," she said. "Let's take a couple of minutes and look at the states and their capitals before you have to leave to catch the bus." My mother tried her level best to turn everyday life into learning situations, even breakfast. All I wanted to do was fish, hunt, trap, and gather whatever nature provided to carve out a livelihood around the creeks, marshes, and reefs in the sound around the island. At that point, a future in education was completely impossible for me to conceive. It was a chilly morning with a northwest wind of at least ten to fifteen miles per hour as I boarded the bus for the twenty-mile ride to school.

That whole week seemed to crawl by; it dragged on and on until finally it was Friday. I was so excited I could not sit still at the breakfast table that morning. I grabbed two pieces of toast, put cheese between them, and was out the door before the questions about states could be asked. My mother called me back, "You forgot your bag of hunting clothes," she said. She had packed a green canvas army bag, given to me by my cousin Raymond, with my gear for the hunt. The bus driver, Ella Porter, allowed me to leave my bag on the bus until that afternoon. On the way home that evening she let me off the bus at Bay Landing, where my father was waiting along the side road for me. He had the *Dolphin* anchored fifty yards offshore, and he brought a pair of waders and a slicker for me. I put on the gear and we walked to the anchored boat.

When we tied up at the dock on the island it was near dusk. I could smell the aroma of the evening meal drifting down the dock, carried by a now light west wind. My father and I came in the small mudroom where all the guns, shells, and foul weather gear was kept. The hunt crew was seated at a small table playing a card game called gin rummy. Mr. Kotarides was manning the galley. My cousin Pudding Head was setting the table.

When we walked into the main room, Mr. Kotarides called me to the galley. He told me I could help him serve up the chow, as he called it. He handed me a large plate of roasted pork spare ribs. He told me to tell the crew they were cut-back ribs. They were going to be served with offshore stewed potatoes, over-the-bar boiled cabbage, and in-the-slot lace corn-bread. At that time I did not have any idea what he was talking about. I just placed all the food platters on the table and relayed his message to the letter to the hunt crew. They all broke out in laughter, but after my father blessed the food, they all dove in.

As I ate I realized what a fantastic cook Mr. Kotarides was. The food contained spices that I was not used to, but it seemed to enhance the flavor of the meal. I commented on how good it was, and he just smiled and said, "Wait until you taste dessert." After we finished he asked me to help him in the galley a few minutes. Out of the oven he took a long tubular-shaped piece of dough baked golden brown. It was plump and easy to detect that it contained some type of filling. He placed a number of glass bowls on the counter. He cut into the roll, and blueberries came oozing out, bathed in heavy syrup. In each bowl he placed a generous portion of the roll and topped each with a thick, sweet cream sauce that he whipped up. As he handed me each bowl, he told me to tell the crew that this was out-of-sight strudel. I did as I was told, and they broke out in laughter once again, but soon gobbled down the dessert. As I ate my portion, again the taste buds were aroused.

As cousin Pudding Head and I cleaned off the table, Mr. Kotarides said to me, "Son, the best part is still baked to the bottom and sides of the pan. It would be a shame to waste any; you need to scrape that pan really good before you wash it," he said with a smile. He was right; the baked scrapings were as good as the dessert itself. During the washing of the dishes I commented to my cousin Floyd how delicious the meal had been.

"So that is the first time you have had Greek cooking," he said.

"What do you mean?" I asked.

"Mr. Kotarides comes from a Greek family background. The Greeks are all excellent cooks, with years and years of experience passed down from generation to generation. That is why they are so successful in the baking business; they keep their formula very secretive," he told me.

We finished up the dishes, and the hunters settled down at the big table and began to play cards. The conversation drifted to the next day's hunt. The wind was supposed to come around to the northeast and moderate to ten to fifteen miles per hour. The wind from this direction would lower the water to a level favorable to hunt the stilt blind on the north reef. It was decided that Mr. Bowman and Mr. Hodges would be the shooters, and I would shag or retrieve their downed fowl for them. My father had baited one of the small white clam containers all week, and no one had hunted the stilt blind the entire hunt because the water level had been too high to wade.

When we left the dock that morning I could tell it would be a good day to hunt the north reef. The water level was low, which allowed the geese to dip their bodies halfway under the feed, and the diving ducks could easily dive and feed. When we reached the stilt blind I jumped over the side; the water level was just past my knees. I took hold of the bowline attached to the decoy boat and allowed my father to transfer from the powerboat, while Pudding Head and my cousin Floyd helped the hunters into the stilt blind with their gear. Under directions from my father, I pulled the decoy boat around as he placed the decoys. They were all diving duck decoys, a mixture of redheads, blackheads, and canvasbacks. He arranged the decoys in a large group to the windward of the blind. Then he placed a string of decoys running from the end of the large group along the side of the blind ending downwind. In all we placed about seventy-five diving duck decoys. He had me move the boat to the leeward side of the blind where he placed about a dozen geese decoys. Then, true to the plan, I joined the hunters in the blind. My father and Pudding Head anchored the decoy boat and retrieved the white clam container from the baited area and anchored it in front of the decoy group.

As my dad and Pudding Head were leaving, I asked Mr. Bowman why my father placed a string of decoys along the windward side of the blind. "The diving ducks will approach us from upwind, circle the box to the leeward, and fly right up that string and try to light in that space between the head of the decoy group and that clam container. The fowl have found corn around that container all week long; they will continue to look for it there," he said. "Your father is a master hunting guide," Mr. Bowman told me. "He really knows his business. He baits his markers heavy, and the birds get accustomed to feeding around them, and he moves them within range on hunt days and buoys their bait location. There aren't any hunting regulations concerning the use of markers. When the game warden checks the blind locations, he finds them to be free of grain."

Just about that time, a flock of six redheads headed for us from upwind. Just as Mr. Bowman said, they circled down and flew right up the string. The hunters downed four of the ducks. They made my job easy by waiting until the ducks were upwind of the box before they shot. By the time I got down the ladder to water level, the ducks floated right up to me. I walked to the clam container and placed the ducks in a burlap bag that had already been placed there for that purpose. When the hunters had reached their limit, I waved the flag for the boat to come.

The hunters traded places, and the hunt continued into the afternoon. I shagged or retrieved all the downed fowl for the four hunters that day. When the limit was reached, the fowl were taken to the camp and the hunters switched places until we took up the rig just before sunset.

Pudding Head took the last two hunters back to the camp while I pulled the decoy boat around, and my father gathered all the decoys. The last thing we did was load the signal flag and the adjustable sitting stools in the decoy boat. Then I took the clam container and pulled it back on location, anchored it, and took up the marker and walked back to my father and the decoy boat. He wanted to know right away if I anchored it in back in the corn. I told him I had because I could feel it crunching against the bottom as I walked. Then Pudding Head came with the powerboat. We tied on and he towed us back to camp. I tied up the decoy skiff and scooped out what water was in the bottom and went into the mudroom to shed my waders and slicker. A slicker is a waterproof jacket with hood. I had been in both all day long; it was a relief to get them off.

My father said he would help Pudding Head set the table. I was to clean and lightly oil the guns that had been used on the day's hunt.

Hunters are particular when it comes to the care of their guns. I had four twelve-gauge shotguns to clean and case before the evening meal, so I got straight to work. At the end of a day's hunt, most all hunters stand their guns vertically, resting against something that will support them with the barrels in the downward position so any excess water will run off the guns in a direction away from the working parts. This is how I found the guns positioned. There was a Winchester model 58 pump gun, a Remington three-inch magnum automatic, a Browning automatic, and a double-barrel Savage three-inch gun. I used 3-in-One oil on all the moving parts of the guns, and whipped the exteriors with a lightly oiled cleaning swab. I checked all moving parts for excess oil and whipped it off to prevent possible jamming of the shells during the next use. Then I hung them on the rack to dry while I hung up all the waders and slickers and generally cleaned the mudroom. It's a funny thing about people who have money, I noticed at an early age: they expect to be pampered and hardly ever clean up after themselves.

There was always plenty of work for me at the camp. I finished up early and was able to take a shower before supper. My father had started up the generator for the hunters to clean up. Now it was my turn. There was plenty of hot water, and it really felt good to shower off a full day's worth of salt spray from my body. All the water was fresh-caught rainwater from the roof stored in lard containers from Mr. Kotarides's bakery. All the containers were connected at the bottoms with an-inch-and-a-quarter pipe for water equalization from container to container. There were about fifty of these containers connected to an old piston-type water pump and a fifty-gallon water heater. Everyone had a chance to shower, then my father shut down the generator. The lights were gas supplied as well as the icebox. We all could eat in the quiet; the generator would have to be brought back on line for anyone taking a late shower and to be used during galley cleanup. I had a little time before the evening meal. One of my favorite things to do was to walk out on the back porch and just listen to the noises at night. Even on windy days, the wind seems to fall out at dusk. Most nights were still on Gull Island. There were no main island noises such as songbirds, crickets, or frogs croaking. This particular night I could hear flocks of geese and swans talking as they fed on eel grass and grain at the north reef. On the back side of the island I heard the high ball quack of a female black duck. Off to the left I could hear the faint whistles of sprigtails and widgeons. At the mouth of the creek I heard the cry of a female otter calling to her pups as they foraged for food in the darkness. I heard a funny cracking noise. I asked my father to come out and explain that noise to me. It seems that the otters had collected mussels—a type of shellfish—climbed up on the end of the dock, and were cracking the mussels against the deck boards to open them. The last thing I heard before I went in to eat was the cry of a couple of marsh hens on the far side of the dock searching the water's edge for food. Experiencing these nighttime sounds on the island are some of my most treasured memories of time spent with my father during these hunts.

We had another fine evening meal. Pudding Head and I cleaned up after the feast. The next day was Sunday. This was traveling day for the hunters, time for them to return home. We were up by six o'clock, finished breakfast, and loaded the luggage and gear on the *Dolphin* and the hunters on my father's houseboat. We left the harbor at Salvo by 7 a.m. We did not do any cleaning at the camp before we left; even the dishes were left on the table. Only the perishable food was placed in the icebox. After church on Sunday, my father, mother, and I would go back to the camp and thoroughly clean up and prepare for the next week's hunt. We always finished and returned to Salvo in time so that my father could leave with the next party. During hunting season he hardly ever got a day off. My father kept a large chest freezer in his small fish house at the harbor. The hunters would select the type and number of fowl they wanted to carry home with them. During the hunt Pudding Head's wife, Janie, cleaned all the fowl and stored them in the freezer.

# CHAPTER TEN

# The Bluebird Hunt

Things went along fine on the first hunt, and by now Father had completed three hunts. I had been involved as much as humanly possible. Thanksgiving vacation from school was approaching; all of my friends and I were excited about having a few days off from school duties. On the bus ride home we were discussing what to do with our upcoming time off. My friends shared their plans with me. Some were taking trips off the island, others had family coming for the holidays with big feeds planned. They wanted to know what my plans were. I told them my folks planned to spend the holiday on Gull Island. We were going to clean up the camp and make ready for my father's guests after the holiday hunt.

"You are going to spend Thanksgiving on that isolated island?" one of my friends asked.

Before I had a chance to answer, another of my friends said, "You better watch what you say about that island around him. He thinks it's the most precious place in the world."

"That's true," I responded. "I can't think of any place I would rather spend Thanksgiving." I tried to explain the magic the island held for me. They just laughed and kidded me about it all the way on the bus ride home. Our bus ride was one of the longest home-to-school rides on the island, about twenty miles one way. The only other route I know of that was equal in distance was the Eastlake to Manteo school bus ride. I believe both places faced about a forty-mile round trip per school day. Finally, we reached Salvo.

I ran up the lane to my house. As I opened the door, my mother called to me, "Wipe your feet, mister. I just this minute finished scrubbing the floor. Stand there on that scatter rug for a few minutes until it dries. If you are too impatient to wait, walk around to the kitchen door. Your father is in the kitchen," she said.

I entered the kitchen, and my father was thumping the barometer with his finger. "What's up, Pop?" I asked.

"The bottom fell out of the barometer in the last few hours," he responded. "I think we are in for a blow: Probably a strong northwester in the initial shift, then slowly coming around and ending up in the northeast," he said.

"Does this mean we will not be able to go to the island tomorrow?" I asked.

"We can still go, but I would rather leave tonight. Check with your mother and see if she has everything packed and ready." My mother overheard our conversation and told us everything was ready. We closed the house up and loaded up the boat and headed for the island. The wind was light from the northeast, a quarter off our stern, which made for a smooth ride over. When we arrived and off-loaded our gear, my mother and I began cleaning up the kitchen from the hunt. Everything was left on the table after the hunters had finished their midday meal. We had a fine meal from the leftovers in the icebox. While my father checked and secured the decoy boats with extra lines for the upcoming blow, my mother and I finished cleaning up the camp. We would wait to scrub the floor just before we left. When my father came in he told me, "I think we will have a rainy day tomorrow. After the shift, you and I can walk out back to the sand beach and shoot ducks all day until the wind goes to the northeast," he said to my delight.

Mom and I finished cleaning the kitchen and put all the leftovers back in the icebox and generally straightened up the camp. My father tidied up the mudroom and cleaned and stored all the weatherproof hunting gear. After we had things straightened up, my father and I walked outside on the leeside porch and just listened to the nighttime melody of noises. Already you could see the clouds racing across the moonlit sky from the northwest toward the southeast. "That, my boy," began my dad, "is the beginning of the shift." Looking up to the northwest you could see the dark clouds of the shift approaching. We all retired for the night. The small camp shook as the northwester took control. The wind began to howl, and the rain came down in buckets. By daylight the wind was blowing steadily thirty to forty miles per hour from the northwest, the temperature had dropped, and the rain had turned to periods of snow and sleet. The weather was much too rough to move any of the boats. "Before we go out in this," my dad said, "we both need to see if your mother has a few cellophane bread bags we can have."

"What do we need bread bags for?" I asked.

"If we put our bare feet inside the bags and put our boot socks over the bags, the bags will hold in our body heat and keep our feet warm," he answered. I did as I was told, and to my surprise, my toes never got cold all day. My father and I took a lunch my mom packed: sandwiches, hot soup, and coffee in thermos bottles. There was snow all over the marsh grass and patches of ice in the sound; it was extremely cold. Every now and then I had to walk out in the water and clean the ice off the decoys. As they faced the wind on their spans, all the water that splashed up on their bills froze solid. The extra weight of the ice caused them to go down, some even rolled over. This caused approaching ducks to flare off instead of coming in. Just as my father had said, we could have shot ducks all day. By about noon he asked me if I had enough. We had two burlap bags full of game, enough fowl to share with the folks back home, he said. We ate our lunch, stored the decoys back in the blind, and were on our way back to the camp. When we approached the side porch, my dad climbed up first, and I handed him the bags of ducks. "We will store these in the generator house until we go home; they are frozen and will keep fine until we head home tomorrow," he said.

The camp was as warm as toast. My mom had been baking most of the day. She had fixed a swan with all the trimmings, and an apple pie for our Thanksgiving dinner the next day. That night the wind shifted around to the northeast, the temperature rose, and it began raining. All the snow and ice melted. At daylight the wind had gone around to the southwest and moderated, and it was even warmer. After we had our Thanksgiving feast, we cleaned up, scrubbed the floors, and left for home. We arrived home in time for me to meet up with my friends and see what they were up to.

My father kept about a dozen ducks. My friends and I walked around the village and gave the rest to the neighbors.

The Thanksgiving vacation slipped by quickly, and I found myself back in school. My dad was back at the island with another group of hunters. Early in December that year, something strange happened to the weather. The northern branch of the upper polar jet stream winds shifted much farther north than usual for that time of year. We did not experience the low pressures normally carried by the northern jet stream that season. Most of the cold, blustery weather retreated up north of our location. The southern branch of the jet stream winds brought warmer than usual Gulf Coast air up over our area. It was almost springtime weather in December. My father called it the days of the bluebird hunts. He tied out several of the blinds during the remainder of the month with rather poor results. Most days the wind fell out about an hour after sunrise, the sky would clear; there was hardly a ripple on the sound. The birds would come in early in the morning and late in the afternoon with hardly any flights during the course of the day. The hunters would get one shot at the birds; it was so calm that the report of the hunters' guns could be heard for miles, even in the villages. Each morning after the hunters got their first shot, the noise of their guns would scare everything up to flight. The birds stayed in much larger flocks than normal and disappeared miles out in the sound to spend their day in calm water. They would return after dark to feed.

This cycle continued for the first three weeks in December. The hunters would get so bored during the day that my dad would have to bring them back to the camp and return them to the blinds just before dark for a twilight shoot. The long-range weather forecasts showed no improvement in the weather patterns. It looked like the remainder of the season would offer the same type of bluebird weather with limited game. Mr. Kotarides was involved in a bluebird hunt the last week in December that winter. On one of my Friday night trips out to the island, I overheard them discussing the curse of the bluebird. Mr. Kotarides wanted to know if my father had ever experienced beautiful weather such as this during the winter months. My dad explained that the whole eastern portion of the country was under the influence of extreme high pressure, and the polar jet had moved way up north, bringing warm moist Gulf air over the area. In the animal way of life, the chance of survival increases when critters form up in large groups. In this situation they are much harder to approach, more easily frightened, and they are much more difficult to manage. It is next to impossible to predict their movements. My dad told Mr. Kotarides he had never before been under the influence of the bluebird for such a long period of time. "It is going to take a few shifts from the northwest and some heavy weather to break up those large rafts of fowl into smaller, manageable flocks," my father told him.

"We have to do something to harvest a few more birds this season," Mr. Kotarides told my father. "I want you to give it some thought, and we will talk about it tomorrow. I need a few good hunts. I am planning to offer shares for sale to some of my good hunting friends. I want to build a much larger clubhouse, buy two new hunting boats, dig out and bulkhead this small creek, and build all new docks and have a small front yard with grass in front of the house. The shares will help offset the cost of the improvements, and we will have a much nicer gunning club," he said. Mr. Kotarides had the Brown Brothers from Tennessee scheduled to hunt the last week in December. This was the first group he planned to offer shares to, and he wanted them to have a good hunt. "We need to put our heads together to battle this weather, and produce some birds for them," he said to my dad.

"I have a couple of things that we can try," my dad said in response. "We will begin with one method tomorrow." Before daylight the next morning we tied out the north reef stilt blind. The wind was light out of the north, five to ten miles per hour. When it lightened up a little, there was not a cloud in the sky. When the hunters were set, my dad and I retrieved the clam float and anchored it in front of the decoy spread. When we arrived at the float to move it, we flushed one of the largest rafts of diving ducks that I had ever seen. "Boy," my dad said, "that many can sure take care of some grain during the course of the night." I believe there were at least two thousand of them in that large raft. They were mixed blackheads, redheads, and canvasbacks. When they took flight it reminded me of the mosquito clouds I had seen over the marshes at the beginning of the summer. The entire raft of ducks took back to the water about two to three hundred yards offshore from us.

My dad eased up to the blind. Mr. Kotarides and Mr. Bowman were the hunters that day. My dad told them that we would circle to the south of the ducks, and come at them from the offshore side slowly and try to divide them in smaller groups with the boat. They all agreed, and we were off to try this method. Slowly we circled the ducks, and my father turned the boat toward the center of the large raft. We began to approach them at a very slow speed. At first they just swam away from us to the north. My father turned the boat northward to cut them off. In a few minutes he had the whole raft of fowl swimming straight toward the blind. As soon as a few of them were within range, the hunters fired on them. They were able to harvest a few, but when their shots rang out, everything took flight. It was so calm that the geese and swan on the south reef, along with the puddle ducks and brant out back of the island, all went skyward with the report of the guns.

We went to pick up the downed ducks and watched the diving ducks disappear from sight toward the middle of the sound. All the geese, swan, and puddle ducks took to the shore side and began heading up the island in the direction of the refuge at Pea Island. My father told the hunters that they might as well go back to the camp and wait for the evening shoot. It was so calm that with the echo of the guns, most all the game had left the island seeking a safe haven. "That's the way it's been with all my hunts since this bluebird weather pattern has had the upper hand," said my dad. "I am afraid that is the way it's going to stay unless the weather changes and we get a few shifts. We need wind to break up the fowl into smaller groups so their movements can be managed."

We took the hunters back to camp. They spent the day playing cards. We returned them to the blinds for the afternoon shoot; they harvested a few ducks and a goose or two. The supper table conversation that night was monopolized by Mr. Kotarides and my father; they were concerned about the upcoming hunt with the Brown Brothers. "We have to do something if the weather is the same when they arrive here," Mr. Kotarides said to my dad.

"I have another idea that I want to try," my dad responded. "Tomorrow morning Floyd will take you and Harry to the shore so you can go home. I think Elvin and I will follow the diving ducks when they make their flight and see where they are spending their day before we go home for church," Dad said. "If I find out where they are spending their daylight hours, perhaps I can improve the Brown boys' hunt," Dad told Mr. Kotarides.

Just after first light the next morning my cousin Pudding Head took the hunters and their gear back to Salvo in my dad's houseboat from his long net rig. My dad and I finished cleaning up the camp and headed for the north reef. Sure enough, the large raft of diving ducks were feeding on the grain near the clam float. My dad fired a couple of shots in the air, and just as usual, all the fowl for miles took flight at the noise of the gun. The diving ducks settled back on the water about three hundred yards offshore from us. Dad headed the boat slowly toward them. At first they began swimming away from us. We got just about seventy-five yards from them, and Dad fired more shots. This time the raft took flight and gained altitude as soon as they left the water. "They are headed offshore this time," my father said. "Here, you take the wheel and I will watch them with the field glasses. Give her a little more throttle; I don't want to lose sight of them." I opened her up to about half throttle. The *Dolphin* slid easily out on a plane skimming along on the calm water. "Give her more speed," Dad said. Now I pushed her up about three-quarters of the way open and it felt like we were flying. My father was up near the bow holding on to the tie-up line with one hand, and gripping the field glasses with his other hand, his legs spread wide apart as we bounced along trying to keep the ducks in sight. The raft of ducks turned to the northwest and disappeared from eyesight. He had me slow to about half throttle and we cruised on up in a northwest direction. He released his hand from the field glasses and allowed them to hang down from his neck on their strap. His hand went up in the air and he signaled for me to slow down. Just as I slowed the boat, the ducks came into eyesight. The entire raft was settled on the calm waters northwest of the island about five miles out in the sound. We got about sixty yards from them and he had me cut the motor to an idle. Then he tossed a large balsa wood float with a weight tied to it over the side. We baited around the float with ten bags of large-grain yellow corn. I watched as the grains sank to the bottom in the prop wash. The ducks were on the grain before we were a hundred yards away from them.

# CHAPTER ELEVEN

# The Deepwater Blind

My father and I arrived back to the harbor in Salvo about 9 a.m. Sunday. We entered the back door that led to the kitchen. Mom told us to wash up, breakfast was ready, and then we were all going to Sunday school and church. After church that Sunday I noticed my father talking to Mr. Perry Farrow and Uncle Bill. I eased up near them so that I could overhear their conversation. They were discussing the construction of a type of deepwater float blind. My father wanted them to build a type of pen out of two-by-fours on the corners, with one-by-fours connecting them. He wanted one end of it nailed fast and the other end on hinges, so it could swing open and closed. Also, he told them that he didn't want them to install any bottom in it. He wanted them to bush it, and have it ready by midday the next day. They would have to get up early on Monday morning in order to complete the work on time. He told them that he didn't have time to work on it or help. He promised them a full day's wages if they completed it on time. My father planned to tie out the north reef curtain box and leave Pudding Head to wait on the hunters while he came back to Salvo to load and place the new float blind. He explained that he had an important hunting party arriving that Sunday afternoon, and this blind would determine the successes of their hunt. On the way home I noticed he was in a hurry. "What's up, Pop?" I asked.

"Come on. Hurry up and change your Sunday clothes and you can help me," he said.

"Help you do what?" I asked.

"Come on and you will see," he said. As we were going out the back door my mother caught up with us.

"Just where do you two think you are going?" she asked my dad.

"Just to the harbor," he answered. "Set the table; we will be back up here by the time you have dinner ready." When we got to the storage house at the harbor he told me to get the wheelbarrow out. He wanted the roll of parachute cord, the bucket of leather span material we used to put lines on the decoys with, and as many diving duck decoys that would fit. "Take them up to the picnic table on the outside porch," he told me. He filled up the other wheelbarrow with more diving ducks and followed me. When we got to the porch, my mom opened the back door and told us dinner was ready. After we finished Sunday dinner we began our portion of the work. He wanted me to put a piece of span leather in the front eyelet of each of the decoys, and he passed it back to me to place a piece of span leather in the back eyelet he had just put in. When we had all the decoys modified like this, he placed ten of them in rows of five, lined about three feet apart. The next step was to connect them from decoy to decoy with the parachute cord from the front of the last one to the back of the next one in line until all ten were connected. On the decoy positioned at the front, he tied a piece of cord about ten to twelve feet long and attached a heavy weight to it. The weight was heavy enough to hold all ten decoys on station, and the span was long enough to reach bottom in the deeper water. As we finished up a string of decoys, I loaded them in one of the wheelbarrows until it was full, then I took them to the harbor.

Dad told me that we had three hours to complete our portion of the work before the hunters arrived. If we ran out of time I would have to finish it up on my own. My father had to leave with the hunting party; all I had left to do was take the last load of decoys to the harbor and stack them. The decoys were ready to be loaded and used at the deepwater blind location.

The next day at noon my father came back to the harbor at Salvo. Mr. Perry, Uncle Bill, and my dad loaded the decoys in my grandfather's sixteen-foot skiff and pushed the blind into the water. They opened the hinged end of the blind and positioned the skiff inside the bushed frame of the blind. Under my father's directions they had attached larger lines to the bottom rails of the blind. They were placed at three locations on each side. The lines were pulled tight over the washboards of the skiff and made fast to the gunnels halfway down the inside of the skiff. This allowed the blind to ride much higher up in the water, supported by the flotation of the skiff. My father towed it to the buoyed location, anchored it, and added ten more bags of corn for the diving ducks. He then returned to the club to help our cousin, Floyd, at the curtain box, with the afternoon hunt.

That night at the supper table the conversation began with comments from the Brown Brothers about the limited number of ducks taken during their first day at the club. The Brown Brothers were from Knoxville, Tennessee. Both of them had brought their sons along on the hunt. They were the owners of the Kerns Baking Company located in that city. They were good friends of Mr. Kotarides's, and were interested in purchasing shares in the club here at Gull Island. My father told them that he felt fairly confident that their second day would be much better. He explained the problem the club had been experiencing during their hunts under the influence of the bluebird weather. "Tomorrow," he told them, "I will put one of you, along with your son, in the north reef stilt blind, and the other with his son, in the new deepwater blind offshore. We will have both locations covered. When the diving ducks leave the north reef location, hopefully they follow their movements of the past few weeks and stop at the offshore location. I believe tomorrow will be a much better day as far as the hunt is concerned," Dad told the hunters.

On Tuesday morning, the second day of the hunt for the Brown Brothers, my father and Pudding Head tied one of the Brown Brothers and his son out in the north reef stilt blind, the other, along with his son, in the new location at the deepwater blind. As they approached the deepwater blind my dad marked the grain locations with a buoy, and towed the float blind about seven hundred yards to the north and anchored it. He helped the hunters get in the skiff with their guns, hunting gear, and a signal flag. Dad placed the fifty diving duck decoys around the blind. He told the hunters not to even think about getting out of the blind; the water was much too deep. If they needed anything all they had to do was wave the flag. He would be down wind in the powerboat out of eyesight watching them with field glasses. All downed fowl would be gathered by him in the boat. Just after daylight the diving ducks came out of the northwest and made a pass at the stilt blind where a few were harvested. The large raft headed offshore just as they had for the past weeks. Many of them settled on the water just out of range and began to swim toward the float blind. When they were within range, a few more were taken. The ducks jumped and flew back to the reef, settling on the water; a few swam within range of the stilt blind, and a few more were downed. The larger raft divided into four smaller groups, and some went offshore; some settled back on the water and swam back to the float blind. This process continued until the morning turned into a successful hunt. At noon the hunters exchanged stories. The younger Brown Boys were amazed at the vast number of ducks and were impressed how the ducks flew up the decoy strings, providing many good wing shots. All the Brown boys were satisfied with their morning hunt.

The next few days of the week's hunt continued to be good for the Brown boys. They were able to take diving ducks each day. The younger Brown boys wanted to hunt geese; neither of them had ever shot a goose. It was decided that on Friday, to give the diving ducks a rest on the reef and out in the sound, the younger Brown boys were placed in a shore blind on the southeast end of the island where small flocks of geese visited daily. The shore blind location was baited heavily around a small cedar tree secured to a wooden stake about seven hundred yards from the blind. My father and Pudding Head took the boys there and tied out the goose rig, moving the cedar tree marker within range of the blind. The weather was still bluebird-influenced, so they only had a morning and an afternoon shoot. The hunters were able to take several geese during the morning and afternoon sessions.

The Brown Brothers were pleased with their hunt on the island. They decided to leave a day early on Saturday instead of Sunday. They were flying back to Tennessee from Manteo on a plane owned by their company. Pudding Head and I stayed and cleaned up the camp while my father took the hunters ashore to connect with their flight. After we finished up the cleaning we had to place corn around all the bait markers before we came ashore. On the offshore float blind location we baited it heavy right next to the blind. On the next hunt the blind could be moved five hundred yards from the baited site, and it would be within hunting regulations to hunt it. We finished our baiting duties, and we secured the boat by three o'clock that afternoon. This gave me a little time to catch up with my friends to see what they were up to. I walked over to my grandfather's house to search for Woody, my cousin Elwood. It was four o'clock when I got there. We decided that it was too late in the afternoon to get our friends together to do anything; dark was soon approaching. We walked over to the store owned by Miss Louise Roundtree and purchased a pack of salted peanuts and a Pepsi-Cola each. We proceeded to pour the peanuts in the Pepsi bottle, which was a typical snack in those days. As you took a drink of Pepsi, you also ate a peanut or two. I still pour peanuts into soft drinks to this day. We left the store and headed for home. We parted at my grandfather's as I went down the path to my house.

The next day was Sunday, and off to Sunday school and church. The old church echoed meeting time all around the village on a still December morning. My father's hunters arrived around three o'clock in the afternoon. This hunt during the second week of December also had several hunters who were interested in purchasing shares in the club. My dad wanted them to have a successful hunt as well. I was in the process of helping my cousin, Pudding Head, load the hunters' gear in the *Dolphin*. I noticed that Mr. Kotarides and my father had their heads together discussing the upcoming hunt. Mr. Kotarides saw me helping with the luggage and called to me. He wanted me to come over, and he introduced me to the hunters. He told them I was the son of their hunting guide, and gave them my name. One of the hunters was named Mr. Harrell; he owned the franchise for all the Below Meat Markets in the state of Virginia. Another hunter was named Mr. Sam

Johnson; he was the owner of several auto body shops in eastern Virginia. A third hunter was his son, Mr. Joseph Johnson, who was involved in the wholesale oil markets. These were very important prospects to buy shares in the club. Mr. Kotarides wanted everything to go smoothly for them. I shook hands with them and answered a few questions they asked about the island. It seemed they were always interested in the type of school system we had in the area. They wanted to know first of all if we had a school, and the number of students who were enrolled.

We finished loading the gear in the *Dolphin*, and Pudding Head left for the island. All the hunters boarded the *Vivian Marie*, my father's house-boat, to ferry over to the island. The hunt went well. With utilization of the deepwater float blind, used along with the north reef stilt blind, the hunters bagged their limits in diving ducks each day of the hunt. They were able to take geese from the shore blinds on the eastern side of the island early in the morning and during the late afternoon shoots. The hunters were satisfied and interested in becoming paid members of the hunt club.

Mr. Kotarides was happy with the results of the last two hunts. He told my father that the hunters from the last two hunts had already pledged to become shareholders. With these new pledges there would be enough money to make all the improvements they had previously discussed. The hunting party left early on Saturday morning.

After we got ashore, my mother, father, and I went back to the island to clean and prepare for the next hunt. We spent the night at the club, finished up cleaning, and made it back home in time for Sunday school and church. On this particular Sunday I was singing at the dinner table. My mother told me to let my food stop my mouth. She wanted me to stop singing at the table. I was in a singing mood because I was on Christmas vacation from school and would be allowed to attend the entire hunt.

On that Sunday afternoon I got my hunting gear together, loaded it early, and was already at the harbor helping pump gas for the boats. I looked up and saw the hunters' cars approaching the harbor. Mr. Harry Bowman was in the first vehicle; he had one of his hunting buddies from Virginia with him. We began to load their hunting gear in the *Dolphin* when three more vehicles pulled up. My father greeted the men as they got out of the cars. They were local hunters from Hatteras Island whom Mr. Kotarides had invited to the club to hunt. Their names were Mr. Donald Oden, Mr. Lee Peele, Mr. Edgar Styron, Mr. Clarence Jennette, Mr. Dudley Burrus, and Mr. Charles Williams. Some of these men lived in the village of Hatteras and some in the village of Avon.

We arrived at the camp and had a big supper. After we finished eating, my cousin and I cleared off the table, washed the dishes, and the hunters settled in for a poker game. As soon as they began playing poker, they had me running, fixing drinks and snacks for them. When I had them all fixed up, I settled in an easy chair near the table so that I could keep an eye on their needs. After a few drinks the stories began to flow. This was the most enjoyable portion of the night for me. I loved to hear the stories of how it was when they were boys and the things they were involved in. There were many stories of past hunts, the types of business they were in, and the many women they all bragged about being with in their younger days. Just before my father turned in for the night he stopped by the chair to talk to me. He reminded me that when men have a few drinks, their tongues begin to loosen up a bit. "Everything you hear them talk about out here at the club under those conditions must absolutely remain here at the club. You never take any of it ashore with you, and most of all, never repeat any of it to your friends. These are all hard-working family men. They are just having fun. They trust you, so you must respect their privacy." To this day I have always remembered what he told me. I waited on them and enjoyed their many stories until they all grew tired and decided to turn in for the night. I cleaned up and headed off to bed myself. My father woke me up about four-thirty in the morning. I asked if I should wake the hunters; he told me they had had a late night, not to wake anyone. "Just put on the coffee and begin frying the bacon. They will get up when they smell the food," he told me. "The first two on deck will be our hunters for the south sink box," he said. "We have a ten- to fifteen-mile-an-hour wind from the west this morning, and the water is full and in the marsh." Sure enough, Mr. Harry Bowman and Mr. Dudley Burrus came out just after I put on the bacon. They asked my dad where the hunt would begin today. He told them that they could hunt geese and pintails from the south reef curtain box until midmorning. "My son and I will tie you out there after you have had your breakfast," he told them. So my father and I took Mr. Bowman and Mr. Burrus to the south reef curtain box. All the hunters on this hunt enjoyed themselves for the entire week. We broke camp and headed home to celebrate Christmas.

# CHAPTER TWELVE

# A Gull Island Christmas

On December 21, which fell on a Friday, Mr. Kotarides called my father by phone from Norfolk, Virginia. He asked my dad about the upcoming weather for Christmas week. My father told him the long-range forecast called for mild weather with light winds, still under the influence of the bluebird. His response was that is exactly what he was looking for; he wanted to bring his family down for a Gull Island Christmas. It was his opinion that it was time for our families to get acquainted. He invited our family to join his family for a Gull Island Christmas celebration. My father readily agreed and told my mother and me that we would be celebrating Christmas with the Kotarides family on Gull Island. They would be arriving on Sunday, December 23. My mother went right to the corner. She began to blast my father about altering our plans on such short notice. "Spend Christmas with a family we've never even met," she barked. "Our families know absolutely nothing about one another. This house is a mess; it's completely out of the question. We couldn't possibly be ready by Sunday," she said.

"Settle down," my father began. "They are folks just like us. Mr. Kotarides is nice; we all like him. He has a wife named Helen, and a daughter named Sandy, about Elvin's age, I believe," he answered. *Lord, a daughter*, I thought to myself. Just my luck. *Why not a son who might go on a hunt with me?* "Besides, I had to except his invitation. He is my boss, and we are going. Santa will have no problem finding his way out there on Christmas Eve night," he said and winked at me.

"My word," said my mother. "I have a million things to do to prepare for their arrival. I have to clean this house from top to bottom. I have pies to bake, I have to get our clothes ready, his wife is probably a high-society-type lady, and I am just a simple coastal woman," my mom said.

"Don't worry," my father said, reassuring her. "She will love you. You will see, everything will be okay. If she is anything like him, we will all get along fine," my father said. During the next day and a half my mother was a ball of energy. She was scurrying around the house cleaning, baking, and washing clothes. She even made me clean up the yard. On Sunday afternoon when they arrived, she was plumb tuckered out. All our gear was packed; the house was clean enough to eat off the floor. The table was full of decorated Christmas cookies, everything was sparkling, and made ready when my father went out to greet them. I walked out with my dad while my mother retreated to the bathroom to check her general appearance one last time.

I saw a big cream-colored Chrysler Newport parked behind my father's Henry-J. The doors opened, and Mr. Kotarides, his wife, and daughter got out of the car. He introduced them to my dad and me. His wife was named Helen, and his daughter was named Sandy; they both seemed nice. I asked my father what Mr. Kotarides's first name was; he told me it was Alexander, Alex for short, but I should always call him Mr. Kotarides. We all walked up to the house, my dad made the introductions there, and Mom invited them in to freshen up after their long drive down to Salvo. She brought out some fresh-baked Christmas cookies and lemonade.

My father and Mr. Kotarides walked down to the harbor to look at the boats and discuss future plans for the growth of the club. My mother and Helen were involved in conversation concerning the upcoming stay at the club for Christmas. I was munching on cookies and relaxing in a rocking chair when Sandy broke the silence and asked me a question. She first wanted to know about the chickens we had out in the chicken pound, near the garden, in the backyard. It seemed her father told her that we raised chickens and collected our own eggs, and even sold some of the eggs to other folks. She wanted to see the chickens; my mother passed her an egg basket and told me to show her the chickens and the egg collecting process. We walked out back to the chicken pound, I told her we kept about one hundred chickens. She asked a ton of questions. She wanted to know why the pound had a wire cover over the top of it. I explained that the cover kept the hawks, coons, and possums from catching the chickens, and it kept the crows from eating the eggs. She was curious about the chicken coop, the egg-laying boxes, and the seaweed that was strewn all around the pound. I explained that the weatherproof chicken coop was where the chickens roosted or slept at night, and the egg-laying boxes is where they laid the eggs. The seaweed provided them a soft place to rest, under a large oak tree, which provided them shade from the sun during the heat of the summer months.

We stopped by an outside hand pump my dad had installed to provide water for the things or animals we kept. As I ran water in the bucket, I explained it was for washing off the eggs and checking to see if any of them were bad. She questioned me about what was meant by an egg being bad. I explained that an egg that was bad would float, and the good ones settled to the bottom of the bucket. A bad egg has gas that forms inside the egg as the decaying process begins, making it impossible to eat.

I opened the gate to the chicken pound, and we walked in. The chickens immediately came over and surrounded us. She was a little scared and wanted to know what they were doing. I reassured her by telling her that they were just curious and thought we had feed for them. Not to worry; she was perfectly safe. When the chickens realized that it was not feeding time they slowly wandered off. We went to the first egg boxes and began to remove the eggs, wash them off, and test them. All of them were good, and soon we had a whole basket of eggs.

She wanted to see the garden; she couldn't believe that we grew our own vegetables. I told her that my father had the green thumb in our family, and I just helped him in the garden. This time of year wasn't much to see, only rows of harvested vegetables. She asked about the structures my father had provided for the bean vines to wrap around and climb. And the grape barber, which is a flat slated platform about five feet above the ground for the grapevine to grow on. We had a long discussion; I answered all her questions the best I could; then we returned to the house.

My mom told me that we were just about ready to go. I should bring up a wheelbarrow from the harbor, clean it out, and take our luggage and gear to the boats. Mr. Kotarides was going to drive his car to the harbor and load their gear. My mom told me that she, Helen, and Sandy would walk down in a few minutes. I fetched the wheelbarrow and took our gear to the harbor. Dad and I loaded all the gear in the *Dolphin*. Then the women folks showed up and boarded the *Vivian Marie*. I untied the *Dolphin* and took the painter or bowline and made it fast to the stern cleat for the *Vivian Marie*. My father eased the *Vivian Marie* out of the harbor, towing the *Dolphin*. When we cleared the mouth of the harbor, my dad throttled back the *Vivian Marie*, and I lengthened the towline on the *Dolphin*, allowing her to follow a safe distance behind us. When dad throttled up the *Vivian Marie*, the *Dolphin* rose up on an even plane behind us, and we were off on our way to the island.

The weather was amazingly warm and mild for December. There was hardly a ripple on the water. The wind was from the southeast about five to eight miles per hour. The water was as clear as gin; there was not a cloud in the sky. We skimmed along the surface of the water, passing No-Ache Point, soon entering Cedar Hammock Channel. When we passed over Bay Shoals my dad had to throttle back, the water was much shallower on the shoals, and we began to lope, making the ride much rougher. As soon as our forward speed decreased, both boats settled back on an even plane. When we had crossed the shoals and entered Gull Shoal Channel, he had to throttle up again. We soon crossed the channel. My dad throttled back until we were just moving along at an idle. Then we bumped bottom several times before we reached the outside boat stake closest to the edge of the channel. At that point we had to tie the *Vivian Marie* to the boat stake, bring the *Dolphin* alongside, and transfer all passengers. The *Dolphin* was a much shallower draft than the larger boat. Then we were able to slide into the small creek to the clubhouse. We off-loaded all of the luggage and the hunting gear.

The womenfolk began to prepare the evening meal. At the supper table my mother reminded us that tomorrow would be Christmas Eve and we didn't have a tree. My father told us that we would go ashore the next day and bring back a tree to be decorated. The table was cleared, kitchen cleaned up, and my dad fired up the generator for hot water and baths. We relaxed at the table, had a snack, and Helen read "The Night before Christmas" aloud. Mr. Kotarides told us a Christmas story of when he was a small boy back in Greece. He told us that the celebration of Christmas is a little different in Greece; in his country St. Nicholas, which is our Santa Claus, is the patron saint of sailors. On Christmas Eve the boys of the villages usually travel from house to house, beating drums and singing Christmas carols. At each house they are given dried figs, almonds, walnuts, and lots of sweets or sometimes small gifts. Christmas trees are not commonly used. Instead, a shallow wooden bowl, a sprig of basil, and a wooden cross are used. The bowl contains a small amount of water to keep the basil fresh. On Christmas very few presents are exchanged. Instead, gifts are given to hospitals and orphanages. The words "Hronia Polia" (many happy years) are used as a Christmas greeting. Normally gifts can include a Greek nut cookie known as Kourambiethes. The celebration lasts the full twelve days of the Christmas season. I listened to every word that he said.

Then everyone wanted to know about the past Christmases that my father had celebrated on Hatteras Island. He related a story of celebrating the birth of Jesus in the church on Christmas. The children hung one of their stockings on the fireplace mantels. On Christmas morning the stockings would have an apple, an orange, and some hard candy inside them, left by Santa. Some small homemade gifts were usually given, and a Christmas play was performed in the church, including Joseph, Mary, baby Jesus, wise men, and shepherds telling the Christmas story. A huge Christmas dinner was prepared including ham, goose, turkey, and potatoes cooked in many ways, with many types of desserts. After all the Christmas stories were over, we sang "Silent Night," "Jingle Bells," "Up on the Housetop," and a few more carols. Then we decided it was time to retire for the night.

I walked outside for a few minutes before going off to bed. Even though the weather was mild during the daytime, it got cold when the sun went down at night. The temperature was in the middle thirties to the lower forties, and there was no downwind; it was almost dead calm. Before I went inside, I stayed long enough to hear a few swan on the south reef and some geese on the north reef. As I was going in, I heard the whistle and the rustle of wings from a flock of teal as they headed for the south reef.

The next morning I woke up to the smell of coffee perking, bacon frying, and bread baking in the oven. My mother and Helen had the breakfast cooking, and boy did it smell good! It was about eight o'clock in the morning. They had the table set, and everyone was out of bed except for me. I was the "cow's tail," as my mom called me. "Are those cheese biscuits I smell?" I asked, wiping the sleep from my eyes. My mother could bake cheese biscuits to die for; she cut block cheese and rolled it up in dough and baked them to perfection. The cheese melted into the bread as it baked. One of them, along with a cup of good coffee, could serve as a breakfast by itself.

"Yes, sleepy head," my mom said to me. She asked me how long I stayed outside last night before going to bed.

I answered, "Not too long."

"I don't know what in the world you get out of walking around the outside deck in the cold night air," she said.

"It's only on calm nights, Mom," I answered. "If you are real quiet and listen, the island will share its secrets with you."

"You can tell that you are your father's son, with the high regard that you two have for this island. The both of you act as if this place is paradise with magical powers. After you finish eating you can help me clear the table and wash dishes."

Helen winked at me and broke into the conversation. "Oh, I will help you," she said. "I overheard Alex and Ed talking about taking the children to look for a Christmas tree this morning," she added.

I didn't wait for my mother to respond before I said, "Thank you very much, ma'am. That is very nice of you." My dad told us we should be going and asked Mom to pack us a lunch just in case we didn't get back by noon time. Mr. Alex, Sandy, my father, and I left in the *Dolphin* and headed toward the shore in search of a Christmas tree. My dad brought along a hand saw, and sent me to fetch a couple of empty feed bags to bring with us. We came to the shore at the sand beach near Bay Landing, about five miles down south of Salvo. The wind was light from the west; we pulled the bow up on the sand and set the anchor. We were able to step out of the boat without putting waders on. Then we were off to find a tree. Soon we came up on a group of small cedar trees, picked out one that had a good shape, cut it down, and pulled it to the boat. My father suggested we walk across the road and continue on to the beach. We took one of the empty feed bags with us. At the beach we found a number of starfish, small sand dollars, conch egg cases, and skate egg cases washed up near the surf. "The kids can make decorations for the tree from these," my father said, as he placed a couple of sand dollars in the bag. We took these treasures back to the boat, loaded the tree, and pushed off. It was approaching midday. My father picked the paddle and began to shove the *Dolphin* in a northward direction parallel to the shoreline. I knew the water was deep enough to run, so I asked, "Why are you shoving? Where are we going, Pop?"

"Just up the shore a little," he said. "I know a creek that has some oysters in it that would make a nice pan of oyster dressing for the Christmas feed." He continued on until we came to the creek containing the oysters. We gathered about a half a bag full, stopped and ate our lunch, then headed toward the clubhouse: one bag for the beach treasures, another for the oysters. I wondered what else he had up his sleeves. When we arrived back at the clubhouse, my father made a stand for the tree. He helped Sandy and I bleach the articles we found on the beach. The starfish, the sand dollars, the conch egg cases, and the skate egg cases all turned white in the bleach. He had a few cans of paint at the club he used to touch up the decoys when they got scuffed up. He gave us the paint and some small brushes. We painted the bleached items and made decorations out of them. We all pitched in and decorated the tree. We had green and red spotted starfish, yellow and green sand dollars, white and blue skate egg cases, and white and green conch egg cases. All of these items were attached to the tree by string from an old decoy span. When we finished, the tree looked really nice. Helen said that this was the first Christmas tree she had ever seen decorated with sea creatures. My father worried about Santa being able to get across the channel and find us on the island. He was picking on Sandy and me. We had a delicious supper, sang a few more Christmas carols, and Sandy and I left cookies and milk out for Santa. Then we went to bed. We were tired from the day's activity. The next morning Sandy and I got up first. Santa had found his way to the island. If I live to be a hundred years old, I will never forget the Christmas I celebrated on Gull Island.

# CHAPTER THIRTEEN

# Torpedoes in the Channel

After a very fine Christmas celebration on Gull Island, the Kotarides family had to return to Norfolk, Virginia, to finish celebrating the Greek holiday well into the New Year. The Hooper family celebrated the coming of the New Year along with the rest of the villagers of Salvo. The celebration began by the men firing their shotguns in the air several times just after midnight on December 31. On New Year's Day the midday meal always included black-eyed peas for luck during the upcoming year. The festive holiday in the Chicamacomico area—the villages located at the north end of Hatteras Island: Rodanthe, Waves, and Salvo—continues until the first weekend of January, with a large island get-together known as the Old Christmas Celebration. This festive occasion includes a stewed chicken and pie bread supper, a Christmas play, an appearance by Santa Claus, and a dance with live music to finish up the night. During this time of the year my dad enjoyed a few days off.

All the hunters were occupied with holiday celebrations of their own. My father used this period to check all the hunting equipment, materials, and gear. If any repairs were needed we completed them, in order to have the club ready for the first hunt of the New Year. A couple of days before the New Year my father and I made a trip to the island to grain up the blinds. While we were there we checked all the wings or sea breakers at the curtain boxes. We checked the shore blinds, float blinds, and the stilt blinds for signs of disrepair. When my father was satisfied that everything was in good working condition, he made a list of materials that needed to be brought over. This list included one-hundred-pound gas cylinders for the lights, cookstove, and refrigerator. We also had to bring gasoline over in five-gallon cans for the generator. All these materials and supplies had to be boated over to the island from Salvo. My father had converted one of the larger decoy skiffs into a material and supply carrier by building racks and shelves onto it. He reinforced the deck of the skiff at the mid-ship area in order to transport the many five-gallon cans of gasoline for the boats and generator. Above the gas deck, as my father called it, he had constructed a large rack to stack one-hundred-pound cylinders of liquefied petroleum gas. This rack was attached to six four-by-four posts, which elevated it to a level even with the docks. The cylinders could be easily rolled on the boat from the dock and off the boat to the dock, and placed into position with a hand truck. The rack could safely transport six one-hundred-pound cylinders per trip.

My father implemented a safety rule when transporting the fuel to the island. He would never transport a mixed load with the two types of gas; they were always taken over to the island separately. The local gas truck from Manteo delivered a load of cylinders for the club. My father noticed that the cylinders did not have the protective caps that were normally screwed in place on the top of them. These caps were there to protect the valves from damage during the shipping process. These valves were opened when the cylinders were filled with gas at the bulk storage yard, and opened again when they are put in use. He asked the driver about the lack of the protective caps on the cylinders. The driver told him that the gas company was in the process of replacing most of their one-hundred-pound cylinders. Just last week they had sent a large tractor trailer truck of empty cylinders back to the manufacturer to be replaced by new ones. All of the empties had to have a protective cap on them in order to be transported. At the time my father was told that the company didn't have enough caps to go around. He told me that we would wait until they could provide us with the caps before he took any full cylinders out to the island. These plans were quickly changed after we made a trip to the island to place grain around the blinds, and make a gasoline delivery in five-gallon gas cans. My father realized that he only had one cylinder of liquefied petroleum gas that was full. He told me that we had to bring over at least six cylinders from the harbor. We took five empty cylinders back to the shore and made ready to load up the full cylinders the next morning.

My dad thumped the barometer with his index finger on his right hand a couple of times, stood back, and took a good look at it after the evening meal. He was concerned about the weather for the next day. The barometric pressure was high, which called for fair weather, but he had seen a few upper-level clouds racing across the sky in a northwesterly direction. This type of cloud movement is not normal for the winter time. Most all the winter weather patterns, low- and high-pressure areas, move from the west toward the east. My father was concerned about the clouds moving from east to west during the winter season.

The next morning was clear but cold. We loaded the cylinders carefully on the rack, tied them down securely with rope, and chocked them in place with wooden chocks my father had shaped to fit next to the cylinders. The trip to the island was smooth until we passed by Cedar Hammock Island. The wind breezed up from the southeast a bit, making a three- to four-foot chop as we entered Cedar Hammock Channel. We were aboard the *Dolphin* towing the container skiff about twenty-five feet behind us. As we came out of the channel and entered Bay Shoals, the water was much shallower, and the waves suddenly increased to five to six feet, with an occasional eight-footer. We began to rise and fall violently to the point of slamming hard several times. We were about two miles offshore. My father decreased our forward speed, and I let out another twenty-five feet of tow rope, hoping the container boat would ride a little smoother. The stress of the tow was about to rip the stern cleat out of the *Dolphin*. As soon as we crossed Bay Shoals and entered Gull Shoal Channel, our ride smoothed out considerably.

Then my father brought my attention to three dark clouds moving in our direction. The clouds were out over the ocean, just beginning to cross the island near the Little Hills area. We noticed a small tail trailing downward toward the ground from the center cloud. Most of the time this situation is the beginning of a tornado on land or a water spout over the water. When the clouds came off the island they exploded upward and increased to better than five times their original size. The wind increased to around fifty miles per hour, lightning began to flash from cloud to cloud, and from cloud to ground. The booming roar of thunder followed each lightning flash. The tail in the center cloud extended all the way down to the surface of the water and increased drastically in size. Water could be seen swirling from the surface to the base of the cloud in a cone about a half mile in diameter. At this point we knew a large water spout had formed and was heading in our direction at an alarming speed.

My father yelled to me to turn the container boat loose from our tow. He backed down on the *Dolphin* in order to give me slack on the tow rope. As soon as I had enough slack in the towline, I untied it from the cleat, and set the container boat free. The water spout was upon us. The rain began to come down in buckets. We could barely see the bow of the boat in front of us. Then the hail began to pelt us. We were lucky we were wearing heavy clothing, waders, and foul-weather gear. We had to crouch down in the boat and shield our faces from the blinding hail. My dad opened up the throttle on the *Dolphin*; she instantly responded and surged ahead. She was jumping from the crest of one large wave and crashing down with a shudder on the backside of the next. At times her bow was violently pushed deep under the water, forcing her stern to be elevated completely out of the water as the next wave approached. When her bow came back up, the propeller would take another bite, and she would leap forward. As she left the surface of the water you could hear the motor race. We were able to outdistance the water spout and escape to the safety of the middle of the channel. The very second we were in the clear, away from the large water spout, the conditions improved.

Our towboat was not as lucky. My father throttled the *Dolphin* back, and we were able to turn toward the container boat for a look-see. The water spout picked the skiff completely clear of the water's surface up about ten feet, then dropped her bow first back down, shearing off the rack supporting the gas containers. The valves were broken off the cylinders during the spill. The containers surfaced and went speeding off in all directions, propelled by the pressure of the escaping gas. Two of them came surging through the waves in our direction, just missing the boat. They reminded me of the torpedoes I had seen in World War II movies. The torpedoes were launched by German U-boats at Allied shipping, trying to cut off our supply lines along the Atlantic Coast.

The three large thunderclouds continued racing in a northwest direction. We could see the water spout scooping large amounts of water as it sped away from us. The wind fell out and changed direction back five to ten miles per hour from the southwest. The sun came out, and the only evidence that any rough weather had occurred was our sunken, upside-down decoy boat and the scattered cylinders.

I was amazed by the power of the water spout. I had heard stories of fish, frogs, and other water creatures raining down from the sky. I had never witnessed any situations like that, and to say the least, I was always skeptical about the truth of these stories. But at that very moment, it dawned on me how it could possibly occur. This was the first time that torpedolike projectiles had been launched in the Gull Channel. The cylinders kept crashing from wave to wave until they had expended all the pressure from the gas that propelled them.

These powerful water spouts are extremely dangerous to watermen and have been responsible for many deaths in the Pamlico Sound area of the Outer Banks. That day we were lucky to be able to escape serious injury or perhaps death by drowning.

We collected all the empty cylinders and tied them together by threading the towline through holes in the brackets that were welded to the bottom of them. These brackets formed the base they sat upright on. I slacked them off about twenty feet behind the stern of the *Dolphin* and retied them to the stern cleat. My father brought the *Dolphin* downwind of the decoy boat, easing up alongside to check for damage. She seemed to be intact, just bottom side up bobbing along on the waves. The stern line from the decoy boat was floating nearby; I tied the cylinder line to it, and allowed them to drift back out of the way. My father placed a stern line from the *Dolphin* across the bottom of the decoy boat and made it fast to the opposite side of the washboard. He throttled up the *Dolphin*. When the line came tight, the decoy boat was pulled over and righted herself. She settled on the surface full of water. We were able to bring her alongside and began to bail her out by hand with buckets. Slowly, she began to rise higher up in the water. Soon I was able to get aboard and bail from the inside of the boat. In a short time we had the water bailed out of the decoy boat. My father boarded and examined her from stern to stern. When he was satisfied with the condition of the boat, we towed the decoy boat with the cylinders tied to her stern across the channel to the reef. At the reef the water was shallow enough for us to anchor the *Dolphin*, go over the side, and wade to the decoy boat. We were able to load the empty cylinders back inside the decoy boat and begin our trip back home with her in tow.

As we made our way back to the harbor at Salvo, we found five of the six wooden chocks, and most of the material from the rack that we had lost to the water spout. When we arrived back at the harbor we off-loaded the empty cylinders, rebuilt the rack, and loaded up six more full cylinders for a next-day departure from the island.

The next morning my father and I loaded ten bags of grain in the *Dolphin*, took the cylinder boat in tow, and made a successful delivery to the island. That day we were able to regrain all the blinds and off-load and place all the gas cylinders. With everything squared away to my father's satisfaction, we left the island and returned to the harbor at Salvo. The club was ready for the first hunt of the New Year. Plans were in place for the first hunt of the New Year to occur during the second week of January.

When that Sunday morning came around, my father checked the barometer and was pleased with its readings. The barometric pressure was very low, which was an advanced warning of a winter low-pressure system approaching our area. It meant that a strong shift of wind and cold temperatures would be replacing our bluebird-type weather patterns. These conditions would force the large rafts of waterfowl to divide up in much smaller groups. These large rafts of birds sometimes number in the thousands. During calm conditions they tend to form up in these massive flocks. These flocks are difficult to manage, and it is next to impossible to predict their movement. A good hunting guide not only has to know his area, he also has to know how the birds are using his area. This knowledge helps him place his hunters in order to harvest the game during the hunt. When the rough weather forces the larger rafts to divide up, the smaller groups are much easier to manage and hunt. When low pressure approaches, the wind blows hard from the northwest and increases the water levels in the Gull Island area to the point of covering most of the island. This rise in the water level narrows the hunt down to the shore blinds, the high-water curtain boxes of the south reef. In all the rest of the blind locations, the water is much too high to wade and successfully hunt.

On the south reef of Gull Island, my father had installed two curtain boxes. The first was at the edge of the reef and could be hunted when the wind was at medium strength from the northwest. The second one was located in the center of the south reef, rather close to the highest elevation of the reef, and was high and dry most of the time. This box could only be hunted when extreme low pressure was moving over the area. The wind normally blew in excess of thirty miles per hour from the northwest, and the water covered the entire reef. This curtain box could only be used on a hunt during this type of weather. All the larger game such as swan, geese, snow geese, and black ducks would seek this area for gravel. The fowl swallowed the gravel and stored it in their gizzards to aid in their digestion process. When the high-water box was hunted, it had to be constantly monitored. If the barometric pressure suddenly changed and began to rise, this rig had to be immediately taken up and the hunting location moved. The rise in pressure was warning that the wind would soon shift directions, usually from the east. The water on the south reef would quickly recede, and this blind location would return to being high and dry. If this occurred, usually about 150 of the decoys would have to be dragged hundreds of yards to the edge of the reef to the waiting decoy skiff. Water would have to be carried just as far in buckets to flood the box and secure the curtain. The sea breaker, or wing, as it is called, would have to be dragged a sufficient distance from the box and the anchor set. Whenever my father hunted this curtain box, he kept a sharp eye on the barometric pressure. As soon as it began to change, he made sure we moved the hunters to a different location. Then he collected the decoys and secured the box before the water ran off. It was much easier to do all this when there was enough water to bring the decoy boat next to the blind location. My father was thankful the weather had shifted from bluebird back to its normal winter patterns.

# CHAPTER FOURTEEN

# Island Changes

The remainder of the hunting season that year was successful. The sunny, balmy days of the bluebird vanished and were replaced by overcast, blustery, more favorable hunting days. The northern branch of the jet stream moved much farther south, directing the low-pressure areas to track over our location. This type of weather pattern divided the large rafts of waterfowl into smaller, manageable flocks. More fowl was harvested, more successful hunts were completed, and more hunters became interested in the club. That particular January's hunt was one of the best months that my father ever experienced while hunting Gull Island. Hunting season ended at the end of January each year. The interest in the club grew so quickly that Mr. Kotarides had to set limits on its membership. This increase of members enabled him to plan and implement many new changes and improvements to the island.

When the season was over, all the decoys, decoy boats, and hunting gear were brought to Salvo and stored. Mr. Kotarides visited with my father with the planned changes for the island. One of the first changes to be put into place was the digging out of the entrance channel: the digging and shaping of a harbor replacing the small creek near the clubhouse. Mr. Kotarides wanted to begin the work around the first of May as soon as the winter weather broke. He instructed my father to make all the necessary arrangements for the work to begin.

In the middle week of April, when I arrived home from school on Friday afternoon, my dad told me that he had a surprise for me. I began to search the house for a parcel or package of some sort. My mother wanted to know what in the world I was doing. When I told her, she laughed and told me it was not that type of surprise. I begged her to tell me. She laughed some more and informed me that my father would tell me at supper. Just as soon as my dad had finished saying grace, I asked him about the surprise.

"Tomorrow all three of us are catching the first ferry at Oregon Inlet. We will drop your mother off at the Archie Burrus IGA Supermarket in Manteo to grub up." "Grub up" is local Hatteras Island slang for purchasing a month's supply of groceries. Manteo is a town located on the north end of Roanoke Island. "You and I are going to Wanchese, a town located on the south end of Roanoke Island, to meet with a heavy equipment owner." This man owned draglines, bulldozers, dump trucks, and a large barge. All of a sudden, my mind jumped to overdrive. I thought of Manteo as the Fearing Drug Store, where a soda fountain was located, and the Daniels Five and Dime, a toy store. Nothing like that existed on Hatteras Island. After supper I was off to visit all my friends to take orders for the toys they wanted from the Five and Dime store.

The next morning we piled into my father's Henry-J, his car, and caught the ferry to begin the trip. We dropped my mother off at the grocery store and headed south toward Wanchese. My father met with the heavy equipment owner, Mr. Sam Liverman, who lived on Colington Island. Colington is a coastal town located in the northern portion of the Outer Banks of North Carolina. They discussed the upcoming work of improving the depth of the water at Gull Island. They formulated a plan, which included the barge to transport one of his draglines to the island. This barge was in Wanchese Harbor. The owner would be able to load one of his draglines on the barge. He had everything to begin the work except a towboat for the barge. My father told him that a towboat would be no problem; just contact us a couple days before the planned tow.

We returned to Manteo to pick up my mother and load the groceries. The supplies consisted of canned and dry goods, fresh milk, bread, and meats that were bought locally. The dry goods were much cheaper in the larger IGA

Market. We visited the Fearing Drug Store for the midday meal: cheeseburgers, fries, and a large chocolate milkshake. Then to the Five and Dime; I had a list of items to purchase for my friends, and a couple of things for myself. On the way out of town, my mom wanted to stop by the Davis Brothers clothing store. She purchased a few items we needed, and then off to the ferry.

We boarded the very boat that my uncle Luther, my father's younger brother, worked on. He took me up to the pilothouse to meet the captain. The captain's name was Pam Gallop, a Wanchese native. When we were out in the main portion of the inlet, he let me steer the ferry for a short distance. We returned to the car, and my mother gave us a bologna and cheese sandwich, chips, and a drink. She prepared this snack from things she purchased and stored on ice in a small cooler. After we got off the ferry, I mentioned the possibility of accompanying my father on the barge tow from Wanchese. "That just depends on what day of the week the tow falls on, mister," my mother stated. "If it means missing school, the answer is absolutely not," she said. I knew I was in treading on thin ice.

"Suppose I get permission from my teacher and agree to write a paper on the experience," I asked.

"We will see when the time comes," was her answer. My father chuckled, looked at me, and winked. I knew he would help me over this hurdle when the time came. By the time we got home, my mom had to wake me to help with the groceries. I had fallen asleep in the backseat.

The next day was Sunday. After church I delivered the toys to my friends. We all played with our new stuff until it was near dusk and time for supper, then church. As I fell asleep that night, I began to formulate my plans to convince my teacher, Mrs. Hilda Brown, and my mother to give me permission to go with my father on the tow. The next morning I got up early. I knew my father would be sitting at the table around five in the morning, drinking coffee. He wanted to know why I was up so early. I told him I might need his help persuading my mother to let me go with him on the tow. He assured me that he would do all he could, but he also reminded how she felt about me missing school.

I finished breakfast and went to the school bus stop. I had about a one-hour bus ride to school each day. This gave me ample time to formulate a plan to gain permission from Mrs. Hilda Brown to go on the tow with my dad. Just before the bus turned into the school parking lot, I had an idea that linked the tow to geography class. When she announced it was time for recess, all my classmates ran toward the playground. I remained in my seat until all of them had left the room. She wanted to know if I was feeling okay. She remarked that normally I was one of the first ones out the door to the playground. I told her that I felt fine. Then I explained the trip by boat up the sound and the return trip back down the sound with the barge in tow. I also told her that I would be willing to write a paper and read it aloud to the class during geography class. The content of the paper would explain our Islands location in relationship with the Roanoke Island village of Wanchese.

At that point I noticed a smile beginning to develop on her face. First of all, she wanted to know how many days I would be out of school. I told her two, possibly three days. She told me she would approve with three conditions. These conditions were to include a hand-drawn map charting our trip, including the villages and the bodies of water involved. The second condition required the writing of two papers instead of one. The first paper was to be written before the trip, with an explanation of the fine points of geography I was expecting to learn along the way. I would have to read this paper to the class prior to leaving. The second paper would be implemented as planned. Last but not least, a note of permission from my mother would have to be brought to school. We would have to run my first paper, along with the permission slip, by the principal for his approval. I agreed to all her conditions. I asked her to include all this in a note I could take home. I was afraid I would leave something out trying to explain all this to my mother. She agreed and passed the note to me near the end of the school day. She encouraged me to read it before I left to make sure I understood all that she was expecting of me. The note listed all the conditions we had agreed on. There was a section for me to sign showing that I knew, understood, and that I was in agreement with all the terms. Another section was for my mother to sign, giving her approval for me to go, and indicating that she had read and understood the note. It also contained a section for the principal's approval. I read it and told Mrs. Hilda it was fine, and placed it in the safety of my book bag. When I arrived home that afternoon I gave the note to my mother. She was amazed that I had agreed to all the terms that Mrs. Hilda had strapped me with. She wanted to know if I understood all the work that was involved. I assured her that I did and began working on the first paper. My father broke in to the conversation and said, "If he completes all the requirements imposed by his teacher, it will be a learning experience for him."

At this point my mother threw up both of her hands and said, "All right. I know when I am licked." She picked up the pen and signed the permission section of the note. In a couple of days I stood before the class and read my first paper to them. My classmates were interested in the trip and asked me a few questions about it. I answered their questions the best I could. Mrs. Hilda took the paper; she said I had done a good job so far, and promised to give it to the principal for his review that afternoon. The next morning before we began our spelling lesson, she let me see the field trip request with the principal's signed approval. I was so excited. Remember, she told me, "You still have another paper to complete and read after you return." I assured her that I would finish all the work we agreed on. That afternoon when I got off the school bus, I ran all the way up the sandy road to our house. My father was sitting at the picnic table on our back porch. He was splicing a long piece of rope to a length of heavy chain. "I have the approval of my teacher and principal," I told him.

He looked up and smiled, and returned his attention to the splicing. He had a large pile of rope in front of him. I asked him if he was making up a tow rope for the *Dolphin* or the *Vivian Marie*. He laughed and told me that his long net boats were not stout enough, nor did they have the power to tow a crane barge. I was puzzled and wanted to know why he was making long tow rope. He told me he was making an extralong anchor line. "I have made arrangements for a much larger, more powerful towboat," he told me. "Mr. Donald Oden from Hatteras is sending his eighty-five-foot wooden-hull fishing trawler, the *Mitts-E-Kay*, up here next Thursday. She is designed to tow large trawl nets, but has been converted into a freight carrier. There is a boom mounted on the front of her, for on-loading and off-loading freight."

A lot of freight was hauled to Hatteras and Ocracoke Islands by water in those days. In 1963 Oregon Inlet was bridged and freight hauling vessels were replaced by tractor-trailer trucks. The *Mitts-E-Kay* had a twelve-cylinder diesel engine with ample power to tow the crane barge. This piece of line would be used to anchor the *Dolphin* out back of the reef. The reef is a shallow-water sandbar that runs parallel the entire length of the island. This sandbar separates the inshore shallow water from the offshore deep water in the Pamlico Sound. "You and I will meet the captain of the trawler, with one other crew member, back of the reef in deep water. We will anchor the *Dolphin* and crew with them on the trawler. On our return trip we will pick up the *Dolphin*."

I thought I would bust at the seams. Man, was this going to be an adventure. I ran to tell my mother. She smiled and remarked that I was willing to do almost anything, no matter what it took, as long as it involved Gull Island or travel on the Pamlico Sound.

The next few days seemed to crawl by. I didn't think the week would ever end. Finally, the weekend came and went. On Monday morning when I arrived at school, I reminded Mrs. Hilda that this was the week we were going on the tow. She reminded of the work that was due upon my return to school.

My father and I were up early on Thursday morning, loading our gear on the *Dolphin*. We planned to meet the *Mitts-E-Kay* around eight o'clock that morning. When we left the harbor I noticed the wind was blowing from the southwest at five to ten miles per hour. This was a good sign; we would have a fair wind or tailwind all the way up the sound. Just as we crossed the reef I could see the large vessel approaching. She was massive compared to the *Dolphin*. They were just about abreast Gull Island Channel, about five miles to the south, and about four miles to the west of our location. Soon we were far enough offshore that she was due south of us. My father told me to make ready the new anchor line he had spliced. He had a larger than normal Danforth anchor attached to a heavy section chain. He told me to throw it over the side. Then he put the *Dolphin* in reverse and slowly backed up until all one hundred feet of the line were overboard. He throttled up until the anchor was securely embedded in the bottom. "That should hold her," he said and cut off the engine, and we awaited their approach. When they arrived at our location, the trawler circled us and took a position about two hundred feet to the windward of the *Dolphin*. The captain held the large vessel in place. The mate lowered a skiff attached to a large boom. The boom was located on the bow of the trawler. The skiff appeared to have two bows. Both ends were sharp. When the skiff reached the water, the cable became slack, and the hooks on the bridle detached. The mate slacked the skiff back to us, attached to a long line. We loaded our gear and climbed into the skiff. The mate pulled us up to the bridle hanging from the bow of the vessel. My dad reset the hooks of the bridle to the skiff, and the mate lifted us aboard. We came to rest on deck in a cradle that was fashioned for the skiff to rest in. We got out of the skiff with our gear and helped the mate secure the skiff, winch, and boom.

The mate introduced himself as Tom Daniels. He told us that the captain was Charles Daniels, his uncle. Tom told us to follow him and he would show us to our quarters. As we were going below decks, I heard the captain throttle up the vessel. There was plenty of room in the below deck area; it contained a galley, eating area, bathroom, and four births for sleeping. We stored our gear and went to the wheelhouse to meet Captain Daniels. He and his nephew, Tom, had been hauling freight for Mr. Oden for some time aboard the *Mitts-E-Kay*. As we entered the wheel house, the captain introduced himself. He smiled at me and asked me if I would like to steer the vessel. I said, "Yes," and he moved a large wooden box over for me to stand on. He told me to watch the compass, that we were headed a little west of north. I noticed the large boom on the bow. The wench was powered with an air-cooled engine, which turned a large wheel of cable for lifting and lowering of freight. I also noticed a large towing post located on the stern of the vessel. This towing post was also supplied with a large drum full of two-inch-diameter hawser. We were making about eight to ten knots of forward speed. The island could be seen by looking toward the east. It appeared that we were about due west of Rodanthe, the last village to the north leaving Hatteras Island. Captain Daniels told me we would arrive in Wanchese Harbor early afternoon, in about three to four hours. A distant channel marker came into view, and Captain Daniels told me to head for it. As we neared the marker, he took over the wheel. He told me this was the beginning of Old House Channel, which led us into Oregon Inlet. As we crossed Oregon Inlet, we could see the ferries making their crossings. We continued on past the north ferry dock and entered Roanoke Sound, then headed up the sound to Wanchese Harbor.

# CHAPTER FIFTEEN

# The Tow

There was still plenty of light left in the day as we passed the break water and entered Wanchese Harbor. We moved to the inner portion of the harbor. On the way we passed several large fishing trawlers unloading their catch of fish. Captain Daniels eased the *Mitts-E-Kay* alongside the freight dock. A man on the dock tossed us the mooring lines, and we made her fast. The mate fired up the air-cooled engine attached to the wench on the boom. My father scrambled up on the dock and placed the hooks into the bridles that were fastened on the freight bundles. The mate began the task of loading the freight on the vessel. The freight consisted of long pilings and large bundles of lumber. All these materials were treated with creosote. Everything was carried back on our return trip. These materials would be used to construct bulkheads and docks on Ocracoke Island.

It was much more practical and less expensive to ship the material by boat than by truck. By boat it could be off-loaded at its construction location. If the shipment was by truck it would have to cross two inlets by ferry to reach its destination. The length of time required and the lack of equipment to unload the trucks made it impossible to place the material near its desired locations.

When all the freight was loaded and secured, Captain Daniels and his nephew, Tom, left the vessel to spend the night with their families. My father and I prepared the evening meal and quartered aboard the *Mitts-E-Kay* for the night. The next morning Captain Daniels woke us up early. Tom fixed the breakfast, and we soon got under way.

Captain Daniels took the vessel farther up the harbor. Soon a large barge came into view. There was a large dragline and a D-sixteen bulldozer strapped to the deck of the barge. The mats that were designed to support the dragline as it crawled along on marshy areas were also strapped to the deck of the barge beside the dragline. The barge itself was well over one hundred feet long. It had two long, tubular-shaped structures that passed through holes in the deck. Captain Daniels told me these things were called spuds. The spuds were shaped to a point on their bottoms. They could be dropped through the deck to the bottom to hold the barge into place. These structures had a heavy collar on each of them at the deck level. The collars had a pin through them, holding the spuds in place above the bottom of the barge as it was being towed. The dragline was located on the front, and the bulldozer was placed on the back of the barge. There was an empty space between the two pieces of equipment. I figured they were placed in this manner to equalize the weight on the barge. With the weight evenly distributed, the barge would ride properly on the surface of the water as it was towed.

Captain Daniels brought the *Mitts-E-Kay* alongside the barge. Tom secured the vessel to the barge. Mr. Sam Liverman, the heavy equipment owner, boarded the vessel. He came to make arrangements with my father about the proposed work at Gull Island. The equipment operator was with him. Mr. Liverman introduced him to us; his name was Earnest Ambrose. Mr. Ambrose was to accompany us on the tow. Mr. Liverman was concerned about where he would be staying and taking his meals. My dad told him the operator could stay with us at our house. We had two upstairs bedrooms that were not being used. He could also take his meal with us, and my dad would make daily trips to the island to take him to work. The job schedule was all worked out.

Tom attached the towing hawser to the barge bridle. Mr. Liverman untied the barge as he was leaving. Tom let out a small amount of the hawser to keep the barge close to the stern of the vessel. Captain Daniels began to move the vessel slowly toward the harbor entrance with the barge in tow. When we cleared the harbor, Tom released the brake on the towing drum containing the hawser. He allowed the barge to be slacked back about twenty-five feet behind the stern of the vessel. The barge was kept at a short distance behind us. This enabled us to navigate the narrow channels of Roanoke Sound and Oregon Inlet.

Soon we entered the wider and deeper waters of Pamlico Sound. At this point Tom let out a lot more of the hawser. The barge was allowed to fall back about five hundred feet. I asked Captain Daniels why so much slack was let out. He told me this manner of towing created less demand on the towing vessel. He said at this distance the hawser would dip in the water and stay submerged for minutes at a time. This would allow a small amount of slack between the submerged hawser and the barge. The vessel would then pull the slackened hawser to the surface of the water. At this point, the barge would be propelled ahead. This would create slack on the hawser, and it would disappear below the surface again. This process would continue on a repeated cycle. In theory, the vessel was towing one half of the hawser, and the other half of the hawser was towing the barge.

The *Mitts-E-Kay* had her bow loaded down with the creosote lumber for the construction site at Ocracoke. We were bucking a southwest wind of ten to fifteen miles per hour. She would gently rise and fall in a slow rocking motion in the three- to four-foot waves. The bow of the vessel was plowing ahead through the waves, pushing white water five to six feet out in front of us. Each time the stress of the hawser called on her, the stern squatted under the load. When the hawser relaxed, the bow would rise a bit. The entire vessel shuddered as the big diesel engine pushed her ahead about three to four knots.

Captain Daniels told us we would have to tow through the night and would be abreast of Salvo about first light. Tom and my father took a turn at the wheel steering, allowing Captain Daniels to rest. Mr. Ambrose and I slept the entire night.

Just as day was breaking, the *Dolphin* came into view. Captain Daniels throttled down the *Mitts-E-Kay*. He held the vessel in a stall about twenty-five feet behind the *Dolphin*. He talked to my father about leading the larger vessel in close to the island. He was used to traveling out back of the reef in deep water on his freight trips. He knew my dad was accustomed to navigating the shallow channels around Gull Island. He wanted to tow the barge as close to the island as he could. Dad and I got into the skiff and Tom lowered us to the surface of the water. We rowed over to the *Dolphin*, got aboard, and slacked the skiff back about twenty feet. My father started the engine, and I brought the anchor aboard as he eased the boat ahead. We took the skiff in tow and followed the larger vessel south toward Gull Island.

We were lucky that morning; the water level was high due to southwest wind. When we neared the mouth of Cedar Hammock Channel, my father moved the *Dolphin* up alongside the larger vessel. He waved for Captain Daniels to follow us. Tom brought the barge up close to the stern of the *Mitts-E-Kay*. This allowed better maneuverability as we prepared to cross over the reef and enter shallow water. The entrance of Cedar Hammock Channel opened up back of the reef just to the southern edge of Scotts Reef. The entrance to the channel was located between Scotts Reef and Gull Shoal Reef. It was only about thirty yards across. The depth of the water in the entrance was ten to twelve feet with a southwest wind. Cedar Hammock Channel turns south and heads up at the outside edge of Bay Shoals. These shoals separate Cedar Hammock Channel and Gull Shoal Channel. The water across the shoals is about six to seven feet on southerly wind, much shallower on a north wind. We had to slow the larger vessel down considerably and creep across the outer portion of Bay Shoals. We entered Gull Island Channel in much deeper water.

The waves subsided considerably as we approached the lee of the island. Captain Daniels was able to bring the barge right up to the south edge of the channel. We were about one hundred feet from the mouth of the creek that led to the clubhouse. The captain held the vessel in place as Tom winched the barge up to the stern. Mr. Ambrose boarded the barge with his gear. He started the dragline and dropped the spuds. The point of the spuds dug into the bottom, anchoring the barge in place. Captain Daniels maneuvered the *Mitts-E-Kay* around the barge back into deep water. My father brought the

*Dolphin* alongside the larger vessel, and Tom lifted the skiff back aboard. We guided them back across the reef to deep water. We waved to them as they turned south to continue on their way to their freight delivery.

My father and I returned to the barge and Earnest. The spuds, located near the back of the barge, held it in. At the front end there were two one-hundred-danforth anchors. These anchors were attached to large wenches that contained drums of coiled cable. Earnest took the wenches out of gear, slacking up the cables. My dad and I took the anchors ashore on the *Dolphin*. We carried them a good distance from the edge of the marsh. Directed by Earnest, we placed them at forty-five-degree angles from the front corners of the barge. Then we embedded them into the turf. Earnest tightened the cables, setting the anchors. When he was satisfied the barge was securely anchored, he gave us a thumbs-up gesture. We picked him up from the barge and turned the *Dolphin* north toward home.

As we entered the harbor at Salvo, I realized we were in time for one of my mother's midday meals. We tied the *Dolphin* to the dock and walked toward the house. I helped Earnest with his gear and showed him upstairs to his quarters. We came down to the dining room, and I introduced him to my mom. She welcomed Earnest to our home and asked if he liked fried fish. He thanked her and told her he loved fried fish. We all sat down at the table, and my dad blessed the food. The meal consisted of fried bluefish, a plate of fried potatoes and onions mixed, coleslaw, cornbread, and iced tea. For dessert she had apple fritters.

After we ate, I realized it was Saturday afternoon. I asked if I could be excused from the table. I was out the door to find my buds to tell them about the tow. I found my friends in the pasture in front of my grandfather's house. The pasture was a large open area where livestock used to graze. It was a safe distance from all the houses. It was a perfect place to play all types of ball games. My friends and I had filled old flour sacks with sand. We used these for bases to fashion a baseball diamond. When I walked up, my friends were playing a game called "work up." Work up is a type of baseball game. This game can be played with a minimum of twelve or a maximum of fourteen players. It requires four batters, so base runners aren't trapped on base. It can be played with twelve as long as one of the batters assumes the duties of the catcher. It can be played with fourteen by adding another outfield position. The ideal number is thirteen players. The game is played like baseball. When a putout occurs, players advance in a counterclockwise direction. Each player moves from right field to a batter playing each defensive position as they advance. If a batter hits a fly ball that is caught, the person who catches the ball trades place with the batter. The object is to remain in the batter's position as long as possible. The winner is the player who scores the most runs. It was almost impossible to round up enough players for a baseball game.

At times, some of the passing adults would join the game. These games could last for hours, providing an abundance of relaxation and fun. The game that Saturday lasted until dusk. We played until our parents called us in for the evening meal. At the table that night, my father asked me to go over to my grandfather's after we finished eating. He wanted me to ask Uncle Luther to come over to our house. He asked Uncle Luke to give Earnest a ride to Oregon Inlet on his way to work the next day. Earnest was going to pick up his car on the first ferry, from the north side, the next day. A cousin of his was going to put it on the ferry for him. This would enable him to work at the island and return home on Friday evenings for the weekends. My father, mother, and I went to Sunday school and church the next day. Earnest went with Uncle Luke to bring his car back to Salvo.

The following day was Monday; I went to school. My father and Earnest went to Gull Island to begin the task of digging the entrance channel. The entrance channel was to begin at the mouth of the small creek near the clubhouse. It would end in the deeper water of Gull Shoal Channel. When the entrance channel was completed, the small creek would be dug out into a larger harbor.

On Saturday, after the first week of digging was complete, my father and I went to the island to remove the sink box curtains. We removed the curtains from all three sink boxes. My father always stored them on the northwest end of the island. He examined and cleaned all the aquatic growth off of them and made minor repairs if needed. Then he applied a type of flexible water proofer on them after they were completely dried. If any of them required more extensive repairs, he always took them ashore to work on them.

After we dropped the curtains off, we went to the clubhouse. I was amazed at the amount of digging that was completed in just one week. The barge was well out in the channel. The dragline was still on the front, with a large pile of sand on the deck behind it. The bulldozer was off the barge, sitting on marsh near the clubhouse, on a second mound of sand. I noticed a finger of deep water about ten feet wide located on the right side of the barge. My father had to steer the *Dolphin* close to the right side of the barge. This allowed us to pass under the anchor cable and enter the creek.

I was curious about the location of the bulldozer and the pile of sand near the clubhouse. My dad explained the entire situation to me in detail. He began with their arrival at the first of the week. He told me that Earnest started up the dragline. He then dug as far as he could reach, piling the sand behind him on the deck of the barge. Then he lifted the spud on the back left corner of the barge. He slacked off on the left front anchor and tightened the right front anchor. This allowed the barge to swing to the right. At this point, he dug out the right side of the cut. Then he dropped the left spud and raised the right. He tightened the left anchor, and slacked off on the right. This enabled him to swing back to the left edge of the cut. He repeated this process until he walked the barge up inside the creek. Finally he started the bulldozer and pushed the sand off the right side of the barge. He used the sand to make a surface to drive the dozer on. He used the same process in reverse, with the spuds and anchors, to walk the barge back out to the channel.

After listening to my father's explanation of the work, I realized Earnest was a superior heavy equipment operator. He had completed all this work in just one week. If everything went according to plan, his tasks would soon be finished. The entrance channel and the harbor would be finalized in a couple of weeks. As anticipated, Earnest worked a couple of weeks more and finished up all the digging at Gull Island. He used some of the sand to shape up the sides of the harbor entrance. The remainder of the sand was used to form a front yard in front of the clubhouse. At the end of the third week, all of the work was accomplished. He used the bulldozer to break the anchors out of the mud. Then he loaded the anchors and the dozer on the barge.

Captain Daniels and Tom showed up on the *Mitts-E-Kay* at five o'clock on Saturday morning. My father, Earnest, and I met them at the edge of the reef aboard the *Dolphin*. They followed us into the barge at Gull Island. Captain Daniels maneuvered the *Mitts-E-Kay* up to the back of the barge. Tom and Earnest hooked the hawser to the bridle on the barge. Earnest lifted the right spud. Captain Daniels throttled up and eased the vessel forward. The barge pivoted around on the left spud. Earnest lifted the left spud and they were off. The barge tow back to Wanchese was under way.

# CHAPTER SIXTEEN

# Painting the Boats

We guided the *Mitts-E-Kay* a safe distance back of the reef until she was in deep water. Captain Daniels and Tom had a fair wind of about fifteen to twenty miles per hour behind them. This southwester enabled them to make good time going up the sound. Earnest got back on the *Dolphin* with us. He was going ashore with us to Salvo to pack his gear, then drive up to meet the barge. When the barge arrived at Wanchese, it would tie up there until early Monday morning. Then Captain Daniels was going to tow it up Roanoke Sound to Kitty Hawk Bay. Mr. Liverman had a job scheduled in the northern portion of the bay near the Avalon Beach area. All the digging of the harbor and the entrance channel at Gull Island was completed.

My father now turned his attentions to maintenance of the boats. He had a small window of time to complete the annual scraping, painting, and repairs on all the boats. A coat of copper paint had to be applied to their bottoms after the barnacles were scraped off. The inside and hulls had to be scraped, and a coat of battleship-gray paint applied. My father had fashioned a dry dock system for hauling the boats out of the water. He buried two large pilings about thirty feet from the edge of the marsh. Smaller round pilings about six inches in diameter were used as rollers. These rollers rolled along on a bed-way of two-by-twelve creosote planks placed on the marsh. The bottom of the boats rode on the rollers. A ringbolt, located in the center of the bow stem of the boats, would be attached to a chain-driven manual-powered come-along. This come-along was chained to the buried piling and provided the pulling power to haul out the boats. As each boat was hauled out, it would be blocked up to a level position. Any repair work that was needed would be completed before the painting began. When the outside hull was finished, the inside work began. All loose paint would be scraped off, then a fresh coat of paint applied. When all work was completed, the boats would be pushed back into the water. This process would be repeated until all the boats were repaired, scraped, and painted. With two large powerboats and four decoy boats, this work usually lasted well into the summer.

My father always hired a few of my friends and me to help with the boats. The weather was hot and sticky during the workdays. My friends and I usually wore cutoff jeans and a hat of some description. My father kept us supplied with scrapers, brushes, and plenty of paint. Most of the time when he got us all set up, he would leave us to our work. We would have to crawl under the blocked-up boats with a bucket of paint and a brush. The bottom coating was of a marine growth retardant in a reddish color called copper paint.

In those days we had three types of pesky bloodsucking flies that fed on people, animals, and anything else that contained blood. The larger of the two we called greenheads. They were a large fly with a bright green head. When they sunk their bill into you, it felt like you were getting stabbed with an ice pick. To this day I don't know if they were after blood or a small piece of flesh from your body. They were not too fast and could be easily killed with a slap of the hand. But the bite location would rise up in a welt and itch for hours. The second type of fly we called yellow flies or deerflies. There were two varieties of these flies. One was yellow in color; the other was a greenish brown. They were smaller than the greenheads; the bite was about the same, especially the itching afterward. The third type resembled a common house fly. They usually showed up in late July to early August. They were extremely fast. You hardly ever killed one with a slap. They were just as aggravating as the others. It seemed just as you got into position to do a little bottom painting, one of those devils would bite you on the ankle. Usually, you were lying on your back, trying to reach the keel with the paintbrush. From this position all you could do was to scream or cuss. It was impossible to reach the fly to swat him and end the suffering. You had to put down your brush, crawl from under the boat, and swat the fly. Whether you killed it or not, in an instant the location of the bite would form a welt and begin to itch unmercifully. If you were not careful it was very easy to scratch the outer layer of skin completely off the bite area. At this point a little blood would ooze from the welt area. This was an open invitation for the next bite. I believe they could smell the blood. Sure enough, just as soon as you returned to your painting position, another fly would bite you in the same location as the first bite occurred. This resulted in more scratching off of the skin and exposing of more blood. I have seen the legs and ankles of small children covered with scabs, resulting from scratched fly bites.

As long as there was a puff of wind or two, anything that resembled a breeze, the work was bearable. If the wind fell completely out, in a short time your entire body would be covered in sweat. This situation was like ringing the all-you-could-eat bell at the body buffet for gnats and mosquitoes. The gnats would do the backstroke around on your head, stopping only to take random bites from your sweaty scalp. They would be all up in your face to the point of trying to gain access to your eyes. Both of your ears would be filled to capacity with scrambling little gnat bodies. They were on a mission to your brain, entering through your ears, feasting all along the way. The first reaction would be to wipe them from your eyes so that you could see. Then with both hands moving in opposite directions, you had to violently shake your hair to the point of almost ripping it out. This was the only way to remove them from your scalp. Both of your pinky fingers would be used to crush and remove them from your ears. I have seen long black lines of dead gnat bodies, mixed with sweat, running down the faces of my friends. At night when you were trying to sleep, gnats completely ignored the screens in the windows of your bedroom. They would just crawl right through the openings in the screens and feast on you as you slept.

Mosquitoes were the fourth type of bloodsucking predators of the summertime. There were so many of them; they traveled around in huge black clouds. They were so thick; in just seconds they would cover you from head to toe. We used to break off small branches from crape myrtle bushes to swat them off of us. Most all the adult men in the village set up mosquito smokes around their houses to battle them. At that point anyone could purchase liquid or powdered pesticides from the closest hardware store. A few of the men fashioned small tanks on the handles of their lawn mowers. They attached copper tubing down along the handles to the exhaust of the mowers. A hole was drilled through the side of the muffler, and the tubing was placed inside it. The pesticide would be mixed with kerosene, then poured into the tanks. When the mower was started, a small valve would be opened, allowing the pesticide to be fogged all over the yard.

The early mosquito control trucks used by local governments all over the East Coast areas used pesticides. When we were kids we used to ride our bicycles in the fog directly behind the trucks. This method killed all insects it came in contact with. At that point in time, no one knew the hazards created by the use of pesticide and the extent of damage it posed to the environment. I have often wondered about the use of these pesticides, and if it was somehow related to the large number of cancer cases diagnosed in our area. With all these pests and the heat, it was a wonder that we were able to complete any work on the boats at all. We were always taking breaks and diving into the creek to cool off.

Early in the morning my father would lay out the work he wanted us to complete during the day. If he had other pressing matters, he would leave us to attend to them. We used to take turns watching for his return. He would always try to sneak back and catch us loafing. The work area was located across the harbor behind a high, grassed-over dike. The dike provided enough cover for one of us to watch for him, while the rest of us were cooling off by swimming in the creek. When he was able to catch us off task, he would scold us, then laugh and threaten to dock our time. During one of these boat maintenance periods, we had a considerable amount of washboard, stern, chime strip, rib, and inside seat repair to complete. The washboards are located at the top of the sides of the boat. They separate the outside of the hull from the inner sides of the hull. They are normally wide on juniper skiffs, such as the decoy boats. This area of the boat was subjected to more wear and tear than any other portion. Anything that was on loaded or off-loaded had to be drug across the washboards. The sterns of the boats are located in the back. The chime strips consist of a horizontal two-by-three-inch piece of juniper, located halfway up the inside, fastened to the ribs. The ribs are the vertical strips that the planks are fastened to that form the sides. The inside seats are fastened to the chime strips. The seats provide a place to sit on and also provide cross-boat stability. All these areas are subjected to constant wear and tear from physical contact. These areas require the most repair. We were forever replacing boards at all these locations.

All the new board replacements were rough cut with handsaws. They had to be tightly fitted, using hand planes or wood rasps. Then two coats of battleship-dull gray paint had to be applied. We didn't have any source of electrical power at the boat maintenance area. All fitting of new material had to be accomplished by using hand tools.

When all the repair work was finished, the bottoms coated with copper paint, the hulls coated with gray, it was time to paint on the numbers and strike the waterlines. The process of painting on the numbers was fairly easy. My father always made a small plaquelike structure for each boat. He painted the numbers on these plaques. All we had to do was attach these plaques to the sides of the boats near their bows. They were attached with two copper screws, one at each end of the plaque.

The water lines were a different matter. It took the use of a good window sash brush, combined with a firm steady hand. The person striking the water line would have to have prior knowledge of how each boat rested on the surface of the water. The water line height was determined by how far down the boat settled in the water when it was loaded. It was okay for a large portion of the water line to rest above the water with no load on the boat. You had to make sure the water line was a few inches above the water's surface when the boat was loaded. Sometimes the decoy boats would rest in the same location, loaded with decoys, for long periods of time. The top of the water lines had to be horizontally straight and pleasing to the eye, or the boat would have an unbalanced look. My father would let each one of us try our hand at striking a water line. No matter how bad the end result turned out, he could take the brush and make it right. He had a knack for balancing things and making them pleasing to the eye. He always told me, "It's good to use leveling tools as constructing guides, but the final results have to appear good to the eye." One of his favorite things to say was, "If it is good to the eye, it is good."

The larger powerboats were decked over; they had scuppers to allow the water to flow back out whenever it splashed in. The sun had no effect on their bottoms if they rested on the rollers for long periods of time out of the water.

But the decoy boats were a different story. The inside bottom of the decoy boats would dry out in the sun. As the bottom boards shrank in the sun, large cracks would open up on their sides between them. It was important to push them back in the water as soon as the work was completed. The cracks were so large that the boats would immediately sink as soon as they were pushed back in the water. They would normally sink down until the washboards were level with the surface of the water. At this point, the buoyancy of the wood kicked in and kept them from sinking to the bottom of the creek. They would have to be pulled over and tied to the docks full of water. This was one part of the job that my friends and I really liked. The most effective way to pull a sunken boat to the dock was to swim it over. If there was any wind at all, sometimes it would take three of us to swim one boat over. We all had flippers, and my father would allow us to use them to move the boats. The decoy boats would have to remain sunk overnight. Early the next morning we would bail them out. The cracks had swelled up over night, and the boats would remain afloat as long as they stayed in the water. This swelling process always amazed me. The cracks were so large, but they always swelled back into place, floating the boats.

I used to sleep over night at my grandfather's house every now and then. I slept upstairs. His roof was shingled with wooden juniper shakes. The shakes were attached to boards called lathes. These lathes were attached to the roof rafters. The lathes were evenly spaced up the rafters with the width of a lathe between them. During long dry spells in the summer, cracks would become visible along the side of the shakes between the lathes. It was possible to be resting on the bed and see daylight between the shakes. Even on bright, full moon–lit nights you could catch a glint of light between them. But just as soon as it rained, the shakes would absorb all the moisture, immediately swell, and not a drop of water would reach the inside of the house. To this day, it is hard to believe this swelling process. It is truly amazing the effect water has on juniper or white cedar wood.

It took my father, three of my friends, and I most of the summer to complete the work on the boats. These days all the old juniper boats have been replaced by fiberglass and metal boats. These types of boats don't have to be given annual face-lifts. The fiberglass and metal boats are much more durable. They can take a lot more abuse and still remain structurally sound. They might require a power wash now and then, or the fiberglass ones polished and the metal cleaned and a rivet or two be replaced. Over all, the day of the juniper boat is at its end; they have become relics of a forgotten past.

When all the boats were repaired, scraped, and painted, we tied them in their places at the dock. They would remain at the harbor in Salvo until the decoys were loaded into them in September.

My father sent our time sheets to Mr. Kotarides for payment. Two of my friends and I had worked two weeks in the month of June and all four weeks of July. Each of us received a check for $240. Man, we thought we were rich. My mother put most of it away for me, except for a small amount of pocket money for spending.

My father told me that we had finished all the work that he had for us to do that summer. That gave me the whole month of August to crab, fish, swim, play, and run amuck with my friends. We normally started school the day after Labor Day, in the month of September. I asked my dad what he was going to be doing for the rest of the summer. He said he had to build a bulkhead and several docks at Gull Island. I asked if I could be involved in the construction process. He told me that type of work was too physically demanding for me. Long creosote pilings would have to be manhandled into position. Creosote lumber would be attached to the pilings to form the bulkhead and docks. He explained that he didn't want me to work with the creosote material. Our cousin Floyd Hooper—Pudding Head—had left employment at Gull Island. He had gone to work for the state at the Hatteras Inlet Ferry Operation. My older brother, Burtis, was taking his vacation time from the State Highway Department during the month of August to come home and work with my father on the bulkhead and docks. I could come along, but I was not allowed to handle any of the material.

# Bulkhead and Docks

My father and I made a trip to Gull Island the first week of August. The purpose of our visit to the island was to take measurements to create a materials list. This was my first experience of being involved in the creation of a list of materials. When a materials list was created and priced out, it became a "takeoff" as my father called it. He told me to pay close attention to this process. First of all, he made a rough sketch of the structures he planned to build. He showed me the sketch before we left for the island. When I looked at the sketch I could see the harbor at Gull Island. Located on the right side of the entrance, he had drawn the bulkhead and three docks. The docks were placed perpendicular to the bulkhead. They were located inside the protection of the harbor. Along the inside of the harbor he had placed another small bulkhead some distance down the dike. I asked him what that was for. He told me this smaller bulkhead was to form a pond. The pond would be located along the backside of the harbor. A dike of piled-up sand dug by the dragline would separate the pond from the harbor. A small opening was located at the end of the dike. This was the proposed area he wanted to bulkhead off. He wanted to isolate the salt sound water from the newly formed pond. In time, after the influence of enough rain, the pond water would become brackish. He was hoping it would freshen up enough to become drinkable for the fowl. He was planning to place a buried box at the pond's edge for hunting.

I noticed on the drawing he had placed lines and directional arrows. In the center he left a space at the end of the lines. I asked him about these.

"These are for placing the measurements we will take at the island," he explained. "Whenever you have something to build, first you have to make a rough sketch, including accurate measurements of the object. Then you will be able to make up a list of materials in order to complete the work."

When we left the harbor at Salvo, the wind was blowing about ten to fifteen miles per hour from the northeast. The humidity was low, the air temperature was cool; we were experiencing a low-pressure shift in our weather pattern. Any northeast wind shift pushes the water of the sound to its western side. This creates an extreme high-water condition near the mainland. As a result of this condition, on the east side of the sound, near the northern end of Hatteras Island, the water is very low. When we had cleared the mouth of the harbor at Salvo in the *Dolphin*, we began to bump bottom. My father had to throttle down until we crossed the shallow water near the harbor's entrance. As soon as we reached deeper water, he throttled back up and we were off to the island.

The water level was too low for us to take the boat close to shore, across Bay Shoals right to the island. We had to head offshore, across the edge of Scotts Reef into Cedar Hammock Channel. We followed Cedar Hammock Channel until we entered Gull Shoal Channel. Then we headed straight for the harbor's entrance at Gull Island. We entered the newly dug channel connected to the harbor that led right up to the clubhouse. The *Dolphin* had to be anchored inside the harbor. At this point there were no pilings placed to tie up to. My father handed me the end of a 250-foot reel-type tape he brought along to take the measurements with. He had me stand at the end of the dike where it turned ninety degrees and formed the back of the harbor. He walked down the dike to the entrance of the harbor, pulling out the tape as he went. When he reached the end of the marsh, he stopped. I saw him write something down on his sketch. Then he turned and announced a measurement of 104 feet. At this point he walked back to me. We both walked down the dike to the opening he wanted to close off from the harbor. In this location he recorded a measurement of 30 feet.

When he was satisfied with the sketch and the measurements, we went inside the clubhouse and opened the windows. This let in the northeast breeze to air out the inside; it had been closed up for a long period of time. We sat down at the table to eat the midday meal we brought with us. Then he proceeded to show me how to calculate the materials needed for the bulkheads and docks. He used simple math to tally up, as he called it, the number of pilings, whalers, sheeting, bulkhead cap, and the amount of hardware needed for the job. The pilings were to be twenty feet long, six inches in diameter on the small end, and ten inches on the large end. Whalers were the connecters from piling to piling. They would be four inches thick by six inches wide by sixteen feet long. Sheeting would be the vertical two-inch-by-eight-inch-by-eight-foot-long planks attached to the whalers. The bulkhead cap would be the finished top of the bulkhead. All the wood material would be treated with creosote. Hardware for the job consisted of galvanized spools of cable, nails, bolts, nuts, and washers. The final list included all the material needed for the job.

Once he contacted the supplier and had a price on all the material, and added the freight cost, he could send the takeoff to Mr. Kotarides for his approval. Then my father would order the materials. This was my first experience at rough sketching, calculating materials, and pricing them to create an estimate. This was a valuable construction process that my father taught me. All he had to work with was pencil and paper. He kept his pencil point sharpened using the small blade on his Barlow pocket knife. He could put a point on a pencil that would make any pencil sharpener proud.

When we arrived back home that night, my mom made a copy of his takeoff for the work. Her handwriting was much more legible than his. Her copy would be mailed to Mr. Kotarides in the next day's mail. I inherited my father's technique of handwriting. It was no easy task for my teachers to fathom my work assignments. The proper use of grammar, correct spelling, and accurate punctuation were nonexistent in my completed assignments. It was a common practice for some of my teachers to have me read my work to them. All of my papers, if corrected in red ink or red colored pencil, looked as if they bled to death. My mother was constantly after me about the quality of my handwriting. When it was part of the school curriculum to practice cursive or penmanship, I was required to bring my writing book home. Mom saw to it that I set aside ample time to practice writing.

In just a few days my father received a phone call from Mr. Kotarides; he had reviewed the takeoff. The price was to his satisfaction. He was ready to proceed with work at Gull Island. My father contacted his supplier in Elizabeth City and ordered the material. Then he contacted Mr. Donald Oden to arrange the freight pickup and transport on the *Mitts-E-Kay*. The day the material arrived, my father and I boarded the *Dolphin* and met the *Mitts-E-Kay* out back of the reef to the west of Gull Island. Captain Charles Daniels and Tom were aboard the freight vessel. We guided them in, right up to the entrance channel of the harbor. Captain Daniels held the large vessel in place. Tom operated the crane and off-loaded the hardware onto the *Dolphin*. There were many boxes of fasteners and spools of cable. We had to make numerous trips into the shore to transport all the hardware. He off-loaded the large clusters of pilings and lumber into the water. My father and I towed the large bundles of materials inside the harbor. We attached mooring lines to the bundles and anchored them securely on the opposite side of the harbor. In this location the material would be readily accessible, but out of the way of the construction process.

The off-loading of all the material lasted until time for the midday meal. We invited Captain Daniels and Tom to the clubhouse for bologna sandwiches and canned soup. Captain Daniels laughed and invited us aboard the *Mitts-E-Kay* for homemade hambone soup and fresh-baked cheese biscuits. He told us that Tom was an excellent cook. It seemed that Tom had started the soup as soon as they were under way. We had to wait a few minutes for the biscuits to finish baking. The wait was worth it. The soup was delicious, and the biscuits were hot and melted in your mouth.

After we finished eating, we guided them back out back of the reef. We waved to them as they turned the large vessel south to complete other deliveries. My father and I went back to the island and made a last check on the material, then he turned the *Dolphin* toward home.

There were three more weeks left in the month of August. I had time to ramble and create discontent with my friends for the rest of the summer. Instead, I choose to tag along and watch the work progress. My father hired two more men to work with him and my brother. He hired my cousin Leslie Hooper and I. D. Midgett. Both men worked with the ferry operations at Hatteras Inlet. They worked one week on and one week off, but they were on opposite shifts. There were always three men working at Gull Island on any given week.

As the work began, I understood why my father wanted me out of the way. They all had to wear chest waders, long-sleeved shirts, and gloves to work with the creosote materials. The weather was extremely hot and miserable most of the day. There were plenty of gnats, mosquitoes, green head flies, and the little black flies that show up in August each summer. The material was saturated to the point that the creosote film was floating on the surface of the water. It was impossible to dip water from the creek to cool off; there was a constant danger of chemical burn from the floating creosote film. I sat in the shade, bringing them cold water and anything else they needed.

First, they drove a stake into the edge of the marsh on the right side of the harbor, then another stake, about halfway up the side, and the last stake where the harbor's edge turned at ninety degrees. They had a distance of 104 feet to fill in. A twenty-foot piling was manhandled, placed eight feet apart, and pumped eight feet down into the edge of the creek bottom. Then they moved the operation down the dike to the area to be closed off. This area was to form the pond in the shallow portion of the natural creek. No digging by machine occurred behind this gap in the dike. Two rows of pilings were placed in this gap. The pilings were spaced eight feet apart as before. There was a twenty-foot space between the two rows of pilings. When all the pilings were pumped into the bottom, each piling received one hundred blows from a twenty-pound sledgehammer. This was to settle them into the creek bed. Then the whalers or horizontal members were bolted to the pilings. There was a top whaler placed about two feet above the marsh level. The bottom whaler was placed just above the water's surface.

The sheeting was pumped vertically beside the whalers and nailed securely to them. When all the sheeting was in place, a piece of cable about thirty feet long was attached to each piling, supporting the bulkhead. The other end of the cable was attached to a shorter piling buried in the bank behind the bulkhead. A cable puller was used to tighten up the cable, then cable clamps were used to secure the cable under tension in place. This process was used to anchor the bulkhead vertically plumb when it was backfilled with the sand from the dike.

When the longer bulkhead was finished, they began on the area forming the pond. A bulkhead was placed on both rows of pilings. Then cable was attached from one row of pilings across to the other row below the surface of the marsh. The area between the two bulkheads was filled with sand from the dike. At this point the area behind the long bulkhead was filled. All this fill had to be moved by hand with shovels and wheelbarrows. Finally, all the bulkhead work was completed.

Pilings for three docks were then pumped into place. The docks were spaced about twenty feet apart along the bulkhead. They were about twenty feet long, placed from the bulkhead toward the center of the harbor. The dock joists and decking were two-by-eight creosote planks. This configuration allowed the powerboats to be tied to one dock. The four decoy boats could be tied to the other two docks.

When the work on the bulkhead, the pond barrier, and the three docks was completed, the yard work began. All the sand piled up from digging out the harbor had to be spread and leveled. This work was done with shovels, wheelbarrows, and yard rakes. When the yard was raked level, grass seed was planted. A walkway was built along the bulkhead, connecting each dock, and ending at the porch to the clubhouse.

All this work was finally complete by the third week of September. This left a little over a month to clean up and transport all the debris back to the main island. In those days all scrap materials were burned. My father refused to allow any fires on Gull Island. No burning in a barrel, dug pit, or otherwise. He always said if a fire got out of control on the island, it would burn everything up. Just a shift of wind from another direction could spell disaster for the island.

He told me of a time he could remember when he was a boy. They were experiencing a bad thunderstorm. Lightning from cloud to ground struck a group of bushes on Gull Island. Fire quickly spread from the strike and burned up everything on the island. He told me not a sprig of grass or a bush was spared; all vegetation was reduced to ashes. At that time a small, one-room shack with two beds inside was lost in the fire.

We had to load all the construction scraps in one of the decoy boats and bring it back to Salvo. On shore at Salvo we had four burn barrels that were used to burn the scraps. This burning was accomplished in the barrels, in a large, open, sandy field near the harbor. The only time my dad would ever burn was when the wind was light from the east, northeast, or southeast. This wind direction carried all the smoke and fumes away from the village. He insisted that the person watching the fire always tend the fire from the upwind position. The burning of creosote material emits hazards from smoke and toxic fumes if inhaled. He always dug a large hole and raked all the ash from the fire. The creosote residue congealed with the sand and formed lumps. Days after the burning, if you broke open one of the sand lumps, the aroma of creosote would emerge from it. Marine cut worms, termites, or any type of lumber-destroying insects were no match for creosote treating. There are still pilings supporting fishing piers, bulk-heads, sea walls, and many other structures up and down the coast that have lasted well over one hundred years. Creosote is a reliable preservative, but extremely hard on the environment.

There was another drawback to this type of preserving wood product. The problem was with the planking that was installed on the top walking surfaces of any structure. When the walking surface was exposed to the heat from the sun, the treating stuck to anything that came in contact with it. It was impossible to walk on any dock or deck without tracking creosote residue inside any building you entered. This was the case at Gull Island. Even in the wintertime, if it was a sunny day, this was a problem. At first my father placed mineral spirits and rags near the doors of the clubhouse in order to clean the bottoms of the hunters' boots. This became a cumbersome process. Sometimes there would be as many as six pair of waders by the doors to be cleaned. If the guides were busy with other tasks, at times it would be after dark before some of the boots could be cleaned. Then the chemical hardened on the bottom of the waders. They would have to be scraped, then cleaned off with the mineral spirits. My father and Mr. Kotarides had a brainstorming session for a possible solution to this problem. At his bakery in Norfolk, Virginia, Mr. Kotarides had rolled up steel mats on the concrete floors. He sent enough of these to cover the walking surfaces on the docks: problem solved.

# CHAPTER EIGHTEEN

# The Diving Duck Hunt

All the work on the bulkhead and docks at Gull Island was completed. There was plenty of deep water from Gull Shoal Channel to the inside of the harbor at the clubhouse. There was ample dock space to tie up both the powerboats and all the decoy boats. With the addition of the metal walking mats on the surface of the docks, the sticking of creosote residue to the bottom of the boots no longer existed. There was just enough time left at the end of summer to get all the hunting gear ready for the upcoming season. My older brother was working off island with the State Highway Department. He had built up enough annual leave to be off work to help our father run the club that hunting season. Everything was ready.

The weather cooperated; it turned cold at the beginning of November. The low pressures seemed to come in one after the other that winter. First, there would be a couple of days of northwesters, allowing the high-water curtain boxes and shore blinds to be hunted. Then the wind would shift to the northeast as the low pressures exited off the coast. This would allow the low-water curtain boxes and float blinds to be hunted. The waterfowl were being managed effectively, and ample numbers were being harvested. This made the hunters satisfied with their hunts. The season was off to a good start.

I could only join my father and brother at the club on Saturdays. I arrived on Friday nights, just in time to help with the cleanup and aid with the exiting of the hunters at the end of each hunt. There were the only two times during the season I had a chance to spend any time at the club: Thanksgiving and Christmas vacations. During one Thanksgiving vacation period I was permitted to join two hunters in the north reef stilt blind. The wind was out of the northeast, and the water was low enough to walk after the downed fowl. This hunting location had plenty of natural eel grass for food, along with the supplied grain. It was ideal for hunting three species of diving ducks. Blackheads, redheads, and canvasbacks used this reef during low-water periods by the thousands. Diving ducks completely submerge under the water in order to feed. The stilt blind was situated about eight feet above the water. It had a ladder to climb up as well as a trap door in its floor to allow access to the inside of the blind.

The hunters, Mr. Harry Bowman and Mr. Tommy Hodges, took me along to shag, as they called it, or gather the ducks they knocked down. Each time they downed ducks, I was expected to climb down the ladder to walk and gather them. On many occasions there would be crippled fowl shot down, but not dead. I would have to take a gun along with me to finish off the cripples in order to gather them. It was important to get to the downed fowl as soon as possible. Large white seagulls that patrolled the area from the sky would peck holes in the floating ducks. These gulls will eat anything that floats on the surface of the water. This situation would ruin the possibility of using these ducks as the main course for a waterfowl dinner.

Another situation that occurred, creating a problem, was the force of the wind, causing the dead ducks to drift off the reef into deep water. The water on the reef was only about knee deep. If the ducks drifted off into the channel, the depth of the water was well over a person's head. This made it impossible to gather the ducks by using boots to wade after them.

When the legal bag limit of ducks was reached—the number of ducks allowed per person per day—a flag was waved from the stilt blind. A hunting guide always kept an eye on the blinds, using field glasses. The guide would come to the blind in a boat and remove the ducks. The hunters would switch places sometimes two or three times per day, depending on the number of hunters at the camp.

This particular day, the area was completely surrounded by diving ducks. My dad had situated the decoys in what is called a flyby pattern. The main body of the decoys had been placed to the windward of the blind. There were about fifty to sixty in the main body, with a string of them that began at the end of the main body. This string of decoys circled the stilt blind to the windward, about thirty yards out. About a dozen geese decoy ducks were placed to the leeward of the blind. If any geese approached, they would fly downwind and settle on the water. They would begin feeding and eventually swim up to the geese decoys. This would allow the hunters easy water shots, and the geese would have to fly by the blind in order to get off the water. This would also give the hunters flyby shots on the geese.

Geese are much larger than ducks; they are unable to jump vertically like ducks when leaving the water. They have to start similar to an airplane. They have to flap their wings, even using their feet to push them along the water's surface. Then they have to take off facing into the wind to become airborne.

There were thousands of ducks sitting on the water about five miles out in the sound to the windward of our position. Every so often a flock of about twenty-five or thirty would leave the large raft, a body of ducks larger than one hundred in number, and approach our position. They approached from the windward, circled downwind, and flew right up the string in front of the blind. They decreased their forward speed and were constantly looking for a place to land and feed. This provided the hunters with slow, horizontal, flyby shots. One of the hunters commented that it was like shooting ducks in a barrel. The arranging of the decoys in this pattern provided many successful duck hunts on the north reef at Gull Island. I was up and down the ladder all day gathering the ducks the hunters had shot down.

On one of these trips from the blind to gather fowl, I learned something new about diving ducks. I was up to the windward of the blind, chasing down a couple of cripples. I shot and killed one; the other one dove below the surface of the water. I broke down the single-barrel gun I used to shoot cripples and placed in another shell, waiting for the crippled duck to surface. I waited for about fifteen minutes, but the duck never came up again. I walked back toward the ladder to climb up into the blind. I turned and looked in the direction where I last saw the duck. All of a sudden, it popped up on the surface and began to float toward me. I was puzzled to say the least. As I entered the box with the two ducks, I asked Mr. Bowman about what I had just witnessed. He told me that it was not out of the ordinary for wounded diving ducks to dive and disappear for long periods of time. It seems they grab hold of the eel grass. This grass is attached to the bottom. They hold fast with their bills until they die. They either die from their injuries or drown themselves to avoid capture.

During one of these hunts, on a northeast blow, it was not out of the ordinary to keep changing out hunters and harvest over one hundred ducks per day. This type of heavy hunting, combined with all the noise from the shotguns and the boat activity, drove the ducks off the reef. They would retreat to the safety of deep water. Large rafts would form up miles from the reef out in the sound. The grain from baiting the reef kept the large rafts of diving ducks in the area. The guides kept a close eye on the rafts of ducks. Sometimes it would take days before they returned to the reef to feed.

After the hunt was over, the location was allowed to rest for a few days. No hunting was permitted until the ducks returned and became comfortable using the shallow water of the reef near the blind. Overhunting a good spot can drive the waterfowl away for days and ruin a good hunting location. Poor hunting practices can also drive the fowl from your hunting spots. It is considered a bad hunting practice if you shoot into large flocks of ducks numbering fifty or more birds. If a large raft of ducks with numbers much larger than your spread settle on the water to the leeward of your hunting spot and refuse to swim within range, you must scare them into flight. A spread is a hunting setup—decoys, blind, and all the hunting gear required on a hunt. It is better to stand up in the blind and wave your arms and chase the large flock away. If you allow them to remain, all the rest of the approaching birds will join this large flock instead of coming into your spread. Never shoot in the direction of the large raft of fowl to scare them off. This action will drive them away and ruin your day's hunt. If you scare them off without using your gun, they will fly off a couple of hundred yards and resettle on the water. Most of the time a few of them will break off and return to your location. These smaller flocks are more likely to fly to your decoys.

Another poor hunting practice is to chase the fowl with a powerboat in order to get close enough for a shot. This is one of the quickest ways to drive them off, especially during calm days. It is much better to work along with their natural movements, allow them to rest, feed, and return to your hunting locations.

Another popular hunting spot at Gull Island is the southeast reef. Unlike the northwest reef, this location is completely covered with shifting sand. It is similar to any other sandbar in the sound or ocean side of the island. It does not contain any natural grasses for the fowl to feed on. Most days it is completely above the water's surface. On occasions the sand dries out to the point that the wind blows it around. This is a perfect location for the fowl to get on their feet. They can rest, dry out, prune themselves, and gather grains of sand for their gizzards, which helps in their digestion process. They prune themselves to add natural oil to their outside layer of feathers. This oil is secreted from an oil sack located near their tails. This area provides these features for all aquatic birds that visit and use the south reef. It is useless to set out a spread on the south reef on days when it is high and dry. The best time to hunt this reef is during the first few days of an approaching low-pressure area. During this time frame the wind will be blowing gale force from the northwest. The northwesters will blow in high water and completely cover the south reef. On the south reef of Gull Island, my dad had placed a high-water curtain box on the highest point of the reef. This was the spot of choice on hard northwest blows.

It was on one of these hunts that my brother and I found ourselves in somewhat of a situation. Mr. Kotarides had purchased an air-cooled, powered, tunnel stern skiff to be used in shallow water on these reef hunts. My father named her the *Old Anytime*. She had a ten-horsepower Wisconsin air-cooled motor in her. This motor was rather temperamental; the choke had to be pulled all the way out, and at this point the motor had to be cranked three times. Then the choke had to be pushed all the way in, and the motor always started on the fourth crank. The cranking mechanism consisted of a metal hand crank. This crank was similar to the cranks used for starting early-model automobiles, before the invention of the electric self-starter. If this starting process was not followed to the letter, when starting the *Old Anytime*, she would flood very easily. Then you would have to wait about a half hour for the gas to evaporate from the carburetor before the motor would start.

During Thanksgiving vacation one hunting season, a deep, core low-pressure area was approaching from the northwest. The barometer dropped considerably, and the wind breezed up to about twenty to thirty miles per hour from the northwest. These conditions completely flooded the southeast reef. My dad announced that we were setting out the spread for the day, at the southeast reef high-water curtain box. He said it was a perfect day for a goose and sprigtail hunt. Then he took my brother and me aboard the *Old Anytime* and reviewed the starting procedures with us. He warned us about the flooding of the carburetor. We were to follow his instructions to the letter. He even went over them as he primed and started up the motor. I got out of the *Old Anytime* and untied the decoy boat containing the spread for the south reef. I waited in the bow of the decoy boat as my brother approached in the *Old Anytime*. I tossed him the bowline from the decoy boat. He made it fast to the stern cleat. I sat down on the stern seat. He towed me and the decoy boat out of the harbor. We were headed for the south reef. When we arrived at the box, we raised the curtain, and I began to bail it out with a five-gallon bucket. My brother waded around and set out the decoys.

After we finished setting out the spread, my dad brought the hunters in the larger powerboat. We situated the hunters in the box, gave them the two stools to set on, passed them the signal flag, and told them to wave it if they needed anything. My brother and I tied the *Old Anytime* to the stern of the larger powerboat. We rode back to the clubhouse, towing the *Old Anytime* and the decoy boat behind us. After we secured the boats to the docks, I cleared the table and cleaned up the kitchen from breakfast. My dad told me to find a good place out of the wind to monitor the hunters with field glasses. I climbed up on the porch roof, well below the roof's peak, partially out of the wind, and kept watch. The binoculars that Mr. Kotarides had provided were of professional quality. I could see the entire south reef and the village of Avon. The Little Kinnakeet Life Saving Station looked as if it was just a few feet away. The sky was beginning to lighten up as daylight made its appearance. It was overcast and gloomy; the wind was steady—twenty-five to thirty miles per hour from the northwest. It was freezing every drop that flew, as the old folks say to describe a very cold day.

I was looking in the direction of the three villages of Chicamacomico when I spotted the first flock of geese of the day. They were approaching from the north. The flock numbered twelve birds. I counted them as they crossed the outside edge of the channel. They presented me with a side view as they approached the northwest reef to the windward of my position. The lead gander circled his flock around the north reef. It was much too choppy, and the water was too deep for them to land. He directed his flock around the back of the island. They flew down the backside of the reef and approached the curtain box spread from the leeward side. From my position, if you are a hunter, it was something to see. They dropped down to water level and flew right over the box. I could even see them flare as the hunters stood up. The lead gander was the first to go down, then two more geese fell out. The remainder of the flock cupped their wings and sailed off to the south, exiting the area. The new leader must have been a young, inexperienced gander. He directed the remainder of the flock on another flyby of the box; three more of the geese went down. At this point, I went and told my brother. We had only two hunters in the curtain box, and six birds were down. At that time, the bag limit was two geese per hunter per day. We took *Old Anytime* and went to the blind and collected the fowl. The day continued to remain overcast and stormy. We switched out the hunters several times; it was a successful hunt. All the hunters limited out in geese and puddle ducks, such as sprigtails, black ducks, widgeons, and green winged teal.

Early in the afternoon, my dad told my brother and me that we had to take up the spread. I thought this was odd; normally we hunted until twilight or nightfall was beginning. He told us that the barometer had risen sharply and the wind was going to shift to the northeast. In a short time, all the water would run off the south reef. We would have to drag the decoys hundreds of yards across sand to the decoy boat. Also, we would have to carry water in buckets to flood the box if we waited any longer. My father took the larger powerboat and picked up the hunters. By the time my brother and I arrived at the blind, he had flooded and secured the box. He left the stools and signal flag on the sea breaker or wing for us to pick up.

# CHAPTER NINETEEN

# The Lost Crank

The wind shifted to a northeasterly direction just about the same time my brother and I reached the blind. The water was falling off very fast. My brother took the *Old Anytime* back to the edge of the channel and anchored her in the edge of deep water. I pushed the decoy skiff up to the box, picked up the stools and signal flag, and began to take up the geese decoys. My brother hustled back to the box and began picking up the duck decoys. In no time at all, both of us working, we soon had all the decoys loaded in the skiff. He told me to take the decoy skiff to the edge of the reef to deep water while there was still enough water to float her. I did as I was told, then took the skiff out to deep water, and tied her bowline to the stern cleat on the *Old Anytime*. I returned to the box. My brother and I had just enough water to pull the sea breaker or wing a safe distance from the blind. By the time we were ready to anchor it, the wing was hard aground. I walked the anchor chain a short distance from the wing and embedded the anchor in the sand.

The light of day was fading. We could have walked to the boats without wearing boots. The entire reef was completely dry. Another thirty minutes and we would have been facing twice the amount of work in securing the hunting spot. When we made it to the *Old Anytime*, it was completely dark.

My brother told me to crank the motor. He also reminded me about the starting procedures. I pulled the choke all the way out and rolled the motor over three times. I must have not gotten the choke pushed all the way in. On the fourth crank, it started and then died. The aroma of gasoline filled the air. I knew I had flooded the motor. My brother told me to crank it again, but I told him it was flooded and we had to wait awhile. He told me it was too cold to wait, so he began cranking the motor. He cranked with the choke in, and he cranked with the choke out. The more he cranked, the more the motor became flooded with gas. I shined a flashlight on the motor, and you could see gas dripping from the bottom of the carburetor. He cranked, and he cranked. The more he cranked, the madder he got. He cranked until he broke out in a sweat. The sweat immediately froze to his face. All of a sudden, he slammed the crank down into the bottom of the boat. It landed on its handle, which was a little springy, and jumped overboard into the channel.

There we were, freezing, no crank, about two miles from the clubhouse, and all I could do was laugh. He threatened to throw me overboard if I didn't stop laughing. Thank God we were still anchored, or the wind would have washed us high and dry up on the reef. I climbed up on the bow cap of the *Old Anytime* and started blinking my flashlight toward the club. I knew our father would be watching for our return.

It wasn't long before I spotted the beam from the searchlight of the *Dolphin*. The boat was headed down the edge of the channel, the light shining up on the reef searching for us. Soon the light beam picked us up. When he spotted us with the light, he headed right for us. He came downwind of us and brought the boat up close to us on the windward side. He wanted to know why we hadn't started up the boat. First, he asked me. I told him to ask his older son. Then my brother told him we lost the crank overboard. He backed down to us, and my brother tossed him the bowline from the *Old Anytime*. He fastened it to the stern cleat of the *Dolphin* and began towing us back to the club. When we had all the boats secured for the night, he told us he wanted to talk to us before supper. He told us that he wasn't interested in how we lost the crank. But the next day he planned to set up a stand at the curtain box on the northwest reef. Then he told us that no matter how long it took, when we finished helping him at the northwest reef, we were to go down to the southeast reef and not come back until we found the crank.

The next morning as we were approaching the harbor at the club, I was riding in the decoy skiff. I was being towed by my father and brother, who were ahead of me in the *Dolphin*. We had just finished setting out the spread on the northwest reef for the day's hunt. They released the bowline on the decoy skiff. I paddled her over and tied up to the dock. I ran over to the dock where they were approaching. My father backed down on the *Dolphin* and told us to tie her up. I wanted to know why we were tying up the *Dolphin*. I was under the impression that we had to go and search for the crank. Our father told us that we were going to search for the crank, but we were not taking any of the boats. We were walking down the reef to search for it. He told us he wasn't interested in which one of us did it, but there were depression marks on the floorboards of the *Old Anytime*. He figured that some object had been slammed down hard in the bottom of the boat. He thought that it was probably the crank. He was of the opinion that both of us contributed to the loss of the crank. He told us he would watch the hunters on the northwest reef. We were to go clear the table and clean up from breakfast. When we were finished, we should walk to the southeast reef and return when we found the crank.

My brother suggested we take a shotgun and an empty grain bag along with us. He had a couple boxes of number seven-and-one-half shot in his room at the clubhouse. We took one of the single-barrel guns we normally used to shoot cripples. He went to get the shot. I got the gun. We put our waders and weatherproof jumpers on and began to walk. My brother carried the gun. I carried the empty grain bag. We walked down the dock toward the dammed-off area that separated the pond from the harbor. Soon we passed by the end of the dock. He told me to reach under the dock and get one of the flounder gigs. We hid two gigs there during the summer on flounder gigging trips. He wanted to take one of the gigs along with us. We walked down the north side of the island to Thoroughfare Creek. At this creek we crossed a shallow channel that runs by the eastward side of the island. The water in the channel was only up to our knees. Normally, it is impossible to wade across this channel. The water level was still low because of the velocity of the northeast wind.

As we walked up on the edge of the reef, my brother loaded the single-barrel. He hesitated at the edge of the reef and told me to stand still. A flock of willets flew by us about twenty-five yards out. He shot into them, and four fell out. It was then I realized what the empty grain bag was for. I picked them up and placed them inside the bag. He repeated this process until he was satisfied we had enough for a shorebird fried supper. We had a mixed bag of birds— willits, yellow legs, curlews, and snipe. These shorebirds split, battered, and fried are one of the best waterfowl meals anyone could ever sink their teeth into. They were protected and illegal to harvest in those days, with the exception of the snipe. There was a snipe season in effect then and even currently. If the game warden had caught us with those birds that day, they would have put us in jail and thrown away the key. Those types of meals have gone by the wayside. The same situations apply to turtle harvesting. Turtle hash or turtle soup is far better than beef hash or beef stew. We are so overregulated. Our freedom is disappearing.

We continued on down to the center of the reef until we were abreast of the box. We placed the bag of fowl down along with the gun. At that point we started walking a grid pattern in the edge of the channel. On my brother's first offshore turn back to the reef, he stepped on the crank. He hollered, "Hey!" and held the crank above his head. Mission accomplished: We had the crank. Now we could head back to the camp. My brother wanted to walk across the reef to the lee side. Sometimes large fish that are caught in a quick freeze during a shift of wind swim to the lee side of the reef. They swim to the edge of the reef in the shallow water, and they are warmed by the sun. The sudden drop in water temperature has a numbing effect on them. This slows down their body functions, allowing them to be caught easily. When we reached the lee side of the reef, we spotted a couple of all mouths. All mouth is a local name for a large oyster fish. They were numb and swimming very slowly. These large oyster fish or all mouths have a lot of meat in their tail sections. They don't have any scales. They can be easily skinned, and two large fillets can be cut from their tails. The meat is white in color and mild to the taste. It doesn't even taste like fish. As the old saying goes, it tastes just like chicken.

When we got back to the clubhouse, our father was pleased that we found the crank. But he scolded us about the illegal harvesting of the birds. He told me to stay behind and clean the game while he and my brother took up the stand from the northwest reef. I skinned the fish and cut the meat from their tails. I cut the large slabs of white meat up into manageable fillets. There were two large baking pans full of fish. I skinned all the birds and split each one into two equal halves. I mixed up some corn meal and flour together to bread the meat. I salted and peppered all the meat, then rubbed the breading in. My brother fried the birds and fish while my father boiled potatoes and made cornbread. That night the hunters feasted on fried shorebirds, fish, boiled potatoes, and cornbread. I set the table and mixed up the iced tea. After the evening meal, it was my job to clear the table and set it up for card playing. My brother and I washed up all the pots, pans, and dishes. We cleaned the kitchen—dried and put everything away. After we were finished, I asked my father if I was done for the night; I was really tired. He asked me to check the mudroom behind the hunters. He wanted me to make sure all the waders were washed off. Dry them with a towel and hang them up in the racks with the feet up, straps down. Clean and oil all the guns that were used in the hunt that day. When I had finished these few I could shower and go to bed. It was my brother's job to check all of the boats before he could turn in. He had to check the tie-up lines, make sure the bilge pumps were in working order in the powerboats, and check the water level in the bottom of the decoy boats. If the air temperature fell below twenty degrees, he had to remove a freeze plug from the boat motors that were water cooled. This would allow the water to drain from the water jackets on the motors. If this wasn't done the motors would freeze overnight. The ice inside the water jacket would freeze, expand, and crack the engine block.

It had been a really long day for the both of us. We had walked miles along the reef. My father was already in bed asleep when I walked into where the hunting guides sleep. This room was located on the far end of the clubhouse, away from the dining table and the hunters' quarters. The room door could be closed, separating the card game noise and the racket that was generated from the hunters after a few drinks. My brother came into the room before I fell asleep. Both my father and brother began to snore.

I thought to myself as I drifted off, *Man, what a life.* We were all three getting paid for living the life we loved. The next day the wind had moderated and changed directions. It was now blowing less than ten miles per hour from the southwest. The sky cleared, the water level had risen, the sun came out, and it warmed up considerably.

My dad announced that this would be a perfect day to set out a spread at one of the float blinds. He selected the shallow channel location. This was a large sandbar that jutted out in the channel, forming various shoals and sloughs along the edge of the south reef. It was an ideal location for diving ducks. Small flocks of them would land in the edge of the channel to feed on eel grass. Plus, this float blind was supplied regularly with grain. On the day of the hunt, the location would be marked with a buoy. The float blind would be towed by boat, far enough from the grain, to allow it to be hunted. The diving ducks would eventually swim in expecting to find grain near the float blind.

Geese and puddle ducks would be returning from the refuge north of Rodanthe. Many of them would leave the Gull Island Reef and rest in the fields of the refuge during a hard freeze. The fields of the refuge were supplied with corn on a regular basis. The fowl would return to the sound and surrounding reefs when the weather improved. During this type of weather, the fowl flying south from the refuge would follow the shoreline. They always flew about a hundred yards offshore until they approached Cedar Hammock Island. The shoreline curves drastically inshore to the east at this point of the marsh. They would continue south across Cedar Hammock Channel, then Bay Shoals. At Bay Shoals they turned westward and crossed Gull Shoal Channel, then on to the south reef. The float blind at the Point of Shoals was right in the middle of their flight pattern, which is why my dad chose this location for the float blind.

That particular morning we took the *Old Anytime* and the decoy skiff that was rigged for shore and float blind hunting. The spread consisted of about twenty geese decoys. These were always set out on the back side of the blind in the lee. It also contained about fifty diving duck decoys. The divers were set out on the windward side of the blind close to the edge of the channel. Last but not least, about a dozen puddle duck decoys were set to the right side of the blind just inside the shoals. This was an impressive setup. The geese and puddle ducks provided many flyby shots. The diving ducks usually landed on the water and swam up into the decoys. The *Old Anytime* was performing beautifully; if you choked her for four cranks, and one crank with no choke, she fired right up.

After we finished setting up the stand at the Point of Shoals, we returned to the clubhouse. I monitored the hunters from my vantage point on the roof. I noticed my father walking to the *Old Anytime* with a length of decoy span in his hand. Decoy span is a length of nylon cord used to anchor the decoys in place. I hollered down to him and asked him what he was up to. I thought he was replacing some of the decoy spans and offered to help. He told me he was implementing a new type of insurance plan. I told him that he had completely confused me. He told me that he was making a tether for the crank on the *Old Anytime*. This type of plan would ensure that the crank would always remain attached to the boat in all types of rough situations. He threaded the cord through a hole in the crank and secured it by tying it with a bowline knot. Then he made it fast to an eyebolt he installed in the front of the engine box below the cranking opening. There was plenty of slack in the cord for cranking, but there was no way it could be lost over the side of the boat. When he had finished his task, I made a comment about how this situation would prevent losing the crank in the future. I suggested that this tether would make the *Old Anytime* crank proof. He told me that he wasn't worried about the boat being crank proof. His main concern was to make the crank son-proof. There was a familiar twinkle in his eye as he passed under me. He looked up at me and smiled. He reminded me that it was my job to keep an eye on the float blind and not him.

My brother came outside and asked me if anything was happening around the float blind. I told him all was quiet. No fowl had approached the blind from any direction. He told me it was still a little early for any action. Most of the fowl would be returning to the reef from a long distance off. They had a long trip to make to get back to the reef. He figured they would be arriving about midmorning. I told him about the crank tether; he just laughed. But when I told him about our father making the crank son-proof, he thought I had squealed on him. I assured him that I didn't tell on him. I suggested that our father had taken steps to protect the crank from being lost by his sons.

# CHAPTER TWENTY

# Holiday Pranks

We finished up the Thanksgiving hunt that winter, and soon I was back in school. The few days between Thanksgiving and Christmas holidays are torture. You have had a small taste of time off from school, and you are anticipating a much longer period of freedom. The teachers try to keep the students on task, but with the excitement of the holiday season, hardly anything in the classroom is accomplished. The time between the two holidays is usually less than a month in days; to a kid it seems like this particular period would last forever. Finally, the last day approaches. There is a classroom Christmas tree, the rooms are decorated, and a party is scheduled. All types of goodies are prepared and served by a few of the parents. The students draw names from a hat and give a modest gift to the person whose name they have drawn. It is also customary to give your teacher a gift. Most teachers give each of their students a small gift in return. Then the final bell rings and we're out the door to the buses in a dead run. Once you are on the ride home you realize you have almost made it. When you exit the bus, there is no describing the feeling that comes over you. You feel like a million dollars. All sorts of pleasurable things are racing through your mind. Even the teachers are elated. I was slow exiting the classroom on the last day of one Christmas vacation period. As I passed by my teacher's desk, on the way out the door I turned and said, "Merry Christmas" and good-bye to her. She looked at me and smiled, then a long sigh of relief escaped her lips, as she waved and said, "Bye" to me. It was a Friday afternoon when school let out for the Christmas holidays. All I could think about on the long bus ride home was getting out to Gull Island on a hunt.

When I got home my father was waiting for me. My mother had all my hunting gear packed. He wanted to get back to the island before it got dark. Soon we were out the harbor, headed for Gull Island. When we arrived, we secured the boat and went to the clubhouse. One of the hunters had the black-and-white television on, trying to get channel 13 to come in. The television reception was hit and miss; there wasn't cable or dish networks. A television antenna was attached to the roof or some high location in hopes of tuning in a few stations. The antenna at the clubhouse was attached to a long piece of three-inch-diameter galvanized pipe. The pipe was secured to the side of the chimney. My dad assumed the duty of fooling with the channel tuner. The television usually picked up the generator; the screen was full of horizontal lines. These lines were rolling from the bottom of the screen to the top in a rapid motion. He was rather displeased with the reception. He told me that the hunters wanted to watch the Friday night fights that ran on channel 13. The channel was broadcasted from the Norfolk, Virginia, area. If the antenna was turned in a specific direction, the reception improved. Sometimes it improved to the point of being able to make out the characters on the screen. The improvement included tuning the audio to be able to understand the characters' conversations.

In order to maintain decent reception during any program, the antenna had to be anchored into position, as well as turned to the best location. At the clubhouse this procedure was conducted with my father hollering to me from an open window. My job was to be outside turning the antenna pipe with a large pipe wrench to a location that improved the reception. When the picture came into view and the sound was clear, he would yell for me to stop turning. The anchoring process consisted of jamming the wrench against the side of the chimney to hold it in place. This worked fine if the wind wasn't blowing very hard. In windy situations, you were forever turning the pipe and resetting the wrench.

The hunters finished the evening meal one half hour before the fights came on. My mother had prepared snacks for the hunters; she had baked cheese biscuits for them. Usually they were large enough to make a small meal by themselves. My brother prepared a large pot of coffee and set out the platter of biscuits ready for the hunters. I was given instructions to stay close by in case I was needed. The hunters were serious about the Friday night fights. They had just settled down for the first bout of the night. It was more fun for me to watch them rather than following the fights. They would be sitting on the edge of their chairs, eyes fixed on the television, grunting and punching the air as if they were involved in the fight. Every now and then they would make a comment like, "Give it to him, boy," or "That's the way it's done." They were just about at the middle of the bout when a gust of wind dislodged the wrench. Immediately the picture faded, the screen turned snowy white, and the sound became a static roar. At that point, total chaos erupted in the television room at the clubhouse. I was called on to perform my magic. The window was opened; I went outside to operate the pipe wrench. But now, instead of just my father, I had four frantic fight fans yelling instructions. I found myself in a quandary; I didn't know which one of them to listen to for directions. I could hear, "Hush, you're confusing the boy," "Turn just a little more," "Ah, you have gone too far," and "Finally, that is it. Stop!" I was given the all-clear and anchored the wrench into position. The picture cleared on the screen, the sound returned, and harmony was restored to the room. The Friday night fights continued on until the next strong gust of wind. Then the process was repeated until they had seen the last fight of the night.

The hunters moved to the large table in the dining room. The conversation was about the fights, tomorrow's hunt, and soon a card game broke out. As I drifted off to sleep that night, I could hear them talking and laughing as the card game continued to the wee hours of the morning.

The next day dawned very cold, with a steady northeast wind of ten to twenty miles per hour. It was overcast: a perfect day to hunt the northwest reef stilt blind. I was out of bed by five o'clock and dressed. I joined my brother in the galley; he already had the coffee perking. I started to get out a pound of bacon for breakfast. He told me to wait on starting breakfast. The hunters had a few drinks and played cards all night. All of them were still sleeping. The door opened and my father came in. He told us that he had talked to the hunters, and they were too tired to hunt that morning. They were planning to get up later. They told him they were satisfied with the hunt and would be heading back to their homes. When I heard this news I was disappointed. Usually around noon, when the hunters came in for food, my brother would leave me in the blind to hunt. Most of the time I would get a few shots before the hunters returned in the afternoon. There wasn't going to be any hunting for me that day. Dad told us we had an easy day. When the hunters finally got up, he would take them ashore in the larger crew boat. He wanted my brother and me to clean the clubhouse and make it ready for the next hunt. When we were finished, we could return home in the *Dolphin*.

It was around noon when I helped load the hunters' luggage in the crew boat. It didn't take long for my brother and me to spruce up the place. We made sure the decoy boats were all secured. Then we were off toward home. We arrived at the harbor in Salvo just as dark was approaching. When I entered the house through the kitchen door, my father told me that the next hunt would not be until after Christmas.

After supper that night, he told me I could select a Christmas present from the Sears Roebuck catalog. This was the catalog that we ordered everything we needed from. It contained anything that you could possibly need or use. I instantly turned to the section containing the guns. I found a J. C. Higgins, air-chambered, pump-up .22-caliber pellet gun. I showed it to him. I told him this would be a perfect gun for hunting cedar waxwings, robins, and shorebirds. I reminded him that he would be able to use it at times. He checked it out with my mother. She wanted me to show it to her in the catalog. When she saw it, all she saw were the words, ".22-caliber rifle." Instantly, she was against its purchase. I convinced her that it was not a .22 rifle, only a .22-caliber pellet gun. Reluctantly, she agreed on the purchase of the pellet gun. I was happy. Life was good for a twelve-year-old; I was getting a new gun.

When my mother told me she had agreed on the gun, I watched the mail every day. I never saw it arrive. I suspect my cousin Edward Hooper, named after my father, had something to do with that. He picked up everyone's mail every day and delivered it to their homes. I suspect he gave the gun to my father on the sly, and they hid it from me. Every time I mentioned it to my mother, she told me I would have to wait until Christmas and see. Whenever I was alone in the house I searched every nook and cranny looking for that gun. No matter how hard I searched, I always came up empty. I suspect they had hid it over at my brother's or at Edward's house.

Finally, Christmas Eve arrived. That night we all attended the church Christmas program. When we got back home I started in; I wanted the gun that night. My parents told me I could open all the rest of my presents that night before going to bed. As for the new gun, I would have to wait until Christmas morning.

The next morning I was out of bed early. I went straight to the Christmas tree. I spotted a long thin box. The box was wrapped in snowman Christmas wrapping paper. The paper came off with one swipe of the hand. My mother wanted to save the bows, which ended up on the floor. I opened the cardboard box and finally held the pellet rifle in my hand. Man, it was a thing of beauty. It had adjustable rear and front sights—the devices used to aim guns—and a pump-up air chamber. It was a bolt-action barrel loader. The shoulder stock and fore stock were stained blond maple.

My father read the instructions to me. The air chamber was filled from the outside air. It was only to receive fifteen pumps for the first thirty days of use. As the gun aged, more pumps were suggested. My mother called him to the kitchen, something about meat carving. There I was stuck, knowing about half what to do to operate the gun. I walked outside, opened the bolt, and placed a pellet in the gun barrel. I pushed off the trigger safety, aimed, and pulled the trigger. Nothing happened; the gun didn't fire. Man, I was upset. What to do now?

I went into the kitchen seeking my father's help. He was helping my mother and told me to wait a few minutes. I was out the front door in a flash; I knew exactly what to do. I ran over to my brother's house. His house was located right beside ours. I entered the back door that opened into the kitchen of his house. He and his wife, Jean, were at the table eating breakfast. I passed him the new gun. The first thing he asked me was if I had loaded it. I told him, "no," the first mistake. He pulled the trigger, aiming it at the ceiling. The trigger was loose inside the trigger guard; the gun didn't fire. He tried to pump it; it was pumped tight. No more air could be forced into the air chamber. Then he fooled with the safety button and pulled the trigger again. Still, nothing happened. He discovered a safety feature on the gun that I had missed. There was a catch that had to be pushed forward, locking the pump lever into position. This kept the pump handle from springing back and injuring your hand when the gun was fired. He activated this catch, aimed the gun, and pulled the trigger. There was a loud report from the gun, and he shot a quarter-inch hole through the sheetrock ceiling in his kitchen. Boy, I thought he was going to skin me alive. I kind of cowered down in the chair, and took the tongue lashing. When he was finished with me, I begged him and Jean not to tell my mother. If they told her, I knew I would be in for thrashing. Plus, she would take away the gun for a period of time. I had just gotten it that morning. They agreed not to tell my mother, but there were some conditions. I had to promise to use the gun safely. I was never to load it in or near the house. Under no circumstances was I to shoot at the neighbors' pets. If I shot any type of wild animals, it was to be the ones I was planning to use for food. It would be alright to shoot something and give it to someone who was planning to eat it. I crossed my heart and pinky finger swore to follow all their safety conditions to the letter. I made them promise that they would not rat me out.

That pellet gun got plenty of use. My father used it, my brother used it, and I loaned it to one of my younger cousins for a while. Almost all the young boys of the island started hunting with BB guns or pellet guns. This is where they learned to handle guns safely. Normally, birds and small animals were hunted. As the boys grew older, they moved on to larger game and shotguns.

I went on many interesting hunts with the gun. The cedar waxwings flew around in flocks of fifty or more. They ate all types of berries from bushes or trees. They landed in cedar trees and yaupon trees searching for edible berries. Sometimes when enough of them landed in a tree, the men of the village would harvest them. The men used their shotguns loaded with number seven-and-one-half bird shot. All I did was hide beneath one of these trees and wait for the birds to land in the tree above me. I harvested a lot of cedar waxwings in this manner. Robins are hunted in a different manner. They are worm and insect eaters. They normally hop around on the ground looking for food. The shorebirds that I hunted were found on the beach. They looked for food in the water as the waves washed up on the beach. I never shot anything that went to waste.

I still have that gun to this day; the seals are worn out in it. The air chamber will no longer hold any back pressure in order to air up. The gun is just a fond memory of many happy hours hunting birds on the beach, on the sound shore, and in the trees of the northern end of Hatteras Island.

When Christmas had come and gone, it was time to take down all the decorations and store them until next year. My mother, my brother, and I were in the process of taking down the Christmas tree. As we removed the lights, if we came to one that was burned out, she wanted it replaced. My brother was replacing the bad bulbs. He noticed that I was watching him. He screwed out a bad bulb and licked the end of his finger. Then he placed the end of his finger in the socket, or so I thought. Instead, he bent his finger, hiding it behind the socket. Then he handed the string of lights to me. I was just a kid, or that is the excuse I am going to use. Like an idiot, I licked my finger and placed it into the live socket. It shocked the life out of me, even to the point of turning the end of my finger black. I squalled out. My mother's back was turned; she didn't see a thing. I tried to tell her what he had done. She told me to stop fooling around and finish the lights so that they could be packed away in the attic. My brother laughed at me and continued to make a sizzling sound that is normally heard during an electrical short or shock. The more he picked on me, the madder I got. He picked up the last string of lights; none of them would light up. One of the wires on the female end of the string was burned completely in two. He stripped the insulation off the wire; he was going to put a new end on it. Later that night, he was asleep on the couch. He had taken off his socks and shoes. I wrapped the bare wire around one of his big toes and plugged it in. He came up from there screaming and yanked the plug from the socket. My father was just entering the room and saw it all. He yelled at me. He wanted to know if I was trying to electrocute my brother. He pulled off his belt and commenced to thrash me. My brother ended up with a burnt black ring around his toe. Then I made the same sizzling sound to aggravate him.

# CHAPTER TWENTY-ONE

# The Big Freeze

The weather turned bitterly cold after the Christmas holidays. We left the harbor at Salvo, bound for Gull Island for a two-day hunt. My father had three hunters in the crew boat. My brother and I were in the *Dolphin* with their luggage and hunting gear. The *Vivian Marie* was out in front of us. The hunters were huddled in the cabin. My father, dressed in oil skins, piloted the boat from outside the cabin. My brother and I donned oil skins and fired up the *Dolphin*. We headed over to the island behind my father and the hunters, following behind the larger boat. The wind was howling from the northwest; the waves in the sound were about four feet high. Salt spray was flying over both boats. The water droplets from the salt spray instantly froze when they came in contact with any surface. It was freezing every drop that flew. It was so cold that ice was forming on our oilcloth jackets as soon as the spray hit us.

I looked at my brother. His face was beet red; his hair, eyebrows, and sideburns had ice crystals forming in them. It was so rough we had to throttle down and kind of roll from the top of one sea, down in the trough, and climb up on the back of the next one. It turned into a cold, wet, miserable ride over to the island. As the boats ran up on the crest of the waves, their bows would rise completely out of the water. At the point each wave was crested, the boats slammed down in the trough of the next wave. As the old folks would say, we were just about *mommicked* to death. I thought we would freeze before we ever got there.

Finally, we neared the island. As we approached the mouth of the harbor, the entire front of the island was completely white. The end of the marsh was covered in ice. The strong northwest wind was sending two to three feet of water up on the island. As the waves piled on top of the ice, they froze in place. There was a thick layer of ice that extended back about thirty to forty feet. Once we rounded the north point of the harbor entrance, we were in the lee, the water calmed, and the boats leveled off. The hunters scrambled up on the dock, and my father let them into the clubhouse. My brother and I secured the boats and started bringing in their luggage and hunting gear.

I came into the mudroom and could feel a welcome wave of heat from the gas furnace. Boy, what a feeling; the numbness in my cheeks, toes, and hands began to disappear. The ice melted from my jumper and waders. The melting ice formed small puddles of water on the floor. My brother and I took the hunters' luggage to the archway that entered the cabin. We uncased their guns, wiped them off, and stored them in the gun rack. My brother went into the kitchen to help my father prepare some hot food. I remained in the mudroom. It was my job to wipe our oil clothes dry and hang them up. After that I stored all the hunting gear, mopped the floor, and straightened up the room.

After supper my father told my brother to go outside to the powerboats and take a freeze plug out of each of the larger boats' motors. Both the *Vivian Marie* and the *Dolphin* had water-cooled engines in them. He was afraid the extreme low temperature of the outside air would swell the water trapped in the engine blocks and crack them. He told me to go with my brother and hold a flashlight for him. We had to put our heavy clothes back on, but at least we didn't need to wear our foul-weather gear. Man, it was a cold time.

As I walked outside, my face began to tingle from the stinging effects of that cold northwester. The boats were rocking violently, even in the lee of the harbor. My brother warned me to be cautious walking to the boats. The waves were banging against the bulkhead and splashing up on the surface of the docks. When the water separated into droplets, it immediately froze in the air and accumulated on the metal grates on the top of the dock. The walking surface was transformed into a sheet of ice.

We carefully made our way to the boats. I held the light while my brother removed the freeze plugs. It was a welcome feeling to get back inside the warmth of the clubhouse. All we had left to do that night was to help our dad with the after-supper cleanup. The next morning I got up around five o'clock and walked into the kitchen. I normally helped with breakfast. My father told me there was no hurry because we were completely frozen in. He told my brother and me to let the hunters sleep. He didn't want anyone outside walking on any of the docks or porches until after daylight. After everyone had eaten, and it was light enough to see, my brother and I were to clean all the ice off the docks and porches. There were a few bags of rock salt in the generator box. We were to get the salt and spread it around the surface of all the docks and porches. When it lightened up for us to see, my brother and I cleaned and salted the docks and porches. I was amazed at all the boats frozen into place. The entire surface on the water in the harbor was frozen. The end of the ice extended out past the outside boat stake to the inside edge of the channel. The current in the channel was moving too fast for the water to freeze. The sky was full of fowl. Everywhere you looked you could see ducks, geese, and swan looking for a spot to land.

My father told everyone that the shore blind on the southeastern end of the island would be the hunting spot for the day. The boats could not be moved. If the men wanted to hunt, they would have to walk to the blind. He told them that the decoys were already on location at the blind. My brother and I would show them the way and set the decoys out. He fixed hot coffee, soup, and sandwiches for them to take along. The walk would be about a mile through high grass. The oldest man of the three was in his seventies; he decided to remain in the warmth of the club. My dad told them to take plenty of gun shells, and not to worry about their daily bag limit. Just place the downed fowl in empty burlap bags and leave them a short distance away from the blind. It was cold enough that they would not spoil.

We began the walk toward the blind. My brother was out front leading the way; he placed the hunters between us, and I brought up the rear of the line. The hunters carried their cased guns and their lunch. My brother carried two waterproof ammunition containers, encasing eight boxes of gun shells each. I carried an axe and a short-handled boat hook. My brother guided us around the southeast side of the harbor. He warned us about a muddy creek we had to cross. The creek was narrow and extremely shallow. The water was so low in the creek that it was frozen into a thick, muddy slush all the way to its bottom. We sank up past our waist in the water, mud, and ice. The hunters got stuck in the middle of the creek. We handed everything to my brother, who had made it to the other side of the creek. He helped the hunter closest to him, and I helped the other one. We had to instruct them to lean forward, placing all their weight on their front foot. Then pull up on their rear foot in a short, jerky motion, while we gripped their wrist with our hands and pulled forward. It was a struggle, but we finally made it across the creek with all the gear, then out to the back of the marsh, just behind the large sheet of accumulating ice. We were walking through knee-deep grass coated with frozen spray from the sound. Progress was rather slow.

Once we rounded the most northeastern point of marsh, the wind was to our backs. Walking was easy. Soon we arrived at the blind. The water was frozen from the edge of the marsh all the way to the south reef. The south reef was covered in ice as far as the eye could see.

My brother told the hunters to get inside the blind out of the weather. The shore blinds on the island were buried a couple feet down in the marsh. The outside of them was covered completely with the same type of grass that surrounded them. If you didn't know where they were located, it was easy to walk right past them. They had a partial roof over them. They were roomy and dry, and provided sufficient protection from the weather. While the hunters became situated in the blind, my brother began to chop an air hole in the ice with the axe. An air hole is a hole or a space in the ice for the fowl to land in. He started chopping the perimeter of a large hole about one hundred feet to the south of the blind. The ice was about four inches thick. Then he continued about one hundred feet offshore, and then turned in a northerly direction and continued about the same distance. Next, he turned shoreward. It wasn't long before he had the outside edges of a hole about the size of half a football field chopped out. Both of us began to break the ice up into smaller, manageable pieces. We pushed these smaller pieces under the remaining ice around the outside of the hole. This created a large ice-free hole to set the decoys in.

My brother set out six geese decoys and a dozen duck decoys. He told me to remain with the hunters. I would have two jobs: I would retrieve all the downed fowl and keep an eye on the decoys. The decoys tend to sink down in the water at their fronts during periods of extremely cold weather. Whenever a decoy is placed into the water, the span and weight forces it to face into the wind. The splashing of water up on the front of the decoy immediately freezes, and the weight of the ice causes it to sink down in the front and roll over. I had to walk out in the air hole and beat the accumulating ice off the decoys so that the set would look natural to the approaching fowl.

My brother was hardly out of sight; I was just entering the blind when a dozen widgeons lit in the water directly behind the decoys. The hunters' guns were not loaded; this was one of my father's strictest hunting rules. The guns were never loaded until all hunters were in a seated position inside the blinds. The boats or guides had to be in the clear, then he deemed it safe to load the guns. The hunters quietly uncased their guns and loaded them. Then it was on: the hunters stood up and knocked out six of the ducks. I kept the air hole free of ice and the decoys in an upright condition. The hunters could not keep the ducks and geese shot out of the air hole. This was the only location free of ice for them to land and rest. The entire surface of the sound was frozen over as far as you could see.

By two o'clock in the afternoon the hunters ran out of gun shells. They were cold and ready to return to the clubhouse. I stood on top of the blind and waved the signal flag. In about half an hour my brother reached the blind by foot. By the time he got there, I had taken up the decoys and stored the downed fowl in the tall grass a short distance from the blind. The hunters had four one-hundred-pound burlap bags full of ducks. They had two bags full of geese. It had been a successful hunt. As we turned to go, I noticed the air hole was already beginning to freeze and close up. We all walked back to the clubhouse.

After I wiped down all the oil clothes, and cleaned and oiled the guns, I helped with the evening meal. Just as soon as the hunters finished eating, I cleaned up the table. My brother and I did the dishes and cleaned up the kitchen. My father asked my brother to start up the generator for nightly showers. He asked me to turn and lock down the television antenna. We tuned in channel 7 news and weather out of Little Washington, North Carolina. He was concerned about the freeze. He wanted to know how cold the outside temperature was going to get, and how long the freeze was going to last. He said we had enough provisions to last for about five more days. As soon as the water heated up in the hot water heater, I took a shower. Then I went to our bedroom; I was asleep as soon as my head hit the pillow. I had shagged down fowl all day, kept the decoys free of ice, and kept the air hole ice free. I was blistered—extremely tired. When my father and brother came into the room, my dad shook me and rolled me over on my side; he said something to the effect that I sounded like a chainsaw sawing wood.

I woke at five in the morning the next day. The aroma of fresh-perked coffee filled the air. I looked over to my father's bed; it was empty. I walked to the kitchen. My dad was looking out the window. The older hunter was sitting at the table, drinking coffee. He told me there was no need to hurry. He was going to let the other hunters sleep in. They had spent most of the day yesterday hunting in the frigid weather. He thought they needed the rest.

We were still frozen in. The pipes from the battery-powered freshwater pumps were frozen. He had used all the freshwater in the cabin to make coffee. He wanted me to take the top off one of the tanks, break through the ice, and bring in a bucket of freshwater. There was four lag bolts holding the top on each water tank. I had to keep gloves on my hands. I had a time getting the bolts out of the top of the tank. The ice was about six inches thick on the surface of the water. I brought an ice pick along from the kitchen and soon had a bucket of freshwater.

Around nine o'clock, the two younger hunters got out of bed. Dad told my brother and me to make ready the blind located in what we called the pond box. The pond was created with the two small bulkheads parallel to each other. The distance between the bulkheads had been filled with the sand. The fill came from the harbor when it was dug out. These two bulkheads separated the harbor from a large, shallow natural pond located in the side marsh. We had made a sandbag path under the water to the entrance of the buried box. My brother and I broke out a large air hole in the middle of the pond. Then we set out about a dozen duck and six geese decoys. Before we got back to the edge of the pond, we had fowl flying over our heads. Some of the marsh ducks even landed at the far end on the pond while we were walking out.

The pond blind was located at the cabin site. It could be easily monitored from inside the clubhouse. While the two younger hunters were eating breakfast, I took the older hunter to the pond blind. I showed him the sandbag path; it was easy walking to the blind. After they finished eating, the two younger hunters joined him in the blind. I returned to the warmth of the cabin. The hunters had a successful pond-blind hunt that day. At the supper table that night, the hunters expressed concern to my father about getting back to the shore. They were scheduled to leave the next morning. My dad told them he would call my mother on the shortwave radio that was used to communicate with the shore. He called her that night and asked her to call the Coast Guard. After talking to my father, she called the Coast Guard by phone and explained our situation to them. She called him back and told him that a helicopter from Elizabeth City would be coming around noon the next day.

After we cleaned up from the meal, Dad told my brother and me that we had to gather the bags of fowl from the south-shore blind. The next morning we fashioned a type of sled from two-by-fours and a piece of plywood. My brother and I walked to the blind. We loaded the fowl on the sled and easily drug it across the ice to the clubhouse. Just as my mother said, around noon, I spotted a helicopter approaching from the north. They hovered above the yard and lowered an airman in a large metal basket. My father warned me not to touch it until it made ground contact. The buildup of static electricity from the helicopter could cause a harmful shock. The current would be neutralized when the basket made ground contact. The airman told us he was a rescue swimmer assigned to the helicopter. The helicopter was assigned to the Elizabeth City Airbase. They had come to take us back to the main island. The weather was changing; it was going to warm up and rain. My father asked them to take the hunters, me, and their game back to shore. He wanted me to go with the hunters. He and my brother were staying. That was my very first helicopter ride.

# CHAPTER TWENTY-TWO

# Stranded Game Warden

The helicopter ride was quite an experience. I had never been that far above the ground before, with the exception of a lighthouse climb on occasion or an amusement park ride. The rescue swimmer held the lift basket in place. Each hunter with his hunting gear was lifted up to the hovering helicopter. Next, a basket full of fowl was lifted. Last, the swimmer and I were lifted. The noise from the rotors was deafening. The downward spiral of air almost shook you out of the basket. Once you cleared the ground, the basket spun around and around in the direction of the rotor spin. When we reached the sliding doors, we bumped hard on the side of the chopper. Two of the inside crew members pulled us into the coach. I was amazed as the doors closed; the noise was almost completely blocked out. The pilot took us out to the back end of the ice.

The ice extended about two miles out in the sound from the island. There were large chunks of ice drifting southward, driven by the northwest wind. Some of the chunks were rather large. They resembled small icebergs. When we were abreast Salvo, the pilot turned shoreward. There was enough flat space for the helicopter to land at the Salvo harbor. The pilot set the chopper on the ground and shut the machine down. Even though the wind was blowing very hard and the weather was extremely cold, it didn't take long for a few villagers to gather to see the chopper. The off-loading of the hunters and their gear didn't take long.

My mother came to the harbor and talked to the chopper pilot. She wanted to know if they wanted something to eat. He thanked her and said they had food aboard, but some hot coffee would be appreciated. I helped her take four thermos bottles to the house and fill them with coffee. I took the coffee back to the crew. They climbed in and started up the chopper. We had to stand clear as in an instant they were airborne, soon fading out of sight in a northwestward direction.

It took two more days for the massive low pressure to blow itself out. The wind shifted to the southeast; it warmed up and began to rain. The above-freezing temperature and rain began to melt the ice in the sound. By the end of the third day, the warmth of the air and the rain turned the solid ice into a floating slush. This situation allowed my father and brother to return home and bring both powerboats back to the harbor at Salvo.

On their return my dad wanted to know what I thought of my helicopter ride. He knew that I had never flown before. I told him all about it. He was in the navy, and my brother had been in the army, so they had been on many flights. My dad told me that was the reason he chose me to accompany the hunters to shore. He saw the opportunity for me to have the experience of flight. At the time I didn't give it much thought, but the only other time I have been on a helicopter was on a medical flight. That experience I would just as soon forget.

Later that afternoon, my dad asked me to find my brother. He wanted to talk to both of us. In the warmth of the kitchen setting at the table, he told us we had to make a trip back to the island. The ice had melted and broken up in large pieces; the larger pieces had floated off. He wanted to survey the damage, if any, to the curtain boxes and stilt blinds. He told us that large floating ice chunks sometimes damaged the stilt blind pilings as they moved. He was concerned about the wings or sea breakers for the curtain boxes. The floating ice often dislodged the anchors holding the sea breakers in place. At times the ice would carry them miles from their original locations. All the blinds needed to be checked before the next hunt. His plans were to go to the island the next day to check on all the blinds. We had a window of opportunity to check for blind damage. There was ample time to make necessary repairs if any were needed. It was the last day of December;

all the hunters would be returning to their homes for the holidays. The plan was to attend the New Year's celebration that night. The next day we would head to the island to check things out.

The New Year's celebration around our house was a nonalcoholic event. My dad was an ordained Assembly of God minister. The local name for his position was a Holy Roller preacher. Everyone called him Preacher Ed. All our friends would gather up in Rodanthe at the Old Schoolhouse, or the Community Building as it is known now. There would always be a couple of piano players in the group gathered there. There would be huge pots of black-eyed peas on the boil. The aroma of cheese biscuits and coffee filled the air. The adults would talk and fellowship while they would gather around the piano player to sing hymns and songs of good tidings. The teenagers would gather in the next room or closest corner and talk about teenage things. The kids such as myself would stay outside and run amuck as long as possible. Our parents eventually insisted we come indoors. On the stroke of midnight everyone would hug, kiss, shake hands, or exchange the proper greetings. Some of the adult men would fire their shotguns in the night air. All who were present would be wished a Happy New Year. After we had welcomed in the New Year, my father or some other preacher who might be there said a few words of inspiration, graced the food, and we all sat down to a bowl of black-eyed peas and hot cheese biscuits. The black-eyed peas have always been considered a traditional meal of good luck in our little corner of the world. Then everyone pitched in and cleaned up the building. At that point we would all head for home with the thought of what the New Year might mean or bring our way.

The next day my father, brother, and I headed for Gull Island. The plan was to visit each blind site, make a complete list of any damage or changes made by the moving ice. We set out in the *Dolphin*; the weather conditions were mild. It was a sunny day with a light northeast wind. It didn't take us long to get to the island. We entered the harbor at Gull Island and checked all the decoy boats and the *Old Anytime*. We took a quick look around the clubhouse. There were a few busted water pipes under the floor system. Everything else checked out and seemed to be in order. My dad told my brother and me to take the *Old Anytime* and check out all the low-water boxes and shore blinds. He was going to use the *Dolphin* to visit the stilt blinds and the offshore deepwater float blind. We would meet back at the cabin when we completed our evaluation of the blinds.

My brother and I visited all the shore blinds first. They were in good shape. The decoys were still on location; these blinds were ready to hunt. Next we visited the curtain boxes. The bay shoal curtain box was fine, but the wing or sea breaker was gone. It was not within eyesight of the box. The north reef box looked to be in good shape. The wing was also missing. We headed for the high-water box in the center of the south reef. The water was too shallow to get the boat up to the box. We had to anchor it and walk about one mile to the blind location. Everything seemed fine at this location. The wing was still anchored where we had left it. It looked ready to hunt. The Point of Shoals blind appeared to be alright and ready to hunt. We made a list of everything we found to be out of order. Then we met our father back at the clubhouse. He told us that the deepwater float blind was gone. The stilt blinds were leaning badly in a southerly direction. Dad told us that we would not know if the ice had cut holes in the canvas on the curtain boxes until we raised the curtains and bailed the water out of them.

We warmed up some canned soup and made sandwiches for the midday meal. We thawed out the copper water pipes with a torch and fixed all the leaks we could find. Then we rewrapped them with newspaper and secured the paper with wire. It was getting late in the day, so we decided to go on back home. We would return the next day and begin the task of repairing all the blind locations that needed work.

The next day we got an early start. I was just waking up from a nap, sleeping on the life jackets in the bow of the *Dolphin* as we throttled down to enter Gull Island harbor. Dad told my brother and me to take the *Old Anytime* and work on the leaning stilt blinds. He told us to bring one of the air-cooled water pumps with us. On a long piece of flexible hose there was an eight-foot length of inch-and-one-quarter pipe. This pipe could be attached to the discharge of the pump. The end of the pipe had been beaten almost closed with a sledgehammer, which caused a lot more water pressure on the discharge end of the pipe. This setup was normally used to wash the pilings down into the bottom for the stilt blinds. We were to wash the sand from around the high side of the leaning piling, using the water pressure from the end of the pipe. He told us to tie the boat to the high side of the blind as we washed the sand from around the pilings and pull the blinds back to an upright position with the boat. I had my doubts about this process. My mind was wandering on the way to the first stilt blind. My brother brought me back to reality when he yelled to me, above the engine noise, to jump over the side and hold the boat. He took the boat out of gear but left the engine running. I eased her up to the blind from the windward side. He tied the stern of the boat to the two pilings on the high side on the leaning blind. He started and primed the water pump. The water came gushing from the flattened end of the pipe, making a high-pitched hissing sound. When he was satisfied with pressure, he handed me the galvanized pipe. I placed the end of the pipe at the bottom of the closest piling to me and began to wash the sand from around it. I moved the pipe from piling to piling. I repeated this process until I had a deep hole blown out in the bottom, on the high side of each piling. My brother motioned for me to walk back away from the blind. He wanted me far enough away so the rope wouldn't hit me if it parted. He throttled up the *Old Anytime*. To my amazement, slowly, the blind began to right itself. When he slacked off the tension on the ropes, the blind was a little too far over the other way. He turned off the pump, cut the engine to the boat, and jumped over the side. He told me to help him shake the blind. We shook it back and forth until it looked plumb. He walked a short distance away and sighted the blind from both directions. When he was satisfied with the blind's position, he started up the pump, picked up the pipe, and washed sand back around the pilings. We loaded the pump in the boat. Then we filled a dozen or so empty burlap grain bags with sand. He tied them together at the open end with string, and placed them around the pilings and under the blind. This whole process took less than two hours. We set all the stilt blinds back upright in one day's time.

We were on our way back to the clubhouse that afternoon; we saw the *Dolphin* approaching from a southerly direction with the two wings from the curtain boxes in tow. Our father had found them and was in the process of towing them back. The ice had cut the anchor ropes, and both anchors were lost. Dad told us that we would probably find the anchors at the box locations. The ropes had been cut near the chain bridles, and the loose ends of the ropes should be protruding up out on the sand, from the buried anchors. Now all we had left to do was to raise all the curtains on the curtain boxes, bail out all the water, and check the canvas for holes cut by the moving ice. Iron ducks were placed at the corners of the curtain to hold it into place. Hopefully, the weight of the iron ducks had done their job. Window weights enclosed in canvas were placed between the sides of the buried box and the curtain. These weights were placed there to weigh the canvas down. This took the slack out of the canvas and prevented movement from chafing holes in the canvas. If everything worked as if it should have, the moving ice should have flowed over the top of the buried boxes, causing no damage.

My father anchored wings to the outside boat stake at the entrance of the harbor. We decided to spend the night at the club and finish up the work the next day. The next day we checked all the curtain boxes. All the curtains were raised and tied into position. We pumped the water out of all the boxes. This enabled us to check for any holes cut by the ice. The weights had done their job. We were pleased to find that there was no apparent damage to the canvas curtains. We were able to find the cut line from the wing anchors. We cut the line back and respliced it to the chain bridles. Then we reanchored the wings; at this point we had made ready all the blinds for the next hunt. We went back to the clubhouse.

My father was pleased that we had finished all in such a short time. He told my brother and me to place five bags of corn in the pond near the cabin. He had the game managed to the point that he only had to bait two locations on the island: the north reef stilt blind with wheat and cracked corn, and the pond blind with big-grain yellow corn.

The weather conditions created hunts in the curtain box areas. Northeast winds created low water, so the north reef curtain box was used. Southwest winds enable hunts on the south reef high-water boxes. During winter storms with rough conditions and times of extremely high water, the leeward side shore blinds were hunted. After we checked all around the clubhouse and checked the lines on the decoy boats, my father seemed satisfied. We boarded the *Dolphin* and turned her in a northerly direction toward Salvo.

As the *Dolphin* easily skimmed across the small, choppy waves created by the light northeaster, the sun was just beginning to set on a clear horizon. I watched as it slipped out of sight below the water. The light of the afternoon turned into twilight. I looked at my father and brother from the bow of the boat. My brother was operating the boat while my father stood beside him. Both their faces red from the cold, I realized how lucky I was. I was fortunate enough to be growing up in an area such as this, and being able to share it with the two most important people in my life.

It was back to school for me. On the school bus ride the next morning, I gazed out the window as we passed the bay landing area. This was an area where the grass was low, and you could see far enough out in the sound to see Gull Island. When the island came into view, I wondered which blind my father and brother had set out this particular morning. I suspected it was the south reef high-water curtain box. When I walked to the road to board the bus, I noticed the wind was blowing a gale from the southwest. The water was up high in the marsh, almost up to our back garden fence. When this particular hunt was over, my father told me an interesting story. Just as I had thought, they had set out the south reef curtain box. They hunted it for three days. This location produced a good hunt for them. Mr. Kotarides and one of his close friends, T. G. Brown from Tennessee, were the hunters in the curtain box on the third day. They noticed a plane with pontoons attached approaching the reef. The plane circled to the leeward side of the reef, landed, eased up toward the box, and stopped about two hundred yards out. Two game wardens got out and began wading to the curtain box. The barometer had begun to rise sharply, signaling a shift of wind to the northeast. This wind direction would cause all the water to run off the reef. My father and brother hurried to the hunting location. They knew they had to take up the hunting gear to avoid dragging it hundreds of yards across the dry reef. My father warned the game wardens about the falling water. They continued to check the hunters' guns, gear, and hunting licenses. The wind shifted to the northeast. The water ran off swiftly. By the time the game wardens walked back to the plane, it was stuck on the reef. The game wardens became guests of the Gull Island Gunning Club.

# CHAPTER TWENTY-THREE

# Box of Ducks

The game wardens placed themselves in an awkward position. Their plane was high and dry on the south reef of Gull Island. My father took Mr. Brown and the decoy boat to the edge of the channel into deep water. He tied the decoy boat to the stern of the *Old Anytime*. My brother and Mr. Kotarides waded over to the stranded plane. Mr. Kotarides extended an invitation to the game wardens to stay at the club until their plane could be refloated. At first they declined. My brother told them that a winter northeaster sometimes lasted two to three days. He also pointed out that the outside air temperature was about twenty-six degrees. Mr. Kotarides told them that he was the owner of Gull Island Gunning Club, and they were welcome to stay as his guests. He told them they would have hot food and a warm, dry place to sleep. He invited them to stay as long as it took to free their plane. He also reminded them that the plane could be checked daily, and at that point they were out of options. Realizing their choices were limited, they agreed to stay at the club. All four of the men waded over to where my father and Mr. Brown were waiting. When they arrived at the decoy boat, my father gave my brother an anchor with a length of rope spliced to it. He told him to set anchor and tie it to the plane.

When they arrived at the club, introductions were exchanged and they enjoyed the evening meal and became acquainted. During the conversation the wardens told all present that they were federal game wardens, based at Elizabeth City and assigned to the coastal area of North Carolina. It was their job to investigate large hunting operations. They were monitoring the Whale Head Club in Currituck Sound, the Duck Island Club at Oregon Inlet, and this club at Gull Island. They knew that all three clubs were heavily baiting their areas with grain on a regular basis. They had pictures of the baiting operations while they were in progress. They added that it was not against any of the hunting regulations to bait the hunting areas, but it was against the regulations to hunt over the grain. They mentioned the fact that it was easy to see the grain on the bottom from the air. It seemed they knew all about using the grain to attract the waterfowl. They knew where it was, when it was normally set out, and about how much was used each time it was spread. It seemed they had a type of net that was used in baited areas to gather grain from the bottom. The net had been used at all the larger clubs such as Gull Island. They had found grain near the blinds of all the clubs, with the exception of Gull Island. This resulted in the temporary closing of the blinds to hunting for short periods of time. They knew my father was baiting but did not know why there was no grain near the blinds when they checked them. My father just smiled and told them that he knew it was against hunting regulation to shoot over a baited area. He added that they would never find any grain around the blinds. The only reason he baited was to keep a large volume of fowl using the area. He told them it took a lot of grain to feed the large rafts of waterfowl that used the Gull Island area. He added that even without the use of grain, this was a perfect area for the fowl to use during the winter months. After a lengthy conversation, the hunters and wardens retired for the night.

The next morning at the breakfast table, my dad told the hunters that they would set out the north reef stilt blind for the day hunt. The wind from the northeaster was still howling to near gale force. This was a good day for a north reef diving duck hunt. My dad cautioned the hunters to be careful not to exceed their bag limit on the ducks as long as the wardens were still at the club. If they harvested their limit, they were to wave the signal flag immediately. This would tell my father and brother to switch hunters in the blind. The south reef was still completely dry, continuing to hold the plane at the location where it came to rest. During one trip to the stilt blind to exchange hunters, one of the game wardens asked my father if he could come along. As they approached the blind, the game warden asked my father why there was a large white ball anchored at the front of the decoy setup. He told the warden that it was a range marker; the hunters knew the ducks were within range if they flew between the blind and the ball. This was a true statement; the ball was always placed about forty yards to the windward of the decoy set. It was replaced by a smaller buoy and moved from a heavily baited location about five hundred yards away from the stilt blind. This was the legal distance to hunt from any grained area. It was always moved near the blind during the hunt. This is the portion that my dad left out of the conversation. I don't think the wardens ever figured out the relationship of the large painted balsa wood balls to the hunting spreads of Gull Island.

The next morning was the north reef stilt blind second day hunt. The northeaster had slackened up a bit. The water levels were still low but much higher than the day before. My father told my brother that it appeared through the binoculars that the plane had shifted a little from its original position. He told the game wardens that if the water levels continued to get higher, they could possibly refloat the plane by midday. After returning the hunters to the clubhouse to warm up and have their midday meal, my father and brother took the wardens to the plane. They were able to get the *Old Anytime* about fifty feet from the plane when she grounded. They got out of the boat and walked over to the plane. The plane was still grounded but not as bad as before. It had shifted its position, and now the anchor line was tight. It wasn't completely free, but when a larger wave approached, it would bob up and down a bit. The wardens wanted to start the plane's engine and try to move it to deep water. Everyone stood clear as one of them boarded and started up the engine. When the plane was throttled up, the prop tried to move it forward, but in the process, it also pulled the nose of the plane in a downward motion. This grounded the front of the pontoons and held the plane fast. My father suggested using the *Old Anytime* tied to the front of the pontoons to help hold them up while increasing the throttle slowly on the plane. The boat was tied to the struts on the front of the pontoons. When the plane's engine was throttled up, and the nose went down, my father signaled to my brother to throttle up the *Old Anytime*. When the line came tight from the boat, it pulled the pontoons in an upward position. When the nose of the plane came up, the pilot increased the throttle. The plane rocked up and down, as if it was on a seesaw, but it inched forward. This process continued until the plane was free of the reef, floating in deep water. The other warden boarded the plane. Both of them waved good-bye. The pilot turned the plane into the wind. He then throttled up the plane, skimmed the surface, and slowly lifted above the water and became airborne. They flew in a large circle in a southerly direction and came back over the boat. As they passed overhead they tipped their wings, and disappeared from sight in a northwesterly direction. This particular hunting party came to a close on Friday morning. My father and brother ferried the hunters back to Salvo and their vehicles.

On Saturday morning my father, brother, and I went to the island to grain up the hunting locations and make the camp ready for the next group of hunters. We cleaned up the clubhouse and visited the offshore float blind, located offshore to the west of the island. As we were approaching the harbor to load the grain, we heard the noise of a plane approaching. Sure enough, it had pontoons attached to the bottom of it. It circled up above and headed toward the north reef stilt blind area. My father told my brother and me that we were going to bait undercover from now on. Bait undercover? What in the world could that mean? He told me to check the decoy boats out, bail them out if they needed it. While we were checking the decoy boats, he kept an eye on the plane with binoculars. It appeared that the plane had flown off in the northwest and had gone. My brother and I finished tiding up the decoy boats and returned to the front porch of the clubhouse. My dad told us that he thought the plane would return and try to observe us placing the grain. He called my mother on the radio and told her that we wouldn't be returning until well after dark. All of a sudden, it hit me. "Undercover" meant we would be placing the grain after dark, out of eyesight from the air. We sat on the porch and relaxed. Sure enough, about an hour later, my brother spotted the plane with the binoculars, flying southward over the main island. He watched it as it approached the village of Avon. Then it turned out over the sound and headed in our direction straight for the clubhouse. By this time twilight was approaching; soon it would be dark. The plane circled the camp two times, dipped its wings the last time, and we waved as it disappeared in the northwest. We went inside and warmed up some leftovers from the icebox.

Finally, it was dark. My brother and I loaded up the hand truck with five bags of corn. We placed the grain in a small wooden skiff and spread it in the pond near the buried hunting blind. We repeated this process until we had spread fifteen bags of grain in the pond. We then loaded five bags of wheat, five bags of cracked corn, and five bags of milo. We spread all this grain around the large white balsa wood ball, located five hundred yards from the stilt blind on the north reef. After that time we always spread the grain early in the morning before the break of day, or at the end of the day during the night. Each time we grained up, it was always under the cover of darkness. That was the end of the game wardens viewing any baiting activity around the Gull Island area.

In the pond blind by the cabin, we always checked to make sure the geese had eaten all the grain before the hunters were set up in that spot. This location was a prime spot to harvest geese and black ducks. The north stilt blind was always a good location for diving ducks and a few geese during northeast blows. The large balsa wood ball was used to hunt that area.

The end of hunting season was approaching. In those days, duck hunting season normally ended on January 15. Goose season extended to the end of January. When the north stilt blind was set up, after the end of duck season, it was awfully tempting to the hunters to shoot ducks if they came in. My father warned the hunters about the area being patrolled from the air. He set only goose decoys out at the location. Still, the ducks came in, and the hunters shot them. My dad had to station the boat about one hundred yards to the leeward of the blind. The man in the boat kept a sharp lookout with binoculars for the plane. If the plane was spotted, he would wave with a signal flag to the hunters in the blind. If ducks came in, they were not shot until the plane was out of the area. If any ducks were downed, the hunters remained in the blind. The ducks were picked up by the boat. They were placed in weighted empty grain bags. These bags had enough weight inside, along with the ducks, to sink them to bottom of the channel if they had to be thrown overboard. The bags were tied together at the open ends with a decoy line. A very small buoy was tied to the end of the line so that the bags could be retrieved. On one occasion my brother was in the downwind boat waiting on the blind. He had several weighted bags of ducks inside the boat. A large flock of diving ducks landed within range of the blind, and the hunters shot them. My brother gathered them up as they floated by and placed them inside one of the weighted bags. Just as he tied the open end of the bag together, he heard the plane approaching. He spotted it with the binoculars, waved to the hunters, and slowly headed back to the camp. The plane came in from the northwest, circled around the blind, and flew over the boat. Then it proceeded on an easterly course toward the main island. As my brother entered the channel in the boat, he tossed the bags over the side as the plane was flying away from him. He continued to the camp and secured the boat. The plane circled the island and landed outside the entrance of the harbor. The pilot taxied the plane about fifty feet from the end of the marsh. At this point an anchor was tossed in the water. One of the wardens set the anchor, and the plane engine was shut down. They slackened up the line until the back of the plane was against the marsh. They secured the line to the pontoons and walked up to the clubhouse. They examined all the guns and the hunting license of all the hunters present at the camp. They searched all the boats. When they were satisfied, they left and landed the plane at the north stilt blind. My dad and brother followed along in the boat. The wardens checked the guns and the hunting license of the hunters at the blind. They got out a long-handled small mesh net and dug all around the bottom for grain. When they couldn't find anything out of the ordinary, they started up the plane and left the area. After they were gone, my brother retrieved the bags of ducks and hid them in the marsh a good distance from the cabin.

My father discussed the day's events with the hunters at the table during the evening meal. He told them the wardens were looking for ducks shot after the season had been closed. Also, they were examining the blind areas for grain. If they found any ducks shot after the season, the hunters would be heavily fined. If they found any grain being hunted over, they would close the club for the rest of the season. He cautioned the hunters to follow instructions to the letter; they were to keep their eyes on the boat, and he and my brother would watch for the plane. They could have a good hunt and still be protected from the aggravation of fines and appearing in federal court. He told them that the game wardens had checked everything around the gunning club, and they seemed to be satisfied. The only thing left to worry about was the last day as they left for home. He told the hunters that he thought the wardens had a crew watching the activity around the club from the shore side of the main island. They had accumulated a dozen or so bags of ducks and about six bags of geese. They needed to be taken to shore to be cleaned, packed, and frozen for transport along with the hunters. My father formulated a plan to achieve this goal. The hunting party planned to leave the main island on Friday after a morning hunt. My brother and father would transport the game to Salvo on Thursday in the middle of the night. They took the bags of game ashore to the cleaners without a hitch, in the cover of darkness, on Thursday night.

Early on Friday morning the wind was still light from the northeast. My father and brother set up the north reef stilt blind. They told the hunters not to shoot any ducks. They were to shoot only geese. But the first flock of redheads that came in, the hunters fired on them. My brother recovered six ducks from the water. Another flock of ducks came in, and the hunters downed some more. My brother came back to the cabin with fifteen redheads in a bag. My father took the boat back out to the blind. He told the hunters not to shoot any more ducks. They told my dad that they wanted to have the ducks mounted. My father still had the problem of getting the ducks to shore. He knew the wardens would be waiting for them at the dock in Salvo. He loaded the ducks in a large plastic bag and placed them in an empty cardboard box. The box had Havoline Motor Oil written on the side of it. When they reached the dock, sure enough, the wardens were there. My father handed the box to one of the wardens and asked him to pass it to my brother. My brother took the box and locked it up in the storage building. The wardens searched both boats but came up empty.

# CHAPTER TWENTY-FOUR

# New Boats

My brother told me later that when Dad handed the game warden the box of ducks, he almost fainted dead away. My dad asked the warden to pass the case of oil to my brother so that he could place it into the storage shed at the harbor. There were a couple of bags of geese in the *Dolphin*. The wardens opened them both and checked the contents inside. When they didn't find any ducks, they lingered around the harbor for a while, looking over all the gear. They waited until all the hunters had gone. Then they got into their jeep and left the harbor. The hunters stopped at my cousin Floyd's house to pick up the frozen and dressed fowl. His wife, Janie, cleaned, packed, and froze the fowl for transport. Mr. Brown, the hunter from Tennessee, returned to the harbor. My father gave him the box of ducks and told him to take very good care of the case of oil. He laughed and took the box. He planned to purchase a large cooler and pack the ducks in dry ice. He had a private plane waiting for him at the small airport in Manteo. His plans were to have a few of the redheads mounted when he got back home in Tennessee. That was the last hunt for that particular season.

During the months of February, March, April, and May the work began of closing the club until next hunting season. The stilt blinds were cleaned and the screws holding the floors down were removed. The floors were screwed to the side of the boxes in an open vertical position. This made the boxes easy to clean and put into service the next season. All the curtains had to be removed from the curtain boxes. They had to be checked for leaks, repairs made if needed, and stored until next hunting season. The sea breakers or wings had to be pulled up on the low-sided marsh of the island. They had to be examined and repaired if necessary. All the decoys had to be taken to the main island. The decoy spans and weights had to be removed. The decoys were sent to Norfolk, Virginia, for repairs and painting. The off-season was a time for repairs and improving the gear. Gull Island Gunning Club had several successful hunting seasons. The word began to get out among the hunting community. Mr. Kotarides was flooded with new applications from prospective hunters who wanted join the hunt club. He signed up many new members. He called my father and asked him to come to the bakery in Virginia to a business meeting. At the meeting he introduced my father to the new members. The membership had grown to about a dozen regular members, who were allowed to invite three guests along on a hunt. Mr. Kotarides told my father they could make it through a couple more seasons using the small cabin. After that they would have to add on to it or build a new clubhouse. He wanted to have two new hunting boats built right away before the next season began. He told my father that the *Vivian Marie* and the *Dolphin* had served them well. He knew they were designed for commercial fishing. The *Vivian Marie* was my father's houseboat, and the *Dolphin* was his run boat. Both boats were designed to be fished in a commercial long net rig. Mr. Kotarides wanted two boats designed for hunting in the shallow waters of the Pamlico Sound, around the Gull Island area. The first boat would be designed as a passenger vessel, used to ferry the hunters out to the island. During the off-season he wanted to use it to sport fish out of the Hatteras Inlet area. This boat would need a large, protected, closed-in cabin. It needed to have the capability to transport six to eight passengers, plus two crew members. The second boat would be designed as a workboat. It would be used to carry grain, supplies, and hunting gear. Mr. Kotarides wanted both vessels to have a deep flair in their bows. This was to direct the spray away from the interior of the boat during high-speed travel. Most of the boats that were built in our area were of a slight-angle bow design. They were fine when the weather was good. When it was rough they threw considerable amounts of water into the interior of the boats.

One of his friends had told him of a boatbuilding area located down south of us along the coast. The name of the small town was Harkers Island. The boatbuilders of this area had developed a hull design that had a rather pronounced flair in the bow. Mr. Kotarides had seen a couple of these boats and was convinced it was what they needed. He wanted my father to go down there with him and meet with a boatbuilder. They went to Harkers Island to visit with a Mr. Rose and a Mr. Willis. Their families had been involved in boatbuilding for generations. My father and Mr. Kotarides talked to both of these boatbuilders. Both men had boats under construction in their backyard boat shops. Both boatbuilders had way too much work to complete an additional boat before the next hunting season. It was agreed that each builder would construct a boat hull for Mr. Kotarides. The Rose family would complete the larger of the two boats' hulls. The Willis family would build the smaller hull. Both boat hulls would be completed to the floorboard stage, with one coat of primer paint applied. At that point, the boat hulls would be transported by trailer to Oxford, Maryland. In Oxford the boats would be finished at the Meekins Family Boat Yard. The Meekins family had many years of boatbuilding experience. They specialized in designing and building sports fishing and hunting boats. Their boats were designed for use in the Chesapeake and Delaware Bays. The larger boat hull was twenty-six feet long and about eight feet wide at the beam. The beam is the widest portion of the boat near the mid-ship area. A sports fishing design was used to finish off the inside of this boat. She had a spacious closed-in cabin. She was open and had plenty of room in the stern area, designed for fighting game fish. She had a removable fighting chair installed in her stern. The smaller hull was patterned after the hunting workboats of the Back Bay hunting area. She was twenty feet long and six feet wide. She had an open-back small cabin. Both of these boats had the Harkers Island flair in their bows. Their bottoms flattened at the mid-ship area and ended with a tunnel stern in the back of them.

After the boats were finished on the inside, they were taken to the mechanics shop at the Mary Jane Bakery in Virginia to have the motors installed. The larger vessel was equipped with a 400-horsepower Ford

Interceptor Marine engine. She had a keel cooler installed to keep the massive engine at the proper temperature. The smaller of the two boats had a 327-cubic-inch Chevrolet engine for power. Mr. Kotarides named the larger vessel after his daughter. She was called the *Sandy-K*. The smaller boat he named the *Gull Island*. The *Sandy-K* was painted a glossy white. The *Gull Island* was painted battleship gray.

They were both brought to Salvo on large trailers. It was near the end of the month of September when they arrived. It was in the afternoon, on a balmy Saturday. Man, they were a sight to behold. I had never seen such beauty. The *Sandy-K* gleamed in the sunlight. The *Gull Island* looked just as impressive. We were lucky on that Saturday that the wind was five to ten miles per hour from the southwest. The water level was high. The boats were taken to the end of the marsh and floated off of the trailers. My father got in the *Sandy-K*, my brother in the *Gull Island*. The engines were fired up; man, what a sound of power. By the time both boats were docked inside the harbor, a small crowd of folks had gathered to see them. Mr. Kotarides promised to take everyone for a boat ride after a short shakedown cruise on each vessel. He asked my father and brother to board the *Sandy-K*. My heart sank; I thought I was going to be left behind. Then he looked around and spotted me; he waved his hand for me to get aboard. I was elated; a big smile broke out on my face. Mr. Kotarides looked at me, laughed, and said, "You thought you were going to be left behind, didn't you?"

I responded with a big smile, and said, "Yes, sir; at first I did." My father took the helm and eased the *Sandy-K* out of the harbor, past the boat stake and onto the open sound. He turned the boat south head into the wind and throttled up. She immediately jumped up on a smooth even plane. The flair in the bow split through the three- to four-foot chop; all the spray from the waves was thrown far off to the sides of the boat. Even in this choppy situation, this hull design produced a dry, smooth, even ride. We were skimming across the waves at about half throttle.

When we were abreast at No-Ache Point my father turned the boat offshore to make a U-turn to return to the harbor. He didn't down throttle a bit; she made a wide even turn and outran the spray on the windward side. When we arrived back at the harbor, my dad loaded up six men and headed back out into the sound. My brother, Mr. Kotarides, and I boarded the *Gull Island*. When my brother fired up the motor, it had a different sound. The *Gull Island* had a wet exhaust system with a saltwater intake, and two large, half-submerged pipes protruding from the back of the stern. What a sound of power! The hot air from the exhaust manifold made a bubbling, sizzling sound as it mixed with the water of the creek. It sounded as if the *Gull Island* was ready to fly. My brother eased the boat out of the harbor and throttled up. She jumped on top of the waves and achieved the same fast, smooth, completely dry ride as we experienced in the *Sandy-K*. On our way down toward No-Ache Point to make our turn, we passed the *Sandy-K* on her return trip back to the harbor. Man, what a sight; she was an image of beauty. I would like to have a picture of her steaming along under full power. The water was being thrown high in the air away from her sides. You could see small rainbows made by the sunlight shining through the spray from her bow as she steamed along. On our return trip to the harbor, Mr. Kotarides looked at my brother, smiled, and said, "Let Elvin take her for a bit." Man, I almost fainted. My brother told me to steer straight for the boat stake at the entrance of the harbor. Mr. Kotarides laughed and said, "Let him make a couple of turns." My brother instructed to slowly turn her into the wind. I turned the wheel about a quarter. The boat instantly responded with a smooth, even turn to the windward. I turned her back toward the harbor. My brother took the helm after we rounded the boat stake on the approach to the harbor. Mr. Kotarides was completely satisfied with the boat trials and performance of both vessels. True to his word, everyone who came to the harbor that day to see the boats got a boat ride in both boats. When all the rides were completed, everyone remained to talk about the boats. I overheard comments like, "Man, what a smooth ride in that southwest chop." Another comment was, "Did you see how both of them held the water in the turns?"

"Yes," came an answer. "There wasn't any fluctuation in prop speed during hard turns to the windward and to the leeward." All the men present at the harbor that day were impressed with the performance of the vessels.

I noticed the *Gull* had a wide capped area that reached all the way across her stern. I asked Dad why this area was capped off. He told me it was there for two reasons. The first reason was to protect the large gasoline tank that was underneath it. He pointed out the gas cap to me. It was shiny chrome, even on the deck of the cap, and had two small holes drilled into it. "The holes are there to accept a gas cap key such as this," he said. He removed a chromed piece of metal from his pocket. It looked as if it had two legs on it. The legs fit inside the holes in the gas cap, and allowed its removal and replacement during the fueling process. A smile developed on his face, and he said, "The second reason is to have a platform to place the grain bags on." A grain bag was placed on the platform in the center of the stern. The prop wash would speed up the spreading process and help the grain to sink faster when the bags were cut open. Then it all made sense to me. Mr. Kotarides had thought of almost everything when he had the boats designed. I mentioned this to him. He laughed and said, "That was one of your father's many ideas during the designing process. The only thing I had to do with the development of these boats was the hull designs of Harkers Island. Your father implemented the remaining portions of the design. This was the reason I invited him along on the visits to Harkers Island and Oxford, Maryland. I wanted him to share his knowledge of boatbuilding and the Gull Island area with the boatbuilders. I am pleased with the way it worked out. We have two fantastic boats specially designed for use in this area."

Mr. Kotarides and my dad went over to the storage building and sat down on the porch. I overheard their conversation about replacing the small hunting camp. Mr. Kotarides wanted a large clubhouse built that could service as many as eight to ten hunters on each trip. The new clubhouse would replace the small hunting camp located on the island. It was to be a much larger, more modern structure. They sat there and talked a couple of hours until my mother called us for the evening meal. Mr. Kotarides and Dad walked toward the house; I remained at the harbor still gazing at the two new boats. It wasn't long before I saw my mother stick her head out the back door and yell, "Elvin Hooper, you better come double quick."

Whenever she called me by my first and last name, I knew she meant business. I left the harbor and ran to the house. As I opened the kitchen door, I heard my mother say, "Wash your hands and sit down to the table, mister; supper is ready." When we finished with dessert, I excused myself and headed toward the door. She looked at me and said, "Don't stay outside too late; church tomorrow, you know."

"Yes, ma'am," I responded, and eased out the back door. It was a warm night, the moon directly overhead; it was almost as light as day. The southwester had moderated to a light breeze. I had no trouble seeing my way through the narrow path that went to the harbor. When I arrived at the storage building I sat down on the porch. There, gleaming in the moonlight, was the *Sandy-K*, tied closest to the dock on my right. The *Gull Island* was tied to the dock adjacent to her on my left. Both boats looked as if they had magical powers. They were a sight to see in the light of the moon. I heard someone coming down the path toward me. I turned and saw Mr. Kotarides approaching. "They are really something, aren't they?" he said to me.

"Yes," I responded, "they are the two most beautiful boats that I have ever seen."

He had decided to come outside for a smoke and wound up at the harbor. We both sat there for the longest time, not saying a word, just listening to the sounds of the night and gazing at the boats. Our silence was broken by my father's approach.

"Your mother sent me to get you," he said to me. "She wanted to remind you about church tomorrow. Don't worry. They will still be there tied at the dock when you get home from church."

"I know that," I responded. "I just like to look at them."

"Well, you can look at them some more after church tomorrow. Now you need to go to the house and get some rest. You have had a big day." I got up and walked in the direction of the house but hesitated after a few steps. "Go on," my dad said, "your mother is waiting."

"I just wanted one last look tonight," I answered. Both of the boats were bobbing up and down in the small ripples inside the harbor. I continued on up the path toward the house, stopped halfway up, and turned. My father had taken my place beside Mr. Kotarides; they had their gaze fixed on the boats. When I entered the kitchen door, my mother asked me where Mr. Kotarides and my father were.

"Still at the harbor," I responded.

"Still looking at those fool boats, I reckon," she said.

"Yes, ma'am," I replied.

"A boat is a boat as far as I am concerned," she said. "Your crowd acts as if those boats have superpowers."

*Superpowers,* I thought to myself as I went to wash up.

# CHAPTER TWENTY-FIVE

# The Lost Navy Pilot

The month of October came in with light winds and balmy weather. My father and brother were busy getting things ready for the upcoming season. The club had the boats it needed in place to operate efficiently. The *Old Anytime* was perfect for the low-water hunting on the reefs. The *Gull Island* could handle transporting the gear from the main island to the club. Also, she was good for the deepwater blind hunting around the island. The *Sandy-K* was the cat's meow when it came to a passenger vessel. She could be used to transport the hunters out to the island on hunting trips. When the hunts were at their end, she could return the hunters to the main island.

With the arrival of the two new boats, the *Dolphin* and my father's houseboat remained tied to the docks in the harbor at Salvo most of the time. The worst thing that can possibly happen to a boat is to remain tied to the dock and not used. If they are not used, not boarded, and not run on a regular basis, they begin to deteriorate. It's just like a house that is shut up and not lived in for a long period of time. The small problems that occur become big problems, and then major problems. If there is no one living in the house to detect these problems, and they aren't addressed in a timely manner, soon it's too late. The house becomes in such a state of disrepair, and it's difficult to save it. The same situation applies to boats. After a lengthy conversation with my mother, my father announced that he was thinking about selling his long net rig. He told my brother and me that, after a powwow, as he called it, with our mother, we were getting out of the commercial fishing business. The club had grown to the point that it had developed into a full-time job for him. Mr. Kotarides had offered him year-round employment to manage it. His plans were to sell all his boats, nets, and crab pots. He was going to call a few of his friends in various off-island towns around the county to help spread the word about the sale. In no time at all, the men of the villages of Rodanthe, Waves, and Salvo came and bought his set nets and crab pots. He told me he was going to keep all his terrapin traps and steel traps for me to fool with. He knew I liked to set the terrapin traps in the creeks around the shore. I also loved to tramp around in the marsh looking for rat runs to set the steel traps in. There was a commercial market for all terrapins that measured at least six inches or better in length. A commercial marked existed for the fur of muskrat, mink, and otter. These rats are somewhat of a challenge to catch. They have a tremendous sense of smell. If they detect any human scent whatsoever in one of their runs, they will immediately abandon it. Each trap needs to be completely concealed from view when set in a rat run. It must be washed thoroughly to mask the human scent to be effective. It is also a good idea to carry along a small container of shad oil to pour on the set area. This fishy odor blends in with the natural marshy smell, removing all traces of human scent. I caught more rats in the areas that were prepared in this manner.

The only remaining commercial fishing gear my father had left was his net skiff, the long net itself, and the *Vivian Marie*, his houseboat. The *Dolphin*, which he used as a run boat to transport his catch, was owned jointly by my father and Uncle Luke, his brother. The large net skiff he decided to keep for a cargo boat. It was to be used to carry materials and supplies to the island.

He had a few prospective buyers show up to look over the gear. A man by the name of Cecil Sears from Colington turned out to be a serious buyer for the *Dolphin* and the long net. He came to Salvo along with his brother to pick up the gear. They brought a large flatbed trailer with them to carry the net. His brother was going to take the *Dolphin* up the sound to Colington. After this transaction, only the *Vivian Marie* remained. A fellow named

Wilber Cahoon from Eastlake came to see the *Vivian Marie*. He liked her
and purchased her. My dad agreed to take the boat across the sound for
him. On the second Saturday of the month of October my father and I took
the boat to Mans Harbor for Mr. Cahoon. Uncle Luke picked us up in his
car and brought us back home. With all the commercial fishing gear sold,
my father turned his attention to making the club ready for the upcoming
hunting season.

Each hunting season always opened the first week of November. The
clubhouse was stocked with supplies; the decoys and blinds were ready for
the arrival of the first group of hunters. There was only one week left in
the month of October. The only thing left to do was to begin graining up
the hunting locations. My dad noticed that the observation plane had been
spending more time than usual in the Gull Island area. Each time in the past
few weeks whenever he went to the island for anything, the plane was in the
area. It was flying up and down both reefs at a low altitude, even making
passes over the boats when they were there. The wardens were constantly
taking pictures of the entire area. My father changed his process of baiting
the fowl with grain. He stopped using the grain markers, as he called them.
He removed all the balsa wood balls, stopped using the cedar trees attached
to the stakes, and began daylight baiting again. He and my brother loaded
a dozen one-hundred-pound sacks of grain on the *Gull Island*. They towed
the open net skiff, converted into a cargo boat, with a dozen more bags
loaded in her. When they got near the island, my father slowed the *Gull
Island* so that my brother could pull the net skiff up and board her. At that
point my father steamed to the edge of Gull Shoal Channel, near the outer
part of the north reef. They were about one thousand yards away from the
stilt blinds and curtain boxes. As soon as my brother placed the first bag
of grain on the stern of the net skiff, the plane appeared. He continued on
about his business, cutting the end of the bag open with his pocket knife
and allowing the grain to spill overboard. My father eased the boats all
along the entire edge of Gull Channel. When the net skiff was empty, they
anchored her. Then they finished placing grain along the entire edge of the

channel. All the while the plane was flying low passes over the boat and taking pictures. "Well, now they know we are baiting," my father told my brother, "but they know we are legally baiting and they have the pictures to prove it." It was okay to feed the fowl, but illegal to shoot over the feed. All this grain kept the thousands and thousands of diving ducks in the area. My father continued this process for many years.

I have been present on many of these feeding trips to the island. There were many large rafts of blackheads, redheads, and canvasbacks feeding on the grain. As soon as the first bag of grain went over the side, even before the second one could be cut open, the blackheads would be on it. Hundreds of them would land on the water to the leeward of the boat and swim up to the grain. Just as soon as they were over the feed, they would begin diving to the bottom to gather it. The redheads and canvasbacks were a lot more cautious; they would remain hundreds of yards away. As the boat moved slowly away they would jump up in the air and make small short flights, steadily moving in the direction of the feed. When the boat was at a safe distance away, all the ducks were instantly diving on the grain. All the feed would be consumed in a couple of days. The channel was grained up every other day during the course of a hunting season. The entire feeding process was completely legal.

The first hunting party of that particular season was blessed with good hunting weather. A winter low was approaching the area. The wind shifted to the northwest and blew in excess of gale force. The water levels were much too high to hunt any of the off-island blinds. The shore blinds had to be used. The Thara-Fair Creek blind and the Cain Field blind were set up. My brother was given the task of monitoring the blinds with binoculars while my father cleaned up the breakfast mess. There was a perfect spot on the roof, at one of the dormers, in the sun and out of the wind, to watch the southeastward end of the island. This is the location my brother chose to sit and watch the hunters. The hunters only waved the signal flag if they shot over their limit in fowl. My brother spotted a flock of six geese flying southeast along the edge of the channel, headed for the south reef. When they spotted the decoys at Thara-Fair Creek, they circled and settled on the water just behind the decoys. The shots rang out; none of the geese flew off. My brother didn't wait for the flag; he knew there were only two hunters at that location. He took the *Old Anytime* and went to the blind. Sure enough, they had taken all six geese. The limit per day was two geese per hunter. They were two over their limit. My brother gathered the geese and began to make his way back to the clubhouse. He was making his way slowly along the edge of the reef in a westerly direction. The wind was blowing hard from the northwest. The spray was flying from the four- to five-foot chop.

My brother caught a glimpse of bright orange in the corner of his eye, on the crest of the waves, far out on the horizon to the west. He wiped his eyes and strained to spot the object. All he could see was the whitecaps from the huge waves. When he got back to the club, he told Dad about what he had seen. My father told him that sometimes in the cold wind with the water flying, your eyes play tricks on you. He told him to bag the geese, hide them a good distance from the house, and return to his spot to continue watching the hunters. While he was monitoring the hunters, my brother took an occasional gaze through the binoculars up to the west scanning the horizon. On one of these occasions he spotted the orange object. This time he marked the location above a group of bushes on the west end of the island. He continued to watch just above the group of bushes, and it appeared again. He watched it several times disappear behind the waves and emerge again. He climbed down the ladder from the observation area and informed Dad that there was an orange object drifting toward the island from the northwest. Dad and my brother went on the northwest porch with the binoculars, but they failed to spot the object. "I don't see a thing," Dad said to him.

"It is there. I saw it several times," my brother responded. "This porch is not high enough to see it. I saw it from the roof," my brother said.

"All right," said my father. "Let me get my foul weather gear on. We will take the *Gull Island* and go and investigate your orange object." When they left the calmness of the harbor and turned up into the wind, the boat began to feel the waves. My brother was at the helm when he throttled up the *Gull*

*Island* and jumped up on the top of the chop. The spray from the flying water was directed well off to her sides. She leveled off and smoothed out, even in the four-foot chop, and created a comfortable ride. My father had the binoculars scanning the horizon. He spotted the object and directed my brother to correct his heading in a more southerly direction. It appeared to be about four miles to the west of the island. Soon both of them could see it without the use of the binoculars. As they approached the object, it turned out to be a large orange inflated life raft. There was a half cover located on one end of the raft. They could see a man's feet sticking out from under the cover. Dad told my brother to go up to the windward of the raft and hold the boat steadily in place with the engine. His plan was to use the lee of the boat to slow down the drift of the raft. As they neared the raft, Dad called out to the man. There was no response or movement from inside the raft. "He must be unconscious. Be careful with the boat, Son. We don't want to cause the raft to roll over," said my father. My brother guided the boat up to the side of the raft and held her in place. My father used a long-handled boat hook to bring the raft alongside the boat. My brother took the boat out of gear, allowing her to drift. He helped Dad lift the limp man aboard the *Gull Island*. They made a line fast to the raft in order to tow it back to the island.

The navy flyer was unconscious but still breathing. He was shivering violently. They wrapped the flyer in blankets and placed him inside the cabin of the boat. My father always kept a couple of blankets, enclosed in a large plastic bag, stored with the life jackets. It was not out of the ordinary for a hunter to stumble and fall chasing crippled fowl. This resulted in water-filled waders and becoming wet to the skin. These blankets were for such occasions.

My brother turned the *Gull Island* back toward the island and throttled up. She immediately jumped up on a plane. The life raft came bouncing from wave to wave behind the boat. My brother slowed the boat, and they entered the harbor.

They took the flyer inside the clubhouse and placed him in a bunk near one of the gas heaters. Dad asked my brother to open a can of chicken soup and heat it up for the flyer. After a few minutes of warmth, the flyer opened his eyes.

He wanted to know where he was. Dad told him he was safe at the Gull Island Gunning Club. He was weak and unable to stand, but he could talk.

He told my father his name was Leonard Shoemaker. He was a second lieutenant in the Navy Air Corps, stationed out of Oceana Air Base in Virginia. He asked for some water to drink, then told my father that he was the copilot aboard a two-man plane; he and the pilot had ejected after experiencing engine failure. The pilot, Fred Anderson, was still out in the sound somewhere. They were on a routine bombing run over the target area, located to the northwest of the island, in the middle of the sound. On one of their low passes the engine failed for no apparent reason. The pilot could not get it to respond to any of the restarting procedures, and at that point he gave the bailout order. The flyer gave my father a waterproof pouch that contained the name and phone number of his commanding officer at Oceana. He asked my father to call in and update his commander on the situation. My father told him to drink some of the warm soup and lie back and rest. At this point he had done all he could do.

Dad called my mother by radio and passed on the information to her. She called the air base at Oceana, and also called the Coast Guard Station at Oregon Inlet. She gave both places the information and her home number as a contact location. The Coast Guard initiated an immediate search the next morning. The helicopter from Elizabeth City flew a grid pattern to the northwest of the island. After setting up the day's hunting location, my father sent my brother and one of the hunters out in the *Gull Island* to join the search. He told my brother to concentrate on areas to the southeast of the island. If the pilot was in a similar raft; he would have drifted past the island by now. My brother headed around the back of the island. He went through the Gold Mine Opening in the reef and as far south as Kinnakeet; then he turned toward shore. The Gold Mine Opening is the name of a slough in the reef containing deep water. It is an opening between Kinnakeet Reef and Gull Shoal Reef. The water is deep enough to allow large boats to pass through the shallow reef. My brother followed the shoreline northward beginning at the Little Hills area. The helicopter had continued its search up to the shoreline. It was hovering in place above the Bay Landing area. The copter was lowering a swimmer on a cable as my brother approached the area. On his approach, my brother could see another orange raft washed up in the high grass a few yards back of the sand beach area. He anchored the *Gull Island* and waded inshore toward the raft. He arrived at the raft about the same time as the Coast Guardsman. The raft was empty; there was no sign of life around it. There were no footprints in the sand. The grass around the raft was undisturbed. The navy sent a car to Salvo for the copilot. After three days of extensive searching, neither the plane nor the pilot were ever found.

# CHAPTER TWENTY-SIX

# Market Gunning

There were only two more hunts before the Thanksgiving vacation from school began. My father and brother completed the first week's hunt. I helped them clean the clubhouse and prepare for the second week. School let out on Tuesday afternoon, followed by five straight days of vacation. Man, I thought I had died and gone to heaven. That Tuesday afternoon the school bus driver dropped me off at the Bay Landing Sand Beach. My father was waiting for me with waders and a slicker. We waded out to the *Old Anytime*, which he anchored one hundred yards from the end of the marsh. I would be able to spend the night at the club. I could assist in the Wednesday morning hunt and help clean and secure the club for the holiday. That night the wind shifted to the northeast and blew fifteen to twenty miles per hour. At first light it moderated and held a steady velocity of five to ten miles per hour. This was a perfect wind for the north stilt blind. My father set up the rig and placed two hunters in the blind. Soon they had their limit in diving ducks, and the hunters were rotated until all six hunters had limited out.

My father told me he had a treat for me. He wanted me to pack enough food to last the entire afternoon. He told me to load one of the ammo boxes with two boxes of two- and three-quarter-inch shells. The shells were to be size number-five shot. I was to bring him his gun from the boat. I went to the *Old Anytime* and got his gun. It was a model 11 square-back Remington with a twenty-eight-inch full choke barrel. I handed him the gun.

He changed out the barrel to a twenty-eight-inch modified duck and bird bore. Then he told me that he was going to leave me in the north reef blind. He and my brother were going to take the hunters and their gear to Salvo. When the hunters got in the boat, I climbed up into the stilt blind. He told me to be careful not to walk off the reef into the channel chasing crippled fowl. He gave me an empty grain bag that was weighted with a decoy cord and a small float tied to it. His instructions were not to keep over my limit of ducks inside the blind with me. I was to put them in the bag, walk to the edge of the channel, and toss them into the water. I passed the extra stool to him to make more room in the blind. He left fifteen redhead decoys in place and took up all the rest; then they headed for the clubhouse.

The boat was just entering the edge of the channel when five blackheads landed on the water just outside the decoys. I didn't even have the gun loaded. I fumbled with the ammo box lid to get the shells. All the noise that I was making spooked the ducks. They jumped and flew away before I could get a shot off. I finished loading the gun, engaged the safety button, and leaned it in the corner of the box. I stood up as the two boats left Gull Island Harbor. My father was out front in the *Sandy-K* ferrying the hunters to Salvo. My brother followed in the *Gull Island*, loaded with all the hunter's gear and luggage.

When the boats entered the channel and throttled up, thousands of diving ducks took flight. It was a magnificent sight for a duck hunter's eyes to behold. They had been feeding on the grain that my father had placed around the edge of the channel. The grain began on the outside edge of the north reef, extended along the entire channel, and ended along the edge of the south reef. The baited area formed a horseshoe shape around the island. It was located about 750 yards from any of the hunting locations. Dad had told me many times that the federal game wardens were keeping a watchful eye on the club. He had switched to this graining procedure to be within the legal limits of baiting, and to keep a large volume of waterfowl in the area.

I watched the boats disappear from sight in the direction of Salvo. They were hardly out of sight when I spotted about fifty blackheads approaching upwind from the west of my position. They settled on the water at the edge of the channel and began swimming toward the edge of the reef. As they approached the edge of the reef, they began to dive and feed. The closest edge of the flock was about one hundred yards away from me. I watched as they fed and frolicked. They would take short flights while splashing and scooting along the surface of the water. I could hear their low-pitch babbling as they communicated with each other. Then I spotted a much larger flock of redheads approaching from downwind. They flew to the east side of the blind about eighty yards out and settled on the water with the blackheads. None of the ducks swam close enough to get a good shot. I knew what I had to do. My father and brother had told me many times: If a flock of fowl approaches your location, settles on the water, and refuses to swim to your decoys, you must scare them off. If you allow them to remain, any other fowl that approaches will be drawn to them. You will end up watching the flock grow larger, they will not approach your decoys, and you will not get a shot at them. So I stood up, waved my arms, and shouted. Immediately, the redheads took flight and disappeared out in the sound. The blackheads stretched their necks, bunched up, and turned into the wind. I thought they were going to fly off. Instead, they relaxed, spread out, and resumed feeding. It didn't matter how much noise I made or how much I waved my arms; they would not take flight. I didn't want to fire the gun at them in fear of spooking any other fowl that may be approaching from downwind. I got out of the blind and began to walk toward the blackheads. Finally, after waving my arms and shouting, they flew off toward the east.

I began walking back to the blind. A flock of a dozen blackheads approached from the southeast and lit right in my decoys. I knew instantly that I had made another mistake. I could hear my father's words echoing in my ears. "Never leave the blind without taking your gun with you." Mine was still leaning in the corner of the blind. As I approached the blind, the ducks swam out of the decoys, then jumped and flew off. I climbed back up into the blind. Three geese approached from the south. They adjusted their flight to water level and flew by about twenty yards to my left. This time I was ready. I shot the lead goose in the head; the other two flared. I shot the second goose down and crippled the third one. Two of them were dead, and the third one was badly hurt. He was floating on his back, kicking both feet in the air. I got out of the blind and gave chase. By the time I climbed down the ladder to the water, the cripple had righted himself and was swimming hard toward the edge of the channel. I collected the two dead geese, tied their necks together, and used one of the bag weights to hold them in place. Then I took after the cripple. The closest I could get was within about forty yards of him. He flattened out on the water with just his bill sticking up. I wrapped him up in shot several times, but he continued swimming in the direction of the channel. I chased him until I almost went over the top of my waders and had to give up. I went back for the other two geese and returned to the blind. I was a little upset. I knew if the goose swam off and died, the seagulls would peck his breast off and ruin him.

Soon my attention was averted to a flock of canvasbacks that landed on the water to my leeward and began swimming toward my decoys. This was the beginning of a good duck hunting afternoon for me. I shot all the shells I had. I bagged two bags of assorted redheads, canvasbacks, and blackheads, and two geese.

About an hour before dark I saw my father and brother returning from Salvo in the *Gull Island*. As the boat was about halfway across the channel, she slowed for a second, then throttled up again. They went into the harbor; soon my brother returned towing the decoy skiff. We loaded up the decoys, then picked up the two bags of ducks I had placed in the channel. On the way back to the clubhouse he told me they had picked up a dead goose floating in the middle of the channel. He had spotted a seagull circling over the goose. The seagulls had not picked at the dead goose. I was glad that it would not go to waste. I told him about chasing the cripple. He laughed and told me I should have shot the cripple from the blind when it was closest to me. A good hunter, if possible, makes sure his downed fowl is dead before he leaves the blind. We cleaned up the clubhouse and made it ready for the first hunt after Thanksgiving. I settled inside the cabin, up in the bow, on a couple of life jackets, where I drifted off. They had to wake me up as we entered the harbor at Salvo. We secured the *Gull Island* at the dock and walked up to the house to join my mother.

The next day was Thanksgiving. My grandfather joined us for a big Thanksgiving feast. It was intensely cold outside, and a fine mist of frozen rain was beginning to fall. It was a perfect afternoon to stay indoors. My grandfather and I played a few games of checkers; he normally beat the pants off me. But every now and then, he would let me win a couple of games just to keep me interested. Soon I grew tired of playing and begged him to tell me stories of when he was a boy. I could listen to his stories for hours on end, telling me about growing up in Clarks, now called Salvo, when he was young. He finally gave in and began to tell me about my great-grandfather, the market gunner.

It seems that my ancestors were fishermen, hunters, and gatherers. They used what the land had to offer and never wasted anything they harvested. They worked in harmony with nature and were able to survive and raise their families in harsh and lean times. My great-grandfather was one of the well-known market gunners of his time. His name was Abram Hooper. He and his brother, Rowan Hooper, harvested thousands of waterfowl and shipped them to the northern markets. There was a huge demand for wild fowl on the menus of restaurants in the large cities up north. My great-grandfather and his brother hunted in the Pamlico Sound around the Gull Island area. The Gull Island Reef was one of their favorite locations for market gunning.

They built a twenty-four-foot-long, six-foot-wide at her beam sailboat with a large closed-in cabin. The beam is the widest part of a boat near the center. She had a much longer mast and a larger jib than most boats of her time. They named her the *Black Skimmer*. She was given this name because the way she skimmed along the surface of the water when she was under sail. She was patterned after the smaller single-mast sprit sailboats of the time. The *Black Skimmer* had a large center board with several adjustable height levels. This enabled her to navigate in shallow water. She had a wooden tiller and rudder system attached to her stern for the purpose of steering.

They also built another vessel that was towed around by the *Black Skimmer*. This vessel was twenty-four feet long and fourteen feet wide at the beam. The vessel was bargelike, having a complete house built on her. The house was sixteen feet long and ten feet wide. It had a gable roof and six-foot ceiling height, and was equipped with a woodstove and sleeping quarters to sleep four adults. She was sharp at both ends, or you could say she had two bows. They named her the *Ark*. The two bows gave way to a flat bottom, with four-foot-high sides. The sides were capped over with two feet of washboards on each side. The washboards were designed to enable two adults to push the vessel along with shove sticks on the shallow reefs. The bows were capped over with four feet of flat surface at each end. There was a bolted, heavy constructed metal carriage mounted to each bow cap. These carriages were designed to rotate in a 360-degree circle. They could hold securely in place a six-gauge single-barrel shotgun. These guns were called punt guns. The barrels were four feet long, with a six-inch-diameter bore across the barrels. They were black powder cannons. They broke down like smaller double-barrel shotguns. Six-inch brass shell casings were loaded with many ounces of black powder, and pounds of shot. The ends of the casings contained caps to ignite or light off the powder. These caps could be replaced each time the shell casings were reloaded. The punt guns fit into two carriages mounted on each end of the *Ark*. These guns could not be fired from the shoulder. They had to be securely mounted to the boat.

It normally took three people to complete a market hunt. There would be one person on each side of the *Ark* pushing it along and a gunner on the bow to operate the gun. There was a bracket attached to each side of the house that held a double-barrel ten-gauge shotgun. These guns were used when the hunters walked to the fowl, as well as on the cripples after the larger gun was discharged. Two wheelbarrows were attached to the vessel. One was secured on either side of the entry door to the shack.

The *Black Skimmer* and the *Ark* were much too large to navigate the shallow inshore ditches. These ditches harbored most of the smaller skiffs. They had to be anchored offshore at the edge of deeper water. Their location was a few hundred yards from the shoreline. All the supplies and hunting gear had to be transported out to them in smaller shove skiffs. Before each hunt the vessels would be stocked with enough supplies to last for a couple of weeks. In those days the weather was bitter cold. It got cold near the beginning of November and stayed cold until the end of April. It was not out of the ordinary for the temperature to remain well below freezing until the middle of March. Refrigeration was not a problem.

On one of these hunts my grandfather was allowed to go along. Every other hunt would be in the Gull Island area. The other preferred location was the Pea Island area. This particular hunt was bound for the Gull Island reefs. The vessels were stocked with provisions and began the trip southward toward the island. They left Clarks around midday. The *Black Skimmer* moved smoothly along through the two-foot waves. She was being propelled by a ten- to fifteen-mile-per-hour northeast wind. The *Ark* was under tow about forty-five yards to the stern of the *Skimmer*. My grandfather and his uncle Rowan were aboard the *Ark*, fixing the evening meal. The meal consisted of a large pot of big lima beans and hot biscuits. They sailed along the shoreline until they reached Cedar Hammock Marsh. Then they changed course to the wind and sailed around the outside of the north reef at Gull Island. They continued on around the back of the island and anchored the *Skimmer* behind the south reef in deep water. My great-grandfather Abram joined him, brother Rowan, and his son, Aaron, on the *Ark*. Aaron and Rowan began to shove the *Ark* along the back edge of the south reef with shove poles. Abram was perched on the bow scanning the reef with a spyglass. He was looking for flocks of fowl returning to the reef after feeding on the eel grasses in the shallow portions of the sound. Soon he spotted a large raft of geese gathering near the center of the reef. He gave the command to anchor the *Ark*. They all went inside the shack, sat to the table, and dished out the beans and biscuits. Over their evening meal they discussed the plan for the first night's hunt.

Abram decided that his son, Aaron, would carry the light. Abram and his brother, Rowan, would do the shooting with the two double-barrel twelve-gauge shotguns. The plan was to watch the mounting flock of geese, wait until after dark, light up the fire lighting box, and slowly walk to the geese. The fire lighting box consisted of a rectangular box with one side open. Mirrors were attached inside of the box on the back and both sides. It had a strap that fastened around the carrier's midsection. There were two shoulder straps that were placed over the shoulders and crossed in the center of the back. These two straps were designed to fasten to the top of the midsection strap. The carrier of the lighting box placed it on himself like a backpack in reverse. A kerosene lantern was placed in the center of the box. It was always lighted just after dark. As soon as it was dark enough, the three hunters began making their walk toward the large flock of geese. This plan was used because the reef itself was completely dry. The northeast wind pushed the water to different portions of the sound, away from Gull Island. Aaron placed the lighting box on the front of his body and fastened the straps. Another kerosene lantern was always lit and attached to the bow of the *Ark* before the hunters left the boat.

Cautiously, the hunters inched forward in the direction of the geese. The approach was always made from downwind. The hunters were guided by the constant cackling. With this method the hunters were able to walk within a few yards of the geese. On the ready from Abram, the shots were fired. All four barrels of the ten-gauge shotguns were discharged into the flock of geese. Dead geese were everywhere; cripples were flopping in all directions. When all the cripples were harvested, all the geese were placed into a pile. Abram sent Aaron and Rowan back to the *Ark* to fetch the two wheelbarrows. He remained with the fowl and the fire lighting box. Aaron and Rowan carried three wheelbarrow loads of fowl each back to the *Ark*.

When all three hunters returned to the *Ark*, they prepared the geese for shipment. The fowl were put into light canvas bags, one dozen per bag, and placed into wooded shipping crates. The top of each of these crates were nailed securely in place. The crates were stacked outside the shack. There were twenty-five crates of geese harvested on the first night's hunt. The hunters, exhausted, retired for the night.

The daytime hours were used up watching the movements of the fowl: when they left the reef and when they returned. Abram observed a large raft of diving ducks feeding on the eel grass beds to the southeast of their location. At dark he placed the lighted fire lighting box on the bow of the *Ark*. He attached both punt guns in their brackets. The anchor was brought aboard the *Ark*, and they were on their way to the second hunt of the trip. Aaron and Rowan, at the direction of Abram, pushed the *Ark* down past the large raft of diving ducks on the leeward side of the flock. They approached from downwind as quietly as possible. When they were within range, Aaron held the *Ark* in place with a shove pole. Rowan joined Abram on the bow and manned the other punt gun. Both punt guns were fired into the flock of diving ducks. Aaron hastily passed both ten-gauge guns forward to his father and uncle. He stood ready with extra shells in hand as the two men finished off all the crippled fowl. They retrieved all the ducks and packed them in the same manner as the geese. The ducks were packed two dozen per crate. There were thirty crates of ducks stored. The three hunters stayed at the Gull Island reefs for a two-week hunt. At the end of the hunt they sailed back to Clarks with a deck full of packed crates. The crates of fowl were shipped on a larger vessel to the northern markets.

# CHAPTER TWENTY-SEVEN

# The Lacey Act

My grandfather was interrupted by my mother asking if we wanted anything else to eat before she put the food away for the night. I looked outside; it was twilight, almost dark. In November darkness comes early. We ate a few leftovers from the midday Thanksgiving feast. I asked him about resuming his tales about his experiences with market gunning. He told me to go home with him for the night and he would continue with the stories. My mother packed some food so that we could have a nighttime snack. We walked over to Grandpop's house. He was living alone these days; my grandmother had passed a couple of years before. The warmth from his potbellied woodstove was a welcome change from the bitter cold outside. We sat at his kitchen table. He put a pot of coffee on. A smile developed on his face, and he resumed telling me about his childhood adventures with his father.

During the warmer months when the waterfowl left the area, they did a lot of fishing. In the summertime they would fish out back of the reef in deep water. Long nets would let out from the back end of the *Ark* as they sailed along. The nets would be allowed to remain for a couple of hours. Then they would be pulled aboard and the fish taken out of them. The fish had to be immediately gutted, salted, and placed in a brine box. The brine box was like a modern-day fish box. Instead of using ice, salt was used to preserve the catch. Layers and layers of salted fish were usually inside the brine box. The *Ark* was equipped with ten brine boxes. A fishing trip would not be concluded until all the brine boxes were full of fish. When the brine boxes were topped off, the fishermen returned home. The salted catch had to be transferred to wooden crates for shipping.

My grandfather began telling me of a summer fishing trip for bluefish down near the Cape. The Cape is the former name for the town of Buxton. The town was given this name because of its close proximity to Cape Point. The northern part of Hatteras Island runs almost in a north/south direction. The Cape is the turning point to an almost east/west direction. There is an area located just to the north of the Cape called the Haul Over. This is a thin, flat strip of land separating the ocean from the sound. This strip of land was narrow enough to allow small boats to be hauled across the sand to the ocean.

My great-grandfather Abram, my grandfather Aaron, and my grandfather's uncle Rowan set out on a bluefishing trip down to the Cape. They formulated a plan for Abram and Aaron to sail the *Black Skimmer* down to the Cape. They took the *Ark* and a smaller sea skiff in tow down to the Haul Over. Rowan would travel down in a horse and cart. They began their journey in the first week of the month of June. Word had been passed along that thousands of bluefish were migrating north along the beach. Abram and Aaron had a fair wind from the northeast. They sailed along making good time without very many tacks. They reached the Cape area before Rowan. The *Skimmer* and the *Ark* were anchored offshore in deep water. The smaller sea skiff was rowed to shore to gather information about the location of the fish and to wait for Rowan. Abram talked to a couple of fisherman who lived at the Cape. They had made daily sets, but caught small numbers of fish. It seemed that the larger schools of fish were close, but they had not made it around the point of the beach at the Cape. They were still located in the south beach area.

This news gave them time to make everything ready. Abram and Aaron went back to the *Ark* and made sure the gear was ready to be used. They checked the boats to make sure they were moored securely and returned to shore. They waited for Rowan to arrive. When he arrived, they set up a shore camp. They would camp on the shore unless heavy weather forced them back aboard the *Ark*. They made ready to set the nets the next day.

At first light they hitched the horse to the sea skiff, with the nets inside, and pulled her over to the beach. They waited until it was good and light and looked for signs of fish. The northeast wind had the ocean chopped up. There was a two- to three-foot shore break. The sea was running strong in a southerly direction. There was an outside bar about one hundred yards offshore. It was about two hundred yards in length, with four- to five-foot waves breaking near its center. An occasional wave of six to eight feet in height would form on the backside of the bar. The larger waves would come crashing down, causing two feet of whitewater to roll across the bar. After each of these larger waves broke, there was a lull until the next one formed.

There was an outlet at each end of the bar. They pulled their skiff to the most northerly located outlet and made ready to launch. They were soon joined by two other sea skiffs. Still there was no sign of fish. Abram was standing on the bow of the sea skiff. He was scanning the horizon in a southerly direction with a spyglass. He indicated that he could see large flocks of gulls circling out of eyesight to the south. It looked like a large school of fish was approaching about an hour away. The men made a last check of their gear. The birds were soon visible to the eye. They were working the outside edge of the bar. All three boats put to sea. The men strained on their oars to gain a favorable position ahead of the large school of fish. Abram's crew was located between the two other boats. The three skiffs were swept south by the tide. By the time they reached the inside edge of the bar, they were located near its center. All three crews held their position just inside the bar as they slowly drifted southward. After a huge wave crashed and a lull came, the crew out in front pulled for the bar. They were trying to row across before another wave formed. As they neared the center of the bar, they topped a couple of four- to five-foot waves. It appeared that they were going to make it out past the outside break. Then a couple of larger waves formed outside and came swirling toward the skiff. The crew inside the skiff rowed with all the strength they could muster. As the first wave approached the bow of the small sea skiff, it rose up to an almost vertical position. The skiff just did make it over the top of the wave. It made a loud crashing sound as it slammed back down on the bar. The men in the skiff hardly had enough time to recover from the first monster-size wave when they were faced with another. This wave rose up to about ten feet above the bar. Again, they pulled on the oars with all their might, but this time it was not meant to be. The skiff rose up the front side of the wave. It appeared for a moment that the skiff might make it over the top. Once again, the small skiff was almost in a vertical position when it began to slide backward. It slid down the front side of the wave, turned parallel to the beach, and was drawn up to the crest of the wave. When the wave broke, the skiff was slammed upside down on the shallow bar. All three men were thrown out with the nets and gear landing on top of them. The fishing trip for Abram, Aaron, and Rowan quickly turned into a rescue mission.

The third skiff was too far away to be of any assistance. The overturned skiff was quickly washed past them, propelled by the foaming whitewater. The fishermen were tangled in the yards of net webbing, in water over their heads, in the middle of the bar. Wave after wave broke on them. Each wave forced them below the surface. It was a struggle for them to catch a breath of air. Abram's crew was able to secure one end of the webbing to their skiff. They began to row parallel with the beach with the flow of the tide. The tidal flow, along with the rowing of the skiff, enabled them to begin pulling the tangled net out into a straight line. When the men in the water realized what was happening, they grabbed the end of the net as it straightened out. Two of them were pulled off the bar in calmer water. The eldest of the three fishermen in the water was not close enough to the end of the net to grasp. He was able to make his way to the beachside edge of the sandbar. Waves were constantly breaking behind him; the depth of the water was well over his head. He was able to allow himself to sink to the bottom and push hard with his feet, and propel himself to the surface for a breath between waves. When the two men were clear of the net, Abram ordered his crew to return and pick them up. The elder fisherman was able to continue his bobbing to the surface until he was picked up by Abram's skiff. It was mid-afternoon when all the men and the gear were straightened out and back on the beach. They would have to wait and try to make a set the next day.

The next day was more favorable for the fishermen. The northeast wind had moderated, and the waves decreased in size. The fishermen were able to make successful sets on the bluefish. They rowed out past the bar and set their nets in front of the large schools of fish. Abram, Aaron, and Rowan stayed in the Cape area until all their crates were full of salt-cured bluefish. They shipped their catch and returned home to Clarks.

When summertime fishing came to an end, their attention shifted to the large schools of mullet migrating along the shoreline. Lord knows how far the mullets travel south. During the months of September and October, large schools of them form up. These schools travel in a southerly direction along the marsh on the sound side and along the beach on the ocean side of the island. Abram, Aaron, and Rowan planned to make a trip up the sound side of the island to the Oregon Inlet Bay area to fish for mullet.

At this point my grandfather stopped his story and announced it was time for bed. I begged him to continue, but he told me he would continue with the Oregon Inlet mullet trip another time. I slept upstairs at my grandfather's house. It was an ancient structure. The cooking and eating area was built separate from the sitting and sleeping areas. It consisted of two structures separated by a breezeway. My quarters were very warm. The bedroom where I slept was located directly above the woodstove that heated the house. It was normally warm as toast up there.

I was awakened by voices the next morning around six o'clock. I went down to the living area of the house. My father had come over from our house. They were just heading over to the kitchen as I walked down the steps. When we went outside to the breezeway, the cold hit me like a ton of bricks. Freezing mist was still falling, but the wind had shifted to the southeast. It had increased in velocity to about forty-five to fifty miles per hour. As we entered the kitchen, the smell of fresh-perked coffee filled the room. My grandfather had a pan of cheese biscuits in the oven. One of these biscuits and a cup of coffee was all the breakfast anyone needed. As we ate, I listened to the conversation they were having. My father wanted to make a trip to the island to feed the fowl. The hard southeaster had pushed all the water to the other side of the sound. The boats were resting on the bottom in the harbor. The shoals were exposed as far as you could see. My father had to change his plans until the wind changed and the water came back in. He was going to walk out on the shoals and gather oysters and any fish he could find trapped in shallow pools of water. He wanted to know if I wanted to go along with him. He told me ahead of time that we would be in waders and oilskins all afternoon. I jumped at the chance to go along with him. He told my grandfather we would bring him some oysters and fish if we found any.

We went over to our house and dressed for our walk out on the shoals. My father took a yard rake along. He had fastened chicken wire into it to form a basket to pick up oysters with. He also took along a hammer to beat oyster clusters apart. He placed these items inside a wheelbarrow. Then he told me to bring the other wheelbarrow and follow him. I followed him across the marsh to the edge of the sound. We easily pushed the wheelbarrows across the shallows. As soon as we were a short distance from the marsh, we began to come up on single oysters embedded in the bottom. He began to dig them out with the rake. Soon we had a wheelbarrow full. We left the first wheelbarrow full of oysters and continued on. We checked each shallow pool of water that we approached. In one pool we caught four good-size flounders and two speckled trout. When the last wheelbarrow was full of oysters and a number of fish, we started back. When we returned home, we all went over to my grandfather's house. My mother came along to cook the evening meal. My grandfather began to open oysters, and my father cleaned the fish. My mom had me peeling potatoes as she mixed up cornmeal for cornbread. We had a fine meal of fried oysters, fried fish, coleslaw, and cornbread. My father put half of the oysters that were left in baskets and placed them in Grandpop's outside shed. My grandfather and I remained at the table for a piece of apple pie. I began to aggravate him about the mullet trip to the Oregon Inlet area. He smiled, rolled his eyes and asked my mom for another cup of coffee. He folded his hands together and began.

Abram, Aaron, and Rowan sailed the *Black Skimmer*, towing the *Ark* and a mullet skiff up to the Oregon Inlet Bay area. They anchored the *Skimmer* and *Ark* in deep water. It took most of the day to get to sail up to the mullet grounds. They were facing into a light northeast wind and had to make a few tacks to get there. After the evening meal on the *Ark* they settled in for the night. At first light the next morning they took the mullet skiff and paddled up alongside the shore. Just after daylight they spotted a large school of mullet. The fish were moving down the shoreline in a southerly direction. Aaron jumped out on the shore, pulling the wooden staff behind him. The wooden staff was fastened to the end of the mullet net. Abram shoved the skiff with a shove paddle offshore and turned in a northerly direction. Rowan remained in the stern of the skiff. His job was to watch the net play out over the stern without any overlays or tangles. Abram continued on and circled the fish, then shoved the skiff back to shore. They pulled the net ashore and caught the entire school of mullet. They repeated this process several times during the next week. Soon all their shipping crates were full of salted mullet. My grandfather finished up his story.

We had another piece of pie and a last cup of coffee for the night. My mother finished cleaning up the kitchen. We said good night to my grandfather and left for our house. The wind had shifted to the west; the depth of the water increased in the sound. My father and I would be able take grain to the island the next day.

My grandfather told me many tales of his childhood days growing up in Clarks. I enjoyed them so much; I would sit for hours on end listening and asking questions of how it was back then. In those days everyone lived off the land and used the products it provided for their livelihoods. Most of the occupants all along the Eastern Seaboard made a living harvesting waterfowl and fish. They shipped them to out-of-state markets up north. The Lacey Act of 1900 made this practice illegal. It was introduced into Congress by John F. Lacey, a Republican from Iowa. It was signed into law by President William McKinley on May 25, 1900. With the passing of this law, my ancestors were out of the market hunting business. Fish houses were established on the local level. Commercial fisherman sold their catch to a fish buyer. Then the fish were packed and shipped. But the thrill of market hunting and shipping large numbers of waterfowl came to an end. My relatives continued to fish commercially, gathering and selling oysters, clams, and scallops. They became commercial sport hunting guides. All types of blinds were set up, and hunting trips for well-to-do sportsmen, who could pay, were scheduled. On occasions, market gunning trips still occurred, and the fowl were shipped on the sly.

# CHAPTER TWENTY-EIGHT

# Live Decoys

One Sunday afternoon after church, my grandfather came over to have Sunday dinner with us. After the meal I begged him to tell me more hunting and fishing stories. My mom told me to leave him alone and at least let him finish his dessert. When he finished his pie, he agreed to tell me more stories. To my delight, he began by telling my about my father as a boy hunting and fishing with him. He settled in a padded rocking chair and began to spin his yarn.

When my great-grandfather Abram passed away, my grandfather Aaron inherited the *Ark* and the sailing vessel, the *Black Skimmer*. My grandfather Aaron and his eldest son, Edward, my father, hunted and fished the Pamlico Sound area near Gull Island. They had two prime hunting locations near the Clarks area. One of these was located on the Opening Shoals just to the north of Clarks. The Opening Shoals blind was located about five hundred yards from the back of the marsh. The other was located on the center of Sheep's Head Shoals, about a mile straight to the west of my grandfather's ditch. They hunted the Bay Shoals area northeast of Gull Island, the northwest Gull Island Reef, and the south reef between Little Hills and Gull Island. These locations were hunted with a battery box.

The battery box was a boat type of lay-down blind. It was decked over with watertight compartments. These compartments could be flooded to cause the box to sink down level with the surface of the water. It was equipped with an adjustable, waterproof canvas curtain. This curtain could be raised and lowered from the hunting compartment. The top of the blind was kept just above the water's surface. There was a wing or a wooden slatted sea breaker. The wing was constructed of one-by-four and it fit completely around the blind, with the exception of the back. This sea breaker was always anchored into the wind in front of the blind. Its purpose was to keep the waves from splashing over the top of the submerged blind.

When the blind was fixed into place, the hunters would rest on their backs on cushions, facing each other. Each hunter had the responsibility of watching 180 degrees in two directions. One hunter kept an eye out north and east, while the other watched south and west. This type of hunting blind was so effective because it was portable. It could be moved to any desired location.

Another concept that made these blinds so effective was the use of live fowl for decoys. The hunting guides raised waterfowl from gosling and duckling stage to adult geese and ducks. The guides trained these fowl to leave their pens in the morning hours and follow them to the hunting boats. In the boats they had fowl coops, or enclosed boxes, that the fowl rode inside to the hunting location. The training took many long, patient hours of work with the fowl. In each flock of geese there is a dominant gander, or male goose. The same applies with ducks. Mallards were chosen to train. The task of the hunting guide was to train these lead males in each stand of live decoys. Once these leaders were trained, most of the flock would follow. The left wing flight feathers of each bird were kept cut short to prevent flight. Each bird was equipped with a soft leather band around its left leg. This band would be attached to a tether that was fastened to a wooden peg that was driven into the bottom. This arrangement kept the live decoys from swimming off. Normally, the ducks were set to the windward of the blind. The geese would be set to the leeward of the box.

The hunters had to be extremely careful when they harvested fowl. The best idea was to shoot everything in the air before it landed. If water shots were taken, they were taken only if all the live decoys were in the clear, and there was no chance they would be hit by the shot. These live decoys were a prized possession of the hunting guides. They raised them like pets and worked many long hours training them.

My grandfather told me about the stand of live decoys he and my father trained and worked. Both of them were involved in the training of the fowl. They first worked with the geese. The dominant gander was chosen. They tamed him so that either of them could handle him at will and pick him up with their hands. Then they isolated him from the flock and gave him only water for a day, no food. The next day they placed a trail of corn from the gander's pen to the boat. He followed the corn trail to the boat. They kept placing less and less corn along the trail until the only grain was placed inside the traveling coop, aboard the boat.

Weeks before the hunting season the geese were only fed each morning inside the coops, located on the hunting boat. My grandfather told me it was a sight to see on any given hunting morning. First, the grain was placed in a galvanized ten-quart water bucket. The geese were let out of the pen. He shook the bucket as he walked toward the boat. This allowed the geese to hear the grain in the bucket. The lead gander followed along behind him, and the rest of the geese followed the gander like marching soldiers. The coop door was opened and the geese walked inside; then they were fed the grain. My father followed at the rear of the procession to keep any stragglers from wandering off. The mallard ducks were trained in the same manner.

At this particular time there was no daily bag limit on the fowl. During hunts it was not out of the ordinary for over one hundred fowl to be harvested in a day's time. The location of the battery blind setup was determined by the existing weather conditions on any given hunting day. The wind velocity, direction, and the depth of the water were the three main factors deciding the day's hunting spot. If the wind blew hard from the north, the depth of the water was very low at the northern end of Hatteras Island. A location was selected that had ample natural food. The low water levels allowed shallow water feeding on eel grass and other natural food. The water levels were much too deep on average tides to hunt these locations. Any strong winds from the west created high water levels and permitted hunting on reefs that were high and dry on normal tidal days. The battery box location would be decided, and the gear set up. The box itself would be located on a shallow reef to allow wading to retrieve downed fowl. The blind would be anchored from the front with a boat anchor. There were two lines attached to the back of the blind. These lines had a long metal pin at the end of them. These pins were driven into the bottom, creating a three-point anchoring system for the floating battery box. At point, the curtain attached to the hunting area would be raised to its highest position. Then the sealed compartments were flooded, settling the blind just above the surface of the water. The wing or sea breaker would be placed around the box and anchored at three locations like the box. The waterproof curtain would be adjusted and secured at this point. Then each live bird would be set out around the secured hunting blind. Each tether had to be attached, and the pegs driven into the bottom.

As soon as the live decoys were set out, they began to flap their wings and dip their heads under the surface of the water. They were constantly talking to each other and any wild fowl that approached. When you were off a short distance from such a setup, it was truly a natural flock of fowl sitting on the water's surface.

These hunting setups were successful in the commercial sport hunting business. With the adoption of the migratory bird hunting laws of the 1930s came a flood of waterfowl laws. Soon there was legislation prohibiting battery box hunting. A short time after that, the use of live decoys for hunting was banned. The next set of regulations set aside certain months of the year for hunting. This was the implementation of the first hunting seasons. Hunters could no longer hunt until the fowl left at the end of cold weather. They had to hunt during the months set aside for hunting season. The hunting seasons usually began sometime in November and lasted until late January.

This put a huge crimp in my grandfather's commercial hunting guide service. The hunting parties were restricted to a three-month period. My father grew up hunting and fishing commercially with my grandfather. He was involved in this activity until 1918, when he enlisted in the navy. My father remained in the navy for a period of four years. He received his discharge and returned home to resume work with my grandfather. During the next three years they hunted and fished the area around Gull Island.

Since they were no longer able to use live fowl for decoys, my grandfather came up with a plan that implemented one live calling goose, as he called it, and one rather vocal female mallard duck. He trained them as pets and could handle them at will. He kept these two fowl isolated from the rest of the fowl in their flocks. They were kept in separate pens with their chosen mates. Whenever he separated them from their mates, they began calling, and their mates would answer them. At the blind locations he turned them loose among the wooden decoys. Their flight feathers were clipped on their left wing to prevent flight. He trained them to be accustomed to the discharge of a shotgun by shooting close to them many times. Whenever a flock of fowl would approach, they would begin calling to them. If they were approached by the game wardens, the hunters were instructed to shoot the live decoys. The two pet fowl would hang around the blind setup until each hunt was ended. All my grandfather had to do was call to them. They would swim over to him and allow him to place them in their travel coops. This was a successful method, and was used by my grandfather for many years. The game wardens never came, and his pet fowl lived long and happy lives.

At the end of three years, my father rejoined the military. He signed up for a stint in the Coast Guard.

At this point my grandfather ended his tale for the night. He told me that he was tired and promised to tell me more stories at a later date. He had one last cup of coffee and left for home. I watched him walk down the narrow path that separated his house from ours. I was shocked back to reality by my mother's voice. She told me it was bed time; tomorrow was a school day. It was that awkward time of year between Thanksgiving vacation and Christmas vacation: the aggravation of being cooped up in the classroom after a short taste of freedom, with the anticipation of more freedom on the way. Hardly anything ever gets accomplished in the classroom during this period of time. In just a few days I would be on Christmas vacation and able to hunt with my brother and father out at Gull Island.

Finally, after what seemed to be a lifetime, the last day of school before Christmas arrived. My father and brother were out at the island with a hunting party. When I arrived home my mother told me that my brother would be coming to shore the next morning. She helped me pack my hunting gear. My brother arrived mid-morning the next day. I was already at the harbor waiting for him. He had several bags of fowl to drop off to the lady who cleaned and packed them. He had a dozen empty five-gallon gas cans. While he took the fowl to be dressed, he wanted me to fill up the cans from the buried bulk tank. The bulk tank was buried to ground level with a hand-operated push-and-pull filler pump. I filled each can and loaded them on the *Gull Island* while waiting for my brother. As soon as he came back, I untied the boat, and he guided it out of the harbor. He told me I could pilot the boat out to the island. Operating the boats was always a treat for me. In those days I really thought I was doing something. I imagined myself as a hunting guide. The real deal was that my father and brother both had to keep a constant eye on me. They watched me, taught me everything I know about fishing and hunting, and tried to involve me as much as possible in their daily duties as hunting guides. They assigned me tasks that I could handle, and made me feel as if I was an important part of the club.

The hunt before Christmas ended, and we celebrated the holiday. Then we returned to the island for the week-after-Christmas hunt. On this hunt, a low-pressure area was approaching. On the first day the wind blew from the southeast and rained all day. The water levels were so low that we were unable to get a boat out of the harbor at the island. The air temperature outside was mild for winter time. My father knew the game wardens could not fly in weather and could not reach us in a boat because of the low water. He gave me a single-barrel cripple gun and a shell belt filled with seven-and-one-half-size shot. He told me to dress light, walk to the south reef, and harvest a mess of shorebirds. I was delighted. As I made ready to go, my brother gave me some last-minute instructions. He cautioned me about handling the gun and told me to take an empty feed bag for the birds. If I saw anyone approaching I was to drop the bag and walk straight back to the clubhouse.

I left the clubhouse and walked to the south reef, which was high and dry. As long as you walked slowly, it was not out of the ordinary to get within good gunshot range of the shorebirds. I walked almost to the end of the south reef and harvested about half of a bag of willets, curlews, and snipe. When I returned, my father and I skinned the birds, and he put the pie bread to them. This is a meal similar to Hatteras Island–style stewed chicken and pastry. But for anyone who has acquired a taste for wild game, this shorebird stew is an outstanding meal.

The wind shifted to the northwest during the night. The temperature dropped about fifteen to twenty degrees. The water levels increased to the point that everything was covered with the exception of the southeast reef. This was a perfect morning to hunt the south reef high-water curtain box. That was the location chosen for the day's hunt. My father and brother left the hunters inside the protection of the cabin of the *Gull Island*, anchored at the edge of the channel. They pulled the curtain above the surface of the water and gave me a five-gallon bucket to begin bailing out the box. They adjusted the wing and began setting out the decoys. I had to bail the box down where I could use a small scoop, then a sponge to remove all the water. Then my brother used the decoy boat to bring the hunters to the box. We left the blind and returned to the club. My brother kept an eye on the blind while my father and I cleaned up from breakfast. When the galley was squared away, I went outside and climbed on the roof where my brother was. I relieved him; he went inside to warm up and have coffee. I wiped off the lens on the binoculars and looked in the direction of the sink box. I checked to the south and north of the blind. I didn't see any fowl in either direction. Then I spotted what looked to be a small flock of sprigtails approaching the blind from the east. They didn't land to the blind; they just flew by. I don't think the hunters even saw them. Soon after that, another flock came in and landed to the decoys. It is funny how the laws of physics apply even to hunting. Looking at the blind you could see the water spray up into the air as the shot struck the surface, but it took several seconds before you could hear the report of the guns. This is just another situation that proves that light travels faster than sound. This was the beginning of a good hunt on the south reef for that day. We replaced the hunters several times that day as they reached their daily bag limits of fowl. Just before dusk we went to take up the spread. My brother took the hunters to the clubhouse aboard the *Gull Island*. My father and I took up the decoys, moved the wing, and flooded and stabilized the sink box. I got my feet tangled up in one of the chains to the wing and fell head-first down in the water. I was wet to the skin. I thought I was going to freeze before we got back to the clubhouse.

# The New Clubhouse

It was a cold ride back to the clubhouse. All my clothes were wet. My father secured the boats so that I could get inside. The warmth of the gas heater began to thaw me out. I quickly undressed, showered, and put on dry clothes. I dried my hunting clothes by the heater, dumped the water from my waders, and dried my jumper. I sat close by the heater and drank a cup of hot coffee. I could feel my feet and lower body begin to return to normal.

That season, and the next four or five seasons, were successful ones. These seasons ended with a large number of waterfowl harvested. Membership in the club had increased to over two dozen charter members. All of these members had family and friends they wanted to invite on hunts. There was just not enough room in the tarpaper shack to accommodate all the hunters.

Mr. Kotarides decided it was time for a new clubhouse. When the current hunting season came to an end, Mr. Kotarides stayed an extra week at the club. He discussed his plan with my father for the construction of a new clubhouse. He wanted my father to close all the blinds and secure all the hunting gear, just as he did at the end of any season. Then, as soon as possible, he wanted my father to hire extra men and begin to demolish the existing shack that they had been using as a clubhouse. He was going back to Norfolk, Virginia, to meet with an architect to begin planning the new clubhouse. He wanted my father to try to find a builder who could manage a large group of men and complete the clubhouse before the next hunting season. It took a bit of time to remove the curtain from the sink boxes. The wings or sea breakers had to be pulled up on the island, and repairs made if needed. The shore blinds and stilt blinds had to be secured. All the decoys had to be taken to Salvo. There they were removed from the decoy boats. All of the spans and weights were removed. Then they were sent to Norfolk for repairs and repainting. Normally we would take about two months to complete all this work. However, this year, finishing the work in a timely manner was a concern. Everything was completed in one month's time.

It was the end of the 1963 hunting season. My father hired my cousin, Leslie Hooper, as well as Uncle Bill Hennant, Mr. Perry Farrow, and I. D. Midgett to help with the demolition of the tarpaper shack that had served us well as a clubhouse. At the end of each hunting season my brother had to report back to work. He worked with the State Highway Department, usually at an off-island location. He saved up his vacation days each year and took off to help my father each hunting season. I could only be involved on the weekends because I was still in school. The first week my father and his crew built huge racks on two of the larger decoy boats. They converted them into lumber carriers.

Then the demolition began. The first step was to remove anything of value from inside the clubhouse. These items were taken back to Salvo and stored for future use. All these items were loaded on the two decoy skiffs and towed back to the main island. At this point, taking apart the shack began. First, all the ninety-weight rolled roofing was taken off the roof and sides. This was messy work: the roof was not only nailed, it was attached to the roof deck with liquid tar. This tar had cured over the years, and the roofing came off in small pieces. A few of the members of the crew wanted to cut the roof off in chunks. My father insisted that the roofing material be removed and each roof board be taken off separately. When all the rolled roofing was removed from the roof and sides, then came the roof deck boards and the rafters. At this point, the ceiling joists were removed. The next step was the removal of the interior walls. The exterior walls were braced and removed one by one. He insisted that all the nails be removed from each board separately. He placed all nails in buckets and saved them. All the pine boards that he thought could be reused were stacked separately. Boatload after boatload of scraps were taken to Salvo. This scrap was burned in watched burn barrels.

The last phase of demolition was the pumping up of the creosote pilings. They had been used to hold the floor in place. An air-cooled powered water pump equipped with long rubber hose and a galvanized metal pipe was attached to the discharge. This metal pipe was about eight feet long. The end of it had been pounded with a sledgehammer to squeeze it together, creating more pressure as the water was pumped through it. This piece of metal was called a jet. The process of removing the pilings was a lengthy and difficult job. They were sixteen feet long and had been pumped at least eight feet below the surface of the muddy soil. They were much easier to install than to remove. When they are installed, the weight of the piling and gravity help in the process of pumping them in. In the removal process there are three forces that work against the pulling up of a piling: the weight of the piling, gravity, and the suction of the muddy soil on the sides of each piling, which has to be broken. The process involves many gallons of water pumped along the sides of each piling. They had to be pushed and pulled back and forth in a rapid manner to loosen up the forces of suction on their sides. A long piece of chain was placed over the top of each piling. The chain was tied to the piling using two half hitches. Two half hitches are usually used as a boat mooring knot. The chain was attached to a long six-by-six piling used as a pry to place upward forces on the piling. As the suction was broken, and the piling began to come up, the chain would drop down on the piling when the end of pry was lifted. Then the chain would come tight and grip the side of the piling when downward pressure was placed on the pry. This removal process took four men to extract each piling—one man on the pump, two men working the piling, and one man applying the upward force with the pry. As the piling inched to the surface and the end came out of the mud, it had to be man handled and placed horizontally on the ground. In the old shack there were twenty-four pilings that made up the foundation.

The process was repeated until all the pilings had been removed. The pilings and any other type of material that my father decided could be reused was stacked in organized piles.

On one of the weekends when my brother was home, he introduced my father to a builder who had just moved to the area. This man's name was Hubert Conner. He had moved his family to Salvo from Churchland, Virginia. My brother had met him and his family in church. They were Methodist and had joined Clark's Bethel Church in Salvo. My brother's wife, Jean, and her family have always been a main part of this church and its operation over the years. Mr. Conner had purchased a large piece of land and was building a huge structure that would serve as a store and a dwelling combination. His family had temporary lodging in a travel trailer they brought with them. The travel trailer also served as their construction headquarters. Mr. Conner had finished the construction phase of his project by the middle of May. The store was about forty feet wide by sixty feet long. The dwelling unit was built on the north end of the store above a two-car garage. His family moved in the dwelling at the end of May. They stocked and opened the store by the first of April. They named it Conner's Stop and Shop. The store today is named the Blue Whale.

Mr. Hubert Conner and his family were new to the area. He had a brother, Mr. John Frank Conner, who had moved to the area some years earlier. Mr. John Frank and his family were also storekeepers. They first operated a large store and tackle shop located near the ferry landing on the south side of Oregon Inlet. Their son, Johnny, and daughter, Merian, drove the family car each day eighteen miles one way down to Rodanthe. In Rodanthe they caught the school bus to the school that was located in Buxton. That family moved to the town of Buxton and opened another store. Today this store is Conner's Supermarket, a modern, thriving business providing jobs for a number of Hatteras Island residents.

It was the spring of 1963. The Oregon Inlet ferry system had been replaced by a bridge. This began to open the island to a multitude of changes. The demand on the gunning club would be greater than ever. The planning for the construction of a bigger and better clubhouse at Gull Island was being implemented in the nick of time.

Mr. Kotarides had finished up the work with the architect on the blue prints for the new clubhouse. He mailed two copies of the construction plans to my father. One copy my father would keep, and the other he would give to the prospective builder. My father asked my brother to invite Mr. Hubert Conner and his family over for supper. My father wanted to meet his family, have a meal with them, and discuss the possibility of him being the builder of the new clubhouse. It would be similar to the project he had just finished. My father asked my mother about a time for the meeting. She told him the upcoming Saturday night would be good if the Conners could make it. They agreed to my brother's invitation and arrived at our house Saturday around six o'clock in the evening. There were three of them in the family: Mr. Conner, his wife, Norma, and one son named Bud. My mother told us it would be about thirty minutes before we ate. She told us she would call when it was time to assemble at the table. Mrs. Conner joined my mom in the kitchen; my dad, Mr. Conner, Bud, and I walked down to the harbor. My dad wanted Mr. Conner to understand this project would be constructed on an island out in the sound. He told him that it would be a hunting lodge replacement, and all the material would have to be loaded on boats and taken out to the island. Bud wanted to get a closer look at all the boats. I answered his questions, and we boarded each of the boats. He wanted to know when we could ride in one of them. I told him I would ask my father to take us for a ride after church the next day. At about that time my mom hollered for us: the food was ready. We walked back to the house for supper. After we finished eating, the table was cleared. My dad and Mr. Conner sat at the table to look over the clubhouse prints. After a lengthy discussion, Mr. Conner told my father he was interested in building the clubhouse. He was not concerned about building on an island. However, he would like to see the building site before making his final decision. My dad agreed. After church the next day they would ride out to the island. Bud and I looked at each other and smiled.

The next day around two o'clock in the afternoon, my dad, Mr. Conner, Bud, and I took a boat ride out to the island. It was the beginning of April. The wind was light out of the southwest. We made good time aboard the *Gull Island*. Soon we were entering the harbor at the island. Mr. Conner looked over the construction site. He agreed to build the structure from the floor system to a finished product. He only had two areas of concern. One was hiring a construction crew. He had hired a crew from Virginia to help with his store. They had to return because of the work they had lined up for the summer. The other was the piling foundation. He didn't have any experience installing pilings. He suggested hiring a piling contractor to complete the piling installation. My father told him that he already had a construction crew. Installing the pilings was a job they had completed many times. The deal was sealed with a handshake. Mr. Conner would have a complete materials list, or takeoff as he called it, for my father in a couple of days. My dad called Mr. Kotarides that night with the news. He was satisfied with my father's choice of the builder and his construction crew. He gave my father the go-ahead for the project.

Mr. Conner returned a few days later with two copies of the takeoff. My dad mailed a copy of the takeoff to Mr. Kotarides. All the materials would be purchased in Virginia and shipped to Salvo by truck. The structure required seventy-four eight-inch diameter pilings that were sixteen feet long. My father told Mr. Kotarides he needed fifty pilings as soon as he could get them down to Salvo. There were twenty-four pilings from the old building already out at the building site. The floor framing package was scheduled to arrive by the first of May. That gave my dad and his crew two weeks to install all the pilings. The clubhouse had to be completely finished by the beginning of the next hunting season, in about six months' time.

The main structure measured forty feet wide by eighty feet long. It required sixty-six pilings. They were to be spaced eight feet on center to complete the foundation. Eleven rows of pilings, six in each row, had to be pumped down eight feet into the muddy soil. Eight more pilings were installed on the front side of the structure. These were to support a twenty-four-foot-long-by-sixteen-foot-wide screened porch centered on the front of the structure.

A gas-powered generator was taken out to the island in order to operate the power tools. My dad and his crew began work on the foundation using the pilings they had on site. All of the pilings and the girder material was creosote-treated lumber. The batter boards were erected, strings attached, piling installation begun. The first truckload of twenty-five pilings arrived. They were taken out to the job site and work continued. All the piling work was finished just as the first truckload of floor framing arrived. The girder material was loaded on the two largest decoy skiffs and taken out to the island. Each morning the workday would begin by loading both decoy skiffs with the material needed for that particular workday. After the girders were bolted to the pilings, the floor joist and box band were installed. The subfloor was placed next; it was three-quarter-by-one-by-eight tongue-and-groove pine boards. These boards were nailed on at a forty-five-degree angle across the joists. When the exterior walls were erected and braced, the structure began to take shape. The interior walls divided the structure into the separate rooms. There were four decent-size bedrooms. A spacious galley, large dining area, a day room, a mudroom, and guides' bedroom completed the room layout. The ceiling joist and rafters came next. Pine boards were nailed on the exterior walls and roof like the floor. Then tarpaper and shingles were placed on the roof. Windows, doors, and tarpaper on the exterior walls completed the drying-in phase of the structure. All this work was completed by the end of June.

At this point in time, Mr. Kotarides visited the project and met Mr. Conner for the first time. He was pleased with the progress of the structure. Two men who worked in the bakery came along with him. They had experience in the electrical, plumbing, and pipe fitting trades. These men completed rough plumbing in the bathroom, the rough-in of the electric wiring, and the gas piping installation. The clubhouse would be equipped with gas lights, a gas cookstove, gas refrigerator, and gas heating. A few electrical lights and receptacles were roughed in to be powered by a generator.

There was a blind located in a heavily baited pond very close to the house location. Mr. Kotarides wanted the clubhouse to be able to operate silently when hunters were in this blind. When all the rough-in work was complete, the insulation was installed. The exterior walls and trim were finished off in bald cypress. The walls were sealed using a construction method known as board and batten. The interior walls were finished using tongue-and-groove ponderosa pine. The interior trim and doors were clear pine. White oak double tongue-and-grooved flooring was the finish floor of choice. All the interior woods were coated with three coats of clear sealer. The finished product was something to see. It was beautiful. All this work was completed by the middle of October, just in time for the upcoming hunting season!

# CHAPTER THIRTY

# November Trout

My father divided the work crew into two groups. My cousin Leslie Hooper, I. D. Midgett, and Uncle Bill Hennant worked with Mr. Conner to finish up the punch list items on the clubhouse. Mr. Perry, my father, and my brother completed all the work to make the club ready for the upcoming hunting season. The furnishings and a huge sign for the new clubhouse arrived in Salvo near the end of October. They were taken over to the island. The sign read, "Gull Island Gunning Club." My father and a couple of his workers installed it on the front side of the clubhouse, which overlooked the harbor. My mother insisted that she had to go to the island to oversee the setup of the clubhouse. She barked orders to the work crew as they placed the furniture, put the beds together, installed the curtains on the windows, and set up the galley. When she was satisfied with everything, she hung a Cherokee Harmony ring over the front door, blessed the structure, and announced the club was officially open.

The hunters began to schedule their trips to the island. They were impressed with the new clubhouse. There was plenty of room for at least a dozen hunters and three guides per trip. Each of the four large bedrooms had a double bed and two bunk beds set up in them. The galley was spacious and was equipped with all stainless-steel wall panels for easy cleanup. It had a complete assortment of pots and pans, enabling the preparation of any dish imaginable. Mr. Kotarides was a good cook. He did most of the cooking, with the exception of breakfast. The guides usually cooked a hearty breakfast for the hunters each morning before setting them up for the day's hunt. All the cleanup was left to the guides: the washing of the dishes, pots, and pans, and the general cleanup of the galley and dining room. It always amazed me how almost every pot and pan in the galley had to be used to prepare the evening meals Mr. Kotarides cooked.

This particular season began with bitter cold weather in the beginning of November. The diving duck hunts on the north reef were outstanding in the early part of the season. The last week of November the weather turned mild and unusually warm. The duck hunting on the north reef fizzled to a few ducks in the morning and a few just ahead of dark. This left the hunters hanging around the club, bored and playing cards in the middle of the day.

One Saturday, about mid-morning, my father asked me if my two fishing rods were still in the shower room. I told him they were. He wanted to know if I had any of the artificial baits, such as the rubber grubs that I used for trout. I told him I would go to the shower room storage closet and check. The two rods were leaning in the corner of the shower room closet. The tackle box was resting on one of the shelves just as I had left it. I opened the box. It had a good supply of buck tails, rubber grubs, and mirror lures inside. He asked if I wanted to go fishing in the northwest edge of the channel. I was puzzled: Fishing during hunting season? He told me that he had seen a couple of loons and several cormorants catching baitfish in the edge of the channel. When we picked up the hunters after the morning hunt, he saw a fish break the surface of the water and caught a flash of silver in the corner of his eye. He was convinced he had seen a large speckled trout feeding on baitfish. He told me to ask the hunters if anyone in their group was interested in going fishing.

I approached the table where they were playing cards and asked them. One of them wanted to know if we could catch anything out here in the wintertime. I told him we could possibly catch a few speckled trout.

"Speckled trout," he repeated excitedly, and instantly agreed to go along. He indicated that he was tired of playing cards. His name was Ted Sluder; he was the owner of a dog food company located in Savannah, Georgia.

He had caught speckled trout fishing in the Savannah River when he was a boy. His father had taken him up to South Carolina to fish for trout in the Santee Cooper River. He knew that the large trout had to be lifted aboard the boat with a landing net.

The outside air temperature was in the middle fifties. There was a brisk ten- to fifteen-mile-per-hour breeze from the northeast. The water was as clear as gin. We took the *Old Anytime* to the northwest end of the island. We spotted a half-dozen tern gulls diving in the water about a half mile to the northwest of us. My dad turned the boat toward the gulls. As we approached, we saw the two loons surface long enough to swallow something and dive again. The small tern gulls were steadily diving and feeding on what I thought to be baitfish. Each time one of the tern gulls came up with something in its mouth, it would be chased by a larger laughing gull trying to steal a meal. The two gulls displayed dips, dives, and sharp turns of amazing acrobatic flying that would have impressed the most experienced wartime dogfight aviator. The smaller gull would be trying to get away to swallow his dinner. The larger gull tried to fly close enough to the smaller gull to snatch the food from its beak.

My dad took the boat a little past where the terns were feeding and turned off the motor. We began a slow drift back in the direction of the island. He tossed a small buoy into the water to mark the beginning of our drift. I tied a white rubber grub, with a quarter-ounce red lead head on the line of one of the trout rod, and handed it to Ted. He cast it a short distance upwind of the drifting boat. As soon as the grub hit the water, the rod instantly bent double. He had hooked a three- to four-pound speckled trout. The fish put up a strong fight, mostly on the top of the water. Soon he was able to wear down the fish. I placed the large rim dip net into the water and he glided the fish into the net. As soon as we brought the trout into the boat, it began to spit small brown shrimp out of its mouth. At that moment we knew what the fish were feeding on. I took the fish off the line and placed it into a cardboard box we had brought with us. Before I could tie a grub on the second rod, Ted had hooked another fish.

That afternoon we caught twenty-five speckled trout in the three- to four-pound class. We also landed four nicely sized puppy drum. One of the drum was in the ten-pound class. When we returned to the clubhouse, the other hunters were surprised at our catch. The next day was Sunday; no hunting was allowed on Sunday. All of the hunters wanted to go fishing. That night I went home with my brother. He took fowl ashore to be cleaned and packed. I sent three more fishing poles back to the island with him on his return trip. My father told me that the hunters hunted in the morning and evening for diving ducks. They were ready to go fishing during the quiet midday time when the ducks stopped flying. The small, brown shrimp were in the area the rest of November and the first week of December that hunting season. As long as the shrimp remained, the hunters caught fish in the channel.

The weather turned bitter cold the second week of December. The southern branch of the jet stream dug deep in the southern portion of the country that week. A large low pressure full of moisture traveled along the Gulf Coast, turned north, and moved up the East Coast. The two fronts collided near the Florida and Georgia coast lines. This produced gale-force winds, extreme low temperatures, freezing rain, and deep snow for the East Coast. Most of the southern coastal states were snowed in and brought to a standstill.

It began raining a steady drizzle early Saturday morning at Gull Island. My father checked the barometer and the weather radio forecasts. He told the hunters who were at the club of the bad weather approaching. They were scheduled to fly out of the Norfolk, Virginia, airport the next day. My dad told the hunters they should consider leaving a day early. He advised them that whenever a winter storm approaches from the south, our area is usually in for a bad time. The hunters agreed, and my dad took them ashore. My brother and I remained and cleaned up the clubhouse.

That Saturday evening, just about dusk, my brother and I arrived at the harbor in Salvo. As we were off-loading the gear from the last hunt, the steady drizzle turned into freezing rain. The freezing rain continued all night long that Saturday night. My father left the hot and cold faucets dripping. During the night the electrical power went out. There was an electric water pump installed in the house; when the power went out, the pipes froze. The house was heated by a liquefied petroleum gas furnace. Without electricity the furnace blower would not work. We had to depend on the heat radiating off the furnace. We had a large rainwater tank located close to our house. There was an ample supply of water. When daylight approached we could see that the ground was covered with two to three inches of ice. The sound was frozen out from the end of the marsh as far as the eye could see. The boats were trapped in small holes in the ice inside the harbor. These holes were created by the movement of the boats due to the wind effect on them. Then it began to snow; it snowed all day long on Sunday. We had about four to five inches of snow.

Everything was reduced to a standstill. The entry doors to everyone's vehicles were frozen in the closed position. People had to heat water and pour it on their door frames to gain entrance to their vehicles. In order to thaw out the vehicles, the engines were started and the heaters turned on for a period of time. All the roads were impassable on the island for a period of three days. School was cancelled; all the kids donned warm clothes and went outside to play in the snow.

My mom told me to collect a pot full of snow for snow cream. She had placed a large pot outside on the porch about an hour before. She wanted me to fill it with clean snow. The reason for placing the pot outside was to adjust the metal pot to the outside temperature. If you fill a room-temperature pot with snow, it immediately forms ice inside the pot, making your snow cream icy. When I told her I had the pot full of snow ready, she handed me a large tea pitcher with her favorite homemade ice cream recipe mixed inside the pitcher. I poured the mixture into the pot and folded it into the snow until it was soft and creamy. This is a winter treat that we still enjoy today if we have sufficient snow.

Then I left the house and went looking for my friends. I walked down the road to find my friend Larry Midgett. Together we went to my cousin Richard Austin's house. All three of us set out on an adventure to find fun things to do in the snow. We decided that we would go over to the ocean side and slide down the beach hills. In those days there were only natural hills that formed on the beach. There wasn't a line of connecting hills or a dune line parallel to the ocean. These natural hills were usually large and high, had a steep side, and normally were located some distance apart. One of these hills was just south of Salvo. We named it the big hill. None of us owned a snow sled. We went looking for something to use for a sled. On the way back down the road we spotted an oval shaped sign leaning on the side of the local store. They were two sides to the sign. It had Nu-grape written on both sides of it. It was a soda replacement sign to be erected at the store. That day the two oval-shaped pieces of metal became two snow sleds. We punched two holes in one end of both signs, and attached a piece of rope through the holes on each sign. This gave us a rope handle to pull the sleds over to the big hill.

Then we fashioned a sled course down the steep face of the hill. The steep side of the hill dropped almost vertically for the first few yards. We used this area to build up speed. Where the hill leveled out a bit, we created a large circle from left to right. Then near the center of the hill we fashioned several sharp turns. After a couple of runs this course became hard packed and very fast. Each run began with a sudden drop. This drop created a sharp, speedy turn to the left. The left turn banked around to the right, then completed a circle back to the original course. The ride made several more sharp turns and ended on a slow straightaway almost to the water's edge. The oval signs with turned-up edges produced faster runs each time they flew down the course. Extremely fast rides took place when two of us rode on one sign together. If the ropes were not on the signs to grasp, we would have been thrown off many times. All three of us enjoyed this creation until well after lunchtime. The only reason we abandoned this line of fun was that we all got hungry.

On the way back to the village we formulated a plan for a big snowball fight. It was decided that after we ate we would meet in the center of the village near the church. After the midday meal I walked over to the church.

Larry was already there. We began discussing the possibility of rounding up more kids for the planned snowball fight. Then we saw Richard coming toward the church. He had two more people with him. He had gone over to Johnny Hooper's house and recruited him. Johnny had brought one of his friends along who was staying at his house for the weekend. Now we had five people; things were looking up. We still needed a few more to really choose sides and have a good time. The faint sound of kids having fun could be heard up to the windward of us. We decided to go and investigate. As we approached the yard of my cousin Leslie Hooper, we could see five more people. My cousin Leslie was helping his daughter, Sharon, and his son, Jimmy, build a snowman. His brother, William, was pulling Leslie's youngest daughter, Bertie Kay, around the yard on an old inner tube. We saw Uncle Bill Hennant walking down the road about that time; we called to him to come over. We all got our heads together and came up with a plan. William was going to stay in the yard and watch the two girls. That left eight of us to be involved in the snowball fight. It was decided that the four youngest kids would be against the older folks in the snowball fight. Richard, Larry, Jimmy, and I would be on the same side.

We took up our positions, and the barrage began. We rolled snow up into large balls, packed loose snow between the balls, and created a wall-like snow fort to hide behind. Each side broke off a small limb from the closest clump of bushes and pushed it into the snow wall near the center of the fort. This was a representation of the fort's flag. The idea was to protect your flag while trying to capture the opposing flag. The initial attack consisted of lobbing snowballs at the opponent from the protection of cover. This quickly changed into an open field attack. You would charge the opponent and fire two or three quick shots while ducking the return fire. The idea was to try to get close enough to snatch the opposing flag. If either team was successful, the stolen flag had to be taken back to the home fort. The snowball fight lasted the rest of the afternoon. We formulated a plan to flank the opposition in order to steal their flag. We would conceal Jimmy, and he would capture their flag. All four of us made all the snow balls we could carry. We launched an all-out attack. Cousin Richard was in the middle; I was to his right; Larry, being left handed, was to his left. We were screaming and charging their position. Jimmy was hidden behind us. We fired a barrage of snowballs as we charged. We suffered many hits from their return fire. We ran right up to their fort. At the last second, Jimmy dove behind the cover of their outside wall. Richard held his position in the center. Larry ran to the left; I ran to the right. We continued to pelt them with snowballs while suffering many hits ourselves from their return fire. Their attention was diverted long enough to allow Jimmy to grab their branch. At that point we retreated to our fort, planted their bush beside ours, and claimed the victory. The light was fading. We all had a good laugh and said good-bye for the night. As we left for home, the wind shifted to the southeast and it stopped snowing. The air temperature warmed, and a drizzle of rain began to fall.

# CHAPTER THIRTY-ONE

# Black Duck Moon

The combination of sunshine and the southeast drizzle of rain provided warmth that melted all the snow by nightfall the next day. The road was passable the day after that, and all the kids of the island were able to return to school. I attended a few weekend hunts before duck season ended January 15. Hunting continued at Gull Island until the end of goose season, which was January 31. Only geese decoys were set out during those last days of the season. A few ducks were harvested, very carefully and on the sly.

At the end of the season, we began to dismantle and store the hunting gear. My father, my brother, and I would spend a few nights out at the club after the hunting season was over each year. It took us most of the month of February to secure the blinds and decoys and close down the club. We continued to bait the pond box, a short walk from the clubhouse, with corn until the end of February. This gave us a chance to take advantage of the Black Duck Moon.

The Black Duck Moon is a period of time in the month of February. This period extends from the first quarter through the full moon to the last quarter. These nights offer good twilight hunts. This is the time of year the wild fowl can sense warm weather approaching. They begin to gather in much larger flocks, visit their favorite feeding areas, and feed for days at a time. They rest for long periods, preparing for the lengthy flights of their northern migration. This is a perfect time to harvest waterfowl under the cover of darkness.

My father, brother, and I would go over to the island on Friday nights. We hunted the pond box by the light of moon, worked during the daytime on Saturday, and hunted again on Saturday night. The February nights were usually cold and windy. The pond provided calm water, free of wind chop. The shallow depth allowed easy feeding. Just about dusk, flocks of fowl would begin to circle the club high in the air. If everything looked natural to them, they would drop down to the grass line and begin landing in the pond. You could stand outside on the porch and listen to them talking as they fed on the corn.

We would stay inside the clubhouse and remain completely quiet until the moon came up. My dad remained inside the clubhouse while my brother and I went to hunt in the pond blind. We would always go out the back door of the house as quietly as possible and walk around the far side of the house. At this point we eased down the steps and crawled up to the edge of the pond with extreme caution. We raised our heads up just far enough to get a look at the fowl that was close enough to take a shot at. We decided our shots and we went into action. After the initial surprise attack, we made sure all cripples were dead. With the noise of the guns, all the remaindering fowl took flight. Then we proceeded to the blind and got inside for the night's hunt. At the end of the night's hunt, we gathered all the fowl from around the edge of the pond. Usually we harvested about four empty grain bags of fowl. We tied the open end of the bags together with string. The bags were hidden in the marsh some distance from the clubhouse. Even though hunting season was over, it was not out of the ordinary to have a visit from the game wardens during our workdays.

We harvested numbers of waterfowl after the season using the light from the Black Duck Moon. All that we harvested was put to good use. We packed our freezers with fowl and gave the villagers enough for their freezers. This allowed many families to have something other than hamburger or chicken to eat for the winter.

I was in the process of delivering fowl to my grandfather. That particular time I delivered six geese and a dozen ducks. It was early in the afternoon on a Sunday after church. As I entered his house, I smelled the aroma of something from the kitchen. I asked him what he was cooking. "A pot of large lima beans," he replied. "We will have a bowl later." I stayed over to help him prepare the birds for the freezer.

We went out back of the main house into a small shed. The first step in the process was to pick all the feathers off the fowl. I always despised picking the feathers off of the front top of their wings. In my opinion this is the most difficult portion when picking wild fowl. My grandfather was patient; he slowly picked the top of the wings clean. I always had random feathers left in place along the top edge of their wings. We finished picking all the fowl; he then singed them over the open flame of a portable two-burner gas stove he had. After the singeing we rubbed the remainder of stubble off their skin. Then we gutted them, saving the gizzards and the livers from all the cleaned birds. My grandfather loved to eat fried gizzards and livers. He would have that dish with stewed potatoes, and a vegetable on another occasion. They were washed thoroughly, wrapped in heavy wax paper, and placed in his freezer. We returned to the kitchen, where he worked up a pan of cheese biscuits to go along with the beans.

He asked me about the latest twilight hunt out at the island. I told him the whole story about how my brother and I crawled up on the pond and surprised the birds to begin the hunt. He added, "That brother of yours is a good shot as I remember," he added. "Once when he was just a teenager I saw him knock down two sprigtails with one shot. The two ducks were checking out a spread we had set out. I told him to go ahead and take them. They were circling directly over our heads. He waited until they flew together in a crossing pattern. He fired and both ducks fell, tumbling down. I haven't seen anyone else ever make that shot, before or since," he said.

As he dished up the beans he began telling me about a Black Duck Moon hunt he and my great grandfather went on. They towed the *Ark* behind the *Black Skimmer* up island to the New Inlet area in the beginning of the month of February. The wind was light from the northeast, five to ten miles per hour. Thousands of geese would leave the protection of the sound and congregate in the flat fields near the Inlet to feed on the new grass shoots that had begun coming up. This would be the last market gunning trip of the winter. The Black Duck Moon provided them with the light they needed to harvest their shipment of geese.

They anchored the two larger vessels in New Inlet Bay just before nightfall. A smaller shove skiff was taken to shore. A wheelbarrow and spyglass were among the items they brought in their hunting gear. After landing on the closest sand beach, they proceeded to the highest hill to wait for the moon to rise. When the moon came up, they began to hear the call of the lead ganders to their flock members as large flocks of geese approached. Soon the whistle of their wings could be heard as they passed high overhead. The geese flew toward the oceanside of the island, then circled and landed head into the wind. The idea of the hunt was to determine the direction the geese were working. Almost like grazing cattle, geese of this magnitude would eat the grass shoots off a given area, then move along to another area, always traveling in a straight line. The idea of the hunt was to flank a moving flock and wait for them to approach.

My great-grandfather Abram and my grandfather Aaron spotted a large flock of grazing geese. They began their flanking maneuver around the flock. They walked to the far right side of the geese as quietly as possible, staying in the shadows. The geese stopped feeding and began walking away in a different direction. This action by the geese made it impossible for the hunters to gain advantage in order to get a clear shot at them. The hunters tried many times to flank the flock of geese, but the geese always walked away, always changing directions. Finally, the hunters gave up and walked back to the shoreline. They boarded the *Ark* for the night.

Just before they went to sleep, Abram said to Aaron, "We haven't had any rain in a few days. I believe they heard the rustle of our feet in the grass as we walked. Tomorrow we will have to come up with a better plan."

The next day a mixture of freezing rain and snow was falling. The hunters broke the ice on the surface of a large freshwater pond. This pond provided the fowl with drinking water and gravel they needed for digestion.

They hunted till midday. Then they collected the fowl they harvested. The fowl were taken back to the *Ark* where they were packed for shipping. The hunters rested until the moon came up around midnight. The wind had shifted to the east. The air temperature had risen, and the mist had turned to rain. This provided Abram and Aaron the opportunity to flank the geese. They finished up a successful two-week hunt. On the return trip home they met up with the freight boat and shipped their harvest of fowl.

We finished up our meal of large lima beans, cheese biscuits, and coffee. I said goodnight to my grandfather and began walking down the narrow path home. The Black Duck Moon was high overhead. It was almost as light as daytime. On the way home I had to pass the small family cemetery where my grandmother was buried. I could see the reflection of the moonlight on the headstone at her grave site. A slight feeling of fear began to come over me. Before I realized it, I was in a dead run for my back kitchen door. I decreased my forward speed on occasions to look over my shoulders at the empty path behind me. I flung open the door and entered the kitchen out of breath.

"Why in the world have you been running?" asked my mother.

"So I could get home faster and see your pretty face," I replied as I kissed her forehead.

"Yeah, right," she said. "It's time for you to take a shower. Tomorrow is a school day for you, mister."

I smiled and walked in the direction of the bathroom. I don't know what it is about cemeteries at night, but they seemed to always quicken my youthful steps as I neared one.

The work of closing down the club for the season was finished up in three weeks by my dad and brother. I went on the last moonlight hunt with them the last weekend of February. On the return trip back to Salvo just after midnight, we bumped bottom kind of hard aboard the *Gull Island*. "This harbor entrance in becoming very shallow," my dad said to my brother and me. "I need to advise Mr. Kotarides of the fact that we have been having trouble getting in and out of here," he said. I had noticed that even on a hard northwester, with the water levels high, my dad always slowed the boat and eased the boat in and out of the harbor. Even at this late hour you could see the water being sucked down behind the boat. A small breaking wave formed on either side of the back of the boat. Two sandbars were visible, one on each side, as the waves followed us. It was just about fifty yards from the mouth of the harbor to the edge of deep water. The depth of the entrance channel remained fairly constant during hunting season. This was from the boat traffic going in and out of the harbor. During the off-season with less boat traffic, the entrance channel would fill in to match surrounding bottom. We bumped several more times before we entered Gull Shoal Channel. Then my brother took the wheel and throttled up while my father and I settled into the cabin out of the wind. We entered the harbor at Salvo, stored the fowl inside the storage shed and went home for the night.

My brother had to leave the next afternoon to return to his off-island job with the State Department of Transportation. My father began to organize his postseason work on the boats and the hunting gear. He also returned to his off-island church duties. He was the pastor of the Eastlake Holly Roller Church. The church is located in the inland portion of North Carolina about sixty miles from Hatteras Island. My mother filled in for him at the church during hunting season.

There was one more Black Duck Moon weekend left in February. I was in a quandary. Two more nights of good moonlight hunting were coming up. There was a possibility that I might miss out on hunting them. I was not allowed to hunt unless I went with a responsible adult.

When Friday afternoon came around, my mother and father prepared to leave for the weekend. They were going to Eastlake to conduct church services. I begged them before they left to let me stay at my brother's house while they were gone. My mother told me to go ask Jean, my sister-in-law, if I could stay with them. She said that they would be glad to have me for the weekend. I returned home and told my mother what Jean had said. Mom told me I could stay in our house during the day. I was allowed to make cold sandwiches, but under no circumstances was I to use the cookstove. I was to lock the house and spend the night at my brother's.

When my parents left, I ran over to my brother's house to talk to Jean. I asked her if she knew about what time my brother would be home. She told me it would be late; she thought they were working around the Roanoke Rapids area. This town is located in inland North Carolina, just south of the Virginia state line. I knew it would take him several hours to drive home. I had just about given up, but then I spotted my cousin Raymond's car pulling into my grandfather's driveway. Raymond is my first cousin, my aunt Lucy's son. Aunt Lucy is one of my father's sisters. Raymond, his wife Barbara, and their daughter, Theresa, lived in the Little Kinnakeet Coast Guard Station. This station had been taken over by the National Park Service. Raymond worked for them and was the caretaker of the station. They had come up to visit his mother and my grandfather. My grandfather's health was deteriorating; he had lived alone since Uncle Luther and his family moved to Wanchese. He was having difficulty taking care of himself. Raymond was thinking about moving his family into my grandfather's house to care for him. I ran over to meet them. I asked Raymond about a moonlight hunt down at Cedar Hammock Marsh. He told me he was thinking about it. He had brought his hunting gear with him. He asked me if I wanted to go with him. I was delighted and told him I was off to ask Jean's permission to go along.

We waited until about eight o'clock as the moon was coming up. Raymond's wife, Barbara, drove us down to Cedar Hammock in their car. The plan was to hunt till around twelve o'clock, then walk back out to Highway 12. Barbara would pick us up around twelve-thirty. We carried two burlap bags with us to put the fowl in. We walked carefully around the floating marsh near the entrance of Cedar Hammock Marsh. This was a matted growth of interwoven grasses that completely floated on top of a bottomless bog. If you fell through, it was almost impossible to get out without help from someone. Our destination was the Long Pond area. This pond was shallow enough for the fowl to feed on the new shoots of the marsh grasses. The pond also provided freshwater for them and a lee out of the wind where they could rest. Even before we arrived at the pond, the rustle of wings could be heard overhead. The puddle ducks were filling up the pond. These consisted of black ducks, sprigtails, gadwall, teal, and widgeons. We crawled up to the south edge of the pond. Raymond told me to line up at least two ducks sitting on the water in the moon glade. He had an automatic with the plug removed. I had a single-barrel gun. I was to shoot first and he would back me up. After the first barrage was over, I collected eight ducks from the pond. We would shoot, and before we could load up, there would be more ducks landing on the pond. Each time I waited until I could see two ducks close enough together to take with one shot. Raymond told me to try holding a reserve shell on my mouth after I shot, break the gun down, and quickly put the shell in the barrel. This process provided me with another opportunity to get a shot as the ducks flew from the pond. I was able to knock down a few more ducks using this tactic. We filled our bags with ducks. The hunt continued until around midnight; then we walked out to the road to be picked up.

# CHAPTER THIRTY-TWO

# The *Contraption*

I hunted the last weekend of the Black Duck Moon that year with my cousin Raymond. We bagged enough ducks for our family and most of our neighbors. At the end of February each year we cleaned our guns and put them away until next season. The month of March was the beginning of the migration period for the wild fowl of our area. My grandfather often told me never to hunt the fowl in the month of March. The female of the species begin to transform into the nesting mode. During this period their reproductive organs begin to produce a hormone that enhances the egg production process. This was the beginning of the reproductive cycle for them. We respected this time period. All serious hunters love to harvest fowl but will do anything within their power to make sure there are ample birds for future hunts.

My father contacted Mr. Kotarides and advised him of the shallow-water problem developing at Gull Island. Mr. Kotarides came to Salvo. My father and I took him out to the island to have a look at the entrance channel. They were both of the opinion that it needed to be dug out before next hunting season. They also observed that a lot of the sand in the front yard had washed under the clubhouse. It was decided that a retaining wall would be built across the front of the clubhouse. The fill from digging out the entrance channel would be used to replace the sand in the front yard. Mr. Kotarides instructed my father to go ahead with the project. My father began looking for someone to do the work.

One Friday afternoon Cousin Floyd—Pudding Head—came over to visit my dad. He had some interesting news. Two of my father's first cousins, Richard, or Dick as he was called for short, and Ray Austin were in the process of building a small dredge. The three of us climbed into Pudding Head's truck and rode up the road to see the dredge. As we pulled into the yard, we saw three people working on a funny-looking metal bargelike vessel. It appeared to be a small landing craft or troop carrier. Ray Austin was retired from the Norfolk Navy Yard as a machinist and welder. His brother Dick was a retired New York policeman. They both moved back to Salvo, which was their childhood home, and brought their families with them. Cousin Richie, who was helping them, is Dick's youngest son. The older of the two brothers, Ray, had bought the craft from a navy auction held in Norfolk, Virginia. He had purchased a trailer and towed this funny-looking craft home to Salvo. They were retrofitting it into a small dredge. They had installed an eight-inch suction pump equipped with a ten-inch discharge. Ray had rebuilt a 671 diesel engine that had been used to power the troop carrier. He planned to use this engine to power the pump. He had welded a spud frame on the back of the craft. The frame was equipped with two eight-inch-diameter spuds. He attached swing anchors to the front. Two eight-horsepower air-cooled engines were used to power the spuds and swing anchors. They hooked the engines up to hydraulic wenches and extended the lines to control in the lever room area. The only thing this little dredge lacked was a cutter head on the end of the suction pipe. Ray had finished up with all the mechanic work and welding. They were painting the hull a battleship-gray color. Ray himself was painting the name of the vessel on her sides at her mid-ship area. He was naming her the *Contraption*. "Well, boys, what do you think of her?" he asked as he completed his painting.

"Looks impressive," my father responded. "But will she dig a proper channel?" he asked.

"Don't know," Ray answered. "Everything on her works. We are going to try her out tomorrow." My dad asked him if he might be interested in dredging the entrance channel to Gull Island Channel. "We have a small job to do for a fellow in Rodanthe," Ray said. "After we finish that, I will take a look at your job." He estimated the work in Rodanthe would take about three weeks. On Saturday, the second weekend in March, my dad and I took Ray out to the island to see the job. He gave my dad an estimate of the cost and the length of time to complete the job. My dad called Mr. Kotarides with the estimate, and he gave the go-ahead to start the work. While the *Contraption* was completing her work in the Rodanthe area, my dad, Mr. Perry, and Uncle Bill were busy working out at Gull Island. They were building a containment area for the sand that would be pumped by the dredge. My dad wanted to create a large front yard. They constructed a retaining wall attached to the pilings at the front of the clubhouse. There was quite a bit of material left over after the wall was finished. My dad had ordered extra in case he had to expand the fill area. He had a couple of stacks of sixteen-foot creosote pilings and three stacks of bulkhead sheeting stored near the clubhouse.

At the beginning of April, on a Monday, Ray and Dick towed the *Contraption* out to Gull Island. My dad, Ray, and Dick stayed at the clubhouse during the work week and came home late on Friday afternoons. They towed the *Contraption* into the harbor and faced her bow outward toward the deep water. During the first week while Ray and Dick completed the prep work for the job range, stakes were placed to mark the size of the channel to be dredged. The *Contraption* was placed into position at the harbor entrance, and work commenced.

Easter vacation was just a few days away. We had Good Friday and Easter Monday off from school. Richie and I went to the island with my dad on Friday morning. He had come ashore with a couple of empty propane gas cylinders. We returned with the full ones. As we neared the *Contraption*, the smooth sound of machinery at work could be heard. Ray was on a starboard swing, and we passed on the port side of him. It was quite an operation to see. The spill pipe was positioned over the bulkhead. A combination of sand and water was pouring out the end of the pipe. The sand settled as the water spilled over the retaining wall into the surrounding marsh. The front yard was indeed building up.

After we helped Dad install the propane tanks, the three of us took a skiff and shoved it out of the dredge. We tied the skiff alongside the *Contraption* as she moved back and forth, working. We climbed up a side ladder and stood on the deck. She was decked over with the exception of a six-foot-by-six-foot open hatch with the cover pulled back. We were able to look down inside the dredge. We saw Dick working below decks. He was watching the winches and cables, greasing the moving parts, keeping an eye on all the machinery. He had on earmuffs for protection from the ear-piercing sound of the motors.

We continued up the side of the *Contraption* into the lever room area. This area was enclosed by a wooden, insulated cabin. We entered the cabin and closed the door. Two small vents were framed into the surface of the floor. The lever room was heated by warm air rising through these vents from the engine room. Ray was operating the dredge with a system of levers attached to wench cables. He pointed out the fact that the section pipe didn't have a cutter head on the end of it. The only adjustment on the suction pipe was an up-and-down motion. He told us that the dredge was only capable removing five feet of sand at a time. He said that they would have to make two cuts from the harbor out to Gull Shoal Channel. The desired size of the entrance channel was to be ten feet deep, fifty feet wide, and about two hundred feet long. The *Contraption* was about halfway out to deep water on its first five-foot cut.

Ray brought our attention to a large glass gauge that was fastened to the top of a pipe. The pipe was one half inch in diameter and extended below the deck. He explained that it was a vacuum gauge, and the pipe was welded to the suction side of the pump. There was a delicate mixture of sand and water that had to be maintained inside the dredge pipe. If this mixture had too much sand and not enough water, the entire system could possibly become clogged with sand. If this occurred, the pump had to be taken apart and all the pipes disconnected and washed out with a smaller pump. The gauge needed to register below thirty inches of vacuum while dredging. This would keep the operation running smoothly. He explained that the mixture was about 50 percent sand and 50 percent water. Normally, when everything was working properly, the gauge registered around eighteen to twenty-five inches of vacuum. Ray watched the gauge and dug carefully, keeping the vacuum level below thirty inches.

It was amazing to look around this vessel and realize that Ray actually planned and assembled, with the help from his brother, Dick, the *Contraption*. It was a mass of cables, winches, levers, engines, and mechanical parts that all worked together in a synchronized motion. This enabled the *Contraption* to perform her dredging operations. I really believe that Ray could have built or assembled anything that he put his mind to.

We stayed for a while watching Ray operate the dredge. My dad, Richie, and I went back to the clubhouse to keep an eye on the sand filling up the front yard from the discharge pipe. The yard was filling up with sand at a rapid rate. My dad realized that he would have to expand the retaining wall in order to contain the large amount of fill that was being pumped in. He told Richie and me that he would hire us to begin helping him to expand the fill area. My dad, with our help, set up stakes and attached strings to expand the fill area completely around the clubhouse. This area included two sizable side yards and spacious backyard. We used a small pump to install pilings eight feet apart along the strings. We worked a half day on Friday and stayed at the club Friday night. We got up early and worked all day on Saturday, finishing all the pilings. The pilings were ready to be topped, and the top and bottom rails or whalers installed. Then the sheeting would be assembled. Ray and Dick stopped pumping late Saturday evening and we all went home for the rest of the weekend. We attended church on Easter Sunday and had an Easter egg hunt after services.

On Monday morning seven of us boarded the *Gull Island* and cruised out to the island to work. Ray and Dick boarded the *Contraption* and began dredging. My father, Richie, Uncle Bill, Mr. Perry, and I worked on the retaining wall enlargement. We were able to complete all the sheeting down the right side and the back by late Monday afternoon. My dad took Richie and me ashore. Easter vacation was at an end. We had to return to school the next day.

By the time the next weekend rolled around, Richie and I were able to return with my dad out to the island. On our approach to the island, we set a couple of large mesh drum nets. Drum is a local name for channel bass. We set them on the backside of the island, along the edge of the south reef. During their annual spring migration north, large schools of drum or channel bass swam along the edge of this reef.

After the nets were set, we headed for the harbor entrance. The *Contraption* had finished her first cut to deep water. Ray and Dick were in the process of moving her back into the harbor. They positioned the dredge to begin the finishing cut out to the start of deeper water. With this last cut, the entrance of the channel would have about ten feet of depth. It would be around fifty feet wide. This should allow the boats to easily pass in and out of the harbor. My dad and his work crew had finished all of the vertical sheeting in the retaining wall enlargement. The only thing left to install was cap rail along the top of the wall. When this task was finished, we removed every other piece of vertical sheeting from the original wall in front of the clubhouse. This would allow the water and sand to flow into the enlargement when the *Contraption* resumed pumping. Ray and Dick finished; the dredge was set up about the same time the work finished on the retaining wall.

On our way home we boarded the *Gull Island* and went to fish over the drum nets. From a distance I could make out the large colored floats at each end of the drum nets. As we got closer, a dozen or so large fish tails came into view. My heart quickened; I became excited, as I did each time I saw one of these large fish. They appeared to be in the forty-pound class, maybe a couple of fifty-pounders. These large fish are something to see. When we began pulling the first net into the boat the thrashing commenced. Four of them thrashed so violently, they tore large holes in the webbing, allowing them to get away. The fish were slippery and hard to handle. We forgot to bring a gaff with us. The fish had to be held down on the washboard of the boat by at least two people. Then someone had to place their hands inside their gill plates to pull them inside the boat. When the first one was pulled aboard he began making a loud drumming noise from deep in his throat. This is why local folks gave them the nickname of drum fish. When large schools of them are moving during calm weather, and you happen to be close to them, the drumming noise can be heard. I don't know if this is a means of communication or a noise they make when they feel threatened. We caught an even dozen of these large drum in the two nets. We all had a large drum to eat and a few left to share with our neighbors.

On the boat ride home I couldn't take my eyes off the fish. They have a torpedolike shape and are covered with armorlike scales. Each one has a large black spot located near the end of its tail. Several of them were mul-tispotted; the spots extended well up their sides. Fresh out of the water they had a magical silver-reddish color. Each one had a wide silver streak from its upper stabilizing fin reaching to the edge of its tail. As time goes by and they begin to dry out, they turn a more brownish-red color. They looked magical lying on the deck of the boat near the stern. An exciting thought flashed through my mind. I pondered the thought of hooking, fighting, wearing down, and landing one of these monsters on a rod and reel. Up to this point the largest one that I had ever caught only weighed ten pounds.

My angling dreams were interrupted by the throttling down and turning of the boat. I looked up from the fish and noticed we were entering the harbor at Salvo. Richie and I placed the fish on the dock. My dad kept three of the drum to clean up for our family connections. The remaining seven fish were placed in the back of Ray's pickup to be given to other villagers. My dad sent me to the house to tell my mother that we would be having fresh boiled drum for supper. She told me she had made beef hash for supper, but could refrigerate it for another time. She gave me a sharp knife and a large pan. When I got back to the harbor my cousin Floyd, or Pudding Head, was helping my dad scale the fish. He had walked down to the harbor when he saw the boat come in. They had nailed a piece of two-by-four across two pilings and tied the tails of the fish to it. Each of them had a hatchet and was scaling the drum. When all three drum were scaled, the meat was cut from the backbone. Then it was cut into small enough chunks to cook. The cheek meat was scooped out from the sides of their heads. It was placed with the backbones and livers, and saved for backbone stew.

My father told me about the stonelike bone structure located in their heads that was used as balance indicators. This information had been passed along since the stones had been discovered inside the fish. He explained that they worked like the components of the inner ear in humans. These stones were inside a small hallow cavity, floating in fluid, located near their eyes. The theory is that they help the drum maintain proper balance as they swim along. True or not, there is a matched pair in the head of all drum. They are white in color, elongated, curved, and have a small indented grove near one edge. This is a prized item and collected by all drum fishermen. Scales are sometimes strung on strings by children; almost everything was used on the fish we caught.

# CHAPTER THIRTY-THREE

# Campground Girls

The *Contraption* finished up its dredging at Gull Island in the middle of May. The entrance channel was complete. It extended from the deep water inside Gull Island Harbor to the deep water of Gull Shoal Channel. The boats could easily navigate and even make a broadside pass in the entrance channel. The pumped sand had filled the front yard containment area and filtered through the open spaces in the sheeting to the side yards, filling them. When the backyard had become filled, Ray and Dick pumped excess sand in the marsh out back of the clubhouse. The sand formed up into three large piles in this area. My dad said he could put that area to a practical use. I asked him what he planned to do in that area. With a twinkle in his eye, he said, "You will see in good time."

All the dredge pipe and dredging gear was loaded on the upper deck of the *Contraption*. Everything was latched securely in place by rope on the dredge deck. She was going to be towed back to Salvo to await her next dredging job. This particular Saturday was unusually cold for the month of May. The weather had been mild, then all of a sudden turned violently cold. The wind was light from the southeast, and a frozen mixture was falling. Ray fastened the tow rope from the *Contraption* to his towboat. We secured everything at the clubhouse. My dad wanted to follow along with the tow in case the help of a second boat was needed. The tow went smoothly. We did help on the turn into the creek at the back of Ray's house. Ray slowed the towboat, and Dick shortened the tow rope. Just before the turn, my dad eased the *Gull Island* up to the leeward side of the *Contraption*. Dick tossed me a rope and I made it fast to the cleat mounted on the stern of the *Gull Island*. At the beginning of the turn, my dad throttled up and held the stern of the *Contraption* into the wind. This allowed Ray to make a smooth entrance in the creek. As the dredge entered the mouth of the creek I untied the rope from the cleat. Dick coiled in the slack on the rope. As they entered the mouth of their creek, I waved to them and dad turned the boat toward the harbor behind our house.

Soon the summer was upon us. There had been some changes around the Salvo area. The National Park Service had constructed a campground just to the south of the village. Suddenly the summer population of the Salvo area increased drastically. There were several hundred campsites in the campground, and it stayed full of campers most of the time. That summer I turned twelve years of age. My two closest buds, Larry Midgett and Richie Austin, and I stopped chasing land varmints and water critters. We had a new quarry to chase after.

I still had my responsibilities of helping my dad with the repair and painting of the decoy boats, but every afternoon my buds and I headed for the campground. We always walked to the south end of the village and entered the north end of the campground. There were two wooden board-walks extending to the beach. One was at the north end of the campground. The other began at the north end of the campground and extended to the south beach access. We checked the sound-side bathing beach first. This is a shallow, sandy beach located in the north end of the campground on the sound side. This area was a much calmer area without parallel current or rip tides, and best for swimming and waterside enjoyment. If the weather was nice, quite a few people would be there enjoying the afternoon. Mostly the older folks, such as parents, would be lounging on blankets or towels talking or reading. Their teenage kids, such as daughters, would be standing near the water's edge watching their younger brothers and sisters. This is exactly what we were looking for: the daughters.

Using extreme caution, we would size up the situation. We approached the attractive daughters and engaged them in conversation while keeping an eye on the parents. If the conversation went well, most of the time one of their parents approached us. They were curious to see who their daughter was talking to. As soon as they found out we were local residents, the questions began. We answered all their questions about the area. Then we invited the whole family to a beach bonfire that night.

Then we headed south on the wooden boardwalk that began at the bathing beach. The boardwalk extended over a bridged creek through the campsites and ended at the south end of the campground leading to the beach. Next, we always stopped at the bridge over the small creek. At times there would be parents and their kids crabbing or fishing from the bridge. If we found girls at the bridge, we repeated the conversational process, always inviting them to the nighttime beach fire.

Our journey then took us through the campsites. Sometimes we saw girls at the comfort stations or walking down the boardwalk to the beach near the south access. We tried to talk to as many good-looking girls as possible and invite them to the bonfire. They usually asked us the same question: How would they find the fire? Our answer was always the same. It would be located midway between the beach access boardwalks. It would be huge and probably the only fire on the beach at night. After swimming and enjoying the beach, we would begin to collect scrap wood. The wood was placed halfway between the ocean and the dune line. At this point we usually would walk home and begin to prepare for a night of fun.

The summer afternoons were lengthy. It got dark around nine o'clock in the evening. Our return was normally timed just as it was getting dark. Along with us we brought an old guitar. The three of us could make some guitar chords and murder a few songs. We brought scrap newspaper and matches to start the fire. Before too long, the fire would be roaring. It could be seen from anywhere along the beach. There was no way anyone could cross the dune line on either boardwalk without seeing the fire. Most of the time about half of the people we invited would actually show up at the fire. They evolved out of the darkness, taking form in the glow that extended out about twenty feet around the fire. Parents usually came along with the kids.

We would hang around the fire sitting on blankets. One of us—Richie, Larry, or I—would be plucking on the guitar attempting to play and sing a few songs. At times there would be a guitar player who walked up. If so, they were given a chance to display their talent. We usually brought a couple of bags of marshmallows and a few wire coat hangers to roast them on. If we had a few extra coins, we purchased a few containers of Jiffy Pop popcorn in the round tinfoil containers. This was a premixed brand of popcorn with a soft foil top that expanded as it popped. The containers came equipped with a wire handle, which allowed the contents to be shaken while placed on hot coals near the edge of the fire. Parents would continue to question us about the area and usually leave in a couple of hours. When they left, most of the time the parents would insist that their daughters accompany them back to the campsite. Once in a while, they would allow their daughters to remain. The parents usually left a younger brother or sister for them to watch and insisted that all of them be back at camp by midnight. This is usually when we moved in. We talked among ourselves and decided which one of us would take the initiative. When the decision was made, it was on.

We became acquainted with all the kids who were left at the fire. After talking to everyone for a short length of time, each one of us would approach a young lady of our choice, ask if we could sit beside her, and engage her in conversation. We normally talked until it was time for them to start back to the campsite. It was standard procedure to walk them back to camp. We always made sure that we traveled in a group. This accomplished two things: it let us know the location of their campsite. It also let their parents, who were always waiting up, see that we were not paired off but one big group of kids. Even as we approached the last campsite, the parents saw their daughter with at least three other kids. When we said goodnight, we invited them to another fire the next night. Before we left, we offered to stop by the campsite for them the next afternoon.

All three of us were also together when we arrived at the first campsite the next afternoon. The parents saw at least three kids leaving for the beach. We stopped at each campsite we visited the night before. Our numbers grew as we neared the south end of the campground. The group now went to the beach and gathered scrap wood. The wood was piled in the same location as the night before. The plan was to meet just as it was getting dark at this location. Before leaving for the village, we asked the kids in the group to spread the word about the upcoming bonfire.

On our way home Larry, Richie, and I talked about which one of the girls we liked the best. We needed this conversation so that we wouldn't get our wires crossed. It was always better to have smooth sailing among your crew when you were ready to choose a first mate for your cruise. After the decisions had been made, we were ready to stalk our query.

At the fire that night we had to size up the situation. At times one of our intended targets had already paired off with one of the campground boys. This was only a minor setback; there were always plenty of girls to choose from. Once you made your move, holding hands on the way back to the campsite was customary.

I became friendly with the families of several girls I met at the Campground. Most of their fathers were interested in angling or rod and reel fishing. I would invite the whole family on a fishing outing out near Gull Island. My father trusted me with one of the boats. It was the *Old Anytime*; she was slow, but she was spacious and dependable. At first the fathers of the girls were suspicious and usually questioned me about the fishing trip. I invited them to meet my dad. Once they met my dad and saw that everything was on the level, they became excited. The family outing had to be scheduled for a Saturday. I worked during the week with my dad, but I had Saturdays off. My parents left the island on Friday afternoons. They were off the island for the weekend, attending the church where my dad preached. I normally stayed at my brother's house.

Early on Saturday morning my invited guests met me at the harbor. It was normally hot and sunny; severe sunburn was a constant problem. I made sure that everyone going on the outing had a hat and sunscreen. I had five people on this particular trip. There was the daughter I had been playing up to; her name was Peggy Golden. She was a blue-eyed, blond-haired, fair-skinned beauty. Her parents and two younger sisters came along on the outing. Her parents' names were Arthur and Julie. The two younger sisters were named Casey and Carla. They were from Akron, Ohio. They brought food; I supplied the fishing poles and tackle.

We left in the *Old Anytime*, bound for Gull Island. Summertime fishing is outstanding around the Gull Island area. My guests had many questions. They wanted to know about all the boats that were moored in the harbor. They were amazed that my father was a commercial hunting guide. Many of their questions were about the club and how it all worked. I answered all their questions to the best of my knowledge. Then I took them to all the hunting locations and explained the functions of the hunting blinds to them. The last hunting location we visited was the stilt blind located on the northwest reef. The first fishing location was along the edge of the northeast reef. Speckled trout, puppy drum, and bluefish were in abundance in this location. They cruised along the edge of this reef searching for food. They were easily caught with light tackle, and baited with a quarter-ounce lead head and a rubber grub. These fish were always boated with a landing net. We fished a few hours along the reef, caught quite a few large fish, and placed them on ice in a cooler. The two younger children began complaining of being hot, tired, and hungry. I fired up the *Old Anytime* and took her into the harbor at Gull Island.

We tied the boat up at the dock and walked up to the large covered screened porch. The wind was light from the northeast, providing a nice breeze. It was cooler on the porch out of the sun. It was equipped with a picnic table, so we decided to have our lunch there. I filled up several large containers with freshwater from the rainwater collection tanks. Julie was able to wash the saltwater spray created by the boat from the kids' faces and feed them, and they were much more comfortable. She asked me if we were finished fishing for the day. The younger girls were tired from getting up so early in the morning. Peggy indicated that she was bored with fishing. The girls were ready to head back home. I was afraid that our outing was about to come to an abrupt end.

I knew that I needed to score a few more points with Mr. Golden, so I told them that I wanted to take Mr. Golden to fish one more spot before we left. I indicated to the girls that they could wait on the porch, out of the afternoon sun, and we would return to pick them up. They agreed to wait for us in the coolness of the clubhouse porch. Mr. Golden asked me what type of fish we were looking for. I replied that they would be of the same species of some we had in the cooler. The only difference was hopefully the ones we caught would be much larger. "But we only brought light tackle," he said.

"I have two heavy, seven-foot-long rods, equipped with a couple of open-faced Penn reels on the boat," I replied.

"I didn't see any such rods on the boat," he added.

"They are on a rack, one on either side of the boat, hidden under the washboards. They remain on the boat all the time. It is not out of the ordinary to spot a school of large fish at the beginning of hunting season," I replied. "The gear has to be handy in situations such as that," I said.

"So I see," replied Mr. Goldman. "Always prepared," he added.

"Yes," I answered, "some sort of Coast Guard motto my father lives by." I used to mention that I wish I had a rod when these fish were spotted.

"Why don't you stash a couple on the boat?" my dad told me one day. The *Old Anytime* had large washboards. The rods had been there since that day. They were only removed for cleaning purposes. Then they were replaced in their racks hidden from view. Mr. Golden and I boarded the *Old Anytime*. I told him that I was not going to fire up the engine. This time I would shove the boat with the paddle to our new fishing location. The *Old Anytime* was flat bottomed, wide at the beam, and she glided along with little effort using a shove paddle. I pushed the boat out of the harbor, turned her to the east, and kept her close to the edge of the marsh. We passed the buried hunting box at Thoroughfare Creek and continued to the east side of the island. I anchored the boat along the marsh at the cane field area. I asked Mr. Golden to bring along the bait bucket, and I retrieved cast net from under the bow cap of the boat. We got out of the boat and walked down the marsh a few yards. The cane field area is situated near a deep gulley. This gulley runs between the east end of the island and the southeast reef. It provides the only water route, for about a mile. which is deep enough to allow schools of baitfish to cross the reef. These schools of fish are easy prey for a cast netter standing on the marsh. In no time at all we had a variety of baitfish in our bucket. We had a few jumping mullets, some spots, and number of fatbacks or menhaden. This was ample bait for the afternoon. We glided the *Old Anytime* through the gulley. I dropped the anchor in calm water behind the south point of the south reef. We walked a few feet on the dry reed to the water's edge. The deep water of the sound ran along the backside of the reef. We baited the two large rods, placed them in sand spikes, and waited. I told Mr. Golden that whatever hit either rod was his to fight. It wasn't long before one of the rods bent double. The drag on the reel was screaming. Mr. Golden grabbed it, and the fight was on.

# CHAPTER THIRTY-FOUR

# Gas Episode

Mr. Golden arched his back and began to turn the handle on the reel. The line was peeling off the reel at a rapid rate. I walked over to him and tightened the drag slightly. The line loss on the reel slowed. I adjusted the drag to allow more pressure to be put on the fish, but at the same time, if the fish decided to run, the line would slowly peel off the reel before it broke. After about forty-five minutes the fish came to the surface and continued the fight on the top of the water. It was about fifty yards away from us. That is when we first caught sight of him. It was a big drum, or channel bass. I shouted to Mr. Golden, "Don't give him any slack." The fish rolled and swirled around ninety degrees from us and began a surface run parallel to the reef. The silver-reddish color on its back glistened in the sunlight as the fish swam rapidly to the left. Mr. Golden had to walk, holding pressure on the rod, to the left following the fish. When he caught up with the fish he was able to turn it toward shore and gain the last few yards of line. The drum rolled over on its side about ten feet from us. I was able to wade out in the water, place my hands inside its gill slits, and drag it up on the reef using both hands. I turned and looked at Mr. Golden; there was a big grin on his face. I congratulated him on his catch. "It looks to be at least in the fifty-pound class," I told him. I threaded a fish stringer from the gills of the fish and brought it out of its mouth. The stringer was a heavier piece of cord that we used during hunting season as a decoy span. I walked the fish back out to deep water to keep it alive as long as possible. It was much too large to place in the cooler. It wasn't long before we got another bite. This time he landed a bluefish, about fifteen pounds. He was very satisfied with his catch.

We headed back to the clubhouse to pick up the girls. Mrs. Golden had prepared an evening meal for us. We ate, talked, and laughed, and Mr. Golden gave a complete account of his battle with the big drum. We loaded all the gear in the *Old Anytime*. Mr. Golden got into the boat and helped the two younger girls aboard. Peggy was standing beside me on the dock. Her mother came up to board the boat. I took her hand and supported her as she stepped on the washboard to get in. She looked at me, smiled, and said, "You are okay in my book, young man. I think my husband likes you. I know for a fact my daughter does." On the way home Mr. Golden supported the two small girls on the bow cap of the boat as we steamed along.

Peggy sat beside me in the stern; she wanted to steer the boat. The *Old Anytime* had a rudder and tiller system. To turn the boat you pulled the tiller in the opposite direction you wanted the bow to go. It took her a few minutes to get the hang of it. When we had crossed Gull Island channel, I pointed and told her to steer for the north point of Bay Landing. I wanted to take the inside route home along the marsh. She turned around and said, "Will you look at that?" We had turned toward the east just enough for the sun to be right over the top of the clubhouse. It almost made a complete border around the sides of the structure as it was beginning to set for the afternoon. "Hey, Dad," she hollered above the engine noise, "take a picture of the sunset." Mr. Golden snapped the picture. Peggy looked up at me with those big blue eyes and said, "This has been a perfect day." As we entered the harbor at Salvo, my cousin Pudding Head and my brother walked down to meet us.

"Nice drum," Pudding Head said as we docked the boat. My brother looked at me and Peggy standing on the stern of the boat.

"You had a fun day. I can see it all over your face," he said to me as he smiled.

I introduced both of them to the Golden family. They helped us load the gear into Mr. Golden's vehicle. My brother and I hung the drum from one of the pilings. I handed Mr. Golden one of the rods so he could pose for pictures with his catch. My brother and I cleaned the smaller fish in the cooler for them. Mr. Golden gave the drum to me. He said he had no earthly idea of how to clean it. My cousin Pudding Head volunteered to clean it for us for a portion of the meat. We would all share the drum for future fish dinners. Before the Goldens left for their campsite, they invited me for a fish dinner the next day. I told them I would be unable to come over until after midday. The next day would be Sunday and I had church. Mr. Golden said that would be fine. We said bye to them, and they got in the vehicle. My brother looked at me and said, "What's wrong with you, boy? Invite that girl to go to church with you before she leaves."

I walked over to Mr. Golden's car window. He rolled it down and said, "What is it, Son?"

"I was wondering," I said, and hesitated a little, but finally I got the words out. I was wondering if Peggy would like to attend church with me tomorrow."

"Well, I suggest you ask her," he said, grinning.

I looked at her and said, "Would you like to?"

"Of course. I would love to," she answered.

Mrs. Golden said, "I think that would be very nice. What time should I drop her off in the morning?"

"A few minutes before ten o'clock will be fine," I answered. After that I was a regular at the Golden campsite. Mr. Golden, Peggy, and I went on several more fishing trips during their stay. Peggy and I were spending every afternoon together. Before we knew it, their vacation was at its end. I remember the day they left; I was heartsick. I moped around for days. My grandfather noticed how miserable I was. He told me, "Son, girls are like a bus. If you miss one you can always catch another."

"But this one is special, Pop," I told my grandfather.

"That is because she is the first one you paid any attention to or spent any length of time with," he answered. "In the past you have been interested only in hunting, sports, or hanging with your friends." On the day they left we promised to write each other, and we did. Every summer after that for the next four years, they returned to the campground to vacation the whole month of July. They were always ready to take the Gull Island outing. I think they came to love that island as much as I do. We enjoyed each other's company each summer until our college years. We would have probably ended up together if our young adult lives had been more compatible. The last time I heard from her she had completed medical school. Today she is the chief of staff of the pediatrics department at a large hospital near Akron, Ohio. Over the years since then we have lost contact. I will always have a soft spot in my heart for her. I remember something my grandfather told me many times. "Out of sight, out of mind," was a favorite saying of his. He would back this statement up by saying, "There are events that hurt you so much that only time can bring you any type of ease." That is how I felt at the end of Peggy's vacation after we had first discovered each other.

During the month of August that summer I worked with my dad out at the island. My mother went with us, and we stayed at the clubhouse. My dad and I worked during the day and angled or fished with fishing poles each afternoon. We began work on that special project that he mentioned to me before. This work involved the sand that Ray and Dick had pumped in the marsh behind the clubhouse. We filled empty grain bags with sand. With these we built a sandbag wall around the outside edge of the sandpiles. Then we leveled the remainder of the sand even with the top of the sandbag wall. When this work was completed my dad planted patches of wire grass in the area. We dug this grass from other locations on the island. Wire grass is a type of local grass that spreads fast and grows rapidly. We watered it daily. In a couple of weeks it had covered the area we leveled off. In mid-September my dad built a picnic table and placed it there. He installed a couple of horseshoe pits. We buried a charcoal grill on a galvanized post, embedded in a bucket of concrete. My dad had turned this location into a recreational area for future hunts. On Friday afternoon as we were cleaning the club, my dad said he caught a faint odor of gas. He checked the refrigerator, the cookstove, hot water heater, and all of the gas lights. Just as a precaution we closed all of the gas valves to the appliances before we left for home. He planned to call the gas company to have one of their men come to the island to check things out.

A repairman from the gas company came to look the club over for a possible gas leak. He could not find any leaks around any of the connections of the appliances. He told my dad that he could not find any evidence of a gas leak anywhere inside the clubhouse.

The first of November was always the beginning of hunting season. The first, second, and third group of hunters that came to hunt that year complained of a faint gas odor in one of the bedrooms. My dad contacted the gas company once more, and they sent the repairman back to the island. On this trip he centered his investigation in the bedroom where the complaints came from. The only gas appliance in this room was a gas light. He checked the copper tubing connection and it was fine. A faint odor of gas could be detected around the base of the light, where it was mounted to the wall. My dad and I removed the base mold from the floor on that wall. Then we removed the bed molding from the ceiling on the same wall. We removed the mounting screws from the light. Then we removed several pieces of the wall, vertical installed ponderosa pine, to expose the gas line. There was a slight sag in the copper line and a small split located on the bottom of the sag. The repairman explained that condensation had been trapped in the line at the sag. During bitter cold weather it had frozen and split the copper. He removed a section of the line and replaced it. We reinstalled all the wood components, and the wall was restored to its original condition. The repairman told my father to turn all the valves from the gas supply to the closed position. He asked us to start up the portable generator so that he could have electrical power. He then pulled a vacuum on all of the gas lines with a vacuum pump. The next step was to pressurize the gas lines. He installed a gauge on the lines and pumped fifty pounds of air pressure into them. He told us that if the pressure remained constant for one hour's time, the gas leak problem would be solved. Just as soon as the lines were pressurized they began losing pressure near all the appliances. You could hear the air escaping around the fittings of the gas line connections. The repairman told us to close the valves at the appliance locations. My dad and I began closing these valves. I checked behind the gas range, and there was no valve in that location. But at the same time, there wasn't any air leaking around the fittings. I reported this to the repairman. He said that was not out of the ordinary. He told me that gas ranges were equipped with thick rubber grommets. These grommets pressed against heavy sleeves, when they were under pressure, to seal the gas lines. He gave me a couple of the grommets from his repair container. When the last of the valves was closed, the line began to hold air pressure. The system quickly assumed fifty pounds of pressure and held constant on the gauge. After one hour's time, the repairman removed the pressure gauge from the lines. He released the air pressure, opened all the valves, and checked all the appliances. Everything seemed to be working properly.

I had three days off from school for a total of a five-day Thanksgiving vacation. I was permitted to accompany my dad and brother to my beloved island on a Thanksgiving hunt. We hunted on Wednesday and Thursday of that week without ever using the oven in the gas range. Most of the cooking had been done on the top burners of the stove and on a gas grill on the front porch.

Friday was Thanksgiving for us that year. Mr. Kotarides worked all afternoon on Thursday preparing a huge Thanksgiving meal, including a twenty-pound turkey. He rubbed seasoning on the bird and surrounded it with all his secret herbs and spices. He placed it into the oven that night just before we went to bed. He had me preheat the oven; then he set it on a low temperature. He was planning to cook the bird slowly throughout the night. I cleaned up the galley and dining room after all the hunters had eaten that night. The hunters played a few games of cards, then retired for the night. My father and my brother made a quick check on the boats. I looked around the outside of the club. Then we went to bed ourselves.

In the middle of the night I was awakened by my brother violently shaking me.

"Get up and get outside," he yelled. I jumped up and found that I had a severe headache and felt nauseous. There was a strong odor of gas inside the clubhouse. I staggered to the mudroom door and sat down on the outside deck. My father and brother were busy waking up the hunters. When we were all outside, my dad made a head count. We were all were nauseous, dizzy, and had headaches. A couple of the hunters were even to the point of vomiting. After a few minutes my dad told my brother to open all the windows and close all the gas valves. After we had aired out the clubhouse and it was free of gas odor, my dad turned the gas valves back on while my brother checked for the origin of the odor.

"Cut the valves off," shouted my brother. "It's coming from the cookstove." My brother disconnected the copper gas line from the range, and we carried it out on the screened porch. He installed a plug in the end of the line and turned the valves back on. There was still a lingering odor of gas inside the clubhouse. The windows and doors had to be left open for some time to completely air out the structure.

Soon everyone was beginning to feel better, but no one felt comfortable enough to go back to bed. It was nearing five o'clock, the normal time to begin the hunting day. No one felt well enough to hunt that morning. My dad cooked the bacon and eggs for breakfast on the burner attached to the gas grill. After a good meal the hunters began to feel better, but they still complained of a slight headache and fatigue. The wind was ten to fifteen miles per hour from the northeast. My father and brother set up the north stilt blind. I remained with the hunters and cleaned up from breakfast. Mr. Kotarides retrieved the turkey from the oven. The bird was about half cooked.

"Will you look at that?" Mr. Kotarides said. "This bird is over half cooked; the oven had to be working to get it to this point." I helped him enclose the bird inside tinfoil. He took great pains to preserve all the moisture with the bird. Then he placed it inside the gas grill and set it to the lowest temperature setting. He finished cooking the turkey in the grill. Finally, about lunchtime, a couple of the hunters felt well enough to be taken to the blind. All the hunters were able to have a successful hunt that day. They got their limits in diving ducks on the north reef.

That evening Mr. Kotarides and I set up the Thanksgiving feast. By this time everyone was back to normal. The hunters were enjoying the meal and talking about their day shooting the diving ducks. That was the first time I ever ate turkey roasted on a grill; it was tender and tasty. Mr. Kotarides was an excellent cook. His homemade desserts were simply outstanding.

My brother and I cleaned up from the huge meal. He talked to my dad about the gas range. They were puzzled about the turkey being half cooked before the oven failed. My brother wanted to take the stove apart and look inside the oven compartment. My father agreed as long as he did the work outside on the screened porch. There was still a faint odor of gas around the stove. I helped him take the stove apart. He found the rubber grommets inside the oven's burner compartment. They were pressed almost flat. I told him that the grommets the gas man gave me were much thicker. I went in the galley and got them. "That is the problem," he said as he compared them. "These grommets inside the stove are too thin. They will not seal off the gas when the stove reaches its shutoff temperature. The gas escapes by the altered grommets."

# CHAPTER THIRTY-FIVE

# The *Ramadancer*

My brother told me to go find Mr. Kotarides and Dad. He wanted them to come to the screened porch. When I found them and brought them back, my brother explained the situation to them. "We are very lucky," my father said after examining the grommets. "We all could have taken a very long sleep."

Mr. Kotarides agreed. "It could have turned out a lot worse than it did," he said. He asked my brother why he happened to wake up in the middle of the night.

"I had to answer the call of nature," my brother answered. "When I stood up I noticed I was dizzy and off balance; I almost collapsed on my way to the bathroom," he said. "My head was pounding, and I felt like I was going to throw up. Then I smelled the gas and knew we were in trouble. I woke you and Elvin because you were in the same room with me," he told my dad. "At that point I woke all the hunters and helped them get outside," my brother replied.

The next day was Saturday. We didn't hunt. Everyone got out of bed late. The hunters packed their gear, and my brother took them ashore aboard the *Sandy-K.* My father and I remained and cleaned up the clubhouse for the next group of hunters. The wind shifted and blew a gale from the northeast. The wind from this direction blew most of the water out of the northern Pamlico Sound. By the time my dad and I were ready to go home, the water was too low to take the *Gull Island.* My father decided to take the *Old Anytime* home.

She was a lot slower, but she had a tunnel stern and could operate in shallow water. We had to wear a full set of oil clothes. The spray was completely covering the boat. The waves in the channel were in the four- to five-foot range. The *Old Anytime* was too slow to climb on top of these waves. She just wallowed her way toward Salvo. She would dip down in the trough between waves and rise to the crest of the next one, then back down in the trough again and back up in a slow rocking chair motion. We beat our way across Gull Shoal Channel. Then we crossed the Bay Shoal lumps where the ride was a little smoother. The water levels were much shallower on the lumps. The waves were smaller and closer together. After we crossed the lumps we entered Cedar Hammock Channel, and then the rocking motion resumed. Finally, we made it to the inside of Scotts Reef and entered the Mail Boat Lead. The Mail Boat Lead is a narrow channel that extends from No-Ache Marsh to Southard Channel. The lead runs between Sheep's Head Shoals and Opening Shoals. You are able to pilot your boat from No-Ache, past Salvo, turn offshore near Opening Shoals, and enter Southard Channel to travel northward. This is an inside route well inside the reef.

As we entered the Mail Boat Lead, I noticed the *Sandy-K* anchored in deep water with Mr. Kotarides, my brother, and all the hunters still aboard. My dad eased the *Old Anytime* up close to their stern. This enabled me to toss my brother our bowline. He pulled us up alongside. My brother had taken the larger boat as far in as was possible. Just fifty feet inshore of our location, the water was only inches deep. The only passage into the harbor was a narrow strip of water. It appeared to be just wide enough to accommodate one boat.

My dad instructed me to off-load all the guns, fowl, hunting gear, and the five gallons of gas into the *Sandy-K*. I passed all these objects to my brother. Then he told me to get aboard the larger boat. He was going to take three hunters at a time into the harbor. He began his first trip in with four people in the boat, including himself. He made it halfway in and grounded hard. He had to return and off-load one hunter. His next attempt was successful. There were a total of sixteen people to be ferried in—a dozen hunters, Mr. Kotarides, my dad, my brother, and me—plus all the fowl and gear. My dad made seven trips. On the seventh trip he took Mr. Kotarides and my brother. He left me with the boat and all the gear. My brother returned in the *Old Anytime*. He told me we needed to load only half of the gear into the boat. He had to make three trips to get all the gear in. I came along on the last trip. It took well over an hour to complete all the trips, plus the time they waited for my dad and me to arrive. The time lapse caused the hunters to miss their scheduled flights out of the Norfolk airport.

When everything was loaded into their vehicles, Mr. Kotarides looked at my dad and said, "Ed, we have to do something about this. We either have to dredge a channel to deep water here at Salvo, or we have to purchase a large shallow-draft crew boat for such occasions. I will call you tomorrow, and we will discuss this situation further. In the meantime, think it over. I am interested in your opinion on the matter."

My dad gave Mr. Kotarides a number where he could be reached. They scheduled a three o'clock phone conference. He told Mr. Kotarides that he and my mother would be of-island for the remainder of the weekend. Mr. Kotarides waved and drove away. My dad gave him the phone number of Mr. Wilber Cahoon's store in Eastlake, North Carolina, near his church.

When my parents returned on Monday, my dad had some exciting news for us. Mr. Kotarides was going to have another boat built. This vessel would be large, fast, and able to operate in extremely shallow water.

My brother and I, though, had some disturbing news for him. My grandfather wasn't feeling well. My dad immediately walked over to see him. My grandfather was in his upper eighties. He had heart problems; his health began to deteriorate. On one of his early morning walks he had a massive heart attack and passed away. Cousin Raymond went with him each morning on his walks. This particular morning Grandfather left without having coffee. Raymond filled up two coffee cups and went outside to join him on the walk. He found him lying under a large oak tree, one of his favorite places. This was a blow to us all. Life wouldn't be the same with him gone.

It took a long time for me to become reconciled over the loss of my grandfather. I kept to myself for a few days. I took long walks on the beach and watched the sunset while sitting on the dock at the harbor. I visited the places that I used to go on the walks with Grandfather. He used to share his wisdom and knowledge with me on these occasions. His influence helped me fathom many things that troubled my youthful mind. Our favorite place was sitting on an old bench on the dock at the harbor near sunset.

On one of these occasions after my grandfather had passed, I was at the harbor, and a Mary Jane bakery truck pulled up towing a large trailer. James, the truck driver, backed the trailer down near the bulkhead and stopped. He got out of the truck, unhitched the trailer, and jacked it even with the trailer jack. I asked him if he was staying with us at our house. "Not this time, little man," he replied. "I have to get back to Virginia to haul another load of flour tomorrow. Mr. Ashley and another driver will be arriving here tomorrow." He said bye and in the next instant he had the truck bounding down the sandy road to the highway. As I was waving to him I thought, *Mr. Ashley, I wonder who that is.*

On this trailer sat the most beautiful boat I had ever seen. It was built out of juniper. The outside hull was covered with fiberglass cloth and resin. She was as slick as glass. The exterior was painted a soft powder blue. She was wide with a dead rise bow with a deep flare, flat bottom, and a tunneled stern. The shape of her bottom was unlike any that I had ever seen. It began with a deep, wide tunnel in the back to accommodate the large propeller. The tunnel ran all the way up to her bow. The bow stem extended down to the beginning of a deep concave front on the tunnel. The tunnel edges were sharply curved upward and extended to flat bottom sections that were about four feet wide on each side. These sections were located about two feet above the tunnel. Looking at this design, these structures resembled skis. I asked my dad about the odd shape of the tunnel and how far forward it went. "It looks to me like she will draw much more water than the rest of the boats," I said. "Her bottom is much deeper than theirs are," I added.

"That is true," my dad said. "We will learn all about this new bottom design tomorrow."

"What do you mean by that?" I asked.

"Mr. Kotarides, his chief mechanic, and the hull designer will be here for the launch," he said. The whole concept of the hull design was hard for me to understand, but I thought how lucky I was. We had just got off from school on Christmas vacation. I would be home for the launch. The next morning I slept later than I had planned. I swallowed my breakfast and ran to the harbor. Mr. Kotarides and my dad and the hull designer were looking over the boat. I walked up to them; my dad introduced me to the hull designer. I just kept quiet and listened in on the conversation. He was briefing Mr. Kotarides and my dad on the hull design of the *Ramadancer*. He began by telling us a little about his background. His name was Mr. John Duncan; he was from the state of Florida. He was a design engineer for a boatbuilding firm near the city of Tampa. This manufacturer specialized in the construction of airboats, hydrofoils, and hovercrafts.

He then explained that when the *Ramadancer* came up on a plane, the sharpness of the tunnel near the bow would force more water down into the length of the tunnel. The water would also be forced up the sides of the tunnel, pushing a huge column of air ahead of it. At about three-quarter throttle, the combination of fast-moving water and air would force the boat to rise up on the four-foot structures shaped like skis. The tunnel would be the only portion of the bottom that would remain in the water. The rest of the hull would be completely out of the water riding on the skilike structures, he told us. In very shallow water she would look as if she were on skis. "She has the design of a modified hydrofoil," he added.

"That, I would like to see," I responded.

Then he continued, on a normal tunnel stern boat, when such speeds are reached, the water is forced below the bottom of the boat. Then air is trapped inside the tunnel, so the prop runs out of water and the engine races. The boat hesitates and begins to bang hard up and down in the waves. This is what is meant when someone says the boat ran away from its water. The shape of the tunnel on the *Ramadancer* was fashioned to eliminate this problem. She was designed to operate at high speeds in extremely shallow water. The outside curves and lines of this boat suggested that she was an elite reef runner. I walked around to her stern, and that is when I first saw her name. Painted in lime green, on blue, border in white was the word "Ramadancer." I could not believe my eyes.

Soon my brother joined us. He informed me that this was going to be the new crew boat. My brother told me that this would be by far the fastest boat that I had ever ridden in. Soon the truck driver and the mechanic arrived at the harbor. James was the truck driver, and I did not know the mechanic. We all greeted the two men; I shook hands with them. Mr. Kotarides introduced the mechanic and his helper to us. His name was Mr. Elmer Ashley. The mechanic's helper's name was Fred Andersen; he was also a mechanic and sometimes a truck driver for the bakery. Mr. Kotarides asked Fred if he was ready to tow the trailer to the closest boat ramp and launch her. Fred replied that he was just waiting for the word. My brother rode in the truck with James to show him where the boat ramp was located. My father took the rest of us in the *Gull Island* to the launch location. The boat ramp was located at the Salvo Esso Station. The station was new; it consisted of a gas station, convenience store, and marina. It was located just to the north of our harbor.

We arrived in the *Gull Island* just as Fred was backing the trailer down the boat ramp. He stopped the truck. Fred and my brother gave the boat a little push from the bow. She slid off the trailer smoothly and evenly, as slick as a whistle. She bobbed from stem to stern as she slid into the water. My brother held onto her by the bowline. Fred pulled the trailer up the ramp and headed for the road. My brother got in the *Ramadancer* and tossed me the bowline. I made it fast to the stern cleat on the *Gull Island*, and we began to tow her to our harbor.

When we arrived at the harbor, Mr. Ashley and Mr. Andersen began to check the fluid levels in the engine. Man, what an engine. She had the largest Cadillac engine available. It was over five hundred cubic inches in size. It was a Cadillac Coup de Ville engine. I almost fainted when Mr. Ashley removed the engine box cover. There was a large aluminum tank mounted to the front of the engine. I asked him what it was. He told me it was part of a freshwater cooling system especially designed for the engine. It seems that a saltwater intake was mounted on the bottom of the hull. The salt water was directed to this large tank. Inside the tank was a series of small copper pipes that contained freshwater to cool the engine. He called this a closed cooling system that contained antifreeze like a car. As the freshwater circulated through these pipes inside this tank, it was cooled by the salt water from overboard. Then the salt water was expelled by the two exhaust pipes through her stern at water level. He told us that this was the latest technology in cooling large marine engines. On top of the intake manifold was the largest four-barrel carburetor that I had ever seen.

I said, "This thing looks as if she could fly."

When Mr. Ashley was satisfied that everything had been checked, he fired up the engine. It ran smoothly with a definite sound of power. The exhaust pipes began bubbling at their ends as the hot exhaust mixed with the cold salt water at her stern. Near the bow, the *Ramadancer* had a collapsible canvas canopy. It extended almost back to the engine box and was attached to the edge of the washboards with a grooved stainless-steel track. The canopy could be pulled back and secured in place, creating a covered cabin for cold, rough weather. The canopy could be pushed forward, collapsed, and secured like a convertible top on a vehicle. This could be utilized during fair weather. Mr. Ashley told Mr. Kotarides that the boat was ready for trials. My father and I got aboard the *Gull Island* and went out of the harbor ahead of them. As the *Ramadancer* came out the harbor entrance, Mr. Duncan was at the helm. The wind was light from the west. There was hardly a ripple on the water.

"A perfect day to try her out," my father said. My brother, Mr. Kotarides, Mr. Ashley, Mr. Andersen, and Mr. Duncan were all on board. We followed them into the deep lead; they turned south toward No-Ache Point. My father brought the *Gull Island* up alongside of them, and we began to follow along. All of a sudden, Mr. Duncan throttled up and it looked as if she leaped up on top of the water. She was skimming along on the surface; the entire hull was out of the water. My dad throttled up the *Gull Island* and tried to stay abreast of the *Ramadancer* so that we could get a better look, but it was no use; she left us as if we were still tied to the dock. "Would you look at that?" my father said. She was going so fast that she was kind of skimming along on the surface, trembling from side to side, hardly displacing any water at all. Everyone got a ride in the *Ramadancer* that morning. By noon Mr. Kotarides and his group were satisfied with the break-in trials on the boat. They all left for Virginia: Mr. Duncan had a late flight to Florida that afternoon. My parents left the island, bound for my father's church duties.

As we watched our parents pull out of the driveway, my brother turned to me and said, "After lunch you and I will see what this baby is made of." On our way back to the harbor, my brother said, "I am going to call her the *Dancer*. *Ramadancer* is much too long." That afternoon I enjoyed the fastest boat ride in the shallowest water I had ever experienced. The *Dancer* was truly an elite reef runner.

# CHAPTER THIRTY-SIX

# Chowder

The *Ramadancer* took over the duties as the new crew boat for Gull Island. She could transport a dozen hunters, including their luggage and hunting gear. It didn't matter which way the wind was blowing or how rough the conditions were; she skimmed along on the surface of the water to her destination. This enabled Mr. Kotarides to relocate the *Sandy-K* to Hatteras Village. He rented a boat slip at Hatteras harbor for her. He planned to use her for Gulf Stream fishing in the upcoming summers.

The season continued on with many successful hunts. A problem arose around the shore blinds. This particular season the weather was really nasty. Heavy winds, extreme high-water levels, and rough conditions lasted for many days at Gull Island. This prohibited hunting in the curtain boxes or the stilt blinds. All the hunts were restricted to the shore blinds. When game was harvested, everything was fine as long as the birds were shot over water. Even the cripples could be run down with the boats. When a duck or goose was downed over the marsh, sometimes they were hard to find, especially if they were crippled. It was easy for them to hide in the grass and escape. Most cripples that get away usually are not able to fly. They end up starving to death because they are incapable of searching for food. This really got under my father's skin. He always insisted that my brother and I do everything within our power to harvest all crippled game. He didn't want any of them to go to waste or have to endure unnecessary suffering. My father explained this situation to Mr. Kotarides. Mr. Kotarides asked him what he thought the solution to the problem might be. "What we need is a good hunting dog," my dad responded.

"I will contact my friend, Harry Bowman, when I return to Norfolk from this hunt. You will have one before the next hunt," he told my dad. True to his word, on the very next hunt, Mr. Kotarides not only brought a black Labrador retriever with him, he also brought along the dog's handler. Mr. Kotarides introduced the handler to my dad. His name was Steve Wilkins. He and his family had been in the dog training business for near twenty years. My dad asked Mr. Wilkins what the dog's name was. "He is very young; I haven't named him yet," Steve responded.

"Everything needs a name," my dad said.

"We find it much more successful if we let the new owner or handler choose a name for the dogs," he responded.

"Very well," my dad said. "I will be working with him in the beginning. You can teach me how to properly use him around the shore blinds. After I get the hang of it, I will teach my sons to handle him. When we get to know him, we will figure out a proper name for him."

"The most important thing in the beginning is that you are the only person to feed him. Later you can teach the dog to accept food from your sons," Steve told my dad.

"You mean to tell me that the dog will only take food from you?" Mr. Kotarides asked.

"That is correct, with one exception. He will take food from someone else if the food is placed in a red colored bowl," Steve added. "Sometimes when I am training a dog, I have responsibilities elsewhere and have to be away from it for a few days."

"All your trained dogs will eat food from someone else in red bowls?" asked Mr. Kotarides.

"Each dog is trained with a different colored bowl. They are sometimes all fed together. That way they will not eat each others' food," said Steve. "We feed them together in order to train the aggressiveness out of them.

If they will eat together in harmony, we have discovered they hardly ever fight."(Contrary to what many people think, animals are not colorblind.)

Mr. Kotarides, Steve Wilkins, six hunters, and the dog boarded the *Ramadancer*. My brother joined them to pilot the boat out to the island. My father and I followed them aboard the *Gull Island*. We were transporting a load of grain. As we cleared the mouth of the harbor, I noticed the wind was light from the southwest. The water levels were about average height. I noticed the dog from a distance. He was standing near the stern of the *Ramadancer* reared up on his hind legs with his front paws on the washboards of the boat. His ears were flapping in the breeze. He took it all in. My brother took the *Ramadancer* and his load into the harbor at the island.

My dad and I proceeded to the outward edge of Gull Island Channel and began to spread the grain. After we had grained up, my dad and I joined the hunting party at the clubhouse. My dad went inside to begin putting together an evening meal for the hunters. Usually it was something light the first night, some type of soup and hot dogs or cheeseburgers cooked on the porch grill. My brother and I finished bringing in the luggage and hunting gear. Then we went inside and asked Dad how we could help him. He wanted us to fire up the porch grill and pat out burgers.

Before we could get started, Mr. Kotarides said, "Hold on there, boys. I have some dynamite clam chowder that my cook prepared at home. I have frozen about two gallons of it and brought it along. I will mix up some cornbread and make coleslaw. That should do her for the evening meal." We had a very good meal that evening.

While I was cleaning up the galley, Mr. Kotarides asked me to find the lid for the pot he had warmed up the chowder in. Then I was to put leftover chowder on the front porch; it was cold enough outside that it would not spoil. Neither one of us noticed that the pot was a rose color. About an hour later the dog went to the door and began scratching. Steve let him out and propped the screen door open so he wouldn't scratch the screen out when he returned. He would be able to scratch on the entry door, and we would be able to hear him and allow him to come back inside. The men were playing cards, having a few drinks, and talking about tomorrow's upcoming hunt. My dad told them that low pressure was coming in during the night-time hours. It would be too rough to hunt the offshore blinds the next day. The shore blinds would be their best bet.

"That would be perfect," Steve added. "You will all get a chance to see the dog work. Speaking of the dog, he has been out long enough." Steve decided to go look for him, even though he had not scratched at the door. He went out the door, and I followed him. When we entered the porch we saw the dog lapping up the last bit of the chowder from the pot. There had been about a gallon left over. He let out a tremendous burp and looked up at us with chowder dripping from his nose.

"Oh no," Steve said. "That rose-colored pot, all of that grease from the pork fat used to season the chowder."

The next morning the results were all over the clubhouse floor. There were piles and piles of greasy chowder poop and vomit on the floor. The smell was almost unbearable. Before I could get it all cleaned up, the hunters began to come out of their bedrooms. One of them stepped in a pool of the putrid liquid. It got it all over his boot socks. He placed his hand over his mouth and ran for the door. The sound of his gagging could be heard inside the clubhouse. We had to open the windows and doors for a while and use pine scented floor cleaner to clear the odor.

For the next few days it smelled like a pine-scented privy inside the club-house. The dog was lying near the door on an old blanket my dad left there for him. Steve walked over and stood him on his feet. He collapsed back down on the blanket. His ears were drooping, his eyes were dilated, and he looked too weak to stand.

My dad walked over and looked down at him and said, "This dog is still sick. It is a shame animals suffer because we humans make silly mistakes. He is in no condition to work; he will have to take a sick day." My dad reached down and stroked the dog's head and said, "Boy, you have earned your name." He turned to the group and said, "This dog's name is Chowder."

Everyone in the club laughed and agreed it was a perfect name for the dog. It took a couple of days for Chowder's digestive system to straighten out. When it did, he was ready to go.

I asked my dad if I could go along on the first hunt that Chowder worked. Steve encouraged this. "I can teach your son to how to use the whistle to control Chowder," he told my dad. That day my dad set out the Cane Field blind on the east side of the island. Two hunters, Steve, Chowder, and I sat in the blind waiting for daylight. We heard the heavy whistling of wing beats, then the sound of geese honking. In the next instant we heard the loud splashing sound of large waterfowl settling on the water. It was still too dark to see anything. In a few minutes we could make out five geese sitting on the water, just outside our decoys. The two hunters raised their guns and took the geese. They killed two and crippled three of them. One of the cripples was close enough that a second shot finished him off. The other two flattened out on the water, stretched their necks, lowered their heads, and began swimming off at a rapid rate. The hunters wrapped them up and shot time and time again, but still they swam away.

Chowder was on his feet as soon as the hunters raised their guns. He plunged into the water and began swimming after the cripple that was the longest distance away from us. Steve put the dog whistle to his mouth and prepared to blow on it. It was pitched much too high to be audible to the human ear. The whistle was designed to guide the dog as he swam away from the blind. It was amazing to see Chowder work. As long as he was swimming toward the cripple, no action was necessary on the whistle. If he lost sight of the cripple, one short blast turned him to the left. Two short blasts would turn him to the right. One long blast would return him to the blind. He caught up to the first cripple he was chasing, grabbed it with his mouth, and brought it back to the blind. He then caught and retrieved the second cripple. Then he retrieved the floating dead ones. He placed all the geese one by one at Steve's feet.

A flock of seven sprigtails were the next fowl to approach the blind. They dropped down to water level, cupped their wings, and set down among the duck decoys. The hunters got five of them. Two were taken on the water, and three were winged shots that fell in the marsh. Chowder retrieved all five ducks.

A couple of black ducks flew over the decoys from around the backside of the island. The hunters knocked both ducks down. One was crippled; he made it to the marsh and hid in the grass. Chowder retrieved him still alive from the grass. "That is one we wouldn't have found," said one of the hunters. It is almost impossible to find a crippled duck in the marsh grass, the other hunter agreed.

When we returned to the club that night, I told my father and brother how successful Chowder had worked during the hunt. I told them how well he worked with the whistle. As the result of his work, we didn't lose any fowl that day.

Chowder quickly became a part of the club. My dad took over the duties of feeding him. My brother and I worked him around the shore blinds. The hunting days that we were able to set up the offshore blinds, he roamed free on the island.

On one particular hunt, Mr. Kotarides brought a friend of his to the island who had the most peculiar name I have ever heard: Herman Kettle-Finger. Mr. Kettle-Finger was a wholesale flour supplier for Mr. Kotarides at the bakery. Herman—he insisted that I call him by his first name—aggravated Chowder from the minute he arrived at the clubhouse. He was constantly stepping on the dog's tail each time he walked by him. When we were at the blind, he would stand up quickly as if he were making ready to shoot. This action excited Chowder; he would begin to tremble with anticipation, thinking he was going to work. Then I would have to quiet him down and he would have to return to lying quietly in the floor of the blind. He would constantly try to tempt Chowder with food particles from his hand. My dad explained to Herman that Chowder would only eat food from him. He also reminded Herman that Chowder was a working dog, not a spoiled pet. Herman could not understand. He had dogs of his own and evidently aggravated and spoiled them. It finally got to the point that whenever Herman called Chowder, the dog ignored him. Whenever he tried to approach Chowder and step on his paws or tail, the dog would show his teeth and growl. "If you provoke that dog and he bites you, it is going to be your own fault," my dad warned Herman.

"That dog would never bite me in a hundred years," Herman said. Then he called to the dog, "Come here, Chowder, old boy." Chowder just looked at him and growled.

"He is telling you to stop picking on him," my dad said to Herman.

The remainder of the hunt was successful; the hunters limited out on fowl each day. The last morning arrived; it was the end of the hunt, time for the hunters to return home. Herman had been torturing Chowder all morning. He tried to step on the dog's paws and tail multiple times. All the hunters placed their luggage by the door for my brother and me to load into the boats. I picked up Herman's large, green, military-like canvas clothes bag. He called to me; he wanted me to wait before carrying his bag to the boat. There were a few more things he wanted to put inside it. He left the top of it unzipped. As Herman was returning to his bag, Chowder got on his feet and faced him. The dog looked at him, showed his teeth, walked over, cocked his leg, and proceeded to pee a flood into the top of his clothes bag. Herman yelled and tried to kick at Chowder in order to make him stop. Chowder hopped around to the backside of the bag on three legs, and continued to hose it down. Everyone in the hunting party broke out into uncontrollable laughter. "I am going to kill that dog," Herman said. He threw the remainder of his clothes on top of the urine and zipped it up.

My father looked at Herman, still laughing, and said, "You are not going to touch that dog. You have been asking for that the whole trip. You are lucky he didn't bite you. The unhappiest people in the world are those who get just what's coming to them," my dad added. "I will take the *Dancer* and carry all of you ashore. My wife will wash and dry your clothes when we get there." My dad called Chowder to get aboard the boat with them. The dog saw Herman board the boat; he turned around, walked over, and sat down near my brother and me. "See that," my dad said, looking at Herman.

"The dog refuses to ride in the same boat with you. Okay, boy, you can ride home with Burtis and Elvin," my dad said to the dog. Chowder immediately boarded the *Gull Island* and curled up on top of the engine box. The heat from the engine, along with the sunshine, provided him with a warm, comfortable ride home.

When my brother and I arrived at the harbor in Salvo, all the hunters were gone except Mr. Kotarides and Herman. They were sitting at the table, along with my dad, enjoying a cup of coffee and my mom's apple pie. She was in the process of washing, drying, and packing Herman's clothes in a clean canvas bag. Chowder refused to enter the house as long as Herman was there. "What's wrong with the dog?" my mom asked. "He refuses to come inside the house."

"I will tell you later," my dad answered. My dad and I went outside to see Mr. Kotarides and Herman off. Herman got into the car on the passenger's side and closed the door.

"I think this was Herman's one and only trip hunting at Gull Island," Mr. Kotarides said to my dad.

"That is probably a wise decision if you plan to continue to work Chowder at the shore blinds," my dad answered. After they left, my father told me animals respond to humans according to how we treat them. "Remember, always be kind and gentle toward Chowder; only scold him if he is bad or disobeys. When he does a good job, don't forget to praise and reward him. Hunting dogs are born with the instinct to hunt and retrieve. If you always remember that, you and your dog will have many successful hunts," said my father.

This reminds me of a story that Travis Fulcher, a friend of mine, told me about another black Labrador retriever.

# CHAPTER THIRTY-SEVEN

# Lost Hunters

Travis Fulcher, a friend of mine, lives in the Morehead City area of North Carolina. He comes from a long line of hunters and decoy makers. His father, Joe Fulcher Jr., is one of the premier decoy makers of eastern North Carolina today. Travis told me of a friend of his who had purchased two black Labrador retriever pups—one male, one female. This friend was training the dogs to hunt and retrieve. His friend's next-door neighbor had twin daughters. The girls were ready to celebrate their eighth birthday just before Easter. Their father bought them a couple of white rabbits. The rabbits were a combination of birthday and Easter presents. The girl's father built a rabbit pound well off ground level to protect the rabbits from predators. The girls took good care of the rabbits.

One afternoon Travis's friend came home early from work. There on his back porch was the male pup with one of the rabbits in his mouth. The rabbit was dead and all covered in dirt. The dog owner took the rabbit away from the pup. He washed the rabbit thoroughly and used a hair dryer to dry it. He sneaked over to his neighbor's house and placed the clean rabbit back in the pound. He went back home but kept his eyes peeled for the return of his neighbor. When his neighbor came home from work, he waited a few minutes, then walked over. He found his neighbor in the backyard walking around and around the rabbit pound. He was scratching his head, as if confused, and staring at the dead rabbit in the pound. The dog owner asked his neighbor what happened to his rabbit. Did it die? The neighbor answered, "Yes, and I buried it yesterday afternoon. The wonderment of it is that today when I got home, it's back in the pound."

I trust that some folks reading this might have trouble following this story. The pup dug up the buried rabbit and took it home. Most dogs or cats will do the same thing. They are proud of the booty they find or catch and will bring it home. Usually they will remain close by their prize, expecting praise, when their masters return.

A good hunting dog is a valuable asset for any hunter to own. They not only find and retrieve downed game, they are helpful in locating misplaced items lost by their owner. I recall many times that my dad asked Chowder to help him find a misplaced item. That dog could locate things inside the house or outside of the house. His ability to find things was well known around the Chicamacomico area, the three villages of Rodanthe, Waves, and Salvo.

That hunting season continued on for me until Christmas holidays were almost over. On the last Friday, before school began on the following Monday, the last hunt of the holiday came to an end. After all the hunters had enjoyed a big breakfast, they packed and I loaded all their gear. My brother took the hunters to Salvo in the *Dancer*. My father, Chowder, and I remained at the island to clean up the clubhouse. My father was in a bit of a hurry as we were cleaning. I asked him why he was rushing. He told me that the barometer dropped suddenly in the last couple of hours. He said we were in for a change of wind and a blow: "If we get finished and leave by noon, we could beat the shift home."

I began to hurry along with my duties. We made a couple of sandwiches to eat on the trip and left just ahead of noon. The wind was from the southeast and there was a steady drizzle of rain falling. My father took the inside route home, across the narrow east end of Gull Shoal Channel. We continued across Bay Shoals and neared the marsh at Cedar Hammock Island Point. As we came along parallel to the marsh, we spotted a small boat, a sixteen-foot skiff equipped with an outboard motor, anchored near No-Ache Island. There were two men bushing a blind on the point of the small island. My father slowed the boat and turned inshore toward the men. When we got close enough to talk, he took the boat out of gear and we eased up to them. It was my cousin Richie and a man I had never seen before. Chowder jumped out of the boat and greeted both of them. Richie introduced the man to us; his name was Robert. My dad said to Richie, "Dick, you boys should leave soon; we are in for a shift of wind and a blow." He told them that they should not be caught down the shore in such a small boat.

"We are almost finished, Uncle Ed," Richie answered,

"You should hurry along," my father added. "Come on, boy," my dad said to Chowder, and the dog jumped back into the boat. Just as we were turning to enter the harbor at Salvo, the wind moved around to the south. "Later this afternoon the wind is going to come around to the westward and steadily breeze to gale force, then shift to the northeast," my dad told me. Just about three o'clock in the afternoon the shift came in; the drizzle turned into freezing rain. The temperature dropped drastically, well below freezing. It blew steadily for about two hours, then shifted to the northeast. Just after dark there came a knock at our front door. My mom answered it. There, soaking wet, stood Richie's father. He was my father's first cousin Dick Austin. You could see from the concerned expression on his face that something was wrong. My mom invited him in and offered a cup of hot coffee.

"I am too upset for coffee," he told her. "That fool son of mine and Robert haven't come home yet; I was wondering if you saw them today."

My dad told him we had; they were on the outside point of No-Ache Island working on a blind. "We stopped and talked to them," Dad added.

"I am sick with worry. I just left Dot, Dick's wife, and Richie's mother home wringing her hands and crying. Robert is my brother Rob's son; he is visiting from Southport, a town along the coast, a few miles south of Hatteras Island. Richie wanted to take him hunting before he had to go back home. My brother Ray and I took my boat down the shore awhile, and we couldn't get within a hundred yards of the marsh. This northeast blow has taken all the water to the other side of the sound," he said.

"I will go get Burtis, my older son. You and he can take the *Dancer*; she can run in a tea cup full of water. You two can go down to look for them."

Before they left my mother gave my brother four blankets wrapped up in plastic. "These might come in handy," she said to him. Dick and my brother boarded the *Dancer* and prepared to leave. Chowder jumped into the boat; I called to him to get out. "No," my brother said. "Let him go. He will be our best shot at finding them." My brother throttled up the *Dancer*; she was out of the harbor in a flash. All that could be seen of her through the frozen drizzle was the red and green bow lights, and the white stern light. She disappeared from sight as my brother turned her south along the marsh. As they passed No Ache Point, Chowder began barking and pacing from the bow to the stern of the boat. At one point my brother thought he was going to jump overboard. He asked Dick to get a good grip on the dog and hold him until they found deep enough water to stop.

My brother had to keep the *Dancer* up on a fly. If he slowed her down they might be caught on the shoals. She would skim along in inches of water, as long as you throttled her up in about two feet of water. He had to enter the small channel that ran between Cedar Hammock Island and the shore near the middle of the Pines. This would give him enough water to get the *Dancer* back up.

Just as soon as the boat slowed, Chowder jumped overboard. He took off running along the edge of the marsh and disappeared from sight in a northerly direction. My brother called to him, but he would not stop. "That fool dog is chasing something along the marsh. I was hoping he would stay with us and help find the boys," my brother said. They walked to the outside point of No-Ache Island, but there was no sign of the boat. They started back to the boat. My brother called the dog one last time. "He will have to find his own way back home," my brother said to Dick.

"I don't know what in the world to do," Dick said. "I can't go back home to Dot without them boys. She will have a nervous breakdown; she is all to pieces now."

"Don't worry, we will find them, even if it takes all night," my brother told him.

"That's what I am worried about. They have been exposed to these freezing conditions for several hours now," Dick responded. "I don't know how much longer they can hold on."

"I will get the *Dancer* back up and we will run as close to the edge of the marsh as we can," said my brother. They cruised along the marsh until they approached No Ache Point. There on the edge of the marsh was Chowder. He was pacing back and forth, jumping up and down, barking uncontrollably at the boat. He would run back from the edge of the marsh a few yards, then return, barking all the while. "I think that dog of your father's wants us to follow him," stated Dick.

"This is the exact spot where he went nuts and almost jumped overboard when we were coming down here," my brother said. "I will take the *Dancer* offshore a little and pick up more speed. I think we can get her across that shoal, in the mouth of Cut Thru," my brother added. The *Dancer* skimmed across the shoal, and my brother settled her in the south creek of the Cut Thru in about four feet of water. Chowder jumped into the water and swam across the creek. When he reached the other side of the creek, he resumed barking. He would disappear in the high grass, then return to the edge of the creek and continue barking. "He wants us to follow him into the high grass. I don't believe that boat is that far back up in the marsh," my brother added.

"I am going to follow the dog," Dick said. My brother anchored the boat and both of them followed Chowder. They walked all the way across No Ache Marsh. They were hollering the boy's names as they walked. Chowder kept coming back barking to make sure they were following. They soon approached the tree line. There, lodged between two cypress trees, was the small boat. Chowder jumped inside the boat, still barking. Dick and my brother were relieved when the boys answered their call to them. They were both soaking wet, confused, and shivering from the cold. They didn't know which direction to go to find the shoreline or the road. They chose to stay with the boat until daylight. "You boys would not have made it to daylight," Dick told them. "You would have frozen to death if it wasn't for that dog."

"He came and jumped into the boat a while ago," Richie told them.

"All he did was to bark at us," Robert added.

"He was trying to get you to follow him. He was trying to lead you to us on the back of the marsh," Dick told them.

"The water must have been really high to wash you and the boat to the tree line," my brother said.

Richie began telling them what happened. "The wind was howling from the northwest. The waves jumped up to about four to five feet in size. As we approached No Ache Point, we took a large wave over the bow. The wave swamped the boat. The gas tank washed over the stern, then the outboard cut off. We were at the mercy of the waves. I thought at one time we might be thrown out of the boat. The storm carried us to where you found us, lodged between those two trees."

The walk back to the *Dancer* was brutal for the boys. They were stiff from sitting in the boat so long in the freezing conditions. The hard northeast wind and the driving frozen rain pelted all of them on their way back to the *Dancer*. Finally, they made it back to the boat. Both the boys huddled in the canvas cabin, and my brother wrapped them up in the blankets. Chowder went into the cabin and lay between the two boys. Dick patted the dog's ice-crusted head and said, "Thanks to you, boy, my son and nephew are safe." Chowder nuzzled and licked his hand.

My brother throttled up the *Dancer*. She skipped across the shallow water to the harbor at Salvo. Richie's mother, Dot, had walked all the way down the road to our house. She arrived just after my brother and Dick left in the *Dancer*. She was soaked to the skin, cold and crying uncontrollably. My mom brought her towels and dry clothes, and tried to console her. She wanted to know if my mom had heard anything from the search. Mom told her that my brother and Dick were out searching, and Dad and I were waiting for them at the harbor. She wanted to go down to the harbor to wait for the return of the boat. Mom talked her out of that; she told her there was no heat in the shed where we were waiting.

All of a sudden, the *Dancer* appeared out of the mist. She was skimming along the water's surface up the harbor entrance. As she entered the basin, she created a whooshing sound as she relaxed down into the water. My brother guided her up to the dock. "We found them," Dick called out to us.

I prepared to help them off the boat. Dad stopped me. He told me to run to the house and tell my mother. Then run up the road to Dick's and tell Dot as quick as I could move.

"Yes, sir," I said, and took off. I burst into the kitchen door, and I found Mom and Dot sitting at the table. "They found them. They are cold, but fine," I told them. "They are on their way to the house now," I added. We had to physically hold Dot to keep her from running down to meet them.

"Wait," Mom told her. "They will be here in a few minutes." When the boys entered the kitchen, she began hugging them. Mom had a hard time getting her to let go of them. "Let them get near the stove to warm up," she said to Dot. "They can both take showers and Dick can bring them dry clothes. Now just look at you," Mom said to her. "You are soaked from hugging them. We will have to get you fresh clothes." Chowder was the last to enter the kitchen. The ice began melting from his hair. He stood perfectly still until Mom brought a towel and began drying him off. Then he walked over and lay down on his blanket. Dick told everyone that the dog was the reason that they found the boys.

Dot walked over to the dog and said, "Thank you very much, Chowder, for returning my son and nephew to me." She bent down to hug the dog. Chowder stood up; he was wagging his tail as he licked her face.

The boys soon warmed up. Mom made a fresh pot of coffee and heated up the lima beans we had for supper. They had a bowl of beans along with biscuits. They thanked us and left for home in Dick's car.

Not all the episodes of missing Pamlico Sound watermen turned out as good as this one. No-Ache Marsh is one of the roughest stretches of water near the Salvo area. The water levels on the north reef of Gull Island Reef are too deep to knock down a gale-force southwest swell. The same applies to Scotts Reef. It borders No-Ache Marsh to the north and extends to Sheep's Head Shoals. There isn't any protection from a mounting northwest swell. No-Ache Marsh is located on the shore side between these reefs.

During times of gale-force winds from the northwest or southwest, waves build to five to six feet along the shoreline. There have been numerous watermen who have met their end from Rodanthe to Gull Island in this portion of the sound. The village of Rodanthe has lost more watermen in the sound than the villages of Waves or Salvo. I can recall several from Rodanthe and one from Salvo in recent years. Most of them have been fishermen or crabbers. Their waterman heritage can be traced back as far as anyone in these parts can remember. They are a hearty lot, self-sufficient, and weathered beyond their years by the elements. Most of them have spent almost as much time out on the water as they have on land. This is how these folks support their families. They feel compelled to go out, even in rough conditions. More often than not, they risk their safety for the catch and a paycheck.

The commercial waterman of today faces a lot more than just treacherous waters. The regulations on any type of seafood harvesting have all but put these folks out of business. It is almost impossible to even understand the rules, much less follow them. My ancestors were watermen; everything they harvested was used. They respected and lived in harmony with nature to the end of their existence.

# CHAPTER THIRTY-EIGHT

# Bottlenose Dolphins

It was really hard to board that old school bus on the first day after Christmas vacation. The ride to Buxton is about twenty miles. At thirty-five miles per hour, it takes about forty minutes to get there. Sometimes the heat worked and sometimes it didn't. Most of the windows were stuck in place with a large gap at the top. Most of the time you had to keep your coat zipped up to keep from freezing to death.

Richie and I sat across the center aisle from one another on the bus. It was a long, uncomfortable trip to school. Richie began telling me detail by detail about the awful predicament he and his cousin found themselves in.

"Man, if you think this is cold, you should have been with Robert and me. I was really tickled to see that dog of yours the other night. I wanted to take Robert hunting on No Ache Island. The hunting is really good there when your dad has a party at Gull Island. The fowl fly right across the outside point of No-Ache Island, from Gull Island, on their way to the refuge." The refuge is an area where hunting is banned from north of Rodanthe to Oregon Inlet.

"We drove five two-by-four stakes in the mud and attached plywood to them. We grassed and bushed all sides of the plywood. A small section was left out in the back for entry. A portable wall section was bushed to cover the entrance. We were planning to hunt there Saturday, but we got in that mess Friday night. Both of us slept most of the day on Saturday. Robert's father, Uncle Rob, came and picked him up yesterday, and they left this morning on their return trip home to Southport."

Richie was quite the hand waver when he was telling a story. All I had to do was listen, nod my head, and say "okay" once in a while. He told me he really wanted his cousin Robert to get a crack at those ducks and geese. His account of his cousin's visit lasted all the way to the school parking lot. We got off the bus to begin our first day of classes following the freedom of a two-week Christmas break. I worked at Gull Island with my father and brother every chance that I got. I attended all the weekend hunts and all holiday hunts when school was out. I was able to spend my high school winters out at the island on hunts with them.

At the end of my senior year of high school, my mother was stricken with an aneurysm. It was located in the frontal lobe of her brain. The frontal lobe deals with problem solving, judgment, and motor skills. She had to have brain surgery. After a very complicated operation, she was allowed to return home. My father had to retire in order to take care of her. My brother terminated his employment with the state. He came home to help Dad take care of Mom. I helped with Mom all I could. I was really concerned about her. The doctors told us she would steadily improve. It seemed to me that she was getting weaker by the day. I was hesitant to leave home for my first year of college. I came home every weekend. Mom passed about two months later. I was devastated.

After everything was taken care of, my dad encouraged me to return to college. "That is what your mother wanted," he said. "She was so proud the day you left; she was bubbling over."

I still miss her, especially during the holiday season. Valentine's Day is hard for me; that was her birthday. I told Dad I needed some time by myself. I promised him I would return the next fall semester. It was the beginning of October. My brother replaced Dad in the leadership role at Gull Island. He was very understanding and patient with me; he allowed me to take the *Old Anytime* out to Gull Island. I spent the month of October at the island, mostly alone. I sat for hours on the screened porch of the clubhouse listening to the nighttime sounds of the island. My brother was the only person I saw. He brought supplies for me when he came out on working trips to prepare the club for the upcoming season. I worked with him during hunting season that winter. After the season I came home to spend the rest of the winter with my father. He left the island every Friday night to attend to his church. He returned home on Monday mornings. After that winter, he retired from his church duties.

I picked up a carpenter's helper job working with our distant cousin Burgess Hooper and his son, Johnny. My friend Larry was already working with them. I worked to the end of summer with them and returned to school in the fall.

My brother hired Michael Halminski and Mark McCracken to help him run the club at Gull Island. I was involved every chance I got. During the months of August, September, and November my dad helped me make money for college by flounder fishing. I made sure I scheduled my first class at one o'clock on Mondays, and my last class at two o'clock on Fridays. This gave me ample time to get home before dark. Mr. Kotarides allowed my dad and me to stay at the clubhouse on Friday nights. He gave us permission to use the *Old Anytime*. Each Friday night as we arrived I started the generator. This allowed the icemaker at the club to begin making ice. A lot of ice was needed to preserve the fish. We set flounder nets on the south reef of Gull Island. We had the club to ourselves during the months of August and September. We placed a dozen one-hundred-yard lengths of five-and-a-quarter flounder webbing inside one of the large decoy skiffs. The decoy skiff was towed behind the *Old Anytime*. As my dad steered the motorboat, I set the nets over the stern of the decoy boat.

Early Saturday morning we fished down the nets and iced the flounder in large coolers. We would return to the clubhouse and rest until about ten o'clock Saturday night. Then we fished the nets. Any flounder that were in them were iced with the ones we caught earlier. As I fished the nets I pulled them back aboard the decoy skiff. The decoy skiff with the nets inside was tied up at the Gull Island harbor dock. We left it there to use the next weekend. I added more ice to the coolers when we got back to Salvo. I went to the fish market on my way back to school early Monday morning.

One particular Saturday we noticed four bottlenose dolphins chasing corncob mullets along the edge of the south reef. These are air-breathing mammals with blowholes located on the top of their heads. They are not the type of dolphin caught in the Gulf Stream. Those are fish; they have gills and are used for food. The local folks of the Hatteras area call these mammals "porpoises." It is hard to tell the difference between porpoises and dolphins. They are very similar. The air-breathing dolphin has a long bottle-shaped nose. They have large mouths and are rather talkative. The porpoises have shorter noses and stubbier bodies, and don't make the whistling, clicking sounds that dolphins do. Both have large brains and are very intelligent. There are a lot more species of dolphin than porpoise. Both species travel in pods and communicate with others of their kind by the use of sonar. Two of the Gull Island dolphins looked to be adults accompanied by two younger ones. They were circling the mullets, causing them to form into tight schools. Then they would cut through the center of the mullets, scooping up mouthfuls of them. They were a sight to see, the way they worked the mullets. All four of them were curious and seemed to be interested in what we were doing. They were not afraid of us or the boat. One of the smaller ones swam right up to the boat, rolled on its side, and looked us over. I had just finished the last net. "I believe I could feed them," I said to my dad.

"I doubt that. They like to catch their food and eat it alive," my dad responded. That morning we had a nice catch of flounder, plus a few other assorted fish. There were three trash fish called fatbacks lying in the bottom of the boat. I picked one of them up and threw it as high as I could over the top of the dolphins. When the fish came down close to the surface of the water, one of the larger ones jumped completely out of the water and caught the fish in its mouth. "Did you see that?" I hollered to my dad.

"How could I miss it?" he answered.

Each time we saw the dolphins I threw them a fish, but they never repeated the acrobatic catch. They would take the fish, but only after it landed in the water. The dolphins became regulars on the south reef of Gull Island. Every weekend they were there fishing just off the edge of the reef in about eight feet of water.

I woke up one Saturday morning at the club to the smell of fresh coffee perking. My dad was already up and cooking breakfast. I walked into the galley and he said to me, "We will have to take the nets up this morning." Usually we left them out until late Saturday night to catch more fish. "The barometer has risen sharply fifteen to twenty points in the last hour," he said. "The wind is going to blow a gale from the northeast."

I looked out the window. "It's perfectly calm," I said to him.

"I know, but the water levels are already beginning to run off. The wind has already breezed up to the north of us. By noon the part of the reef where the nets are will be high and dry. We need to hurry along before we lose too much more water." When we came out the mouth of Hull Island harbor there was no wind. There wasn't a ripple on the water; the sound was as slick as glass. We moved along the north edge of the south reef. The boat began bumping bottom a long distance away from the first net. "If we're not careful we are going to get in a mess the way this water is running off," my dad said. "Forget about going across the reef and fishing back this way." He told me to get into the decoy skiff and begin checking the nets from the north and make my way across the reef. He took the power [**QY: powerboat? or something else?**] across the reef and anchored her in deep water off the south edge of the reef. The nets were full of flounder and other assorted fish.

"They are moving ahead of the shift," I said out loud. I didn't have time to take the fish out of the nets. I just pulled them into the boat still hung into the webbing. I worked my way across the reef. I had two nets to go when the skiff began to bump bottom. My weight, along with the fish and the wet webbing, caused her to sink much deeper down into the water. I had to get over the side and pull the skiff the rest of the way to deep water. My dad got overboard and held the skiff into place. I walked back to the nets and drug the ends of both of them to the boat. As I pulled the last net into the boat, the dolphins showed up. They were swimming erratically. They were jumping clear out of the water. The two larger ones were tail walking on the surface. They were constantly chattering.

"I have never seen them acting like that before," my father said. I had to agree. They would swim offshore a short distance, come flying back, and slide up on the reef on their bellies almost out of the water. They would wiggle off the reef and take off at a rapid pace toward the east. Then they would return and return near us and repeat this behavior. Then I noticed there were only three of them.

"One of them is missing," I said to my dad.

"You are right," he answered. "I believe they are trying to get us to follow them to the eastward," Dad said to me. I tied the skiff to the stern of the *Old Anytime*. The dolphins constantly circled the boat, then they raced along the edge of the reef toward the east.

"I think you are right about them wanting us to follow," I said to Dad. We began to follow the three dolphins. The shift of wind appeared in the northeastern sky. The north horizon darkened considerably as the shift came in. The wind breezed to gale force and it began to rain. The water levels began to get drastically low as the wind increased. The dolphins were about one hundred yards ahead of us. One of the adults swam back near the bow of the boat. He surfaced, bobbed his head, and made a series of clicking sounds. When he was satisfied that we were still following them, he turned and continued east. Near the end of the reef they turned and raced up a small slough. When they neared the end of the slough, they slid on their bellies up on the sand completely out of the water. Just about a hundred yards away from them was the fourth one. It was trapped in a shallow pool of water about a foot deep. Evidently they had been chasing a school of fish, and this one swam too far up the slough. The water had run off and left it trapped out of reach of the others. It was floundering helplessly in the shallow pool of water. Large, white heron gulls were already gathering to await its demise. Some of the more aggressive gulls approached the young dolphin and took random pecks at its head. The dolphin was flopping from side to side in order to protect its eyes.

"We have to help it," my father said as he throttled up the boat to drive the bow up on the reef. I jumped out of the boat on the sand and ran toward the dolphin's location. On my approach the gulls took flight. I knelt down by the dolphin. It was completely exhausted and stopped squirming. It seemed to realize that I was there to help. I looked back toward the boat. My dad was setting the anchor.

"His eyes are fine, but he has a few peck marks near them," I said to my dad as he approached. I rubbed the dolphin and constantly splashed water on it.

"We have to carry it to deep water," my dad said. "We have to be careful. If we drop it, we might cause an injury that could result in its death. Go back to the boat and get the canvas tarp we use to cover the coolers with," he said to me. I ran to the boat and brought the tarp back. We folded the tarp and gently rolled the dolphin over on it. We completely wrapped it up in the tarp. Then we picked up the tarp and walked to the edge of the reef. At this point we placed the tarp into the water and unfolded it. The small dolphin just remained there motionless on the tarp.

"He is worn out," my dad said. The other three dolphins had slid back into the water and kept a constant eye on us.

Slowly the little fellow began flapping its tail up and down. After a few strokes it propelled itself off the tarp and swam up to the other three. The others began gently nudging the freed dolphin and making soft whistling, clicking sounds.

"We will go to the back of the island at the sand beach. There we'll have some lee from the wind," Dad said.

I pulled the anchor; Dad started the engine. The dolphins followed us to the back of the island. As we took the fish out of the nets, I threw them one now and then. They were amazing to watch. They allowed the small one that was stranded to take the first fish. Then they took turns eating the food. We finished cleaning the fish out of the nets and loaded them in the coolers. My dad decided to spread the nets out on the marsh on the backside of the island. "Next weekend we will pick them up here," he told me.

We towed the skiff around the west end of the island and entered the harbor at the club. The dolphins followed us to the mouth of the harbor but would not enter. After we tied the skiff to the dock, I filled empty grain bags with ice and iced the coolers. Then we took a few minutes to clean the clubhouse and started for home. The dolphins followed the boat across Gull Shoal Channel, keeping up with us. They played in the wake, swimming back and forth behind the boat. As we came to the other side of the channel, one of the adults jumped completely out of the water. When we entered Bay Shoals, they turned to the west and followed the channel out back of the reef. They circled south and swam out of eyesight behind Gull Island.

The very next weekend, as we were loading the nets in the decoy skiff, there was a large splashing sound in the water behind us. We turned to see what made the noise.

"Our friends are back," my father said. There behind us were the four dolphins bobbing in the water. They came each weekend until the weather cooled off. Then one weekend they were gone. Over the years I have spent many hours in and around the waters of the Hatteras area. I have seen many porpoises, but I believe that the only dolphins I have ever seen were the ones at Gull Island. It is hard for me to distinguish between the species. Each time I saw one, I approached as close as they would allow. They showed no signs of curious behavior or friendship. I just assumed they were all porpoises.

# CHAPTER THIRTY-NINE

# Coffin Boxes

During the following flounder seasons my dad helped me with the nets. We kept our eyes peeled, but the dolphins never returned. Now, many years later, I cherish the memories of that flounder season and the experiences I shared with my father and the dolphins. He told me I probably shouldn't mention the dolphin story to anyone. I asked him why.

"Because no one will ever believe a tale like that," he told me. "If a couple of your cousins told you a story like that, would you believe them?" he asked me.

Instantly I caught his meaning; it was a tall tale at that. My father and I fished on the reef that fall until the flounder had migrated farther south. My brother gave me as much work at the island during hunting season as I could schedule around my classes. On one of these Friday afternoon hunts I was teamed up with Mr. Harry Bowman and Mr. Tommie Hodges. They were hunting in the north reef stilt blind for diving ducks. Both were both getting along in age. They took me along to retrieve their downed fowl. Mr. Bowman asked me if I had noticed the latest shoal that had made up near the channel. I told him that I had seen it and discussed it with my brother. The shoal had made up near the center of the south reef. We noticed a large number of geese and swan feeding on eel grass at the shoal. My brother was concerned about not having a blind in the area. He was afraid that the fowl would be drawn to them instead of the hunting locations.

"He has good reason for concern," Mr. Bowman told me. "Does your brother have any ideas or a solution to address this situation?" he asked me. "That point of shoals is located in the flight path of fowl leaving and returning to the island," Mr. Bowman added.

"I believe I heard him mention something about a float blind for the shoal," I told him.

"I have an idea for a blind that might help him. The hunters of Back Bay call them coffin boxes," Mr. Bowman said.

"What is a coffin box?" I asked him.

"They are portable and can be used in shallow water. I will discuss them with your brother at dinner tonight. Just listen to our conversation," he said. After dinner that night, as I helped clean up the galley, my ears were glued to the conversation between my brother and Mr. Bowman. Mr. Bowman brought up the situation of the new shoal that had formed. My brother voiced his concerns about the fowl being drawn away from the hunting locations. They decided to name the location the Point of Shoals. It was agreed that this new Point of Shoals was located in the primary flight path of the fowl. Mr. Bowman told us of a portable, shallow-water blind called the coffin box. It was a type of small boat, shaped like a coffin, built of marine plywood and fiberglass on the exterior hull. It was about twelve feet long and five feet wide. The front was pointed, like the bow of a boat, and the back was squared off. Near the center was a box six feet long by four feet wide. There was ample room for two hunters to sit facing each other. The rim of the box had a canvas curtain that could be adjusted in height. This feature was similar to the curtain or sink box. The boat was equipped with sealed compartments that could be flooded. Water could be bailed into these areas to submerge the boat below the surface of the water. There was an anchor attached to the bow. Two long pins were fastened to each side of the back. The small boat could be held in place using a three-point anchoring system. A small sea breaker would be installed on the windward side of the blind, when the decoys were set out, and then it would be ready for a hunt.

My brother had a few questions for Mr. Bowman about the coffin boxes. Mr. Bowmen told him that the boxes might be illegal in North Carolina. He knew for sure that they were being used in the marshes of Back Bay in Virginia.

I left them still talking about the boxes and walked out of the side porch of the clubhouse. I always enjoyed the nighttime noises of the island. The wind was fifteen to twenty miles per hour from the northeast. All I could hear that night was the constant slapping of the waves along the marsh on the windward side of the island.

The next morning the water levels were low from the effects of the northeast wind. My brother decided to set out the curtain box on the northwest reef. Just after daylight I was watching the hunters with the aid of binoculars. I swept the horizon on all points looking for approaching fowl. I noticed that flight after flight of geese and swan began to congregate on the newly formed Point of Shoals. About a dozen rafts of diving ducks settled on the water and began feeding along the edge of the channel. The ducks were about a hundred yards off the Point of Shoals. All the fowl that flew around Gull Island that morning decoyed to the ones located at the Point of Shoals. The hunters in the north reef sink box never got a shot the entire day. My brother's fears were confirmed.

The following day was Saturday, the last day of the hunt. It dawned with a brisk northwest wind blowing. The water levels had increased considerably. They were high enough to set out the south reef high-water curtain box. The water was much too rough and deep to allow the fowl to feed at the Point of Shoals. The hunters had a successful hunt, harvesting large numbers of ducks and geese that day. That was the last day of duck season for that year. Goose season extended for two more weeks.

Early Sunday morning my brother took the hunters to the main island so that they could return home. Mr. Bowman promised to obtain a set of plans for a coffin box. He agreed to mail the plans to my brother. The other two guides and I stayed and cleaned up the clubhouse. We completed our work and arrived at Salvo just after ten o'clock. My father was off the island attending to his church services. I washed and dried my week's supply of clothes and bed linens. I packed my old car, locked the house, and went to my brother's house for Sunday dinner. My brother's wife, Jean, is an excellent cook.

During the meal my brother told me we were going to build two coffin boxes. He had contacted Mr. Kotarides and told him about the newly formed shoals on the reef. Mr. Kotarides agreed to fund the project using Mr. Bowman's plans. He told me he would leave the *Gull Island* at Salvo harbor on the next week's hunt. I could bring her over to the island on Friday evening for the weekend hunt. I could hunt with him and his two guides for the last two weeks of goose season. He could arrange payment for me to assist in closing the club for the season. I could also help with the construction of the coffin boxes at the end of the season.

I left for school that Sunday afternoon. Jean gave me a large container of stewed chicken and pie bread to take along. This generous helping would normally last for several meals. The next afternoon after classes I was warming up the mixture, and my roommates smelled it being heated. My normal several meals lasted for only one feed.

The next two weekends I attended the goose hunts at Gull Island. On the last weekend the hunters harvested five grain bags of geese. Also, they shot a couple of bags of diving ducks, two weeks after duck season had ended.

My brother took me aside and said, "You know the game wardens will be waiting for us at the dock tomorrow." I responded with an affirmative head shake. My brother explained his plan to me. "They are always there on the last weekend of the season," he added. They sleep in their vehicles, watching the harbor through the night. "Help me sort these ducks into three grain bags. The boys," meaning the other two guides, "can stay and clean the club. They can come home in the *Gull Island*. I will take the hunters and their gear ashore in the *Dancer*," he said. "You follow in the *Old Anytime* and bring the bagged ducks and geese with you. You can leave here a half hour ahead of us so we will arrive about the same time. I will fly in the harbor in the *Dancer* and back her down at the last minute. Hopefully this will capture their attention. It should allow you to throw the bagged ducks into that group of myrtle bushes at the harbor entrance. Then come on in the harbor with the geese. After they have left, we will pick up the ducks under the cover of darkness."

Sure enough, the wardens were waiting. They were so impressed with the *Dancer* that my brother's plan worked perfectly. They had searched the boats. The hunters had to uncase their guns so they could be checked. Finally they were satisfied that everything was in order. They asked my brother if he had time to take them for a boat ride. He smiled and said, "Sure, hop in." The two wardens got into the boat. As he was leaving, my brother looked at me and nodded his head. He tore out of the harbor, forcing the two wardens to grab anything they could to steady themselves. Soon the boat disappeared from sight in a westward direction. I took the wheelbarrow and retrieved the ducks. We loaded all the gear, luggage, and fowl into the hunters' vehicles, and they left. When my brother returned with the wardens, all was well at the harbor. I heard them asking him about the boat. They wanted to know how such a large boat skimmed along the surface of the water without experiencing any fetch or roll from the choppy waves. He told them it was all in the hull design. They checked our guide license, took a last look at the boat, thanked him for the boat ride, and left the harbor.

"Well, we got away with that by the skin of our teeth," he said.

"Not by the skin of our teeth, but by the skim of the *Dancer*," I added. We both laughed and headed for the house. It took us the month of February to close and secure the club for the season.

Just like he promised, Mr. Bowman mailed my brother a set of plans for the coffin boxes. My brother ordered all the materials, and we were ready to start work at the beginning of March. He borrowed a large army tent from our cousin Myrtle's husband. We set it up under a large oak tree in the lee of our father's house. The tent had a closeable door flap. This provided us protection as well as our material. We had a nice place to work in any type of weather. We installed ten light fixtures suspended a couple of feet down from the ceiling of the tent. In these fixtures we placed one-hundred-watt lightbulbs. On cold days we closed the door flap. The hundred-watt bulbs provided adequate heat inside the tent. The electrical power was provided by heavy extension cords from Dad's house.

The first step was to begin cutting out the spacers for the sealed compartments. The spacers were put together with stainless-steel screws and glue. The spacers graduated in size, spaced two feet apart, from very small to six feet. The smallest was placed near the pointed front, the larger near the front of the hunting box. The back of the hunting box was formed with an additional six-foot-wide spacer. From the back of the box the spacers decreased in size to the last spacer, which was three feet in size. This spacer formed the back or stern of the boat.

Then we cut the marine plywood into six-inch-wide strips that were eight feet long. We mounted the strips of plywood to the spacers, staggering the end cracks. They were fastened with the screws and glued into place. When the entire boat was covered, we applied the sides of the hunting box area. Then we covered the back and front of the box with plywood. When all the plywood was in place, we covered the entire surface of the boat with fiberglass cloth. We brushed the cloth into place with a mixture of polyester resin. Several coats of resin were applied with brushes. Rough sanding was the next step. Then three coats of resin were sprayed on the hull. Before the last coat of resin dried, we used a fiberglass chop gun to apply a rough surface on top of the hull. A chop gun is an electric tool that chops fiberglass fibers into small lengths. It is held over the tacky surfaces and allowed to fall on the resin. Then the fibers are brushed into place, creating a rough non-slippery walking surface. When the coffin box resin was completely cured, we applied a flat, drab gray-green coat of paint on it.

We asked two of our neighbors to come over and help us move it outside of the tent. My brother called Mr. Sam Boomer in Norfolk, Virginia. He gave Mr. Boomer dimensions of the hunting boxes and asked him to build the curtains. It took us all of March and half of April to finish the coffin boxes. We built two sea breakers, or wings—one for each box. They had to fit around the boxes to keep the waves from washing over the rim of the hunting areas. The coffin boxes would be used the next hunting season.

After that work was finished, my brother took on weekend maintenance jobs. He did this to provide me with the funds to continue going to school.

He gave me all the money from the weekend work. If I had any mechanical problems with my old car, he fixed them. We worked together on weekends until the summer breaks came.

During these breaks I returned to work with Burgess Hooper and his son, Johnny, building houses. I spent the months of June, July, and August working with them, surfing, and chasing campground girls. I returned to school in the fall. My dad was retired; he and Chowder were getting along in age. The dog refused to leave my father's side. If you saw my dad's car pass by, Chowder would be sitting in the passenger's seat. My dad was no longer able to help me set the flounder nets. He and Chowder were spending more and more time off the island with his church work. I was still allowed to stay at the club and use the *Old Anytime* and the decoy skiff to set the nets. My brother kept a watchful eye on me and kept me advised on the weather conditions. While I was fishing he and his crew were making the club ready for the season's hunt. When the flounder migrated south, he made a place for me on weekend hunts.

I was fortunate enough to be at the club when the coffin boxes were first used. My brother had placed one at the Point of Shoals. The wind was blowing from the northeast. The water levels were low. It was overcast: a perfect day to hunt the Point of Shoals. Mr. Bowman and Mr. Kotarides were the first hunters to hunt that location. The box was already fixed into place with the three-point anchoring system. I folded the compartments and placed the wing around the box. My brother and his crew placed the decoys. When we were leaving to return to the club, I turned to look at the box. At first glance it resembles a raft of fowl feeding at the edge of the channel.

The hunt that day was quite successful; the coffin box worked like a charm. The fowl decoyed perfectly. Mr. Kotarides was satisfied with the performance of the new blinds. They were portable and were used in many different locations around Gull Island. Each time they were used they resulted in productive hunts the rest of that season. News of the success of the coffin boxes soon spread to the main island. Hunters begin to call my brother asking questions about them. He told all the hunters that they were experimental blinds. This was the first season they had been used at Gull Island. He wasn't sure if they were even legal. They were the talk of the island among all the hunters. My brother tried his best to keep the news from spreading off-island. They were so close in resemblance to the battery boxes that were outlawed. Mr. Kotarides told my brother that he would check on the legality of the new blinds. At the end of the season Mr. Kotarides asked my brother to bring one of the boxes back to the harbor at Salvo. He had scheduled a courtesy visit with one of the game wardens to come and examine the box. A federal game warden came to examine the blind. His name was Joseph Henderson; he told us to call him Joe. He was pleasant, a welcome change from the state game wardens we had been dealing with. Mr. Henderson was of the opinion that the blind was large enough to be classified as a float blind. He said that as far as federal hunting regulations were concerned, it was okay to use them. State wardens came to examine the coffin box. They couldn't come to a decision on their first visit. They said more research was required in order to make the right decision.

# CHAPTER FORTY

# Warmer Winters

My brother asked them if the boxes were illegal. They could not give him a reasonable answer to his question. He told them he was going to use the blinds until they showed him regulations that prohibited their use. They agreed to allow this situation for the present time. They were of the opinion it should be classified as a battery box because it was portable and had an adjustable curtain. But, at the same time, it was large enough to be classified as a float blind. At this point they admitted that they were uncertain of how to classify it. The coffin blinds worked well for the next few seasons while the state wardens pondered the blinds' legal status.

Then Mr. Kotarides and the Gull Island Gunning Club faced a whole new adversary. Each season the weather seamed to get progressively milder. It got to the point that the hunters in the shore blinds were killing more mosquitoes than geese or ducks. The weather was unusually warm with many sunny days. The winter low-pressure areas we normally had ceased to exist. These low-pressure areas typically developed in the Pacific Ocean. They came onto the U.S. West Coast usually bringing rain. Their path of travel brought them across the center of the country. They usually drew moisture up from the Gulf Coast, intensified into deep core lows, and brought cold stormy weather to our area. For a period of about four years, these lows turned up the Delmarva Area. The northeast got all the cold stormy weather. These lows pulled wet, warm air from the Gulf Coast up over our area. We experienced a lot of rainfall each time a low turned toward the northeast. In between these lows the weather was mild and sunny.

This type of weather was disastrous for hunting at Gull Island. The diving ducks didn't return to our area for years. There was ample food for them in locations north of our area. There were a few geese, swan, and puddle ducks that wintered at Gull Island. A few fowl could be harvested just after dawn and just before dusk. The rest of the day the fowl gathered in large groups and sat on the water. They would not decoy to the hunting locations in the middle of the day. The weather was not rough enough to break them up into smaller, manageable groups. The hunters soon grew bored with this type of hunting. The ones who normally hunted the Gull Island area began to shift their interest to clubs up north.

The hunters who came grew accustomed to the routine quickly. They hunted in the morning, then came back to the clubhouse to play cards. They used the horseshoe pits, cooked outside, and enjoyed the mild weather. Then they wanted to return to the blinds to hunt the afternoon shift. Mr. Kotarides wanted to provide the hunters with something more exciting to occupy the midday hours. He talked to me about trout fishing in the channel. He remembered that I had taken Ted Sluder fishing on a previous mild weather hunt. I told him that I was almost sure there were speckled trout and bluefish in the channel east of the island. On the backside of the south reef, there would be drum and Spanish mackerel. Out back of the northwest reef in deep water there would be gray trout. I told him I thought he could renew the interest in the club by offering fishing trips. At dinner that night Mr. Kotarides and my brother discussed the possibility of adding fishing trips to the daytime activity at Gull Island. The fishing trips kept the club at Gull Island going for a couple of seasons.

Gradually the charter members began to lose interest in hunting at Gull Island. One by one left the club and declined to renew their membership. They were all sportsmen and liked to fish, but most of them came to hunt the diving ducks. The thousands and thousands of diving ducks were wintering much farther up the coastline. Mr. Kotarides and Mary Jane Bakery became the sole owners of Gull Island Gunning Club. Hunting parties still came, but the whole atmosphere changed. Most of the hunters who came were Mr. Kotarides's friends. They were nonpaying members, guests of the club. Most of them came from the food supply industry. Many were local Hatteras Island residents. Many of them pitched in and helped with the work of setting up the hunting locations. These were working people of the area who loved to hunt, and Gull Island was one of the best hunting locations in the area. This type of hunter was not the carefree, pocket-full-of-money sportsman.

Most hunting guides in all commercial operations make 50 percent or more of their money from tips, not from salaries. I worked on weekend hunts strictly for tips. These tips provided me with nontaxable cash; they helped keep me in school. My brother's income was largely from tips, at the end of the hunts, on the good-bye handshake. In the days of the true, carefree sportsman at Gull Island, the handshake always contained a twenty-dollar bill, sometimes a fifty. Mr. Kotarides encouraged everyone on the hunt to throw in a few bucks to compensate for the tip loss, but it wasn't the same as getting a good brisk handshake, a smile, and a comment of, "Man, I really had a good time," along with a cash reward.

The hunts became more of a place to go and party. The days of the serious hunts, monitoring and managing the fowl, became a thing of the past. The magic was gone from a lot of the hunting parties. A lot of the working-class hunters wanted to hunt just for one day. More and more of the hunts became before-dawn trips from Salvo: hunt at the island for a day and return to the main island after dark. For the most part, the joy of staying at the island was beginning to dwindle.

As a result, my brother made one of the most difficult decisions of his life. He chose to leave the employment of the Gull Island club. My brother, raised in Pamlico Sound hunting and fishing, loved Gull Island as much as I do, even today. He went back to work with the state of North Carolina, and this time he didn't have to leave Hatteras Island. He was hired as a ferry captain at the Hatteras Inlet Ferry Operation.

With my brother no longer at Gull Island, most of the hunts became hurried one-day trips. As much as I hated the idea, I had to seek part-time employment elsewhere. I applied for a temporary position, during the summer months, at the ferry operation. Mr. George Fuller contacted me for an interview. I was hired as a ferry deckhand with Captain Monroe Stowe the first summer. We had a three-day-on-and-three-day-off work schedule. Mr. Kotarides let me stay at the club and use the boats to flounder fish in the fall of the year. He let me be involved as much as I could on weekend hunts during hunting season.

I got a call from my father in the middle of the week. I knew it was bad news; he hardly ever called me just to chat. He was all upset; he told me that Chowder had passed away. He had lost Mom a few years before; now he had lost his best friend. When I came home that weekend, we wrapped him in his favorite blanket and buried him west of the house, on a hill under a big oak tree. Both of us cried. I would miss that big tail frapping on the floor as he wagged it up and down when he saw me coming. My father would really miss him. That dog had been his constant companion since they both retired from the club. After Chowder passed, my dad spent more and more time off the island. During the wintertime when I left the island to attend classes, he stayed weeks at a time with his church members in Manns Harbor, Eastlake, and Stumpy Point. When I was home, I slept at the house and took meals at my brother's house next door.

Mr. Kotarides had a house trailer on his property at Salvo. He replaced the trailer with a large five-bedroom house. Many of his friends came to stay with him late in the summer and early fall. Mr. Kotarides had work for me. On my days off from the ferry, I took his friends trout fishing in the sound. This was an enjoyable time for both of us. He cooked all types of food for them. This food was packed in lunches and eaten on the fishing trips. Almost anything tastes better on the water while hunting or fishing. These day trips from Salvo were successful fishing trips. In early summer I took them out in the middle of the sound, fishing for gray trout and large croaker. In those days coolers were easily filled with these fish. They were easily caught by gigging bottom rigs baited with squid and equipped with a small silver metal spoon. The rig was allowed to sink vertically to the bottom and gigged up and down a few feet above the bottom. Large gray trout and croaker were all over it.

The sheer number of fish is what pleased the fishermen. There were no limits; you could keep all you could catch. In the late summer we had three spots that produced good catches of speckled trout. The first location was out back of Sheep's Head Shoal. The other spots were the edge of Cedar Hammock Channel and Gull Shoal Channel. In early fall I took them trolling for Spanish mackerel and bluefish back of the south reef. The last hours of daylight on these trips, we baitfished the south reef sloughs. These locations produced good catches of large channel bass or drum.

On one of these trips we were drifting along the edge of Bay Shoals, trout fishing. One of the fishermen caught a small pinfish on a rubber grub trout gig. I made up a float rig and attached it to a larger rod. Then I placed the live pinfish on the hook for bait. Next, I adjusted the float to allow the pinfish to swim about two feet below the surface of the water. All of a sudden, the float disappeared and the preset drag on the reel was peeling off at a rapid rate. I yelled to one of the fisherman to grab the rod. When he picked it up the rod bent double and the fight was on. It was a really large fish; I could tell that by the amount of line being stripped off the reel. The fisherman fought the fish for about an hour. He gained line, then the fish would take it back out. After about another half hour, I tightened up the drag on the reel a considerable amount. The fish was no longer taking line. He began to pull the boat backward at a slow pace. I moved the fisherman to the bow of the boat to keep from breaking the line. That fish pulled the boat with all of us aboard for about another half hour.

Then it surfaced about a hundred yards out from the boat. At first I couldn't make out what it was. It was dark colored on the top with a white underbelly. Then I saw one of the wings break the surface of the water. It was one of the biggest butterfly rays that I had ever seen. I'll bet it weighed better than two hundred pounds. The butterfly ray has two wing-shaped sides. It sort of flaps these large wings, and flies along through the water instead of swimming like other rays. I started the engine and steered the boat toward it. I instructed the fisherman to reel in the line, keeping it tight as he reeled. When we got alongside of this monster, it looked to be eight foot from wing tip to wing tip. The hook was lodged behind one of its tail bones; it had indeed been fowl hooked. I guess he made a pass at the pinfish from underneath and missed it. The hook must have slid along its back and become lodged behind the bone. That is the reason the fishermen had such a tough time trying to reel it in. The group of fishermen took numbers of pictures of the ray. I explained that it was out of the ordinary for such a large butterfly ray to be in the sound. Normally, they are oceangoing rays. When they were satisfied, I touched the line with a bait knife, and just like that, he was gone.

When we returned to Salvo that night, I cleaned all the fish. Mr. Kotarides invited me to stay for a fresh fish supper. The ray was the topic of conversation that evening at the table. Mr. Kotarides wanted to take a trip up to Oregon Inlet for Spanish mackerel. He wanted me to take him and the four other friends who were staying the week with him: a chance to take a trip on the *Dancer*. That night I transferred the fishing gear to the *Dancer*. He told me that they wanted to leave around six in the morning.

By six-thirty the next morning we were skimming along on the *Dancer*. We were headed north toward Oregon Inlet, bucking a twenty-five-mile-an-hour northeast wind. The *Dancer* skimmed smoothly across the top of the waves. It was really a fun experience to operate or ride in this boat at three-quarter throttle or better. It only took us about forty-five minutes to travel the eighteen miles to Oregon Inlet.

We soon slipped out the mouth of the inlet. I spotted a large group of small terns hovering above the north bar. These birds were circling in a feeding pattern along the edge of the whitewater. I instructed the fishermen to select a medium-size rod. I tied a silver spoon tipped with a white feather on the end of the line on each pole. I eased the *Dancer* up to within twenty feet of the circling birds. The plan was to cast the artificial bait into the water below the birds.

The first spoon had hardly hit the water before the rod bent double. Each of the other fishermen followed suit, and we had four fish on at one time. After a fifteen-minute fight, the first fish was alongside. We had found a school of yearling drum. The fish were in the twenty-pound class. A dozen or so fish were landed. Then the school swam off the bar into deep water and disappeared.

I anchored the *Dancer* along the bar. We tied on fish-finder rigs, a type of bottom rig that allows the bait to slide through the sinker swivel. Fresh mullet was used for bait. In no time at all we began to catch the drum again.

Mr. Kotarides wanted to move outside the inlet. He wanted his friends to experience trolling for Spanish mackerel. Three of them wanted to remain at the bar and catch the drum on bait. There was a quandary among the fisherman. There was a dry shoal within casting distance of the location of the feeding drum. The three asked if they could remain on the shoal. I told them that in about an hour the tide was going to change. It was running out the inlet toward low water. When the tide began to run back in the inlet, the water would be much deeper. They were adamant about staying. They took adequate bait to last a couple of hours. I brought the *Dancer* as close to the shoal as I could. When the bow bumped bottom, the three jumped out onto the bar. Mr. Kotarides told them to keep a watchful eye out for sharks and laughed as we pulled away.

I headed the *Dancer* out of the inlet. Once we were past the sea buoy, I turned the boat south. We moved parallel to the outside bar, scanning the horizon for birds. After about twenty minutes we were approaching the old boiler wreck. Mr. Kotarides had the binoculars; he spotted a group of birds about a mile offshore. He pointed out their direction and I turned the *Dancer* toward them. Mr. Kotarides took the wheel while I rigged up two trolling rods with double-ought Clark spoons. I set the rods in the rod holders, and we trolled through the school of fish. One of the rods had a hook-up right away. It was a medium-size bluefish. After we had caught a number of blues, Mr. Kotarides wanted some mackerel. I glanced at the beach and told Mr. Kotarides we should head back. He said, "Okay," but wanted me to go near the surf line and troll for mackerel on the way back to the inlet. I took the boat along the outside bar, and we came upon several small schools of Spanish mackerel.

After we had a number of mackerel in the box, I mentioned we should head back. I told them I was worried about the three anglers we left at the inlet. It was already two hours into flood tide. Mr. Kotarides finally agreed that we should head back. I secured the rods and throttled up the *Dancer*. She responded immediately and came up on a fast plane. We were about five miles down the beach from the entrance to the inlet. It only took us a few minutes to get there. There was no sign of the three anglers. The outside bar where they were fishing was covered with about four feet of water. "I see them," Mr. Kotarides said looking through the binoculars. They had walked about a hundred yards back inside the inlet. All three of them had climbed up on a day marker that marked the edge of the channel. The lowest one was only inches above the surface of the water. They said they had been trapped in that same position for over an hour.

# CHAPTER FORTY-ONE

# Record Catch

All three of the fishermen were soaking wet and cold. They had walked in water deeper than the tops of their waders. They told us that when their waders filled with water they could hardly walk. Climbing up on the pilings was a real challenge for them. Mr. Kotarides was picking on them and said, "You boys looked like three pelicans perched on a post."

One of them answered, "We were lucky. The water got deeper and deeper. We had to make a move. Then we spotted that structure attached to the three pilings. It had metal spikes driven into one of the pilings for the purpose of climbing. We were able to walk over and climb up on the structure," the angler added. "We were able to save the rods by handing them up higher on the structure. The burlap bag that we stored our fish in was attached to this line," one angler added. "All of a sudden, there was a churning in the water below us and the bag was ripped open. Our whole catch was lost," he added.

"What type of fish did you have in the bag?" asked Mr. Kotarides.

"Several of those large fish you call drum," came the reply.

"Near the end we started catching a few large bluefish," another angler said. "One had swallowed the hook and I had to cut it out. That particular fish bleeds a lot."

"Probably bull sharks; they are vicious devils," Mr. Kotarides said, "especially if there is blood involved. You were lucky one of them didn't try to bite you," he said to the angler who was perched lowest on the piling.

"We were lucky to find that structure or we might have been drowned," the angler said.

"You were lucky you didn't get swept off the shoal by the tide. Once you were in deep water, with your waders full, you would have sunk like a rock. Plus, you would have been at the mercy of whatever type of sharks stole your catch," I told them. I guided the *Dancer* through the inlet. Once in the sound, I throttled her up and turned south.

That was the last fall I worked for Mr. Kotarides. During the next few years my cousin Raymond and Michael Halminski operated the club for Mr. Kotarides. There were few hunting parties that hunted at the island. After that time a gentlemen by the name of Charlie Swindell became a type of caretaker of the club and grounds at Salvo. None of the hunting gear, including the decoys, were taken to the island. There were no organized hunting parties during this period. Hunters began to bring their boats, decoys, and gear to hunt at Gull Island on the sly. I was guilty of that; I hunted the island with a couple of my cousins. I bought a sixteen-foot dead-rise hunting skiff. It had an Evinrude ninety-horsepower outboard motor on it. I fashioned a canvas collapsing cover, like the *Dancer's*, on it. I could make it to Gull Island in very short order. I had about twenty geese decoys and forty diving duck decoys. I got permission from Mr. Kotarides to hunt his stilt blinds. Hunting was not very good. No one was feeding the fowl in the area. We only harvested a few ducks and geese.

It had taken me five years to beat my way through school. I had an endorsement in trade and industrial education. I applied at the local school system, but there were no job openings. The very same trades teacher, Mr. Dennett Ransom, was still teaching at the local school. One of my cousins told me about a contractor who had just moved to the area. His name was John Luke. He was in the building and hauling business. He constructed beach cottages and installed septic tanks and driveways. Mr. Luke had a house at the north end of Salvo. I went up to talk to him. I told him I had limited experience in house construction. He hired me as a carpenter's helper. My friend Larry Midgett and my cousin Richie Austin were already working for him. Larry ran one of his construction crews, and Richie drove a dump truck hauling rock and septic tank materials. I learned a lot while working for Mr. Luke. I learned the basics of building, plumbing, and electrical work. I also learned about driveway and septic systems installation. I worked with his company until he left the construction field and became part owner/operator of a local Kampgrounds of America operation.

It was during these few years working with Mr. Luke that my friends and I caught drum fever. When an angler comes down with drum fever, it is something to see. It is similar to a disease. He is obsessed to the point of being driven to the act of chasing these fish. The ones sought after are the large channel bass or drum, usually in excess of forty pounds. (This large fish is a prized meal for local islanders. Boiled drum, potatoes, meat crackling, and raw onions mixed together on a plate is considered nectar of the gods. Add cornbread, coleslaw, cucumbers, and sweet tea, and you are feasting on manna from heaven.) At that time there were few tackle shops on Hatteras Island. Most of the fishing tackle had to be purchased at the three fishing piers. There was a pier located at Rodanthe, Kinnakeet or Avon, and one near Trent or Frisco. They offered a limited selection of rods and reels. Mostly they carried smaller or medium-size rods for rental purposes. My friends and I fished hard during the months of October, November, and December for these large fish. We had to have equipment that was capable of casting a fish-finder rig, bait, and an eight-ounce sinker in excess of one hundred yards. This distance had to be achieved to reach the offshore sandbars along the beach, where the large drum fed. This process required a large open-faced reel that could hold hundreds of yards of line: a rod that was stiff and about ten feet long from butt cap to rod tip. At that time, none of these types of rods were available for purchase in the area. These rods had to be handmade by the anglers. The blanks, reel seats, butt cap, grips, guides, tips, winding cotton, color preserver, glue, and rod varnish had to be ordered from off-island companies.

When you received all your gear, the rod assembly began. The rod blank was about thirteen feet in length when you received it. It was made from spun fiberglass, usually a tan yellow color. It was tapered from about one and a half inches in diameter at the butt end. The smaller end or tip measured about a quarter of an inch in diameter. Normally, the blank was cut off at the tip, leaving it about ten feet in length. The butt cap usually fit snugly over the larger end of the blank and was easily glued into place. The grips were made of soft rubber, usually sized to fit the blank that was shipped. The largest of the three grips was slid over the tip and pushed down the blank. Glue was applied near the butt cap, and the grip slid into place. Then the next largest grip was glued into place about sixteen to eighteen inches above the first grip. The reel seat was slid on the blank and glued in place against the second grip. The last and smallest grip was slid down the blank and glued against the top of the reel seat.

Each angler normally has a favorite color and make their choice for the winding cotton. Guide locations were chosen and the guide underwrap was wound on the blank. The underwrap is the process of winding the guide cotton on the blank by turning it around and around while holding tension on the cotton spool. The underwrap extends far enough to allow the guide wrap to be placed into its center. When the guides are wound into place, the underwrap can be seen, exposed at the ends and center of the guides. At this stage the color preserver is applied. It takes about three coats of color preserver. Then the exposed surfaces of the blank and guide areas receive about three coats of rod varnish.

The choice of reels for this setup was usually a Penn Squidder. These reels were very sturdy. They had a star drag that was easily adjustable for the desired tension. The drag was equipped with a loud, easily heard clicker. It was a wide, open-faced, small-diameter reel. This reel could hold over two hundred yards of twenty-five- to thirty-pound test line on its spool. The line of choice was monofilament. This type of handmade rod equipped with a large, open-face reel allowed the angler to cast far enough to reach the fish.

I can't remember where I saw the first handmade Hatteras Rod. Two people taught me to make these rods. An older man from Pittsburgh, Pennsylvania, who made his home between Rodanthe and Waves, taught me how to attach the guides. His name was Mr. Donald Todd. A friend of mine, Larry Midgett, taught me to make a diamond wrap design between the grips in the reel seat area. My choice of colors was dark blue wrapped over white. I made two of these rods. Larry wrapped the diamond design on the rods for me.

This type of rod soon gained in popularity with all large drum anglers. Everyone who fished big drum wanted one. Some anglers named them Hatteras Heavers. At first they could only be found on Hatteras Island. Soon, the fishing pier tackle shops had them for sale. In the beginning they were very expensive. There were several anglers around the island who made them and sold them to the piers and a few tackle shops in the area. Then the rod makers came up with a system, using a sewing machine motor, to turn the blanks. This increased the production speed of the Hatteras Heavers. Soon, most all anglers could afford to purchase one. Now factory-turned rods similar to the Heaver can be purchased at almost any tackle shop.

I had three fishing friends who had a solid dose of drum fever. They were as crazy as I was about catching these large fish. Their names are Larry Midgett, Ralph Lane—nicknamed Snookie—and my cousin Jimmie Hooper. We made all our rigs by hand. Our bait was caught fresh, mostly with the use of cast nets. At times we set nets close to the sound-side shoreline. A trip to see a local fisherman could also provide us with fresh bait. We promised to trade a drum for a supply of bait. The bait of choice consisted of jumping mullet and fatback, a local name for a bloody, oily fish in the shad family. Fresh spot and sea mullet were also good baits.

A couple of us owned old four-wheel-drive trucks. This enabled us to fish the outside bars and sloughs along the beach in the fall months. We usually fished with two drum rods each. It was customary to pick out a slough with a wide outlet. One of our rigs would be cast out to the backside of the bar along the north edge of the outlet. The other rig would be cast short in the deep water of the slough just behind the shore break. These rods were placed in sand spikes—beach rod holders—and drags set with the clickers on. The big fish swam south along the back edge of the outside bar on their fall migration. The edge of these bars was full of small fish, stone crabs, and shellfish. These are among the drum's favorite foods. They are bottom feeders and will eat any baitfish they can catch. They lack sharp teeth but are equipped with large crushing structures in the back of their throats. These crushers are capable of crushing the shell of clams and other shellfish. If an approaching drum missed your bait along the edge of the entrance of the outlet, there is still a chance he might find your bait in the deep water back of the shore break in the slough. Some of his preferred food is also located near the beach.

If anyone got a run or a strike, the rapid peeling of line off the reel, the loud clicking of the drag, would be heard. All of us immediately wound the other baits into the shore. This maneuver provided the angler who was hooked up ample room to fight the fish.

We fished along the beach in the months of September and October. During the months of November and December we fished on the piers. This type of fishing was especially good during the effects of a northeaster. Waders were not required. The chosen wear was layers of warm clothing under a pair of wind-resistant, hooded coveralls. It didn't make any difference to us what time of night it involved. We fished every night for two hours before the top of tide and two hours after. This seemed to be the feeding periods of the drum on the outer sandbars located near the piers. We harvested many drum during the runs of early November. Some night each of us caught several large drum. We shared them with other islanders, especially the old folks; we cleaned the fish and gave it to them.

I recall one particular night. It was November 6, 1973. I was having an evening meal at Snookie's house. After we finished eating we began to discuss our angling visit to the Rodanthe pier later that night. The wind was ten to fifteen miles per hour out of the northeast. Flood tide that night topped out at about three in the morning. We decided to begin fishing around one o'clock and fish until daylight. The sea was running strong, two- to three-foot chop, but an eight-ounce sinker usually held in these conditions. We had a couple of beers and we got a light buzz on. I told Snookie

I was going to catch a drum larger than any of us had ever seen. We both had a good laugh and popped another top. I fell out on his couch but heard his alarm clock go off at about twelve-thirty. My gear was in my van outside in his driveway. I walked outside, and that cold northeast wind hit me in the face. As he came out, I told him that I felt like going home and sleeping some more. He laughed and said, "Aw, come on. The conditions are perfect. Besides, Jimmy and Larry are already up there waiting for us."

"If they are smart, they are still in bed, as cold as it is," I answered. He placed his gear in the back, and we headed for the pier. We both had two heavers, extra tackle, and a bag of fresh sea mullet heads. I had three large roe mullets that I had bummed from a local drop netter. The pier house was closed for the night.

"No chance for coffee," Snookie said. As we came around the side of the pier house, the mist was so thick we could only see a few feet ahead of us. It appeared that we might have the pier to ourselves. Halfway down the pier two forms began to materialize, sitting on a bench at the end. When we got out to the end, sure enough, Jimmie and Larry were already there.

"Where have you boys been? It's after one," Larry asked. Snookie filled them on what we had been up to. "Yeah, I bet a few beers were involved if I know you birds," he said. Their rigs were already out and their drags set. I baited one of my rods with a fresh sea mullet head. I walked up to the rail and took a look at the break on the bar. I saw some whitewater out about fifty yards off the left corner of the rail. Their rigs were just about straight out.

I am known as a side winder when it comes to casting for distance. I walked up to the left corner of the rail and said, "Heads right." They all took flight along the left rail behind me, leaving the right side clear. I licked my right thumb, placed it along the left side of the spool on the reel, set the reel on free spool, and dropped the rig about three feet from the rod tip. I leaned my body way back until the bait and rig were resting on the deck. I flung the rig seaward with great force. My bail landed about fifteen feet past the whitewater along the edge of the bar. I cast my other rod short, about twenty yards off the pier, and set both drags tight enough so the waves couldn't slacken my line. I joined my friends on the benches and waited for a hit. We were all talking about past drum trips. All of a sudden, the clicker on the rod that I had cast short began making noise. It would make a few short clicks, stop, then make a few more clicks. Usually this indicated a skate, a small bluefish, or the rig had grassed up. Whatever it was, my sinker was dislodged from the bottom, and my rig was drifting south in the tide. I picked it up and wound it in before it became tangled in my friends' rigs. I brought it to the surface and saw it was a skate on the end of the line. Just as I was about to hand over the skate to the top of the rail, my other rod had a screaming run. I put the reel on free spool, set the clicker, and allowed the skate to sink to the bottom. I ran and grabbed my other rod, set the hook, and the fight was on.

# CHAPTER FORTY-TWO

# Outdated Scales

This fish peeled about fifty yards of line before I could slow him down. I pushed the clicker to the off position and the racket stopped, but line kept peeling off the reel. Then I began to slowly tighten the star drag until the rod bent and took on the load of the fish. I set the drag so the line would slip off the reel just before the breaking point. The fish made several runs straight out from the pier. Then it turned south and went with the tide. At this point I began to get some of the line back. It took me about forty-five minutes to tire the fish. It came up to the surface about fifty yards out. We could see it rolling in the northeast chop. "Drum," my cousin Jimmy yelled, "and a big one at that," he said. The fish finished up the fight on the surface. It was just a matter of pulling such a large fish against the tide and not breaking the line. Finally, I had it up on the surface, lying on its side alongside of the pier. Larry and Snookie began to lower the landing net, which consisted of a large circular metal ring with the ends welded together. Netting was attached to the ring, forming a drooping bag to support the catch. Three lines were attached to the metal ring at even distances apart. They connected about six feet above the net to form a bridle, and a single line extended up to the pier. The proper way to net a large fish was to hold it uptide and back it into the net tail first. Once the fish was over the net, the attachment line was pulled tight, trapping it inside. Then the net and the fish would be raised up to the pier. Larry and Snookie had the net lowered to the surface of the water. I had the fish held uptide of the net. I was backing it into the net when, all of a sudden, the hook came loose. This big fish was about halfway inside when a large wave hit the net. The force of the wave wrenched the net from their hands. The end of the rope would have been washed over the side but they had tied it off to the pier rail. The net was carried downtide the entire length of the rope. They quickly grabbed the rope and pulled the net back to the surface, but the fish was gone. It surfaced about twenty yards downtide from the net. It drifted on its side a few yards. Then it rolled over and, with a flip of its tail, disappeared beneath the waves. A feeling of despair settled over me.

"Man, that was the biggest drum I have ever seen," Jimmy said.

"It was a good size," Larry added.

"That was the one you were talking about yesterday evening," Snookie said to me. Then the feeling of despair turned to anger. The thought of flinging the rod and reel as far seaward as I could fling it crossed my mind. Then I thought of slamming it down on the deck.

"That is just my luck," I said out loud. "How in the world did that hook just pop out at that instant?" I sat down on the bench and tried to regain my composure. I examined the rig. The sea mullet head was still on the hook, only crushed flat by the drum's throat crushers. I ran my fingers up and down the line a few yards to check for chafing or frays. The line was fine. I placed it on the left rail, a few feet back out of the way. Then I walked over to my other rod and picked it up. I knew there was a skate on the end of the line. I had seen it and slackened the line to allow it to settle on the bottom between the pilings. I lowered the rod tip and asked my buddies if they wanted to see a skate fly? I yanked the rod upward, but when the line came tight, the rod doubled under a load.

"That skate got big all of a sudden, didn't it?" Larry said.

"Either that or I am piling wrapped," I answered. I thought the skate had swum around the bottom of a piling, but then the line began peeling off the reel in a slow steady pace. "It's moving," I said to them. The line continued to come off the reel until it was about a hundred yards out. I knew then that I had to turn it or possibly be spooled, the process of losing all your line off your reel to a hooked fish while it is swimming away from you. I tightened the drag down enough to hold the fish into place. The rod bent even more under the added load.

"You are going to break your line," my friends yelled to me.

"I don't care if I do," I answered. "I am not going to be spooled tonight," I added. The fish stopped taking line. Oddly, it came to the surface. We couldn't see it but could hear it splashing around on the top of the water.

"What have you hooked into?" Snookie asked me.

"Your guess is as good as mine," I answered.

"It's on the top of the water. I can hear it," Larry said. "I have never seen one act like that," he added.

"I haven't either," I said. "It feels like I have a dump truck on the line." For the next half hour I didn't gain a yard of line. The fish slowly swam parallel to the end of the pier. It allowed itself to be taken south with the tide flow. I had to move to the southside rail to continue the fight. The fish continued to wallow on the surface, not taking any line, but not giving up any either. I lowered the rod tip, held the line in place with my thumb, and pulled it back in an upward motion. I was able to gain a couple feet of line. Each time I repeated this rod-pumping motion, I gained a small portion of line back. "It looks like you are in for a long struggle," Jimmy said. Just as he got the words out of his mouth, his rod took off on a run. He set the hook and his rod bent under a load.

"Jimmy is hooked up," Larry shouted. Thirty minutes later he had about a fifty-five-pound drum on the deck. Then Larry caught one just as large. One of Jimmy's rods had another fish hit it. Jimmy told Snookie to take it. He was the last to get a hit. At this point, everyone but me had a nice fish on the deck. I was still trying to winch that dump truck against the tide close enough to see it. In the meantime they were catching drum. I thought about cutting the line so I could continue to fish. There is an understanding among drum anglers. The line is never cut off until the fish is identified. I kept on pumping and slowly gaining line. I was positioned a few feet back from the rail. I heard Larry say, "Holy smokes, look at the size of that thing."

"Man, that is the biggest drum I have ever seen," Jimmy shouted.

"That is the one you have been talking about," Snookie told me. Then I saw it was about thirty yards out. It was on its side facing the beach. At first glance it looked to be over six feet in length. Then I got nervous. I knew I had to lead it around to the end of the pier to get the net behind it. I gently pumped the last few yards on line in. When they got the net down to the water, the fish was longer than the diameter of the net ring.

"It might be too big for the net," one of my buddies said.

"No," I answered. "It's the net or nothing. I am not dragging this beast to the beach." I gently backed its tail between two of the hoisting lines attached to the ring.

"Here comes a wave," Jimmy said. "You better hurry."

Larry dropped the net down a little until the fish was centered over it. "It's now or never," he said and pulled up on the line. Jimmy and Snookie grabbed the line and helped Larry pull upward. The fish and the net cleared the water just as the wave broke beneath it. The fish's head and tail were positioned well outside the net ring. The only saving grace was it was too tired to even flop. If it had even flopped a little it could have easily rolled out of the net. I had to put down my rod and help them pull the net up to the top of the pier rail. When we got it up to the rail, it was too big lift it over in the normal fashion. We rested the metal ring of the net facing us on the top of the rail. We rotated the net ring until the fish's head was facing us. I held tension on the back net ring line. Larry placed his hands inside its gill plate. Jimmy and Snookie placed their hands under the fish on opposite sides. My angling buddies lifted it like a baby out of the net and gently placed it on the deck. The hook was out of its mouth, tangled in the webbing of the landing net. The skate's tail was sticking out of the fish's mouth. Then we stood there in awe, not saying a word, just staring at the fish. It had a drum's head and tail, but looked to be at least six feet long and as round as a fifty-gallon barrel.

"It tried to swallow that whole skate," Jimmy said.

"You better go wake up Rudy and weigh that thing," I heard one of them say. Rudy Gray was the proprietor of the Rodanthe Fishing Pier. He lived above the pier motel office in an upstairs apartment. The apartment was just a short walk away from the pier. I looked at my watch; it was three-thirty. Rudy normally opened the pier house at six in the morning. It would be another two and a half hours before he opened up. "He will dry out by then in this wind and lose weight," Larry said. "Come on, I will help you load the fish in that shopping cart. You can take it along and show him," he said. We loaded the fish in the cart and I left for Rudy's apartment. I placed the shopping cart under the streetlight so that it would be easily seen from the deck above. I banged on the door that led to the back deck.

Finally, Rudy came to the door. He parted the long curtain attached to the sliding door, peeked out, and saw it was me. He opened the door a little, dressed in his underwear, and said, "This better be good. I have to open up in a couple of hours."

I said to him, "I have caught a drum larger than you have ever seen. My angling buddies and I think it might be bigger than anyone has ever seen. Possibly a new world record."

"Yeah, right," he answered. "You go back to the pier and I will be along after a while, when I am good and awake, then we will weigh it."

"Just take a look at it," I implored him.

"You have it here?" he asked.

"In the shopping cart below," I answered. He walked over to the deck rail and looked down. There, in the glistening in the glow of the streetlight, was the drum. The fish was sagged into a big curve in the middle; its side was against the bottom of the cart. Its head and tail were protruding several feet up in the air above the ends of the shopping cart.

"Good lord," Rudy said, when he saw it. "I'll be right there. Let me grab my pants and shirt." As we were walking back to the pier he asked me if I had taken the skate out of its mouth.

"No," was my response. I began telling him what had happened. "The fish swallowed the skate and it is lodged in its throat. I don't think it was ever hooked. The hook was in the skate's mouth. When we got it up to the pier deck, the wire leader was tangled in the landing net webbing. Sometime during the netting process, the hook was torn from the skate's mouth."

"That story is hard to swallow," he said to me. "There is no need to tell anyone that because they will never believe you anyway," he said. Rudy opened the pier house and we hung the drum in the scales. As we picked it up, the skate fell out of its mouth to the deck. "That is just as well," Rudy said, "now we can get a true weight." The drum topped the scales at ninety-eight pounds. We placed the drum in the large walk-in cooler. "Where are you going now?" Rudy asked me.

"Back out to the end," I told him. "My gear, Larry, Snookie, and Jimmy are still out there fishing," I answered.

"Stop by before you leave. I am going to make a few calls. By the time you are ready to go, I'll have some answers for you."

When I got back to the end, daylight was just making, and my friends had caught several large drum and a few big bluefish. They could hardly believe their ears when I told them how much the drum weighed. "We have to leave soon," Larry said to me. "We need to be at John Luke's house by eight this morning. We will still have to ride to Buxton to work today." We were remodeling the inside of the Buxton Holy Roller Church located alongside the post office. I looked at my watch. It was five o'clock. I gathered my gear, helped them load the fish into the three shopping carts, and we walked up to the pier house.

After all the fish were weighed, we filled out applications for citations. Rudy told us he had called the International Game Fish Association, and the drum was a potential new world record. There was a process we had to complete before they would confirm it. He needed three witnesses to sign the application. I had to provide them with the rig and ten yards of the line it was caught on. The current record was caught off the Virginia Capes in 1949, the year I was born. It weighed sixty nine pounds. The angler's name who caught the fish was Zack Waters Jr. The International Game Fish Association was going to send a representative to Rodanthe to examine the fish in a few weeks, he told us. Rudy came to Salvo looking for me that afternoon. I was at my brother's house, asleep on the couch. I had dozed off waiting for the evening meal. I felt someone shaking my arm. It was my sister-in-law, Jean.

"I hated to wake you," she said, "but I think this is important. Rudy Gray is in the kitchen with your brother. He wants to talk to you." Rudy told us that Aycock Brown, a writer and photographer for the *Coastland Times*, wanted to meet me at the pier tomorrow. He wanted to take pictures and interview me for a story to put in the local paper. When the story came out, it made the front page. Everywhere I went on the island, people were congratulating me. Someone told me that the channel bass was the state fish of North Carolina. I didn't know that fact until then.

Rudy called me and said that a representative from Pflueger Taxidermist had agreed to mount the fish free of charge. They would provide me with a skin mount and make a fiberglass copy for the pier. I had to sign a release so that they could pick up the fish. I asked him about the man from the International Game Fish Association. "We will keep it in the cooler until they examine it," he said. "Then I will call Pflueger to pick the fish up for the mount," he added. Then one afternoon while we were framing a house in Hatteras Colony, a neighborhood of Salvo, I saw my brother's car drive up to the job site. He gave me a piece of paper with a phone number on it. He said that Rudy had called his house and needed to talk to me right away. I went home and dialed the number; it was somewhere in Florida. Some lady answered the phone and said she would find Rudy for me. He was at a tackle buyers' convention in Tampa.

"You have to drive to Nags Head this afternoon," he said.

"What in the world for?" I asked.

"The man from Pflueger came and picked up the fish. Cecil thought it was alright. The men had a copy of the signed release." Cecil Midgett worked for Rudy at the pier. He didn't realize that the International Game Fish representative had not arrived to examine the fish. Rudy had called the pier to check on things, and Cecil told him the taxidermist had the fish.

"The Pflueger truck driver is staying the night at the Sea Ranch Motel in Nags Head. You have to drive up there and bring the fish back to the pier. He is leaving for Baltimore tomorrow morning. If that fish is mounted before it is certified, there's no record," Rudy told me.

"I can't let that happen. I am leaving this minute for Nags Head," I answered.

"See you when you get back," Rudy said, and hung up. I had the fish back in the cooler at the pier by six o'clock that afternoon. I had placed it on a tarp in the back of my van for the trip back to Rodanthe. I noticed it had thawed a little on the trip. There was blood and moisture running out of its mouth as I placed it back in the walk-in freezer. I had to wash my van out with a water hose.

It was six months before an I.G.F.A. inspector arrived to examine my catch. It was the end of May 1974 before he arrived at the pier. He introduced himself as William Walker. He told us we could call him Bill. First he looked the fish over. Next he wanted to see the scales it was weighed on. He asked Rudy where the certification sticker was. The scales were supposed to be inspected and calibrated every six months. The sticker was on the back side of the scales. The last inspection was in July 1971. The man rubbed his chin and said, "This is not good. Where is the closest set of certified scales?"

"At the Avon pier," Rudy said. "I will call them."

"Make sure they check the sticker date," Bill said. The inspection sticker on the Avon pier scales was outdated by one year. "We have a problem," Bill said. "This fish has to be weighed on a set of scales with a current inspection sticker on them," he added. "There is no way the agency will even consider it for a new world record unless it's properly weighed on a set of official scales," he said. Finally, Rudy found scales that had a valid inspection sticker on them.

# CHAPTER FORTY-THREE

# Blues Blitz

The Red Drum Tackle Shop down in Buxton had the official set of scales. Bill said there is only one thing to do. The fish has to be taken there and weighed. "Before we go I want to weigh the fish here. If the weights agree, I can use the original weight," he said. We placed the fish back on the scales; it weighed ninety-four pounds. I told him about the fish's journey to Nags Head and the moisture it lost in my van as it partially thawed, so we put the fish back in my van on the same tarp and took it to Buxton. We arrived at the Red Drum Tackle Shop and removed the fish. When we took it out of my van, we noticed it had partially thawed for the second time. There was more blood and moisture left on the tarp. The fish weighed ninety pounds on the Red Drum scales. "This is the first time the fish has been weighed on official scales, is that right?" Bill asked us.

There was no other answer but "yes" to that question.

"This is the official weight of your catch," he said to me. "Congratulations. You have set a new all-tackle world record for this species. It will be officially announced when the board approves your application. You have probably set several more records also," he stated. "There are three more questions I need to ask you after recording the weight of the fish. What pound test line were you using? Was there a shock leader used? What was the rig made from?"

"I have the rig and ten yards of the line back at the pier," Rudy told him.

"That is good. I will need that sample," Bill said to us.

"I don't use any type of shock leader," I told Bill. Shock leader is several yards of much larger line tied on the end of the fishing line just above the leader. "I use twenty-five-pound test Ande line, and the rig is made of a footlong piece of one-hundred-pound test piano wire," I answered. The purpose of shock line is to prevent the line from parting while the angler is in the process of casting. Some anglers have such a violent cast that the rig is broken off each time they cast. The force of their casts snaps the line, you hear a pop, and the rig is lost to the ocean. The shock leader absorbs the jerkiness of their cast and the line stays intact. During the lengthy certification process of my catch, the fish lost a considerable amount of weight. I thought to myself, *this weight loss could make it easier for a future angler to spoil my record catch!*

In about six weeks from the time Bill left, I heard from the International Game Fish Association, congratulating me on setting several new world records. The first was the all-tackle world record. The second was the twenty-five-pound test line class record. The third was the one-hundred-pound test piano wire. All three of these records were for the largest channel bass ever caught while using that type of fishing gear.

Pflueger provided a promotional skin mount for me. Also, they made a fiberglass mold copy for display at the pier.

Today's fishing regulations prohibit the harvesting of large channel bass over twenty-seven inches long. My large hand drum rods are extremely busy collecting dust in one of my sheds. I am reduced to harvesting a few of these large fish, on small boat rods, under the cover of darkness at several secretive locations.

I wander around the villages of the island in my spare time. I still try to engage my older islander friends into conversations. I love to hear their stories of how it was back then. These older folks are no longer physically capable of catching fish. I always hear the same question: Have you caught one of those big drums lately? I sure would like to have a slab for boiled drum, potatoes, and meat grease. It breaks my heart to realize that I have to poach the food they love so dearly. I never in a million years thought it would be against the law to catch a big drum angling. This meal used to appear on a lot of local holiday tables. These older islanders prefer it to ham or turkey any day of the week.

If there was a large drum permitting program with a daily bag limit to allow the harvesting of a few fish over thirty pounds, this would be a step in the right direction. At least I wouldn't feel like I just robbed a bank, shot someone, or be scared to death each time I caught a large drum. Suppose new regulations prevented the mountain folk from harvesting deer, turkey, and wild boar for food. How long do you think they would stand for it? That is how we coastal people feel about the fish in our area. Before the Food Lions of the world came into existence, people grew their vegetables and harvested wild game. They lived in harmony with the environment and respected their natural resources. What in the world has happened to our government when a man is not allowed to catch enough fish to feed his family? Our coastal way of life is beginning to disintegrate right before our eyes. Sometimes I feel like we, the human race, are the endangered species.

At the beginning of summer season I went down to Hatteras Inlet Ferry Operations to see Mr. George Fuller. I applied for full-time employment with the Ferry Operations. Mr. Fuller told me he didn't have any openings for full-time. There were openings for part-time, seasonal employment. He hired me for the summer season. Near the end of summer, Mr. Fuller introduced me to Mr. Roy Etheridge. Mr. Etheridge was the dredge superintendent. Mr. Etheridge told me there were positions open for full-time employment on the *Dredge Carolina*. The *Carolina* is a state-owned dredge boat. This dredge is used at all ferry operations along the coast. Its job is to keep the ferry channels dredged out. I finished the summer on the ferry. Then I transferred to the *Dredge Carolina*. I worked a week-on-and-week-off schedule. This gave me much more time to fish and hunt during my off time.

Fall fishing of 1974 was a good season. My angling buddies and I caught a generous supply of large drum. Everyone in the villages of the island was given fish to eat. At the end of November, the large bluefish swarmed the surf line from Oregon Inlet to Hatteras Inlet. Every angler along the beach was battling and landing these large bluefish. This process involved riding up and down the beach in a four-wheel-drive vehicle. During these beach rides the angler keeps a close watch on the ocean, from the shoreline to the outer bar. Sometimes binoculars are used. If a large school of big fish are feeding, most of the time there will be a flock of diving gulls above them. When a large fish strikes a smaller baitfish, sometimes the baitfish is cut into small pieces. The gulls pick up these portions of the baitfish that float to the surface. The angler follows the flocks of feeding birds. This will indicate where the fish are.

The birds are followed until they are within casting distance of the beach. Then it is on. You can usually get a strike from the fish below the surface by casting a lure into the middle of the birds. That time of year there are large schools of channel bass, striped bass, and big bluefish on their yearly migration south. The local names for these big fish are as follows: drum, rock, and big blues. They all are powerful fish and put up a tremendous battle when hooked along the surf.

Three of my cousins and I were following a northbound flight of birds one Saturday afternoon. The birds were about two hundred yards out from the beach. They were feeding over a large school of fish along the outside bar. We were riding in Les Hooper's truck. Raymond Midgett was in the front of the truck with Les. Jimmy, Les's son, and I were in the back of the truck. We were in the Rodanthe area. Just as we passed under the pier, the birds turned toward the beach. The fish entered a break in the bar and were swimming parallel to the beach in a slough, about twenty yards out. They were big blues; there were hundreds of them. You could see their bodies suspended in the waves. Their tails and backs were above the surface of the water. Raymond was the first to cast a Hopkins lure, a type of silver-plated spoon, into the school of fish. He immediately hooked up. Les was next to cast with the same results. Jimmy and I grabbed our rods and headed for the water's edge. I was just about to cast my lure when I spied numbers of fish at my feet. The big blues were feeding on everything that was in the slough: large speckled trout, sea mullet, flounder, and all types of fish were beaching themselves. They were trying to escape being eaten alive by the snapping jaws of the big blues. The blues were right behind them, chopping off their tails and biting chunks out of them. I ran back to the truck, placed my rod back in the rod rack, and grabbed a fish basket. I began picking up speckled trout. I soon filled the basket and got another. Jimmy saw what I was doing and he joined me. We soon had a dozen baskets of assorted fish. We filled all the baskets that were in the truck. Then we each dumped a basket of fish into the truck bed, returned to the water's edge, and easily refilled the basket. Soon Les and Raymond joined us. The blues continued their feeding frenzy for about three hours. Just ahead of dark they swam out of the north outlet of the slough and disappeared behind the outer bar. We had the entire bed of cousin Les's pickup rounded off with fish. We gave everyone in the villages all the fish they wanted. There were so many left over we sold them to the local fish house. They were still packing late into the night on that Saturday. We had a great day of fishing and put a few dollars in our pockets at the same time. As we were washing out the bed of our cousin's truck, Raymond said to us, "Those trout will come back in that slough to feed tonight."

"How about the blues?" I asked him.

"They will lay offshore until daylight," he answered.

"What are you getting at?" Les asked him.

"We could catch some more trout on light tackle in the moonlight tonight," he said.

"What in the world would we do with more trout?" Les asked. "Jimmy and I are going home to get some sleep. I have to work tomorrow, and Jimmy has school," he added. Les dropped us off in front of Raymond's house.

"What's on your mind about those trout?" I asked Raymond.

"After you eat, come over to the house and we will talk about it," he said as I was walking away. My cousin Raymond and his family were still living in my grandfather's house. I showered and ate a couple of bowls of lima beans my dad had cooked and left for me. I walked the short distance to Raymond's house. He was sitting at the table with newspaper spread out in front of him. On the newspaper were four mirror lures. This is an artificial lure for trout fishing. They were usually painted red top and bottom with a silver white streak in the middle the length of the lure. The most popular one was a fifty-two M-11. He was in the process of painting them flat black. I asked him what he was doing. It looked to me like he was ruining the lures. He told me that trout feed at night. He said he had caught a few at night when the sky was clear and the moon was out. Just about all of the trout he had caught at night were from an underneath approach. They were hooked in the top of their heads, hitting the lure from below. He was of the belief that a darker lure was better at night. He thought the trout hid near the edge of the sandbars, spotted the dark shapes of baitfish above them silhouetted by the moonlight, and went on the attack. He was convinced this is how they feed at night. "If we used dark-colored lures, we would be able to catch them in the light of the moon at night," he said to me.

"What time does the tide come up tonight?" I asked him.

"Around three o'clock in the morning," he answered. "Do you want to go up to the slough and try it?"

"I am game for a few minutes anyway. If we don't hook up after a few casts, we can always come back home," I added.

"Come back over about two-thirty, and we will go up there."

My cousin Raymond had what we called a beach buggy. It was an older car, a 1953 Chevy. He had cut off the fenders, added split-rimmed tires, and built a wooden trucklike bed on the back of it. When I got back home I washed the fishy smell from my waders and oilcloth jumper. The alarm went off at two. I shut it off and considered rolling over and returning to dreamland. I knew my cousin would be waiting for me. When I arrived at his house, the buggy was running; he was sitting in the driver's seat. I threw my gear in the back and placed my rod in the holder. As I got in he said, "Where have you been, sleepyhead?"

I looked at my watch; it was quarter to three. "Sorry," I said. It is one thing to be late for work now and then, but it is frowned upon to keep your partners waiting when going fishing or hunting, especially family members;

they will put it on you and not give it a second thought. We pulled on the road and headed north toward Rodanthe. It is only about two miles from Salvo to the beach entrance ramp by the pier. I almost dropped back off to the humming sound the oversized tires made on the road surface. These buggies didn't have any insurance or license plates on them. It was tolerated by local law officers at that time to drive short distances on the highway with these buggies. Some of the local commercial fishermen's boat trailers still lack tags today. If you are spotted by a state highway patrolman driving buggies or pulling trailers without tags, that is a different situation entirely. The bump at the beach ramp jarred me back to reality.

"You were drifting again," Raymond said as he laughed. "Get ready. We are almost there. Make sure you tie one of those black lures on your line when we get there," he added. As we drove under the pier I looked out the window in the direction of the ocean. The moon had cleared the water on the horizon. There wasn't a cloud in the sky. The wind was light from the northeast. I lowered the window and breathed deeply to try and wake up. The sharp coldness of wind-laden mist stung my face. The aroma of salt water, sand, and a strong fishy smell filled my nostrils. Raymond drove the middle of the slough and stopped the buggy. I opened the door and got out. The stiff northeast breeze blew the hood on my jumper from my head. The sharpness of the wind traveled around the sides of my neck and down the center of my back. This sent a chill through me and made me shiver. "Not only are you sleepy, but you are cold, too?" asked Raymond. I mumbled a response and tied the black lure on the end of my line. The gear that we used was a light seven-foot rod. These rods were equipped with small Penn spinning reels. The spools on these reels only held about 150 yards of eight-pound test monofilament line. They were designed to cast long distances and fight up to eight-pound trout. We walked to the water's edge, and right off the bat, Raymond hooked up. He beached about a three-pound trout. Then he caught another one. Then he hooked up a third time and landed another fish.

"Alright, what are you doing that I'm not?" I asked.

He laughed and said, "Come over here. Do you see the south end of that sandbar about thirty yards out?"

I said, "Yes."

"Cast your lure up on the middle of the bar; don't retrieve any line at all. Allow the tide to wash it off the edge of the bar into the slough. The trout are waiting in ambush at the edge of the bar. The natural movement of the water is bringing the baitfish to them." Sure enough, I placed the lure on top of the bar. Just as soon as it drifted into deep water, *bang*, he was there. I beached about a four-pounder. We continued this process, one angler moving to the left of the other. We continued to land fish.

"How did you know how they were feeding? I asked.

"Ah, my boy," he said, "you have to think like a fish. Each situation is different. Size up the layout of the slough, then consider the easiest way to catch baitfish if you were a trout. It's not always the fastest trout that catches the finger mullet, but I am sure that it is the smartest ones," he said. "Game fish such as trout are predators. Always remember that predators hide and ambush their prey," he added. My grandfather once told me that Raymond could catch a fish in a mud puddle. The trout stopped feeding for a short time just ahead of daylight. "Better brace yourself. Something much larger has moved into this slough. Baitfish are still here, but the trout have stopped feeding and took off," he said.

# CHAPTER FORTY-FOUR

# Rockfish

As daylight came, a large flock of tern gulls joined us at the slough. They went into feeding mode. They were circling the slough, diving in the water on occasion and catching baitfish. "It's time to take that black lure off your line. It is light enough now to use something white with some silver in it," Raymond said. I tied a fifty-two M-11 morrow lure on the end of my line. That lure has a red top and bottom. The sides have a small white streak separating the red from a silver middle. There was loose line on the spool of my reel forming a small tangle. I flipped it underhand a short distance past the shore break. The loose wraps of the tangle came clear as the line left the spool. As my line came tight, it took off like a rocket. It shot up over the bar and out to sea. The line was peeling off the spool so fast that I was stunned. "What in the world have you hooked?" Raymond asked as he walked over.

"Lord knows," I answered.

"You have a couple of options," he said to me. "You can either tighten up on your drag, which will probably pop your line, or since the tide is low enough now, you can go to the head of the slough and walk out on the bar."

I looked at my reel as the line continued to peel off. I could see the spool. I had about a dozen wraps left. I tightened the drag up a little and ran out on the bar. I gained several yards of line back. Then I lost the line off the spool again, just as quickly as I had gained it back. I walked to the outer edge of the bar until the water was at the very top of my waders. I looked at the reel; there were only two wraps of line left on the spool. In the next instant, my line went totally slack. The next wave washed the loose line behind me. I thought I had lost the fish. My mind raced. I hadn't felt a jolt of the hook pulling lose or the line parting. Then it hit me: The fish was racing straight toward me. I began cranking on the winding handle of the reel for all I was worth. I was gaining all my line back. My line came tight just as the fish was about to cross the bar to the right of me. I saw it for the first time. It was suspended in the middle of a wave, glistening in the early morning sunlight. I could make out a long silvery fish. It had black parallel stripes from its gill plate extending to its tail. It was a striped bass.

"Rockfish," I yelled to Raymond.

"Yes, I see it's about twenty pounds, I would say," he answered. The rock turned south and stripped about twenty yards of line off the reel. Then it entered the slough behind me. For a short time I was fighting the fish between myself and the beach. Then it took off in a northerly direction at a fast pace. It went out over the bar into deep water again. This fish had circled me 180 degrees. On this run it only emptied about half of the line on the spool. I sensed it was beginning to tire. I saw it roll on its side and come to the surface. It began to wallow and shake its head from side to side. I began to gain line slowly. With the help of the tide, I was able to guide it back into the slough. The rock made a couple of short surface runs. Then it rolled on its side, completely exhausted. I retrieved it within a couple of yards of my rod tip. I slowly pulled it to the head of the slough. In this location the water was only inches in depth. I slid my hands inside its gill plates and lifted it out of the water. "Nice fish," Raymond said, as I pulled the treble hooks out of its mouth with pliers. "You were lucky to land it."

"You're telling me," I replied. "It could have just as easily continued seaward and stripped all the line from the reel," I added. "For some unknown reason, it turned and swam straight toward me," I said. I washed the sand off the rock and placed it into the back of the buggy.

"Would you look at that?" Raymond shouted. I turned and looked toward the surf line. The slough was filled with large rockfish. You could see their silvery bodies suspended in the waves on the outer bar. They were as far as the eye could see. They were working their way southward. I had never seen a school of rockfish that large before. "We don't have any gear to handle fish that large," Raymond said. "These small rods and this eight-pound test line will never handle them," he added. "We need much larger gear." The back of his buggy had a dozen baskets of trout. "Let's take these fish to market and get larger rods," Raymond said.

"I have to work today," I told him. I was off from the dredge. On my off weeks I built decks for Wallace Beckham, a local contractor.

We headed back home. When we drove under the pier toward the beach ramp, I could see every fisherman's rod on the pier bent double. He stopped the buggy; we got out and looked. The school of fish was still on top of the water. They extended from the beach out past the end of the pier. "Are you sure you are going to work today?" he asked me.

"I have to finish up a deck for Mr. Beckham. He has a final inspection on an Avon cottage scheduled for tomorrow," I replied. That day I lunched at Willard Gray's hamburger stand. I talked to a couple of anglers from Avon. They told me that the rockfish were caught in the surf near Little Kinnakeet that morning. *The school had made it down that far,* I thought. I had no idea of the magnitude of rockfish that would be migrating south that fall. It wasn't long before anglers were catching them from Oregon Inlet to Hatteras Inlet. The very next week I heard that the rockfish were being caught by anglers in the Ocracoke surf. They were showing up as far south as Ocracoke Inlet.

That fall was a banner year for surf fishing. The speckled trout were abundant in the sloughs. Big blues and rock were being caught all along the beach. The rockfish were high-dollar fish. It didn't take long before commercial beach rigs were on the scene. These rigs consisted of two four-wheel-drive trucks. One truck pulled a trailer containing a beach dory or a wooden sea skiff. These dories had a well—a large hole positioned near the center of the boats. These holes penetrated the boat's bottom and contained an outboard motor. Behind the motor in the stern was a long haul net. The nets were a couple hundred yards in length. The fishermen would patrol the beach. They would cruise the surf line until they spotted a school of fish moving parallel to the beach. The truck with the trailer would speed in front of the approaching fish. The beach dory's stern was always loaded first on the trailer. This made for a much faster launch. The truck turned perpendicular to the surf line and backed the trailer down into the breaking waves. When the truck pulled ahead, the dory unloaded itself. There was a fisherman already inside the dory. This fisherman threw the anchor end of the net out on the beach. Then he started the motor. The truck driver buried the anchor in the sand. The fisherman from the boat jumped out on the beach. Both of the men worked together to wade the dory into deep water. The men climbed into the dory and sped seaward. The dory surrounded the school of fish and returned to the beach.

One of the trucks had large, open steel hooks welded to the front of its chassis. The open portion of the hooks pointed downward. Circular rope straps were spliced and used to haul the net back to the beach. These straps were wrapped around the net a few yards apart. The ends of the straps were placed on the hooks attached to the truck. As the truck backed away from the surf, the net was pulled ashore. When the truck moved forward the straps slackened and fell off the hooks. This was repeated until the entire net was pulled on the beach containing the fish. Then the fish had to be taken out of the net and loaded into the trucks. The next step was to clean and load up the gear. Then the fishermen took their catch to market.

This fishery was enjoyed by anglers and local beach fishermen for the next several years. It seemed that the large blues and rockfish only took to the surf from the mouth of the Chesapeake Bay southward to Ocracoke Inlet. Soon the news spread to many surrounding states. In the next few years the area was flooded with beach rigs. Rigs from as far south as Florida, as far north as New Jersey, and west from Ohio showed for the fall migration of these fish. Soon there were more beach rigs than there were fish. This was unexpected, to say the least. There were no local regulations to prevent the influx of these out-of-state commercial fisherman. The local commercial fishermen were upset with the arrival of these newcomers.

Problems began to develop right away. Some mornings there would be at least two or three of these rigs at each beach ramp. If more than two to three gulls began circling near the shore, there would be a dozen trucks headed in their direction. Two to three beach rigs and the rest of the trucks would be anglers. Open confrontation soon developed. First, it involved problems among the commercial rigs. Two or more of them would be racing ahead of the fish to gain the set position. The engines in the trucks would be racing. Sand would be flying in all directions. At times the sea dories would be flung off the trailers. The first dory to arrive at the desired set location would immediately launch and surround the fish. Sometimes there would be two to three back sets. A back set is setting your net as close as possible to a rig that is already set. I have seen so many fish in a net that the strain caused the webbing to part. Once the net was busted and the fish escaped, which is the reason that back setting was so popular.

Several of the local rigs began to work together. They set their nets straight out from the beach before the break of day. They positioned their nets about one hundred yards apart. When a large school of fish approached, the first rig took in about half of them. The two backup rigs would surround the remainder of the fish. This process of working together in this manner prevented the nets from breaking. It also provided more trucks to transport the fish to market quicker. Moreover, it speeded up the process of clearing and storing the gear. Most local crews had their catch and were off the beach by mid-morning. This helped alleviate some of the friction between the locals and the out-of-state rigs.

The battle of the angler versus the commercial rigs was another story entirely. The best and most exciting way to catch rockfish, on hook and line, is by using an artificial lure. A metal lure is usually used with something silver and shiny. Any type of Hopkins lure tipped with a white feather is really good bait. The preferred method is to cast the lure among the feeding fish and retrieve it rapidly. This will normally create a strike. I have seen beach rigs set around casting anglers. Most of the time these anglers were already on location and catching fish before the beach rigs ever showed up. This type of activity soon created heated situations. At times it led to violence between anglers and commercial fishermen. I have seen anglers casting lines inside of the circled nets. On several occasions I saw anglers' lines cut by netters.

One Saturday afternoon I witnessed a fistfight caused by a line-cutting episode. It started with two men involved. Then friends from both sides came to the aid of their buds. Soon it was an all-out brawl. Several men were injured and had to have medical attention.

Over the next few years these incidents became more commonplace. One of the worst incidents occurred near Oregon Inlet. A large off-island angler was celebrating Thanksgiving with a beach party. They were at Oregon Inlet's south shore. To their delight, a large school of rockfish came through the inlet. They passed the anglers within casting distance of the beach. The anglers began hooking up and landing numbers of large fish. A beach rig came driving up and launched its dory, setting its net around the fish and the anglers. It was a holiday weekend; beers and drinks had been consumed by the anglers and the netters. When small men get a few beers in them, all of a sudden, they get the feeling of being six foot two and bulletproof. When a larger, stronger man gets a buzz on, it can be even worse. One thing led to another, and a bad brawl broke out. Several of the men had to be hospitalized.

As a result of these recurring confrontations, the National Park Service became involved. They had to introduce law and order to the beaches. A few more isolated incidents occurred, but the park rangers kept a lid on the violence for the most part.

In a year or two the problem sort of took care of itself. Something changed. Every year around Thanksgiving you could always count on the big bluefish showing up along the surf. For some reason, the large bluefish and rock began to feed more offshore. They hardly ever came within casting distance of the beach. I don't know what happened. There seems to be ample baitfish in the surf in goodly numbers. The trout and small blues were still feeding along the surf. The larger, more challenging game fish had moved offshore. After about one fall season, the out-of-state beach rigs disappeared. Only a few local rigs made a few sets along the beach with smaller mesh nets. These netters caught smaller bluefish, trout, sea mullets and small drum.

The local commercial outfits soon made adjustments. They took larger mesh nets offshore. These fishermen would locate a school of fish and set their nets ahead of them. The fishermen were able to entangle the larger fish in the net webbing. At times they would stretch many of these nets out and leave them overnight. A popular spot to set the nets was at the shoals near the Cape Point area. The shoals are located a mile or two offshore from the beach. Large schools of baitfish were near this area. The large rock and bluefish fed around the shoals until they migrated north in the spring. Not many of the local anglers took advantage of this fishery. On any given day in the fall, many sport party boats could be spotted near the shoals. Most of them came out of Hatteras Inlet. They approached the shoals from the back side. The boats came within casting range of the shoals but remained in deep water. The fish were plentiful and always feeding if the water was clear. The anglers on these trips seemed to enjoy the short boat trips to the shoals and the abundance of fish. This was a good alternative to traveling twelve to fifteen miles offshore. A few of the anglers soon adapted to launching their smaller boats from the surf at the point. It was just a short trip out to the shoals and the fish.

One of the more successful anglers who used this method was John Robert Hooper. He designed and had a sea skiff built that was perfect for this type of fishing. I was fortunate enough to be invited on several of these rock fishing trips with him at the point. We caught many rockfish on these trips. There was a limit of two rockfish per angler. The bogeyman was always waiting on the beach to examine your catch when you returned. One particular morning John, Joe Lassiter, and I set out to catch our limit in John's boat. We launched the boat in the cove on the south side of the point. The cove was a sheltered area protected by the point itself. We reached the inside shoals in no time at all. John shut off the outboard motor within casting distance of the first group of shoals. Joe was the first to cast his lure into the whitewater along the edge of the shoal. He immediately hooked up. His medium-size rod bent, taking on the load of a very large fish. The line began to scream off the reel in a seaward direction. John had to fire up the motor and give chase to prevent Joe from being spooled. Joe gained about half of a spool of line back. He was able to maintain as long as John kept the throttle at quarter speed. This large fish that Joe hooked into kept leading us farther out to sea. Soon we lost visual sight of the beach. There was no stopping the boat to try and fight the fish. It kept a steady course for the open sea. After about four hours of battling this monster, Joe was ready to give us a turn. We both refused. John decided to speed up the boat. All this time Joe was winding in line. Soon we were above the fish. The line was leading directly down along the side of the boat. We saw a dark shadow, well over ten feet long. The fish never knew he was hooked. Joe tried one last time to force it to the surface. The line parted with a pop. Despair set in.

# CHAPTER FORTY-FIVE

# Ash Wednesday

We all looked at each other for several seconds; no one said a word. We just stared down into the water where we last saw the huge, dark shape. Finally, John broke the silence: "Probably a large bluefin." The bluefin tuna usually frequent the waters of the northern states of the Atlantic Coast. They have an abundant supply of them around the Gloucester, Massachusetts area. They have huge commercial fishery operations located up there. The boats that harvest them at times travel hundreds of miles offshore. The big bluefin tuna are caught on large fishing poles. At times it can take several hours to tire them. There are many careful steps in landing one of these monsters. They must be worn down to a manageable state. They have to be harpooned, then tail wrapped with a rope. Then they are hauled aboard the boat. There are also harpoon boats. These boats search for the schools of tuna feeding on the surface. The boats are designed with a long gang plant protruding from the bow. A harpooner walks out on the walkway and throws the harpoon at swimming tuna. If harpooned, the tuna must be tail wrapped and brought aboard the boat. The tuna can be lost at any point during this process. The larger ones can weigh in excess of a thousand pounds. At the Japanese markets they can bring up to twenty-five dollars a pound, so one large bluefin tuna can be worth thousands of dollars. However, a few of them had been hooked by rockfish anglers such as we were around the Cape Point Shoals area. None had been landed. Most all the anglers who had hooked them were using medium-size tackle.

These monsters had easily stripped all the line off the anglers' fishing reels. Several had been spotted feeding near the surface around the area that Joe had hooked up. It is a real letdown when you or one of your angling buds loses a large fish after a lengthy battle, especially only catching a short glimpse of the adversary instead of a good clear look of what you tied into. It was getting near the noon hour. We were located several miles offshore when Joe's line parted. John turned the boat shoreward, and we returned to the beach—the first time we returned with an empty fish box.

That was the last winter I worked on the dredge for the state. The local school system called me for a job interview. I was hired as the local high school carpentry teacher. I began my teaching career in the month of August that following fall. I taught from the same shop where I took carpentry as a high school student before graduation. I really enjoyed teaching. The local school board was supportive of the construction program. At that time there were only two high schools in Dare County: Manteo and Hatteras High Schools. Both programs constructed homes that were auctioned off at the end of the school terms. These homes were large enough to be used as single-family dwellings, or they could be used as small seasonal rental homes. The community professionals were supportive of the program. Local plumbers, electricians, and heating and air conditioning contractors were involved. They were invited in to teach the students those residential trades. These contractors came in for the rough in and finish work of these projects. We completed a number of these homes. Some still serve as family homes on the island today. Others, at least three, were moved across the bridge and are located off island. Several of my former students entered the construction field after graduation. Most all of them worked in construction-related trades. If they worked in areas not related to construction, at least they were exposed to skills that could help them build their own homes.

The most interesting and challenging educational times I ever experienced were during my elementary student years. My sixth- and seventh-grade years are ones that I will never forget. That was in 1962: the year that the Ash Wednesday storm hit the island. The weather forecasts were all conducted on local radio. Modern satellite technologies were not in place at that time. There were no computer models in place to track storms. It was in the spring of the year. We experienced a couple days of brisk northeast winds. Small-craft warnings were issued for the coastline north of Hatteras. A gale warning was posted for the Hatteras area. No alarms went out. There were no warning signs indicating that such severe weather was approaching the area. The storm struck on the March 7, 1962, on a moonless night.

It hit at the worst possible time. The moon was on an orbit that placed it incredibly close to the earth that night. The moon is in this position once every two years. The effect of the moon's gravity produces one of the highest astronomical tides along the coast during these times. The center of the storm track was inland. It moved northward rather slowly. The western part of the state was blanketed in several feet of snow. The winds along the coast blew in excess of seventy miles per hour for days. The devastation was widespread. Many coastal homes were lost to the giant waves. The entire Eastern Seaboard suffered catastrophically as a result of this storm. The constant pounding of the surf, for several days, opened up a new inlet north of Buxton. This isolated the southern end of Hatteras Island. This inlet began to rapidly expand in width. From the first day it opened, it began to cut south at an alarming pace. Something had to be done to slow it down. At the rate it was widening, the village of Buxton was in jeopardy.

The islanders implemented a plan that involved dumping anything and everything in the inlet that would catch the eroding sand. The Navy Base brig or jail was dumped into the swirling water. Wrecked vehicles from several garages on the island were dumped into the inlet. Most of the materials disappeared from sight as soon as they were dumped. The inlet began to slowly shallow up on its sound-front side. This slowed its rapid acceleration to the southward. As the storm moved farther north, the weather improved on the island.

The Rodanthe kids were all on the school bus traveling the twenty miles for school in Buxton. When we approached the Avon area, Charles Williams stopped the school bus near his store. Ella Porter, the bus driver, opened the side window on the bus. Charles told us, "You kids will not make it to school today. In fact it will be several days before you return to school. As a result of the storm, an inlet has cut through north of Buxton," he said. An immediate roar of celebration erupted on the bus. We knew at that time we would miss numerous days of school. Ella turned the bus around and returned us all to our homes. It took the local school board about a week to formulate a plan. The Department of Transportation had set up ferry service from Hatteras Inlet to Avon Harbor. First, the decision about the high school kids north of the inlet was implemented. They would ride the ferry to Hatteras, stay the school week with friends, and return home on the weekends. Temporary schools were set up in the villages of Avon and Rodanthe for the elementary kids. The school I attended was located at the old schoolhouse in Rodanthe. The schoolmaster's name was Mr. Peele. He was a relative of Mrs. Lilly Peele of Hatteras. He had the task of teaching grades one through eight in a one classroom setting. Ella picked us up every school day on the bus and delivered us to school. She was Mr. Peele's assistant and stayed the entire school day to help him.

It was quite an adventure attending school at the old schoolhouse in Rodanthe. We had lots of fun and learned a lot from Mr. Peele. He was an excellent educator. It wasn't too long before the inlet was bridged. A single land wooden bridge was built crossing the cut. At that point Hatteras Island was reconnected. We returned to the twenty-mile trip to Buxton to attend school.

The relentless undermining and pounding of the waves were a constant threat to the bridge. There were certain hours near midday that the bridge was closed for repairs. A large crane would move out on the bridge and assist in repairs during this time. The crane was on the bridge working, trying to save it from collapse, during a severe northeaster. The northeaster washed the bridge out and took the crane with it. The ferry route from Hatteras to Avon resumed. The high school kids returned to their routine of staying with friends and attending school in Buxton. At this juncture an elementary school was set up at the old Little Kinnakeet Life Saving Station.

This station was decommissioned and now managed by the National Park Service. All kids from the villages of Rodanthe, Waves, Salvo, and Avon attended school there. A teacher named Mr. Clark was assigned as the head schoolmaster. He had a couple of assistants. The seventh- and eighth-grade classroom was located in the upstairs area. First through sixth grades were located in the downstairs portion of the building.

This large number of kids was hard to keep up with and look after. We boys were always getting into hot water. We constantly ran off to the sound shore or the beach. Each time we returned to the classroom our clothes were messed up. We were wet from head to toe and covered with sand or mud. I know we aggravated the living life out of Mr. Clark. One particular prank most of the older boys were involved in I remember well. Charles Williams and Ozzie Gray from Avon were the ringleaders of our bunch. They figured out that the drink bottles we packed in our lunches contained cork in their caps. I don't know which one of them came up with it first. They showed the rest of us how to take out the cork from the bottle caps with a pocket knife, burn it with matches we smuggled from home, and use the charred cork to paint a mustache and full beards on our faces. We all showed up to class one day after lunch in this condition. We were all seated in our desk. Mr. Clark came out of a storage closet he had converted into a small office. Once he caught a glimpse of us, I thought he was going to have a falling-out spell. He went into a zone. His face turned crimson. You could almost visualize the steam erupting from his ears. He was so angry he could hardly speak. After a while he began to spit and sputter and got a few words out. "What in the name of all that's holy are you boys thinking?" he asked. All the girls in the class began to giggle. "What did you use to paint up your faces in such a manner? I want to know who showed you how to do this," he continued on. None of us uttered a word. "If you don't tell me, all of you boys are going to lose your recess privileges for two weeks. During this two-week period you will have plenty of writing assignments to occupy your time," he added. Still there was no response. Everyone knows that when you are a kid it is a carnal sin to rat on your buds. "Alright," he said, "if that's the way you want it, that's

the way it will be. Now get down to the bathroom and wash your faces."
So we suffered. The girls enjoyed their recess while we stayed indoors. The
two weeks we remained inside we improved our writing skills. We had to
write the same sentence five hundred times each day, which read, "I promise
to never paint my face with burnt cork again." Mr. Clark remained in the
classroom with us. He used this time to grade papers. He constantly smiled
at us. Every now and then he would ask us if we were enjoying ourselves.
Finally, the two weeks came to an end. We were pardoned and set free to
enjoy our recess.

It was during one of our recess periods that a small group of us were
checking out an old boathouse located in the backyard. Ozzie Gray was
leading our small pack of explorers. We located a loose board on the side
of the boathouse. Ozzie said, "If you fellers pull out on that board, I think
I can squeeze inside." A couple of us put pressure on the board, but Ozzie
was too big to squeeze through the opening. He looked at the rest of us and
said, "Oley, I bet you could get through there."

Oley Hooper, another boy from Avon, was a tad smaller than the rest of
us. "What do I do if I get through?" Oley asked.

"Check inside and tell us what's in there," Ozzie answered. Ozzie told
Dwight Gray, another Avon boy, that he was the lookout. His job was to
hide in the bushes within sight of the main building and whistle if Mr.
Clark or any adult approached. We pulled out on the board, and Oley was
able to get through the opening. "What do you see?" Ozzie asked.

"A bunch of wood stacked up in piles," Oley answered. "Wait a minute,"
came word from Oley inside the boathouse. "I see gallon buckets of paint
and a few paint brushes."

Ozzie told him, "Pass a couple gallons of paint and two brushes out of
the hole to us." Oley passed the materials out of the opening, then climbed
out himself. At that point Mr. Clark was ringing the alarm that signaled
recess was over. The alarm was used as an attention getter when the station
was manned. It made a perfect bell system for the temporary school. We hid
the paint and brushes in the bushes out back of the boathouse. The next day

when recess rolled around, we took off to the paint buckets. Ozzie found a nail and pried the lids open on the buckets. He broke a couple branches off of a close-by bush and used them to begin stirring the paint. To our amazement, we had a gallon of bright red and green oil-based paint. "We need to be careful with this stuff," Ozzie said. "If we get any on our skin or clothes we will need thinner to clean up with." He looked at us, then at the paint. "Now, what do we want to paint with this stuff? I wonder," he said, as he rubbed his chin, pondering the situation. The entire area was littered with toad frogs. About that time one of the frogs came hopping by chasing a bug. "That's it," he said, as he grabbed up the frog. The frog promptly peed all over Ozzie's hand.

"Now you are going to get warts," Oley said to him.

"You don't believe that crap do you?" Ozzie asked him. "That's just an old wives' tale," he said, before Oley could answer. "We will paint the frogs," Ozzie announced. In a couple of days there were dozens of green- and red-back frogs hopping around.

Mr. Clark asked us if we knew anything about the frog situation. "I know you boys have seen the painted frogs hopping around outside," he said. "I am almost sure that you boys are involved in some way." We acknowledged the fact that we had seen them. At the same time we told him we didn't have an inkling of an idea of how they got that way.

It took a long time for the paint to wear off the frogs. We had painted frogs hopping around for the next several weeks. The temporary school at Little Kinnakeet Life Saving Station was a unique educational experience. We almost caused Mr. Clark and the staff to have a nervous breakdown during our school days at the station. He was an excellent teacher. The well-being and proper education of his students was his top priority.

The Army Corps of Engineers sent a dredge to try and close up the inlet. The dredge began pumping sand from the south shore of the inlet. As it pumped up large sand hills, a bulldozer pushed the sand into the cut. They worked in this manner for months. Then another dredge was sent to the area. It began pumping sand from the north shore. Finally, with the combined efforts of both dredges, the inlet was filled in from the sound side and closed. At this point island life returned back to somewhat normal. The island is still very narrow at this location. All resident islanders hold their breath each time a hurricane approaches. The future of Hatteras and Ocracoke Islands could drastically change as the result of a severe storm or a lengthy northeaster. There is a narrow spot on Ocracoke Island a few miles south of where the ferry from Hatteras docks. Hatteras Island has three sensitive spots. The first spot is just to the east of Hatteras Village. The second location is just outside of the Rodanthe village heading to the north. The third location is up near the new inlet area. The remains of an old wooden ship from a past inlet is there. The Bonner Bridge is not in the best of condition. Ingress and egress is a constant concern during periods of inclement weather.

# CHAPTER FORTY-SIX

# Breeches Buoy Drill

I have always been interested in all types of sailing vessels. I grew up in the village of Salvo. Salvo is the third village along Highway 12 traveling south from Oregon Inlet. My house was located at the head of a creek on the sound side. It was just a short walk to the ocean from where I lived. Growing up during the fifties and sixties in Salvo was quite an experience. Cable television and cell phones did not exist. We all had television antennas on our rooftops. Most of the reception was a snowy screen. Once in a great while a channel would come in clear enough to see. Our telephones were hooked up to party lines. As many as four or five homes were connected to the same phone line. I remember our phone had three short rings in succession. We were the third house connected to the party line. Everyone always listened in on your conversation so they knew your business. With technology the way it was then we kids had no cell phones to text or talk on. We could hardly ever watch television. Most of us read comic and paperback books for pleasure. Some of my favorite books were written by Samuel Clemens (Mark Twain). *Huckleberry Finn* and *Tom Sawyer* are favorites of mine. I really enjoyed their adventures along the Mississippi River. I liked Louis L'Amour's adventures stories about gun fights and life in the old West. The books I liked the best were about swashbuckling pirate adventures. I loved anything that included multimast sailing vessels involving sea battles. I especially enjoyed reading about the adventures of Edward Teach or Blackbeard. Two of my favorite Blackbeard authors are Margaret

Hoffman and Kevin Duffus. The pirate plundered the Caribbean, the coast of Mexico, and coast of North Carolina. He was one of the most notorious sea robbers to plague the Caribbean and the North American coast.

I also read anything I could get my hands on about the U.S. Life Saving Service. Most all goods, materials, and long-distance travel were conducted by sail along the coast. These sailing vessels carried supplies and passengers from Maine to Florida. Some of the vessels traveled farther south to Mexico, the Caribbean and South America. Winter low-pressure areas and hurricanes plagued the shipping industry. Countless vessels and lives were lost to the sea during these times of inclement weather. The government decided to make a move. In 1848 the Treasury Department established the U.S. Lifesaving Service. There were a number of stations positioned along the Eastern Seaboard. The stations were poorly manned and sparsely equipped. It wasn't until 1871 that organization and accountability came to the service. A young lawyer from Maine named Sumner Kimball was appointed chief treasurer of the Marine Division Department of Revenue. He convinced Congress to appropriate two hundred thousand dollars to improve the service. With these funds he placed a lifesaving station every seven miles along the coast. Each station was assigned a six-man crew and issued proper equipment. A set of regulations and standards were drawn up under his direction. A station keeper was established for each station. It was the responsibility of the keeper to hold crew members to these standards. He also implemented the regulations and trained the crews. In very short order the service improved under Kimball's direction. The loss of vessels due to hurricane conditions could not be prevented. As a result of properly trained crew men and adequate equipment, many lives were saved during these adverse conditions. The lifesaving service became a reliable and respected branch of the government.

The closest station to where I lived was the Chicamacomico station. I used to visit it whenever it was possible for me to do so. This particular station was converted into a U.S. Coast Guard station in 1915. Captain John Allen Midgett Jr. was the assigned station captain. In 1938 Captain John

Midgett lost his life in a vehicle accident. Captain Levine Midgett assumed the leadership role at Chicamacomico until it was decommissioned in 1954.

With the implementation of modern equipment and technology the need for many of these stations decreased. The Elizabeth City Air Base was activated to cover the coast line by air. The number of stations on Hatteras Island was decreased to three: one at Oregon Inlet, one in Buxton, and one at Hatteras Inlet. The old lifesaving stations were assigned to the National Park Service. The Park Service assigned their personnel to these stations and gave them the name of caretakers. The caretakers and their families lived at the location where they were assigned.

I became friends with David Fletcher and his family. They were the family assigned to the Chicamacomico Station at Rodanthe. I visited them on a regular basis. The tact room still contained many written accounts of the saves that occurred at the station. David Fletcher allowed me to read these reports. Some of the documents were very fragile. I had to exercise caution when reading them. It was important to keep them in the same order as I found them. I don't know if we violated any government rules or regulations by me viewing these documents. I do know they were well-written. They were exciting accounts of courage and bravery. I could visualize myself being involved in each rescue as I read them.

My favorite rescue was of the crew of the British tanker *Mirlo*. This rescue was conducted by Keeper John Allen Midgett and his crew of surfmen. The wreck occurred in the early morning hours of August 16, 1918. *Mirlo* was torpedoed by a German submarine. The tanker was seven miles due east of Chicamacomico Station. Her cargo was over six thousand tons of petroleum products. A series of explosions caused the tanker to break in half. All the cargo was spilled on the surface of the ocean. It immediately ignited and formed a wall of fire around the wreck. Nine sailors of the ship's crew perished in the inferno minutes after she broke in half.

The lookout in the tower at Chicamacomico Station heard the explosions. He spotted the flames and billows of smoke through his spyglass. He alerted Captain Johnny, as he was called by his men, and the remainder of the surfmen. They scrambled into their oil clothes and life vest and put to sea in the motorized surfboat. It took a few minutes for them to travel the seven miles to the wreck. When they arrived at the scene, the whole section of ocean surrounding the wreck was ablaze. Captain Johnny circled the burning wall of flames several times seeking an opening; there wasn't any. Finally, he just steered the surfboat straight into the raging curtain of fire. The intense heat blistered the paint on the sides of the surfboat. It singed much of the exposed hair off the surfmen's bodies. They began the task of loading burned and injured survivors into the surfboat. They transported these sailors outside the ring of fire to safety. Several times Captain Johnny and his crew penetrated the blaze and loaded survivors. They rescued forty-two of the fifty-one sailors aboard the *Mirlo* during that save.

A lifeboat from the *Mirlo* survived the inferno. This lifeboat was used to help transport survivors to the safety of the beach. It was towed by the surfboat. In his closing notes Captain Johnny simply wrote, "Completed rescue operations around eleven, returned to station, men and myself very tired."

The prestigious American Cross of Honor was a lifesaving medal of the highest degree for that period. Only eleven of them were ever issued. Six of these medals were awarded to the Chicamacomico crew for their efforts during the *Mirlo* rescue. I have enjoyed reading every article I could lay my hands on concerning this operation.

One summer afternoon David Fletcher and I were sitting on the south-facing porch of the Chicamacomico station. We were busy enjoying a large piece of fig pudding. We were washing the pudding down with lemonade, both made by his wife. The figs for the pudding were picked from the fig trees located in the station yard. As we enjoyed the coolness of the moderate southwest breeze, he began telling me a story. This story concerned Captain Levine Midgett, the last man in charge of the station. Captain Midgett had retired from the Coast Guard. His home was located directly across Highway 12 from the station. It seems that Dave and his family were awakened early one morning to the rattling of pots and pans. There was a strong aroma of fresh perking coffee in the air. Dave went downstairs to the galley and found Captain Levine. He was up to his elbows in a pan of dough. The captain looked up and said, "Get a move on. By the time you get the boys up, I'll have the biscuits in the oven. Then hurry back and help me finish breakfast. We have a busy day ahead of us." Dave went upstairs and woke his family. Then he returned to the galley and helped the captain finish cooking breakfast. After they finished eating and cleaning up, he walked the captain back across the road to his home. Dave told me that this had happened on more than one occasion. As far as Captain Levine was concerned, he was still on active duty.

In 1968 the government sold the buildings to the local civic association. They donated them to the newly formed Chicamacomico Historical Association. The property was purchased by the Walter Davis family and donated to the Historical Association. The Breeches buoy reenactment drill was conducted by National Park Service volunteers for a number of years. For some reason the Park Service stopped performing the drill in 1994.

A man by the name of Richard Darcey was a charter member of the association. He had served as the drill interpreter for the Park Service drill team. Dick, as his friends called him, had a vast knowledge of the lifesaving service. He was passionate about the drill. One of his favorite things was to share his knowledge with the spectators who attended the performances. When the drill was cancelled he was crushed. He became proactive and asked for volunteers from the surrounding villages to be trained to conduct the drill. I was the first in line. I was soon joined by seven other local volunteers.

The Park Service loaned two employees from their reenactment drill to the association. They were on loan for training new recruits. These two park employees were the reenactment keeper and the number-one surfman. The keeper's name was Chris Johnston. He was all business and introduced us to a regimented, military-like understanding and performance of our duties. A fellow employee accompanied him who was an expert on all the drill equipment. Chris just introduced him as Fent and told us to let it go at that. Fent was a big, soft-spoken, gentle black man. He was two hundred pounds or better, and stood well over six foot. He knew every aspect about the gear.

Safety was his major concern. He taught us to operate the gear safely according to the prescribed standards listed in the Lifesaving Manual. The crew consisted of a keeper and eight surfmen. The drill itself was conducted from a man-pulled beach cart loaded with the lifesaving gear. The gear consisted of a Lyle gun or black powder cannon. There was a projectile for the gun and a box full of shot line, several hundred yards of one-inch rope called the Hauser, two reels of three-quarter rope called the whip line, a breeches buoy, and a sand anchor. There was a block and tackle, or a fall, as the lifesavers called it. The fall is a tensioning device. A drill pole was situated about two hundred yards away and served as a mast of a disabled vessel.

Chris and Fent walked us through the drill several times, each time switching people around in position until each of us could conduct any position assigned. After about two weeks of observed afternoon drilling, Chris announced that he and Fent would choose the permanent positions the next day.

The next afternoon Chris and Fent called for a close-order muster. We all lined up shoulder to shoulder in a straight line. They choose Larry Grubbs as the keeper. The rest of us filled the positions of the eight surfmen. During the first season we had to use actors from *The Lost Colony*, an outdoor drama, to fill a few positions. Chris and Fent felt confident that we were ready for our first drill with spectators.

Drill day was on Thursday of each week. The performance began at the main station. The interpreter, along with the cook, performed a skit that led the spectators to the boathouse. The boathouse doors were flung open, down the ramp came eight uniformed surfmen pulling the beach cart. The cart was positioned. The gear was arrayed and explained to the gathered spectators. The cart was reloaded, and the surfmen pulled it to the drill location. Once the cart was secured, each surfman explained his duties to the audience. The Keeper then chose the positions for the sand anchor and Lyle gun and gave the command action. The gun was loaded and fired at the wreck pole. The projectile propelled the shot line toward the wreck pole. The sand anchor was being buried into the sand. The hawser was tied in the end of the shot line and pulled to the wreck pole. The hawser was tied to the wreck pole. Tension was applied to the hawser by the fall attached to the sand anchor. The breeches buoy was attached to the traveling block on the hawser. The whip line was attached to the breeches buoy, allowing it to be pulled out to the pole and back cart area. We normally asked for a volunteer from the crowd to ride inside the buoy. Mostly small children were chosen. Surfmen numbers seven and eight worked at the wreck pole and helped the buoy riders inside the buoy.

The whole performance was timed. The time began at the keeper's command of action. It ended when the breeches buoy rider's feet made contact with the sand near the cart. We decided to train buoy riders to improve our time. Chris and Fent attended each performance that summer. After each drill we cleaned and stowed the gear. Then we gathered at a local bar and grill for food and beers. After a few beers, on one of these occasions someone asked Fent if that was his real name. Chris kind of chuckled and said, "You boys better leave that one alone."

Fent held both his massive hands, palms out, high in the air. Then he said, "No, Chris, these boys are good friends of mine. I don't mind telling them." He told us that his first name was Redding and his last name was Fenton. All his friends called him Red for short. His grandfather was named Moses. His dad wanted Moses for his middle name. Somehow it got mixed up on his birth certificate and came out "Roses." To make a long story short, his full name ended up as Red Roses Fenton. He added that we could go ahead and have a good laugh and make sport of him, but after this occasion we were to address him by simply "Fent" or else. We all had a good idea of his meaning of "or else." So, as before, all of us returned to calling him Fent.

We had a good summer season that first year. The spectators usually numbered two hundred or better every Thursday. The breeches buoy reenactment drill was a success. Sales at the gift shop increased drastically. All was well with the Chicamacomico Historical Association. The second season everyone had permanent positions. The drill crew included Larry Grubbs as keeper, Glenn Thompson, Robert Huggett, John Brown, Elvin

Hooper, Mike Lesley, John Contestable, Mike Daugherty, Rick Albaugh, and Steve Simmons as the surfmen. Richard Darcey served as the interpreter, and Michael Finnegan was the chief cook and bottle washer. During the next several seasons we went on the road. We performed at the Life Saving Station located at Little River Inlet, Delaware. The Coast Guard celebration at the Cape Hatteras Lighthouse was another performance location. Even though we traveled, we always kept to our schedule at Chicamacomico.

CHAPTER FORTY-SEVEN

# Too Much Powder

At the beginning of the fourth season we began training our breeches buoy riders. We chose local kids from the island villages. They met with us on Wednesday afternoon before they rode on Thursday. Their training was fairly simple. All they had to do was climb the wreck pole; get inside the breeches buoy, with the help of the surfman; and ride toward the cart until their feet touched the sand. The rider's names were as follows: Casey Midgett, Kristina Hooper, Stan Kee II, and Paxton Gwinn. Paxton was the rider at the lighthouse celebration in Buxton. With the training of our breeches buoy riders our times beat the Life Saving Service standard. We discussed the possibility of this maneuver being inconsistent with the drills procedures manual. After reviewing several accounts of drill-day activity from past keepers' logs, Dick announced that on most drill days the Life Saving Service used the same surfman as its buoy rider. At that point we all decided that we were performing on a level playing field consistent with the regulations. Life was good. The spectator crowds grew in number, and all was running smoothly.

At the close of our fourth season we received some disturbing news. All the gear we had been using belonged to the National Park Service. They were going to relocate the gear to other locations. There were a number of museums located near us, and the Park Service decided that the summer visitors would be better served by this move. We had one more drill before the season ended, and Dick convinced the Park Service to delay their move.

This gave us enough time to perform our last drill of the summer. They came and trucked all the breeches buoy drill equipment away. We had no gear. That put us out of business. The only thing in our favor was time. We had the winter months to formulate a plan.

Dick didn't waste any time. He scheduled a meeting with all surfmen the very next Thursday afternoon. We all met at the station in the tact room. In that meeting we all put our two cents in during a brainstorming session. Good results emerged. It was decided that we would put together our own gear. The most difficult part would be the Lyle gun, and the beach cart wheels. There were skeptics among us. Dick said not to worry. He had a friend in Williamsburg, Virginia, who was in charge of a Civil War reenactment. The Park Service allowed us to visit the gear and make notes. Dick visited his friend in Williamsburg. His friend took him to a cannon foundry and a wheelwright. They acquired a set of original specifications for the gun and cart wheels from Life Saving Service records.

Dick returned home victorious. He had made arrangements with the foundry to cast the gun. The wheelwright agreed to make a set of wheels. All of a sudden there was light at the end of the tunnel. For the first time we all believed we could pull this off. Each of us was assigned a portion of the work in which we had experience. My responsibility had to do with the ropes. I visited Mr. Swartz in Frisco—a net, twine, and rope dealer on the island. He ordered the traveling block, the blocks for the fall, the hardware, and all the grass hemp rope that was needed for the drill. My job was to splice all these ropes, connect the hardware, and attach them to their proper locations. Glenn Thompson, Mike Daughtery, and the remainder of the surfmen ordered the materials for the cart. They did a fantastic job constructing the beach cart. By Christmas the cart, spools for the whip line, and shot line boxes were completed. I had all the splices made up and attached. We were waiting for the gun and wheels to arrive.

Then finally the big day came. The wheels and gun arrived at the station. The wheels quickly bolted up the cart. The gun had been tested several times and was ready for action. At the beginning of April, all our lifesaving gear was in place and we were ready to begin drilling. We all stopped shaving, grew our facial hair, and began drilling in the month of May. By the time June came we were ready.

The first drill of the year went off without a hitch. All our new gear performed perfectly. The best part was that now the Historical Association owned the reenactment gear. That season we were invited back to Little River Inlet Station located in Delaware. We were scheduled to do three drills on Saturday after the Thursday drill at Chicamacomico. We loaded the gear on a utility trailer, lashed it into place, and hooked the trailer to a van owned by Dare County. I was a county employee at the time. I was in luck, as Edward Lee Mann was the county fleet vehicle coordinator. He was a retired Coast Guardsman. One of his assignments was at the Little River Inlet Coast Guard Station. He loaned us one of the county passenger vans for the trip. Five in the morning on Friday we began our trip to Little River Inlet. It took us about seven hours to complete the journey.

Arrangements were made for us to bunk at the state-owned Biden Center. The center is located near Lewes, Delaware. We were able to connect with a taxi service and explore the nightlife at Dewey Beach. It was amazing; there was a party going on at every bar and house all up and down the street. People were wandering in and out of the structures at will. The whole town was in a party mode. That was an eye-opener to say the least. We met a few local folks from the area. They told us it was that way every night all summer long. If you are ever on the Delaware coast at night, you owe it to yourself to check out Dewey Beach.

Our first drill was at eleven o'clock on Saturday morning. They had a cookout for lunch that day at the old lifesaving station. The second one was performed at two o'clock, and the third at five in the afternoon. A Coast Guard admiral from Washington attended all three drills. He was so impressed that he invited all of us to dinner at the Coast Guard station. One of the ladies of the Indian River Historical Association washed and dried our drilling whites. We drove about a mile south to the Coast Guard station. Upon entering the station's galley, the admiral saw us and immediately invited us to his table. He motioned for everyone to stand as we approached the table. We stood behind our chairs, and the admiral explained the activity of the day. He told all gathered that he was so impressed with our drills that he had stayed and watched all three of them. He said they were organized, regimented, and performed at the highest military levels. He took the time to come around the table and shake all of our hands. Then we received a huge round of applause. At one point he introduced the chaplain. The food was blessed, and we sat down to a prime rib dinner. Our trip to Delaware was very gratifying.

Early Sunday morning it was a journey back south to Chicamacomico. We arrived late Sunday afternoon, secured the gear, and prepared for the beginning of our individual workweeks.

The Coast Guard scheduled a celebration at the Cape Hatteras Lighthouse location in Buxton. We were invited to perform a drill during the festivities. A trip to the site to establish our drill field area was necessary. We met with Warren Wren, an upper-brass park ranger at the lighthouse. A drill field area was established. The Cape Hatteras Electrical Membership Cooperative, Hatteras Island's electricity power supplier, donated a drill pole. Dare Building Supply, a local building supply company, donated the material for the drill pole platform. The surfmen made a couple of trips to Buxton to build and attach the platform to the pole. The power company installed the drill pole. We selected Paxton Gwinn, a local girl from Buxton, as the buoy rider. We scheduled a couple of practice sessions before the event. Paxton was very athletic and took to the buoy ride as a duck takes to water.

When the celebration date arrived, we performed three drills with hundreds of spectators looking on. The drills ran as smooth as silk. We were able to provide the audience with a look back into the history of lifesaving techniques. The celebration offered many other activities for the young and the older folks to enjoy. It was a huge success, and everyone who attended had a good time. The local newspapers wrote very good reviews about the event. Local folks and visitors talked about it for days. Everywhere I went on the island during my workweek I was congratulated on the drills. The other surfmen received the same type of feedback from the folks who knew them.

After the very next drill on Thursday at Chicamacomico, we went to the local bar for lunch. I was sitting at a table with Dick Darcey, the interpreter; Robert Huggett, surfman number two; and Larry Grubbs, the keeper. We were chatting about the drill and the gear. The conversation drifted to the Lyle gun, as it always did. We were talking of how far the projectile was propelled on just one and a half ounces of powder. The gun designed, tested, and rated for up to eight ounces of powder.

"Man, I wonder how far the shot, another name for the projectile, would go on eight ounces of powder," I said. I looked around the table, and everyone's face took on a mischievous glow—with the exception of Dick. An expression of concern developed on his face.

"Don't even think about it," he said to all of us. "Do you guys want to get us barred from the drill? The association's board of directors would have a fit."

The three of us just looked at each other and grinned. We finished lunch, and as we were walking out the door, Larry looked at me and said, "Call me later."

"You boys heard what I said," Dick told us. "Stay clear of the gun until next drill day or you will be in for it," he reiterated as he got in his car.

I called Larry later. He told me Glenn and Robert were going to meet him for a beer, and he asked me to join them at the bar. Man, my mind began to race, as I knew we were in for some fun.

I met the three of them at the bar. The conversation went immediately to the gun. It was like having a new car with 120 miles per hour listed on the speedometer. There was always a nagging temptation to try to obtain the top-rated speed.

Robert's duty included weighing out the powder and sewing up the cloth pouches to be loaded in the gun. He was hesitant to make a heavy load of powder for the gun. If an accident occurred, everyone knew he prepared the powder. We aggravated him to the point of agreement. He said that three ounces would be the maximum load of powder that he would make up. "How are we going to gain access to the boathouse?" he asked.

Larry smiled and held up the key. "Dick sent me to the boathouse the other day to check on the amount of NEVR-DULL brass polishing cream and cleaning supplies we had left. I went to Dare Building Supply and duplicated the key," he said as he grinned. After a few more beers we decided to go to the station. Larry was the last to arrive. He took about three hundred yards of nylon line, a big red plastic ball, and a wheelbarrow from the back of his truck. Then he drove his truck back to the far side of the shadowed parking lot. As he walked up he said, "I found this line and net float at the harbor. I figured we could tie it on the end of the shot line box before we fire the gun," he added.

I added my two cents in the mix: "We better use both shot line boxes with a three-ounce powder shot," I said.

So we took the wheelbarrow to the boathouse. There we loaded the Lyle gun and two shot line boxes into the wheelbarrow. At this point we returned to the main station near the cookhouse.

The area around the cookhouse was the logical placement for the gun. It was located between the main building and the massive rainwater tanks. We thought that the noise from the gun would be somewhat muffled by these structures. The surface of the ground was hard-packed soil, unlike the soft sand we normally fired the gun from. There was a cement walkway along the sides of the cookhouse. We placed the gun about twenty feet ahead of the walkway. This location was at least a thousand yards farther back away from the ocean than our usual firing position. Glenn tied both shot line boxes together. Larry tied the float and the nylon line to the end of the second shot line box. We had a thousand yards of shot line and three hundred yards of three-quarter-inch nylon line, with a large net float tied to the end of it.

"Do you think we have enough shot line boys?" Glenn asked, laughing.

Robert said, "Shut up. I hear someone coming."

We all immediately flattened ourselves on the ground. About a dozen people were walking along a sand path within a few feet of us. They were returning from a beach party and were laughing and singing. We remained absolutely silent until they passed for fear of being discovered.

"Boy, that was close," Glenn said.

"Quiet until they get farther away," Robert said.

When the voices faded we all got back to our feet. Robert placed the three-ounce cotton cloth pouch of powder in the end of the gun barrel. Glenn pushed it down the barrel with the rammer. Larry tied the end of the shot line to the projectile or shot. He placed the shot into the barrel and let it slide free of his fingers. The shot made a rattling sound as it slid down the barrel. It made a muffled thud as it came into contact with the pouch of powder. Larry used the powder prick to make a small hole in the powder pouch. He placed the .22-caliber primer against the hole. Then he screwed the spring-loaded grooved firing pin to the top of the igniting chamber. He gingerly raised the firing pin and locked it into position with the lanyard clip. The clip was attached to a four-foot piece of quarter-inch line. This line is tied to a small wooden handle.

"Okay, boys. Are we ready?" he asked all of us.

"Ready," we all answered, except for Robert.

"You all know that they are going to find out," he said. "When we fire the gun, they will hear it," he added.

"At this time of night they are all asleep," Glenn stated.

"As hot as it is, all their windows are closed. Their houses are shut up tight, and their air conditioners are on," I added.

"If they hear they will probably think it's thunder," Glenn said.

Larry said, "Let's relax for a minutes and have a couple of more beers."

"Good idea," Robert agreed.

Larry and Glenn retrieved the cooler from the back of Larry's truck. We could hear the ice, water, and beers sloshing around in the cooler as they walked toward us.

"Just how many beers do you have in that cooler?" Robert asked.

"Enough," was the answer he got.

We sat down on the cookhouse steps and popped a few tops.

About thirty minutes and a few more beers later, Larry said, "Well, boys, are we going to do this or not?"

"Let's do her," Glenn answered.

"I am in," I said.

We all looked at Robert.

"I know when I'm licked," he said. "Let her go."

We all got well away from the gun, and Larry pulled the lanyard. Out popped the lanyard clip, freeing the firing pin. Immediately there was a tremendous ear-splitting explosion. The projectile burst from the end of the gun barrel. It was as if everything suddenly went into slow motion. The two-hundred-pound solid brass Lyle gun was catapulted violently twenty feet backward. It came in contact with the edge of the cement walkway. At this point it was propelled four feet up in the air. The gun, to our astonishment, slammed through the side of the cookhouse wall. The projectile ripped the shot line from both shot line boxes. Then the three hundred yards of nylon line took flight. The last thing we saw was the large net float flying out of sight in the night sky toward the ocean. For a few seconds we all stared at each other in disbelief. There in the side of the cook house wall was a gaping hole. The gun was completely concealed from view inside the building. We didn't have a key for the locked cookhouse door.

"Now what do we do, mister smart guys?" Robert asked. The three of us looked at his concerned face and busted out in uncontrollable laughter.

"You won't be laughing tomorrow when Dick finds out," he said.

"He won't find out," Glenn stated. "I believe we can fix everything if we hustle," he said.

The cookhouse was repaired and painted. We returned the gun and empty shot line boxes to the boathouse, cleaned up the grounds, and left just as daylight was making.

# CHAPTER FORTY-EIGHT

# Island Band

As we were getting into our vehicles to go home, Robert made a suggestion. "Let's go have some breakfast at the Fishing Pier restaurant," he said.

I was the first to respond. "That is a very good idea."

Larry and Glenn agreed. "We still have a lot to talk about," Larry added.

When we entered the restaurant, Sheila Skipper-Dean, one of the owners, greeted us. "My God," she said as she looked at us. "you boys look like you have been through the ringer. You look as if you have been up all night rolling around in a peg pen. The alcohol odor alone is enough to knock you over. A lot of you smell like you just came from a gin mill. Have you guys looked into a mirror this morning?" At that juncture we all took a good look at ourselves and each other. Our clothes were soiled and wrinkled; smudges of sweat-stained dirt were all over our faces.

"Don't move," she told us. "I'll be right back." She returned with a washcloth, towel, and a bar of soap for each of us. "Now go in the bathroom and clean up the best you can," she said. "When you are finished I'll seat you in the back corner, just as far from the customers' line of sight as possible." We thanked her and said we would appreciate the privacy, and did as we were told.

When we emerged from the bathroom she looked us over. "Ah, that's much better. Now follow me," she commanded. She led us to a partly secluded corner at the far side of the restaurant. "Do you need menus, or do you know what you want?" Everyone knew what they wanted and we placed our orders. Then the conversation began.

Larry started off. "We have three problems: the empty shot line boxes, the freshly painted cookhouse, and all the shot line out in the ocean."

"The most pressing problem is retrieving the shot line without Dick finding out," I stated. "I suggest after breakfast we take my binoculars out on the pier to see if we can spot the float." At that point breakfast came and we all gulped our food down, then went out the door and up on the pier. We walked to the end, and I scanned the northeast horizon. I spotted a small speck bobbing in the waves far in the distance. Every now and then when the sunlight hit it just right you could catch a glimpse of red. "That's it," I said and passed the glasses. Everyone looked at the object, and it was jointly decided that it was indeed our float.

"Now to get it back," Robert said.

"Let's all go home, get our surfboards, and come back and park at the drill field near the dunes. We will be seen, but they will think we are just going surfing," Larry said. As I returned to the drill field with my surfboard, Steve Simmons, the youngest surfman in our group, came running up to my truck. "You guys going surfing?" he asked.

"Yes, you want to come?" I asked him.

"Can you give me a ride back home to get my board?" he asked.

"Sure," I said, "hop in." It was just a short ride to Steve's house. On the way I brought him up to speed on the past night's events.

"If you can show me the float I will take your board and retrieve it," he said. My surfboard was a nine-foot, six-inch Hanson. It was longer than the boards my friends had. I took him straight to the pier. We looked at the buoy with my binoculars. His only question was how he would see the buoy from the water.

"I will guide you from the pier," I told him. "When you see the buoy, wave to me. When you get there, go to the end of the line and pull up the shot. Place it on the board in front of you. Don't try to pull the buoy end, dragging the shot on the bottom behind you," I told him. "It will be hard enough dragging all that line in," I added.

"Okay," he said, "let's get under way." He paddled my long board to the end of the pier. I borrowed a fishing pole and a white bait rag from a friend fishing on the pier. I tied the bait rag to the tip of the fishing pole. Steve began paddling toward the float. If he got too far to the left I waved the flag to the right. The same applied if he was off to the right: I waved to the left. As long as he was heading for the float I waved straight ahead. I guided him in this manner until he waved back to me. This was the signal that he had spotted the float. I returned the pole and bait rag to my friend and left to join my friends at the beach.

When I walked over the dune, Glenn saw me and said, "We saw you on the pier directing Steve to get the float."

"He is out there now, but you can only see him using these," I said, handing him the binoculars.

"I can see him, but I can't tell if he is still going out or paddling in," Glenn said. I focused my eyes on the horizon, but I couldn't see him without the binoculars. In about an hour we could make out a speck on the horizon with the naked eye. Slowly the speck grew and materialized into a paddler and a surfboard. Glenn and Larry went out to help Steve when he was within several hundred yards of the beach.

Once the shot was on the beach, we pulled all the line in. Larry took the float and nylon line and placed it into the back of his truck. Glenn took one stretch of the shot, and Robert took the other. They pulled it toward the boathouse across the high grass. The grass suspended the line above the sand. This allowed the wind and sun to dry out both shot lines. We all went to the boathouse and took out the shot line boxes and the gun. Larry and Robert were cleaning the gun. Steve and I were pulling the shot line toward us. We were beating the dried sand out of it with the beater sticks. Glenn was threading the shot line around the shot line box pegs. We looked up, and Dick walked around the side of the boathouse.

"What in the name of God are you guys doing?" he asked. The veins were swelled with blood and enlarged in his temple areas. Rage was written all over his face. We were dumbfounded; he had caught us completely off guard. We all tried to formulate some sort of explanation. The words came out garbled; we were all trying to talk at the same time.

"Hold it, hold it," he said, holding up his hands. "I have already seen the cookhouse. It looks great. Funny thing though. It made a miraculous transformation overnight," Dick said. "What inspired you all to replace most of the boards on the east side and paint it? What do the gun, shot line, and shot line boxes have to do with all of this?" he asked. We all started up talking at the same time again.

"That's it," he said. "I have heard enough. Get this mess cleaned up and stow the gear. Then get out of here until drill day. You all could cause us to lose our drilling privileges." He stomped off in a huff, mumbling something under his breath. From what we could hear it had something to do with the board of directors of the association.

The end of the 2001 summer season rolled around. We were scheduled to perform two drills in September, but our September drills were cancelled by the events of 9/11.

The whole nation was thrown into shock and disbelief. We had been openly attacked by terrorists on our own soil. The terrorists had used our own knowledge and resources against us. Our nation's security was caught completely off guard. They were unable to detect any signs of the attack or protect us from it. Over three thousand people lost their lives. Property damage was in the billions of dollars. Our whole nation's infrastructure was severely interrupted. The average American realized that we are vulnerable and open for attack. All types of new antiterrorist rules and regulations were immediately implemented in our society. We now live in constant fear of future terrorism, captives in our own country. After the attacks of 9/11, it was unlawful to discharge a black powder gun within one thousand feet of a dwelling.

We knew we were in trouble. The liability insurance carrier we had cancelled our policy. Without insurance coverage, our drilling days were over. Then the official word came down from the top. The breeches buoy reenactment drill at Life Saving Station Chicamacomico was officially cancelled. The pressure of terrorism on our insurance company had taken our beloved drill. We turned in our uniforms with heavy hearts.

Even to this day everyone who was connected with the reenactment drill loves that old station, so we decided to do what all good Hatteras Islanders do when they are down and out: have a big party. It was decided that we would give the drill a proper send-off. We invited everyone we knew to the party. The get together was held at the community center in Rodanthe. The wives prepared all types of food. Music was provided by the island band, Chicamacomico. We ate, danced, and partied into the wee hours of the morning. A good time was had by all. A few of us remained to clean up the building. It was daylight when we left for home. The band, of course, was named after the station. The members consist of local musicians from the villages of Rodanthe, Waves, and Salvo who play classic southern rock and country.

I have been a member of this band for well over forty years. We first started playing back in my high school years. My cousin Donald Hooper was the first lead guitar player. The first drummer was my cousin Richie Austin. The bass player was Jack Cahoon Jr. I was the rhythm guitar player. We played for various functions all up and down the island. When we were first learning to play, we practiced in Richie's father's garage. In the winter there were no problems. The garage doors were always closed. There was a small propane heater for heat, but when the summer came around so did the complaints. The summer nights were always hot. We had to open the doors in order to keep cool. In the beginning the complaints were about the racket we were making. In those days all the neighbors opened their windows to catch the cooling southwest breeze. The breeze cooled their homes, but the racket kept them up.

As we began to improve, the young folks began to congregate outside in the yard to listen and sing along. Now, not only music noise, but crowd noise was beginning to become a problem. Richie's father would sometimes have two or three complaints a night from his neighbors. Uncle Dick, as we called Richie's dad, met with us to discuss the problem. He came into the garage one night around eight o'clock as we were setting up our instruments. He asked us if we could begin playing earlier in the evening, around six or seven o'clock, and stop by nine. We usually played until midnight or later. We agreed to start around seven and stop at nine. This seemed to solve the problem.

As we improved even more and began playing around for local parties, our crowds grew. More and more people began to show up for our practice sessions. Now we had another problem. There wasn't adequate parking at the garage for our fans. Something had to be done.

My cousin Donald and I went to a civic association meeting. We asked to use the civic center on our practice nights. Permission was given. The only condition was scheduling. We had to coordinate our practice sessions with other functions that used the building. Our drummer, my cousin Richie, was replaced by my nephew, Kenny Hooper, for a short time. Then, for some length of time, we didn't have a drummer. When you're young, sometimes other things get in the way of practice sessions.

Even without a drummer we had a crowd at our practice sessions on Wednesday nights. A local girl brought her date to one of our practice sessions one time. Her date was in the navy, stationed at the base in Buxton. He approached us after we finished and introduced himself as James Beausoleil from Louisiana. One of his responsibilities was to arrange entertainment at the Driftwood Club on the base. On Friday nights the club was opened to enlisted men and their guests. Saturday night was reserved for officers and their guests. He asked us if we wanted to play on Friday and Saturday nights that week. We agreed to play on Friday night to test the waters. Things went well, and we returned to perform on Saturday night.

A young officer approached us as we were setting up to play Saturday night. He introduced himself as Frank Lorenzo. He was from New York. He was also a drummer. His entire navy career had included playing in officers' club combo bands. His last transfer to Hatteras Island had put the kibosh on his playing. There wasn't an officers' band stationed here that he could be join. He asked us if he could play with us that night. His drums were just a few houses away in his quarters. We were delighted. Donald and I helped him fetch his drums. That particular night we had a blast. That was the beginning of a long friendship and a permanent drummer for the island band, Chicamacomico. We began to play in clubs all around the island and the upper beaches. Two nights a week, in the summertime, were reserved for the navy base club. We used these as our practice sessions and left our gear set up there. We could just walk in, tune up, and play. That was really nice. Then Frank retired from the navy. He got involved in real estate and made Hatteras Island his home. For the first time we had four band members willing to pay the dues to make it work. Our popularity increased in leaps and bounds. We were playing three or four times a month, even in wintertime. Our favorite place to play was at the Old Christmas Celebration held each year in Rodanthe. It was like coming back home for us each year. We played there for at least fifteen years in a row.

Then my cousin Donald began having respiratory problems. The least little thing he physically attempted, and he was out of breath. The rest of us aggravated the life out of him until he agreed to see a doctor. The initial prognosis was very upsetting. The local practitioner determined that he had a lung problem, but he didn't know to what extent, so the doctor sent Larry to a specialist. The results of a battery of tests showed several spots on his lungs. Treatment was scheduled to begin immediately.

Sometimes one wonders if the treatments aren't more harmful that the disease. After several treatments it was determined that he had cancer cells in other organs of his body. He needed a combination of chemo and radiation treatments. The chemo made him nauseous. He threw up everything he ate. The radiation cooked him alive. His lips dried and cracked. He developed raw spots on his skin. Donald's health seemed to deteriorate at a much faster rate after each treatment. We all had to stand by helplessly and watch the life slowly drain from him. Weekly he lost more and more weight until there was almost nothing left. He was a walking skeleton. He fought the brave fight and held out as long as he could. He told me he was bone tired, that he just couldn't stand anymore; he was ready for it to end.

My cousin, my friend, our lead guitar player—we grew up playing music in church together—passed away on my birthday. He was just forty years old. I was devastated; he was like a brother.

As I write this, I am sitting alone in the wee hours of the morning, just me and my laptop, tears streaming down my cheeks. If you have ever gone through this agony with a loved one, you can relate to this experience. He was loved and respected by everyone who lived in the area. There was a gaping hole torn in the psyche of the Chicamacomico area. It was like a dark cloud settled over the northern three villages of Hatteras Island.

Our small, carefree island band went on the skids for a lengthy period of time. The magic was gone. We tried several lead guitar players, but couldn't quite find the right mix. The remaining three of us, drummer Frank Lorenzo, Jack Cahoon Jr. on bass, and me on rhythm guitar, sort of drifted apart for a few years. I tried playing acoustic sets at a few of the local bars, but my heart wasn't in it.

Then a friend of mine, Michael Finnegan, leased an old tackle shop in Buxton. He named it Finnegan's Dining Haul. I was having lunch there one day talking to him. He was telling me how expensive live music had become. I offered to bring in my gear and play for food and beers. He readily agreed. Mike, as I called him, is a good guitar player and singer himself. When business slowed at night, we were able to hit a lick together.

CHAPTER FORTY-NINE

# Shenanigans

With the addition of music, Mike's business picked up to the point that he was always busy preparing food. I played on for several months. During one of my breaks I met a man named Thomas Tripp and his girlfriend, Linda Farmer, who came in to eat. They had just moved to the area. They were staying in a camper at a local campground. They were looking for a house to rent in the northern villages of the island. I had just built a house in the Buxton area and moved my wife, Debra, and daughter, Kristina, there. I still owned a home in Salvo and rented it to them. They asked me how often I played. I told them every Friday and Saturday nights during the summer. The next question was how much was I getting paid. I laughed and told them. They asked if they could join in. I said it was fine by me, but we would have to ask Mike. He agreed, and now we were three. Linda was a good guitar player and country singer. Tom was a fair bass guitar player.

One Friday night a man named Larry Crum and his girlfriend came in. He was interested in joining us. Larry is a fine musician; he can play almost any instrument. He is also an accomplished singer. Now we were four and we played there for a few years.

Then Mike sold the business to a man named Hal Lester from Richmond, Virginia. Hal and his wife, Robin, kept the name and continued it as an eatery. They agreed to let us play there under the same arrangements. We had several tourist bass players join in from time to time. A visiting drummer played with us once in a while. It was really fun; we turned Thursday nights into open mic night. We had visiting fiddlers, and mandolin and harp players drop in and play. Once they played the first time, they always came back and brought their instruments on their next vacation. I called Frank and Jack, and we were able to put a band together to play for three years at the Old Christmas Celebrations in Rodanthe.

Tom Tripp and Linda moved to the state of Georgia. That left Larry Crum and me at Finnegan's to provide the music. Larry is far advanced in skill level and a more serious musician than I am. I am an average guitar player and singer at best. I couldn't keep up with him. He moved on. Soon I was once again by myself at Finnegan's on Friday and Saturday nights.

One night I was munching on a pizza, washing it down with a draft during one of my breaks. Hal Lester, the new owner, joined me. He began telling me about his musical background. He had not only played in a heavy rock band, he was the lead guitar player. He asked how I felt about him joining me later in the night when business slowed. I was delighted. Again, I found myself in the company of a superior musician. He has a good, clean guitar style, and is an excellent singer and a fine musician. There was no way I could elevate myself to his level. He was willing to adapt to my style of classic rock and country music. Together we provided the live music along with a few visitors at Finnegan's. Mike Finnegan returned to play with us. We were joined by Dave Havard, another musician friend of ours. The music was fun again, and everyone was welcome to come in and play. We continued to provide music for the Old Christmas Celebration each year.

Our bass player, Jack Cahoon, lived in Manteo. It was a long trip for him to come to Buxton and play. He began playing with several groups in the Manteo area. His new playing schedule was often demanding and caused him to drift away from us. A visiting bass player from New Jersey retired and moved to the Buxton area. His name was Bruce Pritchard; he began playing with us. My type of old-fashioned music is much too tame for Hal and Bruce. Hal and a local island drummer named Greg Koszykuski created a heavy rock band called Blistered. Hal and Greg had auditioned several bass players with no success. They asked Bruce to join them. They were quite successful playing in clubs around the island.

Then Hal and Robin sold Finnegan's to new owners. Two local girls ran it for a couple of summers. The new owners removed the stage to make room for more tables. They had live music on Saturday nights. We played there a few times, but the convenience of leaving the equipment set up was gone. The regular Friday and Saturday night playing schedule was also gone. We began playing less and less. Off-island musicians and disk jockeys with recorded music had replaced us. It seems that no one wants to listen to classic rock anymore. We only play once a year, on the first Saturday night in January. We play in Rodanthe at the annual Old Christmas Celebration. This is a tradition I hope to keep up till the end. Frank Lorenzo, drummer; Hal Lester, lead guitar; Bruce Pritchard, bass guitar; and Elvin Hooper, rhythm guitar—we are the island band, Chicamacomico. Come see us each January at Old Christmas. Jokes, sea stories, and shenanigans have always been an important part of island life.

When I was a kid, I remember pedaling my bicycle up to Waves. On a wintertime Saturday afternoon I faced a brisk northeast wind for two miles to get to Asa Gray's store. Two miles north of the village of Salvo where I lived is the village of Waves. Asa Gray's was the closest store to my house. I knew that on a cold wintery afternoon, the older men would be gathered there. They would be sitting around a cherry-red potbellied woodstove telling jokes and stories. It was impossible to enter the store without being noticed. When you entered the store, a wave of heat and the aroma of fresh-perked coffee enveloped you. Immediately your outer covering of clothes had to be shed. I always wore coveralls over my clothes on winter bike rides. They had to come off in order to be comfortable. Sometimes even my flannel shirt had to go. I would be down to my undershirt and jeans. Mr. Asa had a hat rack, hangers, and a shelf near the door. I deposited my outer clothes and turned to see if anyone was there. At this instant all was quiet as they sized me up. I waved and said hello. When they recognized me I received a nod. I knew then all was well. I walked over to the drink box and withdrew a

Pepsi-Cola and poured a pack of peanuts inside the bottle. Then I settled in a corner and remained quiet. On this particular afternoon they were telling jokes. One of the men looked in my direction and said, "Hey, you, Hooper boy. Do you know the difference between a fairy tale and a sea story?"

"No, sir," I responded.

"Well, a fairy tale begins with 'Once upon a time.' A sea story begins with 'And this is no shit,'" he said. They all broke out in uncontrollable laughter. When they finally calmed down, one of them began telling a joke he had heard.

"Watch your language around the boy," one of the men said.

"That is Preacher Ed's son from Salvo," he added.

"This is a good, clean one. Even the boy can repeat it," the joke teller said. He took a sip of coffee and a pull on his corncob pipe. The story goes like this:

It seems there was a couple from New Jersey driving through North Carolina headed to Florida. They were driving a big Chrysler Newport. The driver noticed they were almost out of gas. He turned off the main highway at a service station to fill up. When he left the station he made a wrong turn. These Jersey folks found themselves hopelessly lost on rural backroads of North Carolina. The driver stopped the car and backed into a small entry road to a cornfield. The big car was low to the ground and got lodged in the turnoff. The driver couldn't get the car back on the road; the wheels spun around helplessly in the mud. They were stuck on a hot summer afternoon with no help in sight. To their delight an old farm truck came rattling down the road and stopped. The truck driver asked if he could help.

"Could your truck pull us back on the road?" asked the driver of the car.

"I believe so," the old farmer responded. The farmer pulled them back on the road. The Jersey folks thanked the farmer. The farmer agreed to show them how to get back to the main highway. He told them to follow him. The farmer drove in front of them a short distance, and his truck engine cut off. He was able to pull off the road before the truck stopped rolling. The car driver asked the farmer what was wrong. "I think I ran out of gas," the farmer said.

The wife said to her husband, "We can't leave him. He helped us." They offered to take the farmer to the gas station. The farmer agreed but said he had a bucket he needed to bring along. The farmer got into the back seat with his bucket and they were off. Immediately the couple noticed a putrid smell coming from the back of the car. "What in heaven's name have you got in that bucket?" the man asked.

"Cow manure," the farmer answered.

"Do you mean cow poop?" the wife asked.

"That is what it is," the farmer told them.

"May I ask what in the world you plan to do with it?" the woman asked.

"I am going to put it on my strawberries," the farmer answered.

"On your strawberries," the woman gasped.

"Certainly," the farmer said. "What do you folks put on your strawberries in Jersey?" asked the farmer.

"Whipped cream," the woman answered.

Everyone in the store busted out in frantic laughter. When they calmed down, one of them asked me if I had a joke to share. I told them I didn't have a joke, but I had a funny but painful story. They encouraged me to share it. I told them that I was fishing on the pier catching big yellow fin spots and edible panfish the past September. I pulled up a double-hook bottom rig with a spot on the top hook. On the bottom hook clinging to a sliver of bait was one of the largest blue crabs I had ever seen. As soon as he hit the pier deck he scrambled under a nearby bench and partially hid himself close to one of the legs. Two young boys and their parents were walking by and took all this in. The boys walked over to the bench. Before I could get out a word of warning, the youngest boy reached right under the bench and picked up the crab. He let out a blood-curdling scream. The crab had attacked the boy's left hand. It had a death grip on his thumb with one claw. The other claw was clamped on the end of his little finger. He was screaming over and over, "I didn't know they could bite with their arms."

The men kind of chuckled. One of them started to share another joke. He stopped and looked in my direction.

"It's getting on in the afternoon," he said to me. "You don't want to be riding that cycle home after dark," he added. I knew they wanted to tell some jokes that they considered too rank for my ears. This was my signal to be going home.

I nodded and said, "Yes, sir." I asked Mr. Asa to pack a pound of cheese for me. He weighed out the cheese, wrapped it in brown paper, and tied it up with string. I paid for my Pepsi, peanuts, and cheese, donned my overclothes, waved bye to all, and was out the door. The sharp northeast wind bit into my face as I straddled my bike. *Fair wind home*, I thought to myself. Then my mind drifted to the block of cheese that was zipped inside my coveralls. I knew my mom would turn it into delicious cheese biscuits for my dad and me. I was zipping right along; next thing I knew, I was approaching my driveway.

The next time I heard another clean joke, I was with my father down in Kinnakeet Village. We had been to see Mr. Willie Austin about a new decoy boat my father needed. Before we left for home, Dad wanted to visit Mr. Percy Williams at his shop. We began walking to Mr. Percy's house.

"I told your brother to pick us up at Percy's," my dad said.

"When we get to Percy's place, don't you dare ask if his wife, Venus, has baked pone bread dessert."

"Why?" I asked. "She makes the best pone bread I have ever sunk a tooth into," I said.

"It is just not polite," he responded.

"Oh, alright," I said, disappointed. Mr. Percy had a long narrow building beside his house. He was a commercial fisherman; he worked on his gear in this building. In a back corner he had a small barber shop. My father was a self-taught barber. He and Mr. Percy usually traded a haircut. On this occasion he decided that I also needed a haircut. When it was my turn to get in the chair, a stranger walked in. Mr. Percy knew this man. The three of them began talking about fishing, weather conditions, and other topics pertinent to island life. The conversation got around to jokes. The stranger began telling a joke. Mr. Percy stopped him. "This is Preacher Ed and his son from Salvo," Mr. Percy told him.

The stranger laughed and said, "This is a clean joke. Even a preacher could repeat it in the pulpit." Then he began telling us of this man who lived in the mountains. He had worked and saved his money and purchased his dream car. It was a candy-red Corvette. The top speed on the speedometer was marked 130 miles per hour. This marked speed haunted the young man. His curiosity got the best of him one night. Driving along a deserted mountain road he increased his speed up to 100 miles per hour. The vehicle was handling well, sort of floating along. He increased the speed up to 120 miles per hour. As the vehicle flew by a side road, a highway patrolmen gave chase. The man caught sight of the blue lights as the trooper pulled on the road. At this point he made a bad decision; he decided to outrun the trooper. The trooper caught up with him and pulled him over.

"Where is the fire?" the trooper asked. While walking up to the Corvette he asked the man for his license and registration. The man began to babble some sort of response. The trooper looked at him and said, "I get off in fifteen minutes. If you can come up with a reason I haven't heard in the past thirty years as to why you were driving 120 in a 55-mile-an-hour speed zone, I won't give you a speeding ticket." The man thought and thought.

Finally he responded, "My wife ran away with a state trooper ten years ago. I thought you were him bringing her back." Mr. Percy, my father, and the stranger busted out laughing. I kind of chuckled because I didn't quite get the joke.

As I was getting out of the chair, Mr. Percy asked, "Are you feeling alright today, son?"

"Yes, sir," was my response.

"You and your father have been to my shop many times," he said. "This is the first time I can remember that you failed to ask about Venus's pone bread," he added. "I know for sure that she made one this afternoon."

I looked at my father with a sheepish grin on my face. "As long as it is okay with Percy," my father said. I looked at Mr. Percy, and he just nodded his head in the direction of the house.

I was out the door in a flash. I knocked on the back kitchen door. Miss Venus came to the door. When she saw me she said, "Ah, it's my little Rodanthe pone bread boy. You are in luck," she said with a smile. "I have it cooling in the window sill. It's cool enough to cut by now." She cut a generous portion, wrapped it in wax paper, and handed it to me.

I said, "Thank you ever so much, ma'am."

"You are certainly welcome, son," she said, bending down to kiss my forehead. I could feel the warmth through the wax paper. I opened the corner of the paper and took a good whiff of the heavenly aroma. Man, did it ever smell good.

On my return to the shop my father asked me, "Did you at least take time to thank her?"

"Yes, sir," I said. "Hugged her, too."

"Better keep an eye on that boy. I think he might turn out to be a lady's man," Mr. Percy said with a chuckle.

I turned to him and responded, "When I grow up, I am going to marry a lady just like Miss Venus who can make pone bread good," I added. That brought a smile to all of their faces. My brother arrived to pick us up. On our ride home I asked my father how come no one up home baked pone bread.

"I don't know, Son," he said. "It's always been a Kinnakeet thing."

I also asked him about the meaning of the joke.

"It's too complicated to explain now, Son," he said. "As you get older you will understand." He and my brother were discussing possible replacement of the curtain on the Bay Shoal sink box. I knew then his mind was elsewhere and not on my questions. This was a signal for me to hold my tongue and my inquisitiveness for a later time. I fell silent and let my mind drift. I thought of a few weeks back. My friend Larry Midgett and I had ridden our bikes up to Waves. We heard through the grapevine of a tall tower being erected up there. Six men were working at the construction site when we arrived. We settled on a pile of sand and watched them all afternoon.

# CHAPTER FIFTY

# Jersey Connection

Two of the men were sorting the metal supports that would be used to assemble the tower. The other four men were erecting a tall fence completely around the construction site. By the time we headed back toward Salvo, the fence was about halfway complete. The tower itself was bolted together, extending about five feet above the ground. As we were riding home Larry said to me, "Boy, we should climb that tower when it's finished. Are you up for it?" he added.

"What do you think?" I answered. "We have only one problem: how to get over that fence. I noticed that there are supports about every four feet extending out at an angle from the top of it. I'll bet you anything they fasten barbed wire on those supports," I told him.

"That is something to consider. It will take some planning," he answered. In the coming days we kept a watchful eye on the progress of the tower. Sure enough, the workers installed barbed wire on the supports on top of the fence. The tower itself was a thing of beauty. It extended 150 to 200 feet up in the air. The stairs were just wide enough for one person at a time. The steps were metal rungs welded to the tower supports. They extended straight up at a ninety-degree angle without any hand rails. The climb itself would be a challenge, even if we were lucky enough to scale the fence and avoid barbed-wire piercings. Larry and I rode up to Waves on a calm moonlit night in the summertime. On the way we checked a ditch where a local fisherman kept his boat tied. We both knew that on occasions he hid beer in his boat so his wife wouldn't find it and pour it out. I got inside the boat. Under the bow cap I found a case of Blue Ribbon hid under the life jackets.

"Score," I said, holding up a six-pack so that Larry could see.

"Is that all there is?" Larry asked.

"No, but I am only going to take three for each of us. That is all we need if we are to climb that tower," I said. He nodded his head in agreement. We put the cans in our pockets and continued on our way. When we arrived at the tower site, we noticed the workmen had left one of their trucks there. There were two ladders on the top of the truck. Several two-by-tens sixteen feet in length were stacked in a lumber pile near the truck. A coil of rope was positioned on top of the pile of lumber. We stashed our bikes in a clump of myrtle bushes. There was a large oak tree, trimmed by the workmen, located just outside the fence. The tree was located at the back of the fence. Its position was out of the line of sight from the road. Up about the height of the top fence there was a natural shape change in the tree. The large tree trunk divided into a fork shape and grew in opposite directions. We picked up one end of a two-by-ten in a vertical position and raised it up. Then we pushed it under the lowest strand of wire onto the top of the fence. I climbed the oak tree using a ladder off the truck. Larry tied the rope to the other end of the two-by-ten. I pulled on the rope from the tree as he stabilized the two-by-ten while climbing the ladder. We placed it into the fork of the tree. At this point we had a walkway from the tree to the fence. We walked across the board. It was easy to step over the wire strands. Next, we hung from the sides of the two-by-ten vertically and dropped to the ground. Larry approached the step rungs and began to climb. I followed a few feet behind him. We had to pause several times to catch our breath. It was a difficult climb with the beers in our pockets, but finally we reached the top. There was a good-size platform at the top. We were able to sit comfortably on the platform. Several large antennas were attached to the tower top. It was a fairly calm night. Man, you could see for miles. The line of sight included lights at points across the sound. Lights were visible to the north and to the south. There were even lights far out to sea from passing ships. The entire island and its surroundings were visible from that height. The moon was near full; it appeared that you could reach out and touch the stars. We sipped on beers and kind of looked around in silent amazement at our beautiful sleeping island home.

Larry was the first to break the silence. "Man, is it ever pretty up here," he said.

I answered, "I've never seen anything like it. Maybe we should see the island from the air someday," I added.

We were laughing, gulping hot Blue Ribbon and dropping the empty cans in the center of the tower supports. When one of the empties hit a support, it made a clanking noise. It was then propelled to the opposite side of the tower and the process repeated itself. The cans clanked all the way down and created a louder banging sound as they made contact with the concrete below. The next instant we noticed the porch light come on at the nearest house. It was home of Mr. Cecil Midgett.

"I hear you boys talking up there on that tower," he said. "If you don't come down this instant, I am calling the law," he added. I noticed he was constantly frapping mosquitoes. He disappeared in the house. We immediately began to climb down. When we were halfway down the tower, Mr. Cecil returned to the front porch. We took off for the top again. "The law is on the way," he shouted up at us. He sat down in a chair on the porch.

"He is going to stay there till the fuzz gets here," I said to Larry.

"Man, we are in a scrape now," he answered. Soon, in the distance far to the south of Salvo, we spotted emergency lights approaching. In a few minutes the sheriff's car pulled in the driveway. Mr. Raymond Basnight, a Dare County deputy sheriff and the island's only law enforcement officer, got out of the car. Mr. Cecil walked out to meet him. The mosquitoes were so bad at ground level that they both broke off a branch from a nearby bush to swat them. Mr. Raymond shined a spotlight up at us. We covered our faces with our hands.

"I see you boys up there. Now get on down here this instant. You're both in a heap of trouble," he hollered. "I see them beer cans inside that fence, and

I know you boys are under the legal drinking age," he said. We were silent. "I know you heard me. Now who are you? What are your names?"

I thought for a second, and said, "My name is George Midgett."

Larry laughed and said, "My name is Clarence Midgett." We had given the names of two of our friends.

"It's not a laughing matter," Mr. Raymond said. "If you boys fall you will be killed. Now come on down. My patience is getting thin."

It must have been our lucky night. Mr. Raymond got an emergency call on his radio. "I have an emergency at the other end of the island," he yelled to us. "Tomorrow I am going to talk to your parents. You are not out of hot water yet," he said. He got in his car and left. Mr. Cecil tarried on the porch slapping mosquitoes for a short while.

He looked up at us and shouted, "You boys are on your own," and went inside. We waited for about half an hour before we climbed down. We climbed up the inside of the fence. Then we walked across the board. We then put everything back the way it was. All the while mosquitoes were eating us alive. On the way home we didn't get shed of the mosquitoes until we got up a good head of steam. The next few days we heard around that Mr. Raymond visited our friends' parents. They didn't get in any trouble because they were both at home on the night in question. Never have I repeated the tower episode to another living soul—until now.

One of my former students, Brad Doerr, went into business after graduation from high school. He worked and saved enough to purchase a Dairy Queen franchise. His first ice cream shop is located along Highway 12 just outside of Avon. After a couple summers he expanded and placed another shop near the north end of the village of Waves. Some folks from New York were visiting the island. As they drove past the water tower in Rodanthe, they noticed the word "Chicamacomico" written on it. They asked Brad to pronounce the name of the place they were in. He gazed at them with a puzzled look on his face. He didn't know what to say. He asked them if they were serious. "Of course," was the answer he got.

He started out by saying, "Why, folks, you are in Dairy Queen."

Then they exploded in laughter. "No," the man said, as he gasped for breath between chuckles, "not this place. The name on the water tower in the town we just drove through."

Then Brad laughed himself. He told them how to pronounce it. He added that it was an Algonquian phrase that means "land of shifting sands."

As I stated earlier in this work, my mother was from coastal New Jersey. Her father, Caleb Worth, was in the U.S. Life Saving Service assigned to Island Beach station. His interests were similar to my ancestors on Hatteras Island. He was an angler, hunter, and gardener. My mom and uncles told me he bought Penn reels. He chose to make his own fishing poles. He used bamboo blanks; wrapped the guides on using sinew, an animal gut material; and treated the wrappings with banana oil. My grandfather took sportsmen on surf fishing trips. He also guided duck hunters on the Barnegat Bay. I never met him; he passed before I was born. My mother and I used to go up to visit our relatives in the summertime.

The first trip I can remember, Aunt Clara, my grandfather's sister, came to Salvo to pick us up. We had just crossed the Chesapeake Bay ferry and stopped for lunch somewhere in Eastern Shore, Virginia. We had packed food from home and stopped at a roadside rest area. The rest area had picnic tables. All of the tables were taken except for one. This table only had one seat attached for it. We sat out our lunch. Everything was fine until we sat down. The table turned over. Our faces and bodies were covered in potato salad, coleslaw, fried chicken, and iced tea. I jumped up and asked Aunt Clara and Mother if they were okay. They were laughing. I knew they were fine. I looked at them all covered in food and started laughing myself. We cleaned ourselves off, salvaged what food we could, and continued on our way. We stopped for the night in Cambridge, Maryland, at our cousin's farm. The next day we continued on to Bayville, New Jersey, on Route 9.

Aunt Clara lived in the home where she grew up, a large two-story farm—style house with wraparound porches on the ground level. In back of the main house there were several large empty fields. There were five other buildings on the property. They were long and narrow, suggesting a type of poultry-rearing business at one time. I asked Aunt Clara about the buildings. She told me that my great-grandfather raised chickens. He sold chickens, eggs, and fresh vegetables. When she and my grandfather were children, it was a working farm. Now the fields were empty, and the chicken houses were in a state of disrepair. It was fun exploring them.

On that visit we traveled all around eastern Jersey to visit relatives. On our next visit my mother's sister, Laura, and her husband, Sewell Hulse, came to pick us up. That particular summer, the World's Fair was going to take place in New York. They were planning to take us to the fair. On the night before we were to go to New York, I was so excited that I couldn't sleep. The trip north to New York took a couple of hours. We got off to a bad start the next morning. Uncle Sewell and I went to get the car. The garage was located behind the house about fifty yards. When we opened the garage door, three skunks walked right between us into the garage. The largest one brushed my leg as he passed. The two smaller ones hurried under the car. The big one stopped and turned to face us. When he raised his tail, we took off running. We stopped running halfway up the driveway. The putrid odor of skunk filled the air. It was so strong it was difficult to breathe and made our eyes water. At least we didn't come in direct contact with the spray. I ran back to the house to deliver the news to Aunt Laura and Mom. "What is Sewell going to do?" asked Aunt Laura.

"He told me to come tell you while he watches the skunks. If they soon leave, we will wash and air out the car and still go." I returned just as the big skunk was coming out of the garage. From under the car came three smaller ones.

"So that's it," said Uncle Sewell. "I must have locked one of them up in the garage last night." The skunks walked over to the edge of the driveway. The largest one turned to see where we were. Then they disappeared into the deeper grass. Uncle Sewell opened the side door to air out the garage. Soon he was able to back the car out and drive it up to the house. We sprayed the car off and opened all the doors so fresh air could circulate through it.

When we entered the house Aunt Laura said, "You two have to shower and change. You both have a slight skunk smell clinging to you." We finally got under way, but our perils for the day were not over. We drove to New York and took a passenger ferry across the Hudson River. After the ferry ride it was a short walk to the subway station. Uncle Sewell warned us to stay close together. We had to change trains several times. He was the only one who knew the route we had to take to get the fairgrounds. The subway train doors open and close automatically. When changing trains you had to move quickly. We completed the first change smoothly. As we stood on the train platform he told us to get ready to board the next train. The doors opened and we got on. Aunt Laura said, "My bag." She had set her bag down on the platform. Uncle Sewell jumped off to get the bag. The train doors closed. We took off and left him standing there with his mouth gaping open. He ran along keeping up with the train for a few feet. Then he faded from sight behind us, still waving.

"Now we're really in a mess," said Aunt Laura, almost in tears. "We are lost in New York City on the subway system." Then she said, "We will get off at the next stop and wait for him." When the train stopped we got off. It wasn't long before we heard another train approaching. All three of us were waving to get his attention so he would get off. The train entered the station but didn't stop. Uncle Sewell was waving back at us as the train roared right through the station.

We found a uniformed policeman, and he told us that the train was an express. A local train makes stops at each station. The express train makes stops at about every fifth station. "If you have knowledge of the system, you can get to your destination quicker on the express trains," he told us.

"How do you know the difference?" asked Aunt Laura.

"It is written on the front of the trains," he answered.

"I think we should go back to the ferry landing," Aunt Laura said. Sewell will return there sometime today," she added. The policeman said he would go with us so we would arrive safely. We waited at the ferry terminal until Uncle Sewell came back. He finally walked into the terminal around two o'clock in the afternoon. The express took him miles down the track, he told us. He had spent the rest of the time backtracking from station to station searching for us. It was so late in the day that we decided to go back home and try again tomorrow. The next day went off without a hitch. I really enjoyed the fair. I especially remember a household of the future presented by Westinghouse.

Before we returned home that summer, we visited Uncle Linwood and his wife, Aunt Carey. Uncle Linwood preferred to be called Lin. They had two beautiful Siamese cats. He and his family lived in Brigantine. This New Jersey town is located near Atlantic City. Uncle Lin took us to the Atlantic City boardwalk amusement park. The park had a specific attraction he wanted us to see. The attraction was located on the Steel Pier. It was a lady on horseback diving into a pool of water from an elevated platform. We watched this lady climb up an extremely high ladder to the platform. This huge chestnut stallion came walking up a long ramp to the top of the platform. As the horse passed, the lady grabbed his mane and swung up onto his back. The horse continued on and walked off the platform. The lady and horse fell into the large pool of water. They surfaced with the lady still on the horse's back. A large drain opened in the bottom of the pool. All the water drained out. A gate opened in the side of the pool wall. The horse, lady on his back, walked out of the gate.

# CHAPTER FIFTY-ONE

# New Regulations

The lady got off the horse and waved to the crowd. The audience exploded in cheers and applause. That was an experience I will always remember. This attraction was performed two times daily. We had lunch and hung around for the afternoon performance. It was just as impressive as the morning show. It was amazing the way that horse never slowed his pace once he entered the ramp. Even when the lady climbed on his back, he continued on. The tremendous splash and the huge spray of water was something to see, as they hit the water's surface of the pool: well worth staying for the second time. Uncle Linwood wanted us to see the game portion of the boardwalk. The game section contained shooting games and tossing games, as well as games of chance played on big spinning wheels. Uncle Lin won a pouch of catnip by throwing darts. "What is this stuff?" he asked the dart game attendant.

"Its catnip," was the response he got.

"I can see that written on the pouch. What does it do?" asked Uncle Lin.

"It is a stimulant for cats," the attendant responded.

"You mean it makes them drunk and silly," Uncle Lin stated.

"That's right," said the attendant. "Just give them a small portion at a time. If you give a cat too much, it'll drive him nuts," he added.

"I can't wait to try it on your cats," Uncle Lin said to Aunt Carey.

"Only small portions at a time, Lin," said Aunt Carey. "That's what the man said," she added.

"I heard him," Uncle Lin answered. He placed the pouch in his shirt pocket. We played a few more games, then went back to Uncle Linwood's house.

Aunt Carey set the table for the evening meal. Uncle Lin graced the food. The cats were scampering around playing with a ball in the next room. There was an archway separating them from us. Uncle Lin looked up and saw the cats. He reached into his shirt pocket and took out the pouch, opened it up, and sniffed it. "Doesn't have any smell to it," he said. He threw the entire contents into the next room to the cats. It came to rest between them. They approached it with caution and sniffed it. One of the cats reached out with his paw and pushed it around for a short distance. When the catnip remained motionless, the cats lost interest in it. They resumed playing with the ball. "Ah, that stuff is no good," Uncle Lin said. "Look, it doesn't even work."

"Linwood Worth," exclaimed Aunt Carey, "the man said only a small portion." She got up and headed for the cats. She reached down for the catnip. One of the cats grabbed it in his mouth and took off the other at his heels. They ran across the couch. Next, they jumped on an end table, knocking everything off the table. The cats leaped about six feet to the drapes of a bay window. They caught hold of the drapes with their claws in midair. The weight of both cats was too much for the drapes. The drapes came crashing down on top of the cats. They were running blindly, covered by the drapes. The cats jumped up on the dining room table. The drapes came bounding behind them. Everything on the table was turned over and drug off on the floor. "All this is your fault, Lin," Aunt Carey said in a loud voice.

Uncle Lin jumped and looked at me. "Come on, boy," he said. "Help me catch them cats before they completely destroy this house," he shouted. Then he opened the kitchen door and we were able to corral them into the garage. They ran around the garage knocking over tools, buckets, and cans. "Get the cat carrier from that upper shelf," he yelled to me. He put on a pair of leather gloves. Then he grabbed a landing net hanging from a hook on the wall. The net had a four-foot-long handle. The hoop was about three feet in diameter. It had net webbing hanging three feet down from the hoop. Uncle

Lin placed it in front of one of the cats. The cat ran right inside the net. He reached into the webbing and took the cat out. The catnip had to be pried from its mouth. I opened the door to the cat case. Uncle Linwood placed the cat inside. We repeated the process, and both cats were inside the carrier. We straightened up the garage. "Well, let's go in and face the music," Uncle Linwood said. When we came in, Aunt Carey was furious. Her face was blood red, and her hands were shaking. My mother and Aunt Laura were helping her straighten up. Uncle Linwood started to explain.

Aunt Carey held up her hands and said, "Don't say a word. Just help clean up this mess." When order was restored and we returned to the table, Aunt Carey asked Uncle Lin, "What did you do with my cats?"

"I put them in their carrier," he told her.

"How long are you going to leave them in there?" she asked him.

"Until they are calm and that wildness leaves their eyes," he answered. "You have to admit, it was sort of funny," he said to her as he chuckled.

She looked back at him. Anger still flushed across her face. As their eyes met, the pleading for understanding was apparent in his expression. Her eyes softened; the corners of her mouth turned up a little, and she giggled. "I guess so," she said. We all laughed nervously.

"Now let's eat," Uncle Lin said. We finished the evening meal and said bye to Uncle Lin and Aunt Carey. Our vacation was at an end. Uncle Sewell and Aunt Laura brought my mother and me back home. They visited with us for a week and headed back north to Jersey.

I really enjoyed my Jersey trips. The seashore beaches I was used to were empty and deserted most of the year. The beaches of the north were developed for recreational activities. We visited three of them on my vacations up north. Atlantic City, Seaside Heights, and Asbury Park all had large commercial boardwalks. These boardwalks contained arcades, pavilions, gaming areas, and rides, but best of all, they served the most amazing food. At these locations I was introduced to pizza, sausage sandwiches, Carvel ice cream, and funnel cake. Each town had a small owner-operated bakery. Fresh bread, hard rolls, bagels, and sweets could be purchased daily. At that time these foods did not exist in the South. I would bring bags of all types of rolls, bagels, and pastries home with me. I froze them and enjoyed them throughout the winter. I was fortunate to enjoy foods of two cultures at such a young age. Years later, many of these food producers have made their homes in the South. Even on Hatteras Island, we have Italian restaurants. There are at least two or three bakeries on the island. Carvel ice cream and Jersey Mike's sub shops are in the Dare County area. These days all these foods can be purchased fresh or frozen at all the grocery stores of the island. In the days of yesteryear, hunting, fishing, and gardening provided the food to eat.

When I was young there were at least a dozen long-net hauling operations in the Pamlico Sound near my home. Every man in the village either earned their primary living or extra money in the sound. They owned commercial hunting rigs, stands of nets, terrapin traps, steel traps, oyster tongs, and crab pots. Land wasn't worth much. Most all the families divided up their property and passed it on to their children. It was a free and happy lifestyle. You could walk on the beach for hours and only see a handful of people. Then in 1963, Oregon Inlet was bridged. Slowly at first, the tourists came. Then the flood gates opened. Off-island land developers purchased large tracts of land. Local folks thought they received top-dollar prices. They readily sold their property for much more than they thought possible. These land tracts were divided into many lots and the developers tripled their money. The children no longer received family property to build their homes on. It was much too valuable on the real estate market.

During the next forty years Hatteras Island experienced an explosive building boom. A couple of real estate offices opened up. Specialized labor came to the island. Contractors of all trades moved in. Carpenters, plumbers, heating and air installers, and electricians were available by phone for the first time. There was work for anyone who wanted a construction-related job. The houses were small at first. They were two- to three-bedroom single-story dwellings. These structures were erected on piling foundations. Most of the pilings were sixteen feet in length. In the beginning phase of the development, the builder installed the pilings. His crew framed the structures. They completed the rough plumbing and electrical wiring. These small dwellings were finished off inside with sheet paneling. The ceilings were acoustic square block ceiling tile. All the moldings were stained finish-grade pine. The doors had to be hung by hand. Floor coverings were vinyl in kitchens and bathrooms. Carpet was installed in bedrooms and the living area. More and more visitors came to vacation and rent these dwellings. This phase of construction lasted for about twenty years. Everyone was working and making money; life was good. You could buy a lot and have a spacious home built for a fair price.

In the early eighties the boom began. The rental market far exceeded the available housing. The number of real estate offices doubled. There were building contractors coming out of the woodwork. The carpenters, plumbers, and electricians were as thick as hen's teeth. It was not out of the ordinary to see twenty to thirty houses under construction at a time. It was impossible to be in any village on the island without hearing the screeching sound of a circular saw or the banging of hammers.

With all this development came many new regulations. All real estate agents were required to be state certified. The contractors, plumbers, electricians, and heating and air installers had to be state licensed. All of their work had to be inspected and approved. All types of permit fees were implemented. Buildable lots and labor costs doubled. The price of construction materials went up drastically. At this point, the process of completing a dwelling doubled in costs. Even with the increased prices, it was still profitable for off-island people to build rental properties.

Things leveled off again for a few years. Then greed set in. The off-island buyer began to have two- and three-story structures built on the same size lots. These structures contained six and seven bedrooms. Some of the larger ones were five thousand square feet or better. It took up to six hundred amps of electricity to power up these houses. They could accommodate two to three families. All sorts of amenities were added to these mini-hotels. Most all of them contained swimming pools, hot tubs, and a game room, usually with a pool table. This helped offset the cost of the original investment.

Investors began to buy the lots with the smaller structures built on them. They demolished the smaller homes and replaced them with the multistory monsters. It didn't take long for the real estate agents to catch up. The cost of buildable lots went sky high. The permit fees were based on the square footage of the structure being built. Larger dwellings meant more permit costs. Materials went up because of the increased demand. Labor costs skyrocketed to keep up the demand for these larger dwellings. Everyone involved in the construction industry was making money hand over fist. This gravy train lasted through the 1990s well into the 2000s.

Then the rest of the country went into a recession. For the first time ever, trickle-down affected the Hatteras Island area. Construction slowed and almost stopped. For the first time in years, contractors, framers, plumbers, electricians, and heating and air installers were competing for the few available jobs. Only folks who had money continued to build. It was expensive to maintain these larger dwellings. The rental market proceeds fell short of the yearly expenses. Owners began to take out second mortgages to cover the skyrocketing costs. Soon, many loans were in default. The market was flooded with rental homes for sale. The lending institutions would only loan 80 percent of the current appraised value of the homes. The appraisals came in much lower than the amount owed on the homes. The average buyer had to take thirty thousand–plus to closing. The resale market bottomed out. Foreclosures and short sales became the norm.

To this point the rental market has remained strong. New house construction is not a major driver of our island's economy like it once was. The tourist dollar is the mainstay of our economy. All types of new regulations have had an adverse effect on local folks and tourists alike. They no longer have the freedom to wander the beach at their heart's content. The days of nighttime beach parties with bonfires were over. Any fire on the beach must be located below the high-water mark along the surf. It is no longer allowed to roast a hotdog or marshmallow over an open beach fire. The beach angler doesn't have free access to roam the surf line in search of fish. Beach driving is only allowed by permit in limited areas. The East Coast

Surfing Association stopped having surfing contests on the island. They encountered so many restrictions that it wasn't fun anymore. Numbers of channel bass or drum tournaments have gone by the wayside. If a record drum is caught, it is against regulation to keep it. Any drum over twenty-eight inches long must be released alive. There is no way the International Game Fish Association could examine the fish before it is released.

The economy of this area is so fragile to begin with. Anything that limits the ability to attract the tourist is a direct threat to the area's survival. Ingress and egress are crucial to the area's economic stability. The visitors have to be able to get here before they can spend their money. Special-interest groups have caused continuing problems for the Bonner Bridge replacement. Highway 12, south from the bridge to Ocracoke, has several weak locations. There is a bad spot near Pea Island, north of Rodanthe, and as you come into Buxton. On Ocracoke, a mile after departing the ferry from Hatteras, is another trouble spot. One severe hurricane creeping up the coast could open up any or all of these locations.

The aftermath of one of these storms could possibly leave us with multiple inlets. It would take months or even years to recover from such an event. Whenever a hurricane makes its way up to Puerto Rico, the Weather Channel begins to use Hatteras as a reference point. The rental cancellations begin to flow into Hatteras and Ocracoke real estate rental offices while the storm is thousands of miles away. It could choose any path governed by the steering currents.

Problems exist even with favorable weather conditions compromising the entire tourist season. The Bonner Bridge is in such a state of disrepair at times that it is reduced to one lane of vehicle traffic. The pilings near the boat channel are constantly monitored with sonar equipment. When inlet currents scour critical amounts of sand from around the pilings, it results in temporary closures of the bridge. Hatteras Inlet channel has shoaled up to the point that it is impassable to ferry traffic. An alternate channel had to be established. The alternate route doubled the crossing time. This creates problems for the tourist who likes to take day trips to visit Ocracoke to see what the village has to offer. They browse the shops, enjoy the beaches, and have dinner all in a day's time. All these problems have a huge impact on the economic survival of Hatteras and Ocracoke Islands.

The average family visiting our area is trying to escape the pressures of their lives back home. They are in search of a trouble-free, relaxing vacation. They enjoy the area much more if everything goes smoothly. If current regulations prevent them from the freedom of enjoying the area, we are in trouble. Picture this scenario: One summer season without any tourists. The local dollar can't provide enough support to keep the business of the area in operation. Only a few of the larger grocery stores and supply stores remain open all winter long. It is aggravating coping with the summer traffic. Your patience wears thin waiting an hour at your favorite restaurant for dinner. Be patient while giving tourists directions to the lighthouse, even when its location is clearly visible from where you are standing. Exercise a little more tolerance; they are the mainstay of our economy.

# CHAPTER FIFTY-TWO

# Drifting Along

I took a good look in the mirror the other day. I didn't necessarily like what I saw. As I viewed my reflection, a few idle thoughts began to flood my mind. Loose skin hanging under my chin gave the appearance of a turkey's neck. Rings of bags under my eyes and long horizontal wrinkles traveled across my forehead. Deep wrinkles moved off in forty-degree angles from the outside corners of my eyes. All these things added up to a weather-beaten old man's face. My gray matter settled on one train of thought. I said out loud to myself, "Boy, where did your life go?"

It seems like only yesterday I had the facial appearance of a vibrant young man. Now my pace has slowed considerably. I go to bed much earlier and sleep much later in the day than I used to. I no longer have the body of an in-shape athlete. Adult basketball and softball are out of the question with my aching knees. These days I choose walking and sit every chance I get. I have become a sports fan. I enjoy the high school's home soccer matches, basketball games, and baseball games. Traveling to the away games is out of the question. It would keep me up way past my bedtime. Age is beginning to impose its limitations on me. I used to pick at my father and call him an old man. "I am the old man today, but you will be the old man tomorrow," he told me many times. In those days I thought I knew everything. It was amazing how much smarter I thought I was compared to my father and most of the older folk. At this point I can reflect back and realize how silly those thoughts were.

This was a wonderful place to grow up. I had the freedom to roam and enjoy the fruits the island had to offer. Life was good. I grew up on a developing island. There was plenty of work for everyone. I got caught in the romanticism of believing that things would always remain the same. Boy, was I in for a surprise. The new regulations have a direct impact on the freedom I enjoyed since I was a kid. I never thought that I would live to see the day that I was not permitted to freely roam the beaches or the sound-side shoreline. I grew up chasing fish in the sloughs on the ocean side of the island. It was common practice to keep all the fish you could catch. No fish ever went to waste; everything was used. The catch was always cleaned and eaten. My grandfather and I hunted shorebirds on the beaches near Salvo. We dug a hole large enough to hide in, placed carved wooden bird decoys in the wash, shot the shorebirds as they approached, and skinned and fried them up. They are delicious to eat prepared in this manner. If you attempted anything such as this now, the authorities would put you in jail. Some of the best meals I have ever eaten were turtle soup and turtle hash. Turtles are a protected species; they have disappeared from the menus of the restaurants. The sound side of the island provides a variety of edible seafood: mussels, scallops, clams, and oysters can be harvested from the sound. In the summer months, angling is good from the sound shore. Southwest winds bring large schools of baitfish near the shore. The larger game fish cruise the shoreline hunting the baitfish. A fishing license is in effect for rod and reel fishing. A limit on the number and size of fish kept is in effect. A daily limit has been placed on the gathering of scallops, clams, and oysters.

The winter months are usually mild. Every now and then we have harsh weather conditions similar to the winters we used to experience. As I write, this past winter season was one of those. For the first time in many years, my vehicle doors became frozen in place. I had to pour heated water on the edges of the doors to gain access to the vehicle. On several occasions this past winter I saw large pieces of ice floating in the sound. It was an unusually cold winter. The fowl returned, and we had a decent hunting season. I have some friends who live near the Back Bay area on Virginia. They told me that most of the ponds were frozen all the way to the bottom in that hunting area. The fowl had to migrate farther south to find food.

There are limits on the number of waterfowl allowed to be taken. A hunting license is required. Only a three-month period is allowed for the harvesting of waterfowl. Complete bans have been placed on certain species. During these times it is unlawful to harvest the fowl, fish, or shellfish included in these bans. At times, scallop shells are all over the road. The seagulls drop them on the hard surface to break them open to expose the meat inside the shells. Normally the Pamlico is full of these migrating shellfish. Only the muscle that holds the shells together is the edible portion. As the heat is applied to them, they form round balls about the size of your thumbnail. They are so tasty when you sauté them in butter that you almost faint dead away as you eat them. It is an enjoyable trip out in the sound with your friends to harvest them. All you need is a yard rake with chicken wire attached to shape a basket or a clam rake. The scallop shells have a white underside and a dark topside shell. They rest on the surface of the bottom usually in grass beds. The dark side of the shell provides them with camouflage, which makes it harder to spot them for people and seagulls alike. Most winters we are not allowed to harvest scallops.

So many regulations have been placed on the things I used to take for granted. It forces me to operate similar to an outlaw in the old West. I have to gather shellfish, game, and fish on the sly. I have collected baskets of scallops on calm, cloudless, moonlit nights. If the fowl return during a cold winter, I do a lot of pond shooting in the moonlight. During the spring and fall I fish at night for the large drum or channel bass. Moonlit nights have produced satisfactory catches of speckled trout for me. I would check on the location of trout being caught during the day and find out which tide and lures they were hitting on. If the water was clear and the moon full, I would return at night to fish. On these fishing trips at night in the moon glow, darker floating lures seem to produce more trout. Every trout that I have caught at night was always hooked on the bottom hooks of the lure. My opinion is that they cruise near the bottom and strike the lure as it passes over them. They see the dark silhouette of the baitfish illuminated by the moonlight swimming along on the surface.

By operating under the cover of darkness, I have been able to harvest the bounties of the island without harassment. Careful planning must be implemented, though, to pull these episodes off without being caught. I am always looking over my shoulder, suspicious of anyone who material- izes out of the darkness approaching me. At this point you just react and implement the plan you rehearsed for this situation. Usually a friend and I catch big drum in the Pamlico Sound during the fall and spring months. We approach the shore, returning from a trip in the wee hours of the morning. We contact his father by cell phone to make sure the coast is clear. If we get the thumbs up, we come on into the harbor and unload. If he has seen anything suspicious, we are equipped with a coil of parachute cord, weights, and small floats. We thread the cord into the gills of the big fish, bring it out of their mouths, secure a weight to its head, and tie a small float on about four feet of cord and toss it all over the side. At that point we enter the harbor for a short time until we are confident all is normal. Then we return and retrieve our bounty. At times we catch an unusually large number of big drum during our sessions. We clean them and pack the fillets on ice in large coolers. Before we enter the harbor we place the coolers out on the back of the marsh. We return later with a truck for the coolers. All the old folks I know love big drum stew. If we are gathering scallops at night we carry weighted burlap bags. On the beach at night during a trout fishing session, I bury all the fish I catch in the sand. I check the area thoroughly before digging them up and leaving for home.

If you are cautious you can still enjoy the resources of the area and stay out of trouble. That is one thing that the powers that be don't understand. They have protected the channel bass and the striped bass in the sounds for a number of years. There are so many of these fish that they have dimin- ished the blue crab populations to dangerous levels. It's like the situation of having too many mice in certain areas, so cats are brought in to balance the mouse problem. After a while you have a cat problem. Nature has a way of balancing itself. It doesn't need any help from us. When we interfere in the natural order of things, that's when we get into trouble. All of us are bound to the laws of nature. It is a much better mindset to live in harmony with Mother Nature instead of trying to control her.

These days I am just taking it easy and drifting along, enjoying life as it comes. If I continued angling, hunting, and gathering as I was accustomed to, I would be violating every regulation on the books, so I just relax and dream of the glory days Bruce Springsteen sings about. I own a small, sixteen-foot aluminum boat. It is powered with a two-stroke twenty-five-horsepower Johnson outboard motor. Whenever the weather cooperates and the fowl are here, I take one of my nephews, Kyle Smithwick, and his friends out to Gull Island for hunting. When conditions are right, speckled trout show up in the sound. I have two trout fishing buddies: Stan Kee, another nephew, and Sonny Duke, a friend, and I chase them. Once in a while when my daughter, Kristina, comes home for a visit, we burn a tank of gas riding around the sound. She loves to drive the boat. As far as she is concerned, there is only one speed: wide open. On several occasions when I am unable to find a fishing partner, I go on solo trips. One of my buddies, Chester Britt, supplies me with tubs of Gulp-enriched trout baits from Dillon's Corner. He is able to save me a few dollars. These baits are expensive but effective. I hook the boat trailer to my truck and head up the island.

These days I must purchase an off-road permit to drive anywhere off-road. One of my launch locations is on the sound side between Avon and Salvo. It has a small cove with a sand beach; the local name of this area is Percy's net rack. It is named after Mr. Percy Williams, who used to fish commercially there. It's easy to launch a small boat there. It was late in the month of September. This particular day the wind was light from the northeast. I launched the boat, set the anchor, and moved the truck to higher ground. As I was walking back to the boat, I spotted a school of finger mullet swimming nearby. I eased up to the boat, found my cast net, and threw it over the mullets. The catch was enough to fill my live bait container. I got under way toward Gull Island about two miles to the west of my location. When I reached the south edge of Gull Shoal Channel, I turned the boat northeast and steered toward Bay Shoal. I shut off the motor when the boat was abreast of the old abandoned submerged curtain box. The boat swung around side to the wind and began drifting southwest toward Gull Island. I set out two medium-size rods with small floats containing live finger mullet for bait. The drags on the reels were set, and the rods placed in rod holders attached to the boat. The live presentations were in hopes of attracting a large bluefish, trout, or puppy drum. The floats were bobbing along, being pulled by the drifting boat. They were about twenty yards from my position.

After polishing off a can of sardines and crackers, I settled down to serious fishing. I took a smaller trout rod from one of the holders, tied on a red grub head, threaded on Gulp-enhanced rubber shrimp, and began jigging. I heard the sound of a motor behind me. I placed the trout rod in a holder and set the drag on the reel. Then I turned and spotted a sea dory painted white with a net reel mounted inside it. There were two men in the boat; they waved as they passed by. I thought it was odd to see a dory in the sound this time of year. I followed their progress with binoculars as they made steady progress in a westward direction, *probably going out back of the reef drifting*, I thought to myself. When you go drifting, you set the net off the stern and drift along with the tide or wind. The reel is retracted every hour or so, and the catch removed from the net and iced in large coolers. The net then is reset and the process is repeated. Spanish mackerel, gray trout, and bluefish are harvested in this manner. This is commercial night fishing. I watched until the sound of the motor faded and they disappeared from sight. It was a comfortable afternoon: light northeast wind and balmy weather. The slapping of the small waves against the side of the aluminum boat lulled me into a trancelike state. My mind began to fill with thoughts of sea dories and my past experiences with them.

One of the most memorable sea dory episodes carried me back to my childhood, smack in the middle of the dory races at the Pirates Jamboree. This was a huge celebration located near the north end of Hatteras Village. Nearly the entire island's population turned out to celebrate. The older men grew beards for the occasion. A large vessel went out of Hatteras Inlet loaded with bearded men dressed as pirates. Small sea skiffs were launched from the larger vessel and rowed to the beach by the pirates. Once they landed, the pirates chased and captured all the females on the beach they could find. The prisoners were transported out to the anchored vessel and taken back to the docking areas. The pirates and captives returned to join in the festivities. A judging was held, and the best-dressed pirate and a pirate queen were chosen, with prizes awarded. There were all types of good things to eat. The traditional island cuisine is out of this world. Especially tasty were the sweets, cakes, pies, cookies, puddings, and any type of desserts imaginable. A small pig was shaved to the skin and greased with cooking oil, then released inside a pen about fifteen feet square. Any kid who could catch the pig and bring it to an elevated platform was awarded a prize. The older folks stood and laughed hysterically as dozens of kids stumbled over each other trying to catch the pig. A flagpole with a small bell attached to the top was also heavily greased. The first kid who successfully climbed the pole and rang the bell received a prize. In the afternoon there was a beach buggy race around a quarter-mile track near the dune line. These were custom-altered street vehicles equipped with split rims and oversized tires. At the wave of a flag they were off, with sand flying in all directions as the buggies sped around the track. The event I enjoyed most was the beach dory races. Several dories were spaced evenly along the surf line, each with two-man crews. At the sound of a starter pistol, they were off. The men pushed their dory into the surf, jumped inside, and began to row toward a red buoy positioned three hundred yards from the beach. The first crew to successfully round the buoy and return to the beach was the winner. The shore break surf didn't always cooperate. Some of the boats overturned; some washed up high and dry on the beach. I was too young to drive a beach buggy or participate in the dory races. I chased the pig with my friends and tried to climb the flagpole. Some of my fondest childhood memories are of the Pirates Jamboree celebration.

I was jarred back to reality by the line screaming off the spool of the trout rod. The line got caught on one of the rod guides and jumped out of the rod holder. I was able to grab the rod butt just before it went over the side. I hardly had time to react; in the next instant the spool was empty. I had been stripped and had never even seen the fish. I thought of something large and fast. I settled back on the seat and sighed. The boat was at the end of its first drift. I looked up, and I had drifted to the entrance of Gull Island Harbor, or what was left of it. The harbor was almost filled in. There was no sign that a clubhouse ever existed there. Only the docks remain. My parents have been gone for years. Somehow I feel close to them when I am here.

Sometimes I often wonder about the future of the barrier islands we live on. Hatteras and Ocracoke Islands are fighting for their very existence economically. The coastal hurricanes seem to have become more violent. They have created havoc all up and down the Eastern Seaboard. Recent storms are responsible for catastrophic damage costing in the billions of dollars. In the past few years, along with help of northeasters, they have severely eroded and reshaped these sandbars that we call home. I don't think it will occur during my lifetime, but I can visualize Hatteras being reduced to a much smaller place. The highest elevations on the island extend from the hills of Buxton Woods to the hills of Piney Ridge in Frisco. If the erosion continues at its current rate, these areas could be the boundaries of Hatteras in future years. There are numerous narrow locations where the effects of one severe hurricane could cause multiple inlets. Our ability to travel on and off these islands could be interrupted for weeks, even months. It is imperative that our islands be accessible to seasonal visitors. There's a horrifying thought of the loss of electricity for any extended length of time due to storm damage.

We live in an extremely fragile environment. If you live on a sandbar, every now and then you are going to get your feet wet. The next-to-impossible task of replacing the bridges and keeping Highway 12 open has become a constant thorn in our side. How much longer can the Bonner Bridge last? It was originally designed for a life span of thirty years. It just celebrated its fifty-first birthday. We really need help on these barrier islands. Our lifeline to the mainland must be preserved. I never dreamed that our very existence would be in question during my lifetime. We are really in a mess. The future of our island paradise is uncertain.

Elvin Hooper has always lived on Hatteras Island. He grew up in the village of Salvo where commercial hunting and fishing with his father, brother, cousins, and friends molded his childhood years. His family lived in Salvo until 1998. Their home was situated on the sound front and quite vulnerable to sound-side flooding. After coping with storm water damage to the dwellings several times, he moved his family to higher ground in Buxton woods. Now their home is located in the Hatteras Pines area, twenty feet above sea level. Flooding is no longer an issue. During hurricanes and storms, the woods provide adequate protection from the heavy winds.

**CERTIFICATE**

Fishing from
Hatteras Island Pier
at Rodanthe, North Carolina,
Mr. Elvin Hooper of Salvo,
North Carolina caught a
90 pound Channel Bass
(or Red Drum) on
November seventh, nineteen
hundred and seventy-three

*This fish is an all-time,
all-tackle WORLD RECORD
for the species.*

Hooper's hobbies include hunting, sport fishing, gathering shellfish, and spending time out on the sound or in the inlets is his small boat. Surfing is still an option when the waves are small. You will find him on the south side of the point where the water is shallow. He has enjoyed all types of sports, but mostly these days as a spectator. He loves to play music with his friends, and he is still employed at the local high school as a part-time shop teacher. He is a full-time employee with the Department of Transportation Ferry System located at Hatteras Inlet. He has been on the Board of Directors of the Cape Hatteras Electric Membership Cooperative for thirty years. He loves to work a fast-paced schedule, and enjoys the feeling of belonging to all these workplace families. He enjoys writing, and a chance to relive the experiences of his youthful glory days.